Farm and Food Policy

Farm and Food Policy

Issues of the 1980s

Don Paarlberg

University of Nebraska Press
Lincoln and London

Library of Congress Cataloging in Publication Data

Paarlberg, Donald, 1911–
  Farm and food policy.

  Includes index.
  1. Agriculture and state—United States. 2. Food
supply—United States. I. Title.
HD1765   1980.P3   338.1'873   79–17496
ISBN 0–8032–3656–5

First Printing: 1980
Most recent printing indicated by first digit below:
            3   4   5   6   7   8   9   10

Contents

Preface

MOST BOOKS ON FOOD AND AGRICULTURAL POLICY are devoted to analysis of the past. In this book the focus is primarily on the future—what is likely to happen and what can be made to happen.

"Coming events cast their shadows before," said the poet Thomas Campbell. This must be the fundamental assumption of every forecaster. An issue of public policy has a life cycle: conception, birth, infancy, adolescence, maturity, senility, death—and occasionally reincarnation. Given some understanding of the policy process, it should be possible to identify an issue fairly early in its life cycle and prepare to cope with it before it reaches full strength.

The purpose of this book is to identify the issues of farm and food policy in the United States that are likely to be important during the decade of the 1980s—to report the known facts, to outline the alternatives, to foresee the probable alignment of various interested parties, to estimate the relative strength of the contending groups, and, if possible, to anticipate the outcome.

If this can be done with reasonable accuracy, useful research might be started in time to assist decision-making. Organizations and individuals might avoid committing themselves to weak positions. Energy might be conserved for issues of current and prospective importance. There could be clearer understanding of what would otherwise be puzzling events.

Identifying the farm and food policy issues of the next decade is hazardous, but not so much so as one might think. The life cycle of most such issues is considerably longer than a decade, so that many of the issues of the 1980s are already in existence. Some are at an early stage and can be expected to grow.

vii

Others are past full vigor and probably will diminish in importance. But some new issues, not anticipated in this book, will be born. Failure to identify these is unavoidable, and I offer no apologies. In fact, I take great satisfaction from what is spontaneous and unpredictable in human behavior. This continuously demonstrates the self-determination of the individual, an attribute I find gratifying.

The book is intended for those concerned with public policy at each stage in the food system, from supplying input items to farm production and on to final food use. Students of agriculture, government, political science, and public administration may be interested. Farmers, legislators, tradespeople, consumer groups, environmentalists, economic developers, and those with concern for international affairs all might find useful subject matter. Food is for everybody; farm and food policy affects us all, three times a day.

Farm and Food Policy

1. Issues of the Eighties: A Summary

FOR A HUNDRED YEARS, farmers took the initiative in shaping farm policy. But in the 1980s they will be largely on the defensive, and this will require a different strategy. During the eighties farm people will have to comport themselves like the minority they now are. Those who want to extract benefits from the political arena will have to make allies, cooperate, compromise, and keep their friendships in repair. The alternative is glorious defeat, which, however glorious, is still defeat. A strategy of cooperation recommends itself to the rest of the population as well as to farmers. There is no more reason for an adversary relationship between farmers and nonfarmers than there is for a dispute between the hand and the mouth.

Let us look at the various issues that will appear in the text.

Research and education. Research and education in agriculture will be able to cope with the farm and food policies of the 1980s. Publicly supported institutions engaged in these activities have shown themselves to be flexible, but appropriations will be hard to get, and the policy-making as well as the service role will have to be shared more widely. Vehicle, payload, and destination will all undergo change. These developments will place painful but not intolerable stress on the scientific and educational arms of the land grant colleges and the Department of Agriculture.

Commodity programs. The big commodity programs are in for a hard time. Working against them will be the declining political power of farmers, the gradual loss of agriculture's uniqueness, the growing perception that these programs are for the well-to-do rather than for the downtrodden, and the public's

1

inflation-induced feeling that the problem is high prices, not low prices. The tobacco program will be in jeopardy. Marketing orders will be under attack but will continue in much their present form. Hard-fought battles will continue on commodity issues. We will not return to the strong part in the production and pricing of farm products that the government exercised during the fifties and the early sixties. In retrospect it will be clear that, so far as the commodity programs are concerned, we crossed a farm-policy watershed sometime during the sixties.

Increasingly, commodity programs will share top policy billing with a long list of new issues. "Farm policy" has become "farm and food policy." To these new issues we now turn.

Price control. In an inflation-ridden economy there will be public concern about rising prices, especially the price of food. We are likely to launch another effort at direct price control. The food industry will have a difficult time making a case for its exemption from such controls.

The consumer movement. The main thrust of the consumer movement is behind us. During the eighties this movement will consolidate its gains, prune some of its irrational elements, and make further advances here and there. There will be some retreats, but we will not return to things as they were. Consumers will demand and receive a larger role in policy-making.

Food regulation. Gradually, research and reason will play a stronger part in the development of regulations regarding food. Confrontations between the food industry and consumer groups will abate as tempers cool and facts become better known.

Domestic food programs. Most of these programs have gone through the phase of rapid expansion. Domestic feeding programs may grow, but it will be by smaller relative increments than in the past.

The environment. Environmentalists will hold most of the gains they have made. Farm leaders have seriously underestimated the strength of this movement during the past decade; this assessment should be revised. Some of the past intemperate actions will be corrected, and additional advances will occur. Those who consider ecological concern a fad will be proved wrong.

Occupational safety and health. Farmers have won their battle against the excesses of the Occupational Safety and Health Administration (OSHA). If they comport themselves well, they can avert another such initiative. But OSHA will continue to be a strong force in specifying working conditions in food processing and merchandising.

Land use. The assumption since America was first settled has been that agriculture had first claim on land. This premise will be called into question during the eighties. Farmers are likely to lose most confrontations on this subject.

Use of water. As with land, so with water. Agriculture can be outbid by non-farm users of water. In the arid West, farmers will lose most of their battles with nonfarmers for control of this vital resource.

Energy. Farm people and the food industry will get the energy they need, whether in the market or through allocation. Conventional fuels will continue as the major source of energy. Fuel alcohol from grain and farm wastes will develop only modestly during the eighties.

The family farm. There will be much public concern about the family farm, but little effective legislation will be passed. We are likely to see an extension of past trends: farms will grow larger, fewer, and more specialized. Manpower per farm will not change much. Large-scale corporate farms will not become a major factor in American agriculture, but more family farms will be incorporated. Vertical integration will increase but will not become general. Farmer cooperatives will survive attack. Part-time farms will gain recognition as a viable and worthy form of agriculture. Capital needs will increase, and outside capital will continue to come in. The family farm will survive, but not in its traditional form.

Agribusiness issues. Issues regarding agribusiness are worth more to the activists and the politicians if they are unsolved than if solutions are found. For that matter, issues are ill-defined and solutions unlikely. On the subject of agribusiness there will be much talk and little action.

People on the fringe. Benefits of public programs will increasingly be extended to the rural poor, to hired farm labor, to ethnic groups, and to women. Hired farm labor will win the right to bargain collectively. Agriculture's white male tradition will be eroded. Most confrontations will be won by those previously disadvantaged.

The Department of Agriculture. In fact if not in name, the Department of Agriculture will become a Ministry of Food. Only by accepting a broadened constituency will the Department of Agriculture be able to retain cabinet status. Raids on the department by other agencies of government will continue.

International issues. The upsurge of exports during the seventies was not a passing phenomenon; it resulted from a rediscovery of our ability to compete in world markets. Domestic farm policies during the eighties will be shaped so as to give us continued access to the export market. After nearly a half-century of liberalization, trade barriers have been lowered about as much as is possible.

International food aid will be neither greatly reduced nor greatly expanded. We are likely to continue the standoff between the advocates and opponents of technical agricultural assistance. International agricultural development, like overseas food aid, is in a holding pattern while the public decides its degree of responsibility for meeting the food needs of distressed people overseas.

This analysis is based on these assumptions: Weather will be average. Agricultural technology will continue to advance much as it has during the past twenty years. The real gross national product will increase, though at a slower rate than during the past two decades. Inflation will continue. Most of the liberal trade gains made since 1934 will be retained. Major war will be averted. Disillusion will grow regarding the ability of government to solve economic and social problems. Farms that are large enough to be efficient and that are well run will prosper. The reverse will be true for farms that are poorly run or too small. To the degree that these assumptions prove wrong, the analysis is faulted. Unless, that is, this is averted by the forecaster's friend, compensating error.

2. Agriculture Loses Its Uniqueness

SOME TIME AGO a friend asked me, "What is the most important event that has happened in agriculture during your lifetime?" I put him off for a month while I reflected on this provocative question. Then I told him, "The most important event is that agriculture is in the process of losing its uniqueness." My friend looked at me uncomprehending; probably the reader of these lines will be likewise puzzled.

Many years ago agriculture was basically different from other occupations; it was more a way of life than a business. Farmers were self-sufficient. They bought and sold little; they took to market only what was in excess of their family needs. Despite regional differences, there was a generally recognizable rural culture, tradition, and life-style. Farmers were readily distinguishable from other people by speech, dress, and manner.

Farmers had much lower cash incomes than nonfarmers, and they had fewer conveniences. But these disadvantages were not so much the subject of invidious comparisons as accepted attributes of a special way of life.

Farmers were considered uniquely worthy. The Jeffersonian ideal was a nation of family farm operators producing food, the most needed product of all. Farmers were considered good God-fearing citizens, stalwart defenders of the republic, and a stabilizing element in the society. Those who grew up in the country did not need to be taught these values; they absorbed them through their pores. This set of ideas was known by social scientists as agrarianism, or agricultural fundamentalism, or the agricultural creed.

There was much good-natured joking about the farmer. The cartoonist showed him as a simple fellow, with straw hat and pitchfork, at once admirable

5

and amusing. In the poolroom stories of the day, the farmer usually had a daughter who had various adventures with traveling salesmen. Occasionally the farmer came to town, and somebody sold him the Brooklyn Bridge. But in these tales the farmer usually came off rather well, and eventually got the best of the city slicker. Thus did the folklore reinforce the values of the society, as must always be the case. The public felt comfortable with the pro-farmer bias of the early rural tradition; subjectively, the average citizen identified with the farmer and was happy when he did well.

From early times, the economy was delineated into farm and nonfarm sectors. If someone was born into agriculture and left it, the important thing was not whether he became a tradesman or a laborer, but that he became a nonfarmer; and usually there was some stigma associated with the change.

The farm/nonfarm delineation of the society was a logical grouping, whether on economic, political, or social grounds. Farmers were different. They were unique, and worthily so. They knew it, and so did everyone else.

This uniqueness manifested itself in many ways, not least in the political process. Farmers were the most numerous group in the economy. Their spokesmen held the political initiative and controlled the farm policy agenda.

There were few public policy issues about food as such. The assumption, based on the teaching of classical economics, was that producers responded automatically to the needs of the consumer through the mechanism of the marketplace. If the country saw to the needs of the producers, consumer well-being would follow as the night the day. Consumers needed no advocate of their own.

Since farmers were unique, the country set up a group of unique institutions to serve them: a Department of Agriculture, a Homestead Act, a land grant college system, a network of Agricultural Experiment Stations, an Agricultural Extension Service, a Rural Electrification Administration, and a Bureau of Reclamation. Farmers were given preferred access to land and water. We voted price and income supports for farmers, but not for automobile manufacturers or hardware merchants.

When general social legislation was enacted, we often excluded agriculture because of its uniqueness. Consider some of the major exclusions sought by and granted to agriculture:

Exemption from Social Security.

Exemption from a whole set of laws related to hired labor: child labor, working conditions, minimum wages, workmen's compensation, collective bargaining rights, unemployment insurance.

Preference with respect to rate-making in transportation of farm products.

Exemption from laws regarding the restraint of trade, granted to farmer cooperatives.

Exemption from price control.

Exemption from the military draft.

In most states farmers pay heavy taxes on farm property. But at the federal level they come off well, with various exemptions and deductions. In 1974 realized net farm income as estimated by the United States Department of Agriculture (USDA) was $27.7 billion. But net farm profit according to the Internal Revenue Service was $5.0 billion (Gardner 1978).

Preferred treatment having been achieved, the attitude in farm circles was to treat it not as an indication of political favor, but as a form of deserved differentiation from the nonfarm sector. A farm leader or a farm politician would deny with his last breath that agriculture had received any preference. The strategy has been to focus attention on those areas that showed agriculture at a disadvantage, to contrast the existing situation with some ideal, and to claim from government full redress of the disparity. If the claim of agriculture's uniqueness would help in this objective, it was invoked.

A powerful body of rhetoric developed in support of agriculture's unique worthiness. Here are the articles of the agricultural creed (Paarlberg 1964, p. 3):

Farmers are good citizens and a high percentage of our population should be on farms.

Farming is not only a business but a way of life.

Farming should be a family enterprise.

The land should be owned by the man who tills it.

It is good to "make two blades of grass grow where only one grew before."

Anyone who wants to farm should be free to do so.

A farmer should be his own boss.

So we had, until fairly recent times, a coherent, mutually reinforcing agricultural policy, based on the concept of agriculture's uniqueness. There was a body of belief, a set of unique institutions, and the political power to defend the system.

And it worked. In America, agriculture became productive and efficient perhaps to a greater degree than anywhere else in the world. Farm families achieved a social status unknown in most other countries. All of this powerfully supported the policy postulates underlying the structure.

But change was coming. The old policy postulates would be eroded away. And, strangely enough, among the erosive forces were those very agencies the agrarians had set up. The land grant colleges, the experiment stations, and the extension service, established to serve a unique clientele, would in time help deprive that clientele of its uniqueness.

There came the scientist, the technologist, and the engineer. There came the educator and the businessman. The tractor came, and with it a whole new complex of power machinery. The acreage one man could handle doubled, redoubled, and doubled again. Farms increased in size and decreased in number. The farm population diminished.

Rural Free Delivery came, and with it a great expansion of the farm press. There came the radio, the telephone, rural electrification, and television. The paved road and the automobile came, and soon thereafter came the school bus and the consolidated school, so that farm children no longer sat beside other farm children in a one-room school; they mingled with nonfarm children in the classroom and on the athletic field.

The isolation of rural life diminished. Farm people began reading the same papers as nonfarm people, hearing the same radio programs, watching the same television stars, seeing the same commercials, wanting the same amenities. The alleged superiority of farm life no longer provided enough psychic income to compensate for its lower dollar incomes and fewer conveniences.

Farmers began thinking and behaving like nonfarmers. Increasingly they borrowed money, rented land, and hired labor. Farmers began buying more of their inputs—power, fuel, feed, fertilizer. Their wives gave up the kitchen garden and canning—they bought groceries in the supermarket like their city cousins. By degrees the farm family moved away from the older ideas of subsistence and self-sufficiency. Increasingly they entered the money economy.

Formerly it had been assumed that the farm-raised young man would take over the home farm and continue the family name on the old homestead; this tradition gradually faded. The younger generation went off to school and began choosing vocations in much the same fashion as their classmates from town.

Farm people began taking off-farm jobs. Part-time farming grew in importance, and farm wives entered the job market as did women generally.

The changes were profound. From colonial times until late in the nineteenth century farmers outnumbered all other vocational groups combined (U.S. Department of Commerce 1975). The present minority status of agriculture came by decrements. In the census of 1920, for the first time, the urban category exceeded the rural, farm and nonfarm combined. By 1950 farmers were a minority in the rural areas; nonfarmers now outnumber farmers six to one in rural America. And in 1967 an incredible thing happened; for the first time the nonfarm incomes of farm people exceeded their farm incomes (*Economic report of the president* 1978, p. 362).

Farm people have entered the mainstream of American economic, social, and political life. They are no longer readily distinguishable from nonfarm people in speech, dress, or manner. The "city limits" sign, once an indication of economic and cultural differences, now merely marks the boundary between two units of local government.

The institutions set up to serve a unique vocation have had the unforeseen consequence of helping to reduce—indeed, almost to destroy—that uniqueness. The agents of change were so potent that they transformed themselves. The trends were gradual, so that year-to-year changes were not particularly noteworthy. And they are not complete. Agriculture's uniqueness persists, declining gradually through time, like the Geiger count for radioactive material. What is the half-life of an outmoded agrarian idea? Maybe a generation—twenty or thirty years.

A traditionalist (I am one) experiences crosscurrents of feeling as he contemplates these changes. On the one hand, I feel good about removing the disadvantages of income, opportunity, and services that farm people once felt. At the same time, I feel sadness at seeing farmers deprived of a unique sense of worthiness, at seeing them pushed toward becoming an undifferentiated part of a homogenized society. On balance, I raise one cheer, maybe two. Certainly not three.

But what difference would it make whether one cheer, or two or three, or none at all? Or whether there are laments instead of cheers? The change is under way and is irreversible. Turning it around would be about as likely a prospect as putting the chicken back into the egg—or the egg back into the chicken.

Politically and institutionally, agriculture must accommodate to these economic and social changes. It is doing so, at a rate far faster than the traditionalists like to acknowledge. One by one, agriculture is being deprived of its extraordinary advantages: preferred access to land and water, immunity from social legislation, preference with regard to military service, lax enforcement of civil rights laws. The resulting jolt is considerable. Farmers, traditionally independent, are increasingly subjected to the rules of an increasingly regulated society.

Together with the loss of agriculture's uniqueness, and springing from the same causes, has come loss of agriculture's power to control the farm policy agenda. Sometime during the early 1970s, while I was in the Department of Agriculture, the idea gradually began to dawn that most of the policy subject matter we were dealing with had not originated with us or with our farmer friends; it had been generated by nonfarm people. It seems amazing, in retrospect, that we were so slow to perceive and even slower to acknowledge the obvious fact that we had lost control of the policy agenda. These were the policy issues of that time, most of them placed on the agenda over the protests of the agricultural establishment:

Food prices, specifically how to hold them down, an issue placed on the agenda by the consumers.

Food programs, especially food stamps, which grew until they took up two-thirds of the budget of the Department of Agriculture. This issue was placed on the agenda by what has become known as the hunger lobby.

Adulerated foods, which was the code word for foods produced or processed with the use of chemicals, put on the agenda by the natural foods people.

Junk food, the allegation that the food supply carried excessive amounts of fat, sugar, and starch, put on the agenda by the nutritionists.

Ecological questions, placed on the agenda by the environmentalists.

Rural development, primarily a program for the 85 percent of rural people who are not farmers.

Limitations on government payments to farmers, put on the agenda by a coalition of taxpayers, small farmers, and believers in limited government.

Land and water questions, an issue raised by those who opposed the long-held idea that farmers have first claim on the use of these resources.

Grain embargoes, sought and obtained by organized labor. This issue was put forward as a means of holding down domestic food costs.

Civil rights, advocated by those who challenged the white male tradition that has long characterized agriculture.

Occupational safety and health, written into law in behalf of laboring people.

Collective bargaining for hired farm labor, an effort to extend to these people the rights of group action enjoyed by others, an issue raised mostly by Cesar Chavez's United Farm Workers.

Direct price controls on farm products, imposed on agriculture by the president of the United States.

Reorganization of the Department of Agriculture, put on the agenda by the president with the help of a committee of experts. The first proposal was that the department be abolished or dismembered. When this failed, the proposal was to subordinate the department to a new body, headed by a counselor for natural resources.

Meanwhile, the department had been trying to get favorable action from Congress on some initiatives of its own, issues related to the old agenda: streamlining and modernizing the research and education programs to increase the efficiency of agricultural production, and modifying the old commodity programs to make them more cost effective. These efforts were only partially successful.

The conclusion was inescapable that the agricultural establishment—by which I mean the farm organizations, the agricultural committees of Congress, the Department of Agriculture, and the land grant colleges—had lost control of the farm policy agenda.

When we snap on the television set to watch a football game, the first question we ask is, Who's got the ball? The agricultural establishment had the ball for a hundred years or more; but sometime during the sixties and seventies there was a turnover—a turnover so gradual that the public and even the principals have not yet fully recognized it. Nonetheless, the initiative has changed hands.

Control of the public policy agenda is of immense importance. If one controls the agenda, not only can he see that issues vital to him are brought up for action; what is much more important, he can prevent consideration of matters that could be hurtful. If one controls the agenda he holds the intiative; if someone else has the initiative, one is forced into a defensive posture and can only react. The comparison with military strategy and with football is very apt.

One can speculate about the reasons for the turnover. One cause, certainly, is the declining political power of farm people. In 1933, when the big commodity programs were enacted, farmers made up 26 percent of the population. In 1978 the figure was 3.6 percent and declining. In 1926 a majority—251 of the 435 members—of the House of Representatives were from so-called farm districts; that is, districts in which the farm population was 20 percent or more of the total. In 1976 farm districts, thus measured, had fallen to 49, one-fifth as many as fifty years earlier (Knebel 1977). Even in the Senate, the more pro-farm of the two bodies, agriculture's strength has dwindled. There is not now a single one of the fifty states in which farmers are the largest vocational group. In South Dakota, the most agricultural state of the Union, the farm population amounts to one one-fourth of the total. The industrialization of agriculture changed the character of farming and sharply reduced the number of farmers. From this profound change comes both the loss of agriculture's uniqueness and the impairment of its agenda-making power.

From what kind of power base can farmers deal with this situation? Their major asset is goodwill. Repeated surveys have shown that public opinion is favorably disposed toward farmers. There is a large body of "ag alumni"—people who once farmed or who are only a generation or two removed from agriculture. They retain a favorable disposition toward farmers. The historic position favoring agriculture continues but dwindles.

Some people say that, given the continuing favorable attitude toward farmers, declining numbers work to the advantage of agriculture. The argument takes this form: Having only a relatively small number of farmers, we are able to incur substantial public cost in behalf of each one of them. We can afford to be indulgent with a group of people who constitute less than 4 percent of the population; we could not afford to do so if they were very numerous. This hypothesis is compatible with the observed behavior of a number of countries. The wealthy, developed nations (United States, Western Europe, Japan) all pour heavy subsidies into their relatively small and relatively prosperous farm sectors, while poorer countries with relatively large and poverty-stricken agricultural populations (India, Kenya, Mexico) are much less openhanded. By this hypothesis, favored treatment for agriculture is not a prize won by political power; it is a gift conferred by an indulgent state. However this may be, the clear fact demonstrated throughout this book is that agriculture has lost political power.

Charles Hardin suggests that both the high farm-price support policies of the wealthy countries and the low food-price policies of those that are poor result from fear. The rich countries support agriculture because they recall the short rations and threats of famine in two world wars; the poor countries fear the wrath of the urban masses and seek to placate them with "cheap food."

Whatever the political power base may be, during the years ahead we must work out the assimilation of agriculture into the mainstream of American life. As I see it, this is likely to be the major factor affecting farm and food policy for at least the next decade.

The dynamics of change are likely to follow this sequence:

1. Technological change. This is well along. It puts pressure on an institutional complex set up to serve an earlier form of agriculture.

2. Institutional adaptation. This is under way. Slowly, unevenly, and grudgingly, the agencies and the political programs change to accommodate the new technology. The old rhetoric is still voiced, long after technology has invalidated it and even after political action has accepted the change. Praise of the old-fashioned family farm is an example. In part this is a smoke screen. Behind it and obscured by it, the necessary changes can be and are being made. In this respect it serves a useful purpose, and we should not be too critical.

3. Finally, full acceptance of change in all its aspects. This takes a very long time.

So if one wants to know what is really going on or what is likely to happen in terms of public policy, one should look rather than listen. The worst thing to do is to listen to the rhetoric, which is likely to reflect circumstances that have become increasingly obsolete.

REFERENCES

Berry, Wendell. 1977. *The unsettling of America: Culture and agriculture*. San Francisco: Sierra Club.

Bishop, C. E. 1967. The urbanization of rural America: Implications for agricultural economics. *Journal of Farm Economics* 49:999–1008.

Bonnen, James T. 1965. Present and prospective policy problems of U.S. agriculture: As viewed by an economist. *Journal of Farm Economics* 47:1116–29.

Boulding, Kenneth E. 1978. Normative science and agricultural policy. James C. Snyder Memorial Lecture in Agricultural Economics, *Institute of Behavioral Science,* University of Colorado at Boulder.

Breimyer, Harold F. 1965. *Individual freedom and the economic organization of agriculture.* Urbana: University of Illinois Press.

Commission on Country Life. 1911. *Report of the Commission on Country Life.* Chapel Hill: University of North Carolina Press; reprinted 1944.

Economic report of the president. 1978. Washington, D.C.: Government Printing Office.

Ford, Thomas R., ed. 1978. *Rural USA: Persistence and change.* Ames: Iowa State University Press.

Gardner, Bruce L. 1978. Public policy and the control of agricultural production. *American Journal of Agricultural Economics* 60:836–43.

Goldschmidt, Walter. 1947. *As you sow.* New York: Harcourt, Brace.

Griswold, A. Whitney. 1948. *Farming and democracy.* New York: Harcourt, Brace.

Hardin, Charles M. 1952. *The politics of agriculture.* Glencoe, Ill.: Free Press.

Hines, Fred K.; Brown, David L.; and Zimmer, John M. 1975. *Social and economic characteristics of the population of metro and non metro counties.* Report 272. Washington D.C.: USDA Economics Research Service, 272.

Knebel, John A. 1977. Agricultural outlook. In *1977 U.S. agricultural outlook,* prepared for the Committee on Agriculture and Forestry, U.S. Senate, 9th Congr. 2d sess. Washington, D.C.: Government Printing Office.

Larson, Olaf F., and Rogers, Everett M. 1964. Rural society in transition: The American setting. In *Our changing rural society: Perspectives and trends,* James H. Copp. Ames: Iowa State University Press.

Paarlberg, Don. 1964. *American farm policy.* New York: Wiley.

Paulson, Arnold. 1977. *Economic solutions are possible.* Washington, D.C.: National Organization for Raw Materials.

Raup, Philip M. 1978. Some questions of value and scale in American agriculture. *American Journal of Agricultural Economics* 60:303–8.

Ruttan, Vernon W. 1966. Agricultural policy in an affluent society. *Journal of Farm Economics* 48:1100–1120.

U.S. Congress. Senate. USDA. ERS. 1975. *The economic and social condition of non-metropolitan America in the 1970s.* 94th Congr., 1st sess., Committee Print.

U.S. Department of Commerce. Bureau of the Census. 1975. *Historical statistics of the United States, colonial times to 1970, bicentennial edition, part 1.* Washington, D. C. Government Printing Office.

3. The Historic Farm Policy Agenda

HISTORICALLY, American agricultural policy issues have sprung from three evolving and overlapping agendas:

Before 1933: Agricultural development, particularly research and education.

Since 1933: Commodity programs.

Increasingly since the mid-sixties: Issues raised by nonfarmers.

In this brief chapter I shall consider the unfinished business from the first agenda. In terms of broad public policy issues this is not much, for most of the major issues concerning agricultural development in the United States have been resolved, though some have been deferred or finessed. Of course, development is a continuous process, never completed. But the agricultural development questions that will confront those involved with research and education during the next decade are likely to be concerned more with tactics than with strategy, more with means than with ends, more with "how" than with "whether." They are likely to resemble family fights—immensely important to the participants, of some interest to observing neighbors, but of limited significance in a broader sense.

In 1862, at the height of the Civil War, came a major farm policy breakthrough. Before that time the architects of public policy, agricultural and other, had been the big landowners, the industrialists, the politicians, and the professional classes. The working farmers, by far the most numerous group in the country, had little power in agenda-making. In the mid-nineteenth century, advocates of these dirt farmers mounted an initiative that was opposed by virtually all of the contemporary power elite.

14

Farmers wanted a better chance to own land. They wanted recognition at the national levels of government. They wanted a role in decision-making. They wanted improved social status. And they wanted better information on crops and soils and livestock. Some of these desires were actively expressed, others were latent. In any case, they were picked up by politicians who wanted the farmers' votes. These objectives were to be achieved by direct action, coupled with research and education.

The effort succeeded. Farmers got the Homestead Act, which set up a family farming system, despite the opposition of the landed gentry, especially those of the plantation-minded South. They got a Department of Agriculture despite the resistance of the power elite, who resisted this broadening of the political base. They got the federally supported land grant college system, despite the resistance of the established private liberal arts colleges of the East. To this string of victories were later added the experiment stations, the extension service, vocational education, the Farm Credit Administration and other notable service agencies. Farmers expected these institutions to be responsive to their expressed needs.

This was an agrarian revolution, peaceful but potent. Its leaders were Abraham Lincoln and his Republican party, both with roots in the Free Soil movement. They pushed changes through Congress during the Civil War while major adversaries were absent.

This policy initiative had impressive results. It improved the efficiency of agricultural production, increased the flow of food to consumers, and raised the status of farm people so that, as Earl Heady has said: ''The United States has had the best, the most logical, and the most successful program of agricultural development anywhere in the world'' (1976, p. 107).

Out of this yeasty ferment came a series of public and private movements: Populism, the Greenback party, the campaign for free coinage of silver, the Granger movement, and the beginning of farmer cooperatives. These had a mixed and fascinating experience of success and failure. But the focus in this chapter is primarily on agricultural development through research and education.

A crucial question coming from the first farm policy agenda was the degree to which the new institutions would be responsive to the expressed wishes of those for whom they had been created. The answer was to some degree equivocal, but on major issues the new agencies asserted their independence. There were occasional confrontations as the research and educational agencies escaped from narrow constituent advocacy to broader service.

Experiment stations developed new agricultural science that immensely increased the supply of agricultural products, resulting in downward pressure on farm prices. Early adopters were benefited, true enough, but those farmers who would not or could not or in any case *did* not adopt the new technology were squeezed. As it turned out, the consumers rather than the farmers were the prime beneficiaries. Farmers as a whole saw their standard of living rise, but they were helped more as members of an advancing open society than as specific beneficiaries of the experiment stations. Farmers found that they could not, as a vocational group, capture and hold the gains that flowed from the institutions they had set up. The National Farmers Union protested strongly against the research and education community and the price-depressing abundance that flowed from it. But the experiment stations persisted in their scientific inquiry, demonstrating allegiance to the advancement of science.

In 1943 the Iowa Experiment Station did a study that produced results favorable to development of margarine but offensive to the politically powerful dairy interests. After some backing and filling, the principle of research independence was affirmed.

In 1933, when the Department of Agriculture launched the big crop control programs for corn and wheat and cotton, the federal government expected the extension service to take part in support and advocacy. This posed an agonizing problem. The extension service first helped, then wavered, and finally decided it was an educational arm, not an action agency. It has generally maintained this position ever since, despite pressures from within and without.

In the sixties and seventies, the experiment stations and the extension service increasingly served the needs of rural nonfarm people, to the displeasure of their historic farmer constituents. Despite some threats and grumblings, the new initiative persisted.

In California, operators of big irrigated farms sought the support of the land grant system in fighting the acreage limitations imposed by the Interior Department. But support was not forthcoming.

The countries of Asia, Africa, and Latin America, anxious to achieve agricultural development and noting our success, came to the United States for help. Some farm groups feared that if we extended such help we would improve the competitive position of rival exporters or assist importing nations to feed themselves, to the injury of our farmers. Nevertheless, virtually every land grant college became involved in international agricultural development, as did the Department of Agriculture.

Thus, in a series of low-key disputes, the research and educational institutions of the land grant colleges, including the research and extension wings of the Department of Agriculture, established these principles: Responsibility is broad rather than narrow. Independence is coupled with accountability.

Farm operators are the prime but not the only constituents. Research and educational services are to a considerable degree independent both of government and of special interests in agriculture. In a fashion that they have wisely left unspecified, the research and educational arm of agriculture is sympathetic to farm people but not automatically responsive to the expressed needs of the original sponsors.

As I indicated in chapter 2, the new institutions were based on the belief that agriculture was unique. The eventual effect of the information they generated was to deprive agriculture of much of that uniqueness. So the institutions came under stress. Should they insist on retaining the role contemplated for them at the time of their creation? Or should they shed their uniqueness and enter the mainstream of economic, social, and political life, as their farmer constituents were doing? The land grant college system and like agencies did the only feasible thing; they accommodated to change. They did so in laggard fashion, perhaps, and with many creaks and groans, but nevertheless it was effective. The research and education community adapted to the changes that it itself had generated.

A few illustrations will make this clear. As the technological revolution proceeded, farms were consolidated and reduced in number. There were fewer opportunities to farm. An education in agriculture was more often a bridge to get out of farming than a preparation to stay in. By 1978 only 18 percent of the agricultural graduates were going into farming and farm management. Rather than fight this departure from the original goal, the schools adapted their course offerings to meet the needs their students felt. The original idea was to train young men of farm background for farm operation; the objective gradually became an agriculturally oriented education preparing both farm and nonfarm men and women for whatever employment they deemed best. In 1978 two-thirds of the agricultural students at Purdue University had nonfarm backgrounds. Almost one-third were women.

The extension service, which had created the enormously successful 4-H clubs, found that the shrinking farm population put a ceiling on the program. There were millions of young people who could be helped; they just did not happen to be from farms. So the nonfarm rural young people were brought in, as in time were boys and girls from the city. In 1978 only 24 percent of Indiana's 4-H club members lived on farms.

There was an element of self-preservation in this broadened role. Research and education workers understood the arithmetic of public policy. In 1860, when the land grant college system was established, 59 percent of all working people were engaged in agricultural production. By 1978 the farm population was 3.6 percent of the total and declining. For the land grant colleges to tie themselves closely to this shrinking base would have meant sharply restricted budgets and a reduced role in society.

Accommodation to change has gone much further and much faster than one would think if he only listened to the rhetoric. By repeating the familiar litany of agricultural fundamentalism, the research and education community has generally been able to hold the support of the old guard. With this support they have been increasingly able to respond to demands from their new constituents. One can argue whether this is linguistic lag or conscious duplicity, but one can not dispute its effectiveness. In either case the research and educational institutions have established the principles and the deportment with which they can accommodate to whatever lies ahead. The institutions that came from the first farm policy agenda thus equipped themselves to adapt to the second agenda, then to the third.

Consider how great have been the accommodations made by the land grant college system, with its experiment stations and its extension service, which together make up the research and education arm of agriculture. These institutions of the first farm policy agenda, which are biased toward production, reconciled themselves to sharing power with institutions of the second agenda, which are oriented against production. And despite strong commitment toward farming, the research and education people are learning to share power with the architects of the third agenda, who are somewhat anti-farm. The experiment stations, which once had a virtual monopoly on the generation of new agricultural knowledge, have had to share their role with a host of other agencies: other universities, the National Institutes of Health, the International Agricultural Research Network, private agribusiness firms, and the research foundations. The extension service, which once was the prime if not the sole agent of adult education for farm people, has had to share that function with agribusiness firms and private consultants. Meanwhile, as has been said, a larger and larger share of the effort has gone to serve a new nonfarm clientele. And the land grant colleges have somewhat muted their hundred-year-old quarrel with general education and the liberal arts.

These changes were accepted rather than initiated. They came slowly, reluctantly, and by small increments. What can one say of such accommodation? Is it simply instinct for survival? Or does it reflect a higher wisdom, an acceptance of ambivalence? Does it stem from a deep sense of worthiness and mission, which is above pride of place?

Research and education workers in agriculture have been remarkably successful in their original mission, which was to raise the competence, status, and well-being of farm people.

When possible they avoid fights, as in Michigan, when cattle feed was accidentally contaminated with the deadly fire retardant, PBB. In the West they stayed out of the argument over corporate agriculture. In the South they tried to avert confrontation on civil rights. Nationwide, they attempted to keep a low profile on environmental questions. So major confrontations are likely to be few.

There is an important issue remaining from the first farm policy agenda—the structure of American agriculture. Are we to have an owner-operated family type of agriculture, as was intended by the policy architects of a hundred years ago? This and like policy issues will be fought out by protagonists other than those set up a century past. The research and educational institutions have settled into a role that precludes coping with such issues.

Proponents of political, social, and institutional change will get little deliberate help from the research and education people. Defenders of the past or of the existing order will not get much help either. These agencies want no part of direct action; they will do their best to discover and disseminate knowledge. That is their job. But, like good shoemakers, they stick to their last.

REFERENCES

Agricultural Research Policy Advisory Committee. 1975. *Research to meet U.S. and world food needs.* Report of a Working Conference, Kansas City, Missouri, July 9–11, 1975. Vols. 1 and 2.

Barton, Wendell V. 1974. *Coalition-building in the U.S. House of Representatives: Agricultural legislation in 1973.* Paper presented at 1974 annual meeting of the American Political Science Association, Chicago, August 29–September 2, 1974.

Bonnen, James T. 1977. *Observations on the changing nature of national agricultural policy decisions process: 1946–1976.* Presented to conference on Farmers, Bureaucrats and Middlemen: Historical Perspective on American Agriculture, sponsored by the National Archives and the Agricultural History Society, April 27–29, 1977.

Hadwiger, Don F., and Fraenkel, Richard. 1976. In *Economic regulatory policies,* ed. James E. Anderson. Lexington, Mass.: D. C. Heath.

Heady, Earl O. 1976. The agriculture of the U.S. *Scientific American* 235: 106–27.

McCalla, Alex F. 1978. Politics of the agricultural research establishment. In *The new politics of food,* ed. Don F. Hadwiger and William P. Browne. Lexington, Mass.: D. C. Heath.

Vines, C. Austin, and Anderson, Marvin A., eds. 1976. Heritage horizons: Extension's commitment to people. *Journal of Extension* (Madison, Wis.), pp. 1–236.

Youngberg, Garth. 1976. U.S. agriculture in the 1970s: Policy and politics. In *Economic regulatory policies,* ed. James E. Anderson. Lexington, Mass.: D. C. Heath.

4. The Commodity Programs

Unlike the first farm policy agenda, agricultural development—which appeared in the late nineteenth century and is something of a spent volcano—the second agenda, commodity programs, erupted in 1933 and has been belching fire and smoke ever since.

BACKGROUND

Until 1933, the public policy choice was to rely on the market for most economic decisions. Some difficulties were acknowledged, and there were efforts to improve the market's performance, but the system itself was generally considered the best possible way to allocate resources, guide consumption, and reward endeavor.

Then came the Great Depression, worldwide in its effect. Interdependent as international markets were, prices fell both in the United States and in the rest of the world. The statistics were grim. From 1929 to 1932, prices received by American farmers dropped 56 percent. Gross farm income was cut to less than half. Net income of agriculture fell from $6.3 billion to $1.9 billion.

These numbers are impersonal and anonymous. Specifics may serve better. In 1932 the average net farm income on more than five-hundred Indiana farms, of which my family's was one, was only $208. This figure is not synthetic; it is computed from farm accounts kept in cooperation with Purdue University. The figure given is the net return to the farmer for his labor, management, and capital. If he figured a 5 percent return on his capital, the net return to his labor

20

and management was negative; on the average, in 1932, these better-than-ordinary farmers paid $510 for the privilege of working. On our own general farm in Lake County, Indiana, the net return to labor and management in that terrible year was a negative $1,203.

This depression, with some indecisive ups and downs, ground on for a full ten years, despite government efforts to overcome it, until the recovery brought by World War II. During the decade of the 1930s, the yearly average return to labor and management on our farm was $815. During three years of that decade the return was negative. We were more fortunate than many—we managed to escape foreclosure. Many families lost their farms.

The Great Depression often hurt the good farmers more than the poor ones, chiefly because the poor ones had little to lose. The good farmers had generally adopted progressive practices that involved a heavy cash outlay for goods and services: fertilizer, fuel, power machinery, and the like. They had adopted the practices recommended by the extension service. Frequently these better farms were leveraged and had substantial charges for debt service. This meant high and continued cash costs, difficult to meet when receipts fell. The farmers who went broke generally were the venturesome ones who had obligated themselves for large cash outlays. A similar experience occurred on a much smaller scale during 1977 and 1978, touching off the American Agriculture Movement.

The market system had long been considered an intelligent institution. But here were markets gone wild with fear, markets that made no sense, that dealt out the harshest punishment to the best farmers. The system kept generating more supplies when there appeared to be no outlet for what was already in hand. How could one have faith in the allocative merits of a market that behaved like the legendary sorcerer's apprentice, who spoke the magic word to make the broom carry water and then forgot the word to stop it?

Farmers, needing help, undertook a number of desperate acts. In a dramatic protest against legal foreclosures, Iowa farmers threatened to hang a federal judge. They overturned milk trucks, picketed packing plants, and boycotted farm sales. The mood was ominous: anger, frustration, insistence on action.

The first farm policy agenda—agricultural development, research, and education—was incapable of dealing with the problems caused by the Great Depression. Obviously, this was a situation for which research and education could provide no solution. So a new group of activists took over. Relief, Recovery, and Reform were the mood of the times, and they produced the Agricultural Adjustment Administration. The three Rs spawned the three As.

The diagnosis was that agriculture was suffering from overproduction; this was credible both to farmers and to politicians. Farmers knew that excessive production meant low prices and therefore reasoned that the explanation for low prices must be excess production. Objective analysts had some difficulty with this explanation, pointing out that supplies per person were no larger than before. A general consensus today, forty-five years after the event, is that, whatever the original cause, the problem was immensely aggravated by the breakdown of money and credit. But explaining the Great Depression is not my intent in this chapter. My purpose is to trace the consequences of the explanation that *was* adopted.

An idea took hold very powerfully—that American agriculture could not compete with the agriculture of other countries. This was in spite of our great advantages, bestowed by nature and fostered by the people. The idea developed that we should turn inward, reduce production, and create an American farm price structure basically higher than that in the rest of the world. This could not be done through individual decision-making; it had to be done by government. The idea fit in well with the mood that was then on the ascendancy in the world and in the United States—mistrust of the market and a belief that centralized decision-making should supplant the older system of individual responsibility.

Opposed to this approach were a number of groups. Monetary theorists diagnosed the problem as a collapse of money and credit rather than as overproduction and therefore thought that curtailing output was not the solution. Classical economists resisted the control programs because they conflicted with what was then orthodox economics. Rugged individualists resented the expanded role of government. Stalwart Republicans opposed the farm program on political grounds.

The confrontation was brief and the outcome decisive. The new farm policy quickly became, almost totally, the new order of business. The big commodity programs were begun. The idea was to limit output so as to increase the price per unit and thereby raise the net income of farmers. (Details of the programs are given in Cochrane and Ryan 1976; Benedict and Stine 1956; and Benedict 1953.) Output was to be limited by restricting acreage planted. Each farm was given a base, determined by its historical cropping pattern. This method of supply control was focused on six crops that were declared "basic": wheat, corn, cotton, rice, peanuts, and tobacco.

Price supports were established for these and a number of other farm products. The level of support was determined by the relationship of prices farmers received to prices farmers paid during 1910–14, the legally established base period. This is the famous parity relationship.

The devices for assuring that farmers received the legally determined price were generally three: "loans," "target prices," and "purchase and diversion."

"Loans" are nonrecourse loans; that is, no recourse is available to the lender (the government) if the farmer borrower defaults on his loan. The government lends, say, $2 a bushel on a farmer's corn crop. If the market price goes above $2, the farmer sells the corn, repays the loan, and pockets the difference. If the market price falls below $2, the farmer turns the crop over to the government in full repayment of the loan. When markets are weak, the government thus acquires a large inventory. The effect is to keep the market price, in most cases, from falling below the loan level.

"Target prices" are a device for providing assistance to farmers while leaving the market price more or less free to fluctuate. If the average market price falls below the target, farmers receive deficiency payments based on the difference. If the market price rises above the target, the farmer sells for the higher price and owes the government nothing.

"Purchase and diversion" is a method sometimes used to provide assistance to producers of perishable products such as dairy products, fruits, and vegetables. The government purchases the product, thus reducing the amount moving through the commercial market and increasing the price. The government-acquired product is then diverted outside the regular commercial channels, chiefly through donation at home and abroad.

"Commodity programs" as used in this book means programs for the following farm products. They are grouped according to the major techniques used:

1. Wheat, corn and other feed grains, cotton, rice, peanuts, tobacco. The technique used is supply control and price support.

2. Manufactured dairy products, wool. The method used is price assistance without supply control.

3. Sugar. The program involves price assistance, chiefly through limitation of imports.

When "commodity programs" are discussed in this book, I am not referring to marketing orders or to occasional government purchase and diversion of some relatively minor product in temporary surplus. I am referring to programs for the nine commodities named above.

Let us examine the common arguments for and against these programs.

THE CASE FOR THE BIG COMMODITY PROGRAMS

Argument One: These Programs Saved Farmers from Disaster

As has been said, the mood on American farms in 1932 and 1933 was grim. In other countries, notably Germany and Italy, which were also in the grip of the

Great Depression, the open economic system gave way to fascism. How far we were from taking that step is a matter on which historians differ. But anyone who farmed during that time felt the rising tide of anger and the insistence on change.

The Agricultural Adjustment Act was signed by President Roosevelt on May 21, 1933, providing for price supports and production controls on the major crops. The president recognized the novel nature of the bill; he had sent the proposal to Congress with this comment: "I tell you frankly that it is a new and untrod path, but I can tell you with equal frankness that an unprecedented condition calls for the trial of new means" (Halcrow 1977, p. 159).

The crop control initiative gave farmers a role in working out their own chosen solution to their problem. They were put on committees by the thousands. They went to work, for pay, establishing production bases for individual farms. They elected officers and went to meetings. They made fervent speeches. Government officials came out and listened. There were enough government officials to do this; during the term of Secretary Henry A. Wallace employment in the Department of Agriculture increased from 27,000 to 98,000. Government checks began to flow. Checks went for the mortgage payment, or to pay the taxes, or to pay the doctor. Payments were based on volume of production. Hence the biggest checks went to the biggest farmers, whose incomes had fallen the most. On every hand was visible evidence that the government cared. The Depression dragged on, but the mood changed for the better on American farms.

The enormous value of this change in mood was not appreciated by those who disregarded political considerations and viewed the whole experience narrowly in traditional economic terms. Whatever may have been the economic attributes of the commodity programs, politically they were a master stroke.

Most critics acknowledge the beneficial early effects of the commodity programs in improving farm incomes and forestalling what might otherwise have been political upheaval. Of course, when the Great Depression passed farmers were no longer in a desperate position, and that particular rationale for the program lost its validity. But the euphoria generated by early experience carried on for decades. During those early years there were favorable perceptions of the big commodity programs. These would persist through quite different circumstances.

Argument Two: Farmers Are at a Continuous Economic Disadvantage

Impressive statistics are cited in the effort to demonstrate that farmers are chronically disadvantaged relative to other forms of enterprise. A figure often used to describe the economic condition of agriculture is net farm income, which is simply the difference between total income received from farming and the outlay for production expenses. This figure fluctuates considerably from year to year. In 1977 it was one-third below the peak year, 1973. In real terms (corrected for the effects of inflation), it was below the pre-1973 level.

Another set of statistics used in an effort to document the distressed situation in agriculture is the comparison of per capita farm incomes (including income from nonfarm sources) with the per capita incomes of nonfarmers. Since 1934 the Department of Agriculture has computed average per capita incomes, farm and nonfarm. In all but one of these years, the farm figure has been the lower, averaging 40 percent below the nonfarm figure for the period. In 1978 it stood at 91 percent of the nonfarm level.

Additional allegations that agriculture is at a disadvantage arise from yet another set of USDA statistics, the parity ratio. Parity has the connotation of being a fair price. Parity was perhaps most understandably defined by the farmer who said: "If a bushel of wheat would buy a pair of overalls in 1910–14, then, to be at parity, a bushel of wheat should be priced so as to buy a pair of overalls today."

The inference is that parity is a "fair" price and that anything less is "unfair." But farm products have rarely reached parity levels. In July 1978 they were bringing only 72 percent of parity. The variation among commodities was enormous, reflecting vastly different conditions of supply and demand for the various products. Government price supports were no assurance that prices would be high. Apples were selling in the free market for 130 percent of parity; wheat, a supported crop, was selling for 52 percent of parity.

The alleged disadvantage for agriculture, attested by these three statistical series, is often cited as the prime reason for the existence of government farm programs intended to raise farm prices and farm incomes. It is perhaps the most persuasive argument used by the farm lobby. But parity, net farm income, and per capita farm income are in various ways inaccurate measures of the farmers' condition.

First parity. The concept, originally flawed, is now untenable. It assumes that farm and nonfarm prices were properly related to one another during the base period, 1910–14; that production costs in agriculture and nonagricultural activities have changed at the same rate since 1910–14; and that demands for farm and nonfarm products either have not changed since 1910–14 or, if they have changed, the changes are identical.

These are unsupportable assumptions. The period 1910–14 was favorable to agriculture, a kind of golden age marked by growing markets and gradually rising prices for farm products.

Agriculture is dynamic rather than static. One cannot hold price relationships constant for an industry that has gone from horse to tractor and from hoe to herbicide. Luther Tweeten states the situation thus: "Adequate sized, well-managed farms now on the average require approximately 75 percent of 1910–14 price parity to cover all costs of production including land at its current value and a rather generous return to the operator and his family for labor, risk, management, and equity" (Tweeten 1978).

Only about 5 percent of the people living in 1978 were alive when the base period began. Almost no one can remember it.

The Food and Agriculture Act of 1977 virtually abandoned parity, which had become so badly tarnished as to be no longer useful. "Cost of production" was substituted. But this standard also has grave flaws. How do we compute the cost? What interest rate should be charged? What charge should be made for labor and management supplied by the farmer and his family? What charge should be made for land? Price at the time of purchase? Current market value? Rental value? If the land charge is too high, the calculated production cost is too high, income supports are too high, and agricultural production becomes highly profitable. This boosts the price of land in the next cycle so that land charge, production cost, income supports, and profitability rise yet further. The system has the potential of a multistage rocket. Fortunately, the act of 1977 avoids full incorporation of the land charge in determining production cost. However it is computed, some farmers will have a per bushel cost twice as high as some other farmers. Whose cost should be determining? The average? About half the farmers would have costs higher than that. The cost of the least efficient producer? Then windfall gains accrue to the better farmers. Cost of production leaves demand out of the picture altogether. If demand is increasing, as for soybeans, the price should be above production cost, to encourage greater production. The reverse would be true for some product experiencing declining demand, such as butterfat. In time, cost of production will prove to be as flawed a standard as parity.

The net farm income figure also requires scrutiny. It is carefully computed, but in 1977 it related to only 39 percent of the net income received by farm people. Incredible though it may seem, in 1977 the people who were officially classified as farmers received 61 percent of their income from off-farm sources: nonfarm jobs held by farm operators or members of their families, income from investments, and the like. These nonfarm dollars are looked on askance by farm lobbyists, who call them evidence that farming is not as profitable as it should be; "farmers have such low incomes they have to take second jobs." But many of these dollars are earned during the off season, when farm work is slack. Dollars thus received are just as useful for paying bills as dollars from the sale of farm products. The nonfarm income of farm people increases over time. During the ten years from 1967 to 1977, it more than doubled. From 1973 to 1977, income received by farm people from nonfarm sources increased from $19.7 billion to $24.7 billion. This increase, about which very little has been said, offset more than 60 percent of the widely advertised decline in net income received by farmers from farming during that period. Another difficulty with net farm income is that over time the number of farmers declines. Failure to put these figures on a per farm basis makes the income situation appear worse than it is.

The comparison of per capita farm income (which includes incomes of farmers from both farm and nonfarm sources) with per capita incomes of nonfarmers typically shows the farm figure to be low. This is in part because of the way farms are defined. Until 1978 any place that received $250 or more annually from the sale of farm products, or had more than ten acres and sold at least $50 worth of crops and livestock, was defined as a farm. Thus many farms were very small. Nearly a million of them, 35 percent of the total, sold less than $2,500 worth of products in a year's time. They constituted about one-third of the farms and produced only about 1 percent of the products sold. They had substantial off-farm income; on the average they received $10 of nonfarm income for every dollar's worth of farm products sold.

Not only did the farm incomes of these people average low; their total incomes had a low average. If these operators were removed from the farm category, the computed average per capita incomes of farm people would increase 7 percent (Bruce L. Gardner, pers. comm.).

Difficulties of the farm-nonfarm comparison were in part alleviated in 1978 by a change in the definition of a farm. The new definition includes places with annual sales of agricultural products of $1,000 or more. Under the old definition there were 2,672,000 farms in 1978. Under the new definition there were 2,370,000, a reduction of 11 percent. The change in definition will slightly increase the computed per capita incomes of farm people and so improve the calculated ratio of per capita farm income to per capita incomes of nonfarmers.

Finally, there is a piece of statistical information that seldom gets reported. Income is only one dimension of well-being. The other is net worth. One is a flow and the other a stock concept. Having been a livestock farmer, I know there are two important characteristics of a water tank; one is the rate of inflow, and the other is the amount of water in the tank. The same principle applies in financial affairs.

While computations of income show that the farm average is low, computations of net worth show that the farm average is high. This is largely because of the longterm increase in land values. An estimate in 1966 showed net worth per family in agriculture to be four times as high as net worth per nonfarm family

(Jacobson and Paarlberg 1966, p. 127). Since the recent rise in farm land values, the relative net worth position of farm people has no doubt improved. The argument will be made that the increase in net worth arising from increased land values cannot be spent. True, but it can be security for a loan. Stock can be converted to flow, as any financier will attest.

The almost exclusive focus on income, and on the smaller part of the income, has the intent of putting the worst foot forward so as to bolster the argument for government help. The economic position of any occupation as complex as modern agriculture cannot accurately be characterized by a single number, or by a combination of three numbers carefully selected to show the worst case.

All these statistical measures have the defect that they deal with aggregates or averages. The averages obscure the real problem, which is the enormous gap between the poor and the well-to-do, a subject to be taken up later in the chapter.

Argument Three: Agriculture Has a Chronic Tendency to Overproduce

The belief is widespread that agriculture has a built-in tendency toward overproduction. Willard Cochrane has called this the overriding problem. He attributes this tendency to the high value American society places on scientific research and technological development; the market organization or structure within which farmers operate; the extreme inelasticity of demand for food—that is, the sharp farm price increase associated with even a moderate decrease in supply, which results in committing additional resources to agriculture; and the inability of resources previously committed to farm products to shift easily and readily out of farming (Cochrane and Ryan 1976, p. 15).

Farmers, who almost always think the price is too low, contend that this is because the supply is excessive. The inclination to believe in the overproduction thesis is very great. Various estimates are made of the degree to which our farm plant is overexpanded. Luther Tweeten reports that excess production capacity ranged from 4.5 percent to 11.2 percent of farm output from 1955 to 1968 (Tweeten 1977, p. 45). If it is true that there are structural defects that predispose agriculture to overproduction, then the case for government control is persuasive indeed.

Given the price objectives specified in the law, there is undeniably excess production capacity in agriculture. The real question is this: What is the cause of this excess capacity? People who favor the big commodity programs cultivate the feeling, which gained acceptance during the Depression, that overproduction is structural and endemic. But they ignore a number of considerations that cast doubt on the overproduction thesis.

The result of holding farm prices and farm incomes continuously and substantially above equilibrium levels is to create surplus. Artificially high prices have the demonstrable effect of stimulating production and retarding consumption. An increase in price, other things being equal, will result in the commitment of additional productive resources; an increase in price, other things equal, will inhibit consumption. It follows that if price is increased above where it otherwise would be, and if nothing else is changed, excess production will come about, whether or not it previously existed.

If price is stabilized and assured, as it is under the government programs, risk is reduced. Careful studies have confirmed that reduction of risk is a stimulant to production (Brandow 1977 *a*, p. 78; Nelson and Cochrane 1976; Gray, Sorenson, and Cochrane 1954; Johnson 1952).

The gross evidence is contrary to the notion that free agriculture has a structural tendency to overproduce. Consider how farmers, in the absence of control programs, have reduced production:

When the tractor replaced the horse, the need for oats, a horse feed, declined. From 1930 to 1975 the acreage of oats fell 66 percent.

During the past forty-five years farmers and ranchers voluntarily reduced sheep and lamb numbers from 51.6 million to 14.5 million. The reasons were sound from an economic standpoint: consumer preferences for fiber and meat were working against the industry, and other countries could produce at a lower cost.

Farm-separated cream, formerly a major product in much of the country, virtually disappeared.

From 1934 to 1969 the acreage harvested for crops in New York State declined 48 percent.

From 1930 to 1974, the outmigration from agriculture was 33 million persons (Schultz 1978, p. 356).

Retrenchment and reduction of output are difficult for agriculture; this is clearly true. But over time reduction in output is not the major need. The market for agricultural products is increasing overall as population rises and as diets improve. The important thing is to avoid increasing supply faster than demand is increasing.

Finally, even if a chronic tendency toward overproduction were a major attribute of agriculture, the big commodity programs have not solved the problem. They either caused the problem or acquiesced in it. They certainly did not cure it. From 1933, when these programs began, through 1977, $55 billion of public funds has been expended through government payments alone (USDA 1978, p. 52). Additional costs in the form of losses on disposal of commodities, storage charges, and the like are not accounted for in this figure. One is entitled to hope that with so massive an effort more would have been accomplished than to carry the problem along, unsolved.

Argument Four: Government Programs Are Needed to Increase Agricultural Stability

Together, the weeds, the weather, the insects, the diseases, and the gyrations of the market make farming one of the most unstable enterprises a man can undertake. Farmers are very vulnerable to price change, both from changes in the general economy and from changes in supply of particular farm products. Vulnerability to change in the overall economy was demonstrated on the down side during the Great Depression and on the up side during the inflationary surge of the mid-seventies.

Farm income is becoming even more vulnerable to price change. Many years ago, when production expenses were one-third as large as cash receipts, a decline of 10 percent in price received, other things being equal, meant a decline of 15 percent in the net. On today's farms, with current operating expenses equal to 80 percent of cash receipts, a decline of 10 percent in price received means a decline of 50 percent in the net, three times as great a blow as was the case many years earlier.

In most of the nonfarm economy, economic risk is being reduced. Job tenure, unemployment insurance, and a whole set of institutional inventions have had that intention and that result. It is difficult for agriculture to accept increasingly greater risk while the rest of the economy is experiencing less risk. Thus arises the case for commodity programs to reduce the amplitude of fluctuations in farm prices and farm incomes.

The record of farm prices and farm income clearly shows that the commodity programs have resulted in greater stability. Willard Cochrane reports that after World War I, when we had in operation few stabilization efforts for agriculture or anything else, we went through two disastrous price declines: 1920–21 and 1929–32. After World War II, when we had numerous stabilization programs for agriculture (and many other sectors of the economy), such disaster was avoided (Cochrane and Ryan 1976, p. 385).

Temporary extremes in farm prices and farm income give erroneous production signals. The very high prices of grain during 1973–76 overstimulated grain production and led to subsequent price distress. Very low prices of pork in 1971 brought about a subsequent 18 percent reduction in output, with the result that the price of hogs more than doubled. Windfall profits and undeserved losses are the attributes of wild price gyrations. Debts incurred in good times are paid off with great distress when times are hard.

In the absence of commodity programs, which involve accumulation of government-held stocks, there are limited carryover supplies, and so there is great volatility in price. A large crop is forced into use by a sharp decline in price; a short crop is rationed out by a very high price.

These arguments are, for the greater part, valid and persuasive. A doctrinaire classical economist may not agree, because he assumes that economic adjustments take place automatically and for the most part painlessly. He ignores friction in much the same way as the physicist, with his equation for finding the speed of falling objects, ignores the resistance of the air. These assumptions are useful, but they need modification in the real world. When the physicist considers the return to earth after having been in space, he does take the resistance of the air into account, lest he burn up. When the economist enters the world of policy, he must modify his assumption of frictionless and painless change or he too will feel the heat.

But the case for government programs to provide stability is not as simple or as persuasive as those in favor of the programs make it out. In the big commodity programs, government decision-making is substituted for the uncertainty of the market. Government decision-making, however, has itself an uncertain element. And the government decisions may be wrong. The tendency of those who defend the commodity programs is to compare individual decision-making at its worst with centralized decision-making at its best. In the actual case and in the long run, it is not clear which of the two is more prone to error.

In a world of change, fluctuating prices are necessary to allocate production, influence consumption, and guide the product through the channels of trade. Fluctuating prices are needed to provide appropriate signals to farmers in their planting decisions. The question is: How much stability is economically, socially, and politically useful? The answer probably is, more than would come from a completely unregulated farm economy and less than would be imposed by zealous advocates of the big farm programs.

If reducing uncertainty and providing greater stability were indeed the prime objectives, it would be possible to design commodity programs that were in the interest of both farmers and nonfarmers. Price supports or deficiency payments, or both, would be designed that would protect farmers against the sharpest dips. Carryover supplies would be built up to protect farmers from excessively low prices and released to protect consumers against the greatest price increases.

The amplitude of price fluctuations would be reduced and erroneous resource allocations would be minimized, while average farm incomes and average food prices would be little changed from an equilibrium level.

But apparently this is too much to expect from the commodity programs. If the farm lobby has the political power to enact a commodity program, it seems inevitably to have, also, the power to boost the price supports and targets above a moderate and benign level.

Argument Five: The Need for Market Power

Agriculture is the only remaining large sector of the economy that is, for the greater part, competitive in the classical sense. The ability of an individual farmer to influence the total volume of production and so the price of his product is not significantly greater than zero. But he deals with firms that are large enough to have some influence on the market for what he buys and sells.

Most of the prices farmers must pay are determined by others. Transportation rates are set by the Interstate Commerce Commission. Wage rates are set by the unions and minimum wages by the government. The price of tractors is set by the big implement companies. Taxes, another uncontrollable cost, are voted by Congress and by state and local governments.

The farmer goes to the store to buy something and is told how much he is to pay. He takes his crops to market and is told what he will receive. He never gets to name the price. This is baffling and humiliating to him. He wants to have that power. He wants the help of government in achieving something like equivalence of bargaining strength. "Countervailing power" was J. K. Galbraith's apt label for it.

This argument has great emotional appeal. But the effect of the farmer's "powerlessness in the market" is not as adverse as it might first appear. Competent research has shown that increased market power would mean at best only modest income gains for agriculture (Brandow 1977b, pp. 265–66; Hoos 1970, pp. 12–26).

The reasons for this are clear. Governing the market is a tough set of economic laws. The law of demand says that, other things equal, the quantity purchased will vary inversely with price. The law of supply says that, other things equal, the amount produced will vary directly with price. If farmers, through countervailing power, should achieve a sharp increase in price, the amount of the crop purchased would decline and, in the absence of tough production controls, the amount produced would increase. So a surplus would accumulate. Increased bargaining power, to be effective, inevitably means tough restraints on output, which farmers dislike.

No firm can have freedom to name, independently of one another, both price and production. Typically, an industrial firm, operating on the principle of imperfect competition and administered pricing, chooses a selling price and then accepts the level of output that will move at the chosen price. Typically a farmer, operating on principles approaching perfect competition, elects to produce whatever amount seems best and then accepts the price that will move that amount. There is one degree of freedom, not two. An industrial firm, for its own good reasons, elects to take its degree of freedom in naming price. A farmer, for his own good reasons, elects to take his degree of freedom in naming quantity. Having named one of the two, he must accept the other.

The argument is offered that agriculture should be made over in the image of imperfect competition, after the fashion of industry, and should use government to provide the necessary countervailing power. It would be just as logical to contend that industry should make itself over and adopt the classical competitive model that is generally found in agriculture. Neither case is convincing. Circumstances differ between agriculture and industry: size of firm, perishability of product, amenability to production controls, the degree to which the product is imbued with the public interest, and long tradition. To argue that either should make itself over in the image of the other is to ignore these great differences. True enough, there are some specialty crops, in unique circumstances, that have been transformed into something like the industrial pattern: cranberries and walnuts are examples. This is all well and good, but efforts to apply this pattern to the major crops and livestock enterprises have been unsuccessful.

Argument Six: The People Want These Programs

The argument is made that the commodity programs are a product of governmental processes and that, since we have a representative government, their existence is a reflection of public choice. They are thus validated. This view of the legislative process might be found in a sophomore civics text of some years back, but it bears little relationship to the actual political process. Enough has already been said to make clear the likelihood that much legislation will diverge from the public interest.

Argument Seven: Ending the Programs Would Be Disastrous

Defenders of the commodity programs cite numerous studies, the consensus of which is that to terminate the programs would reduce the net income of agriculture by approximately one-third (Robinson 1960; U.S. Senate 1960; Wilcox

1960; Tweeten, Heady, and Meyer 1963; Heady, Mayer, and Madsen 1972; Gardner and Hoover 1975; Brandow 1977*b*). So, they say, we must continue the programs.

This argument makes no positive claims for the programs. It is the argument of the cigarette smoker who says he cannot quit. It is the statement of the pilot who says he has passed the point of no return. He has too little fuel to get back to his base and so must continue on course, even though his original objective may have lost its attractiveness.

Surely, say those opposed to the programs, we are not so hooked on government controls as to preclude all efforts to deescalate them. We could reduce our reliance on some of them, at least. "Gradualism" is recommended as a way of reducing the government's role. To which the people in favor reply that this would be like cutting off the dog's tail an inch at a time. The argument that we "can't quit" illustrates that these programs are habit-forming rather than remedial.

Undeniably, these seven arguments in favor of the programs have enormous attractiveness, which accounts for the longevity of the programs. The major appeal is to distributive justice, the prime mover in public policy. But, as will be shown, the programs are regressive; they add to the incomes of those who already are well off and widen the disparity of income within agriculture. The appeal to stability is, in my judgment, more soundly based. Progress and freedom, the major policy objectives of an earlier day, have been demoted by those who advocate the programs.

Now let us turn to the arguments opposing the big commodity programs. In presenting the antiprogram arguments I shall do as before: offer dissenting views.

The Case against the Big Commodity Programs

Argument One: The Programs Have Priced Us out of Markets

There is no area of the world so well endowed agriculturally as the United States. The American Midwest, stretching from the Appalachians to the Rockies and from Mexico to Canada, is unmatched in the world for its size, its favorable topography, fertility, climate, and transportation, its agricultural institutions, and the managerial capability of its farmers. The American agricultural system is naturally suited to competition in world markets.

But with the coming of the big commodity programs we turned inward. For more than forty years we pursued policies that made us—unfortunately—the residual supplier in world markets. We held our export prices above world levels. Other exporters priced their products a cent or two under ours and sold their supplies. Buyers would purchase these bargain products first, then turn to the United States to round out their needs. To move our products we sometimes resorted to export subsidies, which were strongly resisted by other exporting countries and so were used sparingly. Typically we were' left with unsold stocks. These we carried over. When the stocks became excessive we cut back production. In 1972 we held out of production some sixty-two million acres, 18 percent of our cropland, at a direct cost of $3.5 billion.

The results of these policies, which we were slow to understand, were as follows: (1) We carried the reserve stock of food and fiber for the world, a service to the other nations. (2) We carried, almost single-handedly, the supply-adjustment role for the world food system. (3) We helped stabilize food prices in the world, at no cost to the other countries. (4) We granted to other agricultural exporters most of the growth in world markets.

These policies were more advantageous to the other exporting countries than they were to the United States. But our legislators would never admit that the laws they wrote had this effect. And the other countries claimed their own actions brought the good fortune that in fact emanated from United States policies.

The Canadians and Australians, being good diplomats, even seized the initiative and criticized us severely for certain of our actions in international trade, surplus disposal in particular. The Americans, gullible and full of goodwill, were taken in by this tactic. At numerous international meetings the American delegates were subjected to severe criticism, and they beat their breasts in guilt for all sorts of alleged transgressions. Actually the United States was holding an umbrella, to the advantage of the rest of the world. It is possible, in retrospect, to see some wry humor in this situation.

For no commodity is the adverse effect of this program more drastic than for cotton. Consider these figures:

	1928–30	*1976–77*
United States production of cotton (millions of bales)	14.4	12.6
Foreign production of cotton (millions of bales)	12.2	49.2

Through the cotton program we held our cotton production essentially constant and conceded market growth to our overseas rivals who, under our price umbrella, quadrupled their output.

Not only did we hold the price umbrella for cotton produced in other countries, we also did so for manmade fibers. With the assurance, written into law, that cotton would be scarce and high-priced, the manmade fiber industry invested heavily in research, capital outlay, and market development, and took over 62 percent of the United States fiber market. Once the market for manmade fibers had been established, recapture of the market by cotton became practically impossible. This market erosion is discernible, to a lesser degree, for other controlled crops like tobacco and peanuts.

When we priced our internationally traded products above world levels we attracted these commodities to our shores as a magnet attracts iron filings. To keep from being swamped we found it necessary to impose quotas and other restrictions on international trade, to the irritation of our trading partners.

By limiting output we reduced efficiency and increased costs, the natural consequence of partial use of resources. So, by several steps and stages, the control programs increased our per unit costs. Through the operation of the programs the judgment made in the 1930s that we could not compete in international markets became self-fulfilling.

The program advocates would feed data into their computers, figuring how, by manipulating production and price for the next crop, they could maximize next year's farm income. In the short run they were right, but they neglected the long run. While all this was going on, rival producers at home and abroad were moving in to take over the market. The short-run effect of a cocktail is some degree of stimulation. The long-run effect of repeated drinks is far different.

Faced with a growing world population that was experiencing a rising standard of living, and possessing the world's best agricultural plant with which to meet that growing demand, we turned inward. We made a great problem out of what should have been a great opportunity. The program advocates acknowledge these difficulties. Since 1965 there has been a discernible movement in the direction of competitive pricing. Assistance has increasingly been in the form of direct payments, which permit markets to function more freely. As a result, foreign trade has increased.

Ardent advocates of government controls do not accept competitive pricing and open international trading of farm products as desirable. They endeavor to persuade other countries to join with us in control programs, to enter into international agreements, and to divide up the world market as an international cartel would do. In this view, the foreign trade difficulties experienced under the control program arise not so much from our supply management programs as from the failure of the rest of the world to conform to our initiative.

Argument Two: The Programs Are Inequitable

The big commodity programs are regressive both within agriculture and between farm and nonfarm groups. As Charles Hardin has put it, the windfalls of the wealthy are supported by the pittances of the poor (Hardin 1967, p. 1107).

Most Americans believe in some form of income transfer. Enormous wealth can be associated with inherited property, windfall profits, economic dominance, superior skills, or diligent work, singly or in combination. Dire poverty can be associated with the reverse of all these. The resulting great differences in wealth are repugnant to the rank and file. Hence we have death taxes, progressive income taxes, and tax-supported programs for those in poverty.

What the American people have difficulty accepting, when they are made aware of it, is reverse transfers of income, from the poorer to the more wealthy, particularly if this is achieved through the exercise of power and with the help of government. Government was created to protect the general interest from the special interest; there is disrespect for government if that fundamental role is reversed. Demonstrably, that is what has now happened with the big commodity programs.

To the degree that the programs increase the average of farm income, they do so by widening the dispersion within agriculture. Walter Wilcox of the Legislative Reference Service of the Library of Congress reports that in 1968 more than 90 percent of the payments went to 54 percent of the farmers, the operators of the largest farms. The other 10 percent went to the 46 percent of farmers whose incomes were low. The top 1 percent of farmers got 21 percent of the benefits (Cochrane and Ryan 1976, pp. 366–67).

Poor people spend a larger share of their income on food than do the nonpoor (Hoover 1977, p. 790). The average consumer has lower net worth and less income than do the big farmers, who get most of the benefits of the programs. Professor Tweeten draws the logical inference: "The implication is that substantial net transfers of income were made from lower income nonfarm households to higher income farm households in 1968" (Tweeten 1977, p. 52).

The regressive effect of the commodity programs on income distribution within agriculture has been reported by virtually everyone who has had the courage to investigate it (Cochrane and Ryan 1976, pp. 363–71; Tweeten 1977, p. 52; Carter and Seevers 1971; Findley 1969, H3943 ff.; Hardin 1965, 1967; Fuller 1964).

There are additional forms of inequity; one is the preference given to those who produce certain products: wheat, cotton, corn, rice, peanuts, tobacco, and

dairy products in particular. Farmers who produce other kinds of crops and livestock (especially fruits, vegetables, poultry, hogs, and cattle) are left to fend for
themselves. When the big commodity programs were at their height, the favored products accounted for 20 percent of net farm income; yet they received 75
percent of the government outlay for the commodity programs (Paarlberg 1964,
p. 23).

The programs favor those farmers who sell feed grains, but by decreasing the
supply and increasing the price of feed they work a hardship on the farmers who
must buy feed for their livestock.

Selecting crops for preferred treatment results in geographical preference.
Favored are the South, the Midwest, and the Great Plains. Discriminated
against are the Northeast, the cattle-producing mountain states, and, except for
cotton, California.

The objection that the programs are regressive is not met head on by those
who defend them. The allegation is made that the programs are intended to help
people in commercial agriculture and should not be viewed as a means of reducing income differentials from farm to farm.

Those who defend the programs contend that reduction of the feed grain supply is really helpful to livestock farmers. Limiting the supply of feed, they
argue, reduces the production of meat and increases the price. Thus, they contend, the control programs spread their benefits throughout most of agriculture.
But the livestock producers, paying the higher price for a reduced supply of
feed, have some difficulties with this argument. A higher price for feed looks to
them simply like a higher production cost, much the same as a higher wage for
labor or a higher interest rate.

Argument Three: Production Controls Have Excessive Slippage

Production controls are needed if farm prices and farm incomes are to be supported continuously and substantially above where they otherwise would be.
But mandatory production controls are repugnant to farmers. For most of the
controlled crops, the government can obtain compliance with acreage limitations only by making payments. Even so, the effectiveness of acreage control is
eroded by adverse selectivity and free riding. Together these are called "slippage." Farms and fields that are below average in yield per acre come into the
program in disproportionate numbers. Production is intensified on the acres that
remain in use. Farmers not in the program increase their acreage, offsetting the
cutback on farms that comply.

In 1972 the government was paying for nonproduction on sixty-two million
acres. When controls were removed, only thirty-eight million acres came back

into production, despite the extraordinary inducement of high prices. Obviously, we had been paying for nonproduction on some "phantom acres."

In 1978 the government had a "set-aside" program in effect. That is, farmers were paid to set aside a certain percentage of their cropland. The way this worked is of interest. In the Great Plains there are center-pivot irrigation systems; an overhead pipe walks around the field on giant wheels, sprinkling a circle half a mile in diameter. These circles fit into square 160-acre fields. But most such systems cannot reach the corners; they irrigate only 125 of the 160 acres. Farmers are allowed to consider the other 35 dry and hence unproductive acres as their contribution to nonproduction. They are paid for idling these acres at the same high rate as for irrigated land. "Production control" of this kind involves enormous slippage.

The experience of the mid-seventies is a reasonable assessment of our efforts at production control. We get probably half of two-thirds of the cutback we pay for. Farmers and many of the program advocates do not worry about this. Their objective is to increase farm income. To the degree that we overpay for acreage reduction, farm income is increased.

Argument Four: Gains Are Siphoned Off by Landowners

Numerous studies show that the benefits from the commodity programs tend to become capitalized into higher land values and so constitute a windfall gain to those who held the land when the programs began and are added cost to the next generation (Gafney 1965; Reinsel and Krenz 1972). A 1962 study reported that about half of the income attributable to the tobacco program is capitalized into higher land values. Half of it goes to the operator on a continuing basis (Paarlberg 1964, p. 63). More recent work by Gardner and Hoover shows the estimated rental value of tobacco allotments in North Carolina to be $129 million and of rice in Arkansas to be $30 million (Gardner and Hoover 1975, p. 29).

The mechanics of this are fairly simple. Production controls have long been based on acreage allotments, which in turn are based on history. The allotment is the limiting input item; all other inputs—labor, capital, technology—are unrestricted. So the limiting item takes on value, like the franchise for the San Diego Padres or a taxi medallion in New York City. It is a value created by the government, out of nothing, accruing to those on whom production privileges are conferred.

Here, then, is another inequity in the commodity programs, another regressive feature, in that these programs add to the net worth of the landowner, who in all likelihood is already better off than the other participants in the food production system. They add somewhat to the income of the tenant, who likely is on the middle rung of the income ladder (but, as the program operates, the rent soon gets jacked up because rentable acreage is reduced). The programs reduce opportunities for farm wage workers, who are the low men on the totem pole. None of this should be surprising; the programs are lobbied into law by the big landowning farm operators. It would be naive to expect them to look after the interests of others.

With the big additions to income provided to the large landowning operators and with the increase in net worth resulting from capitalization of program benefits into land values, these large operators have the resources to buy out the small farmers. The big commodity programs speeded up the consolidation of farms and hastened the disappearance of the smaller units (Cochrane and Ryan 1976, pp. 365–66). This is quite a miscarriage for a program whose alleged purpose was to make it possible for the small farm operator to stay in business.

Believers in a market-oriented economic system generally endorse changes in the structure of an industry if these changes result from competitive forces. But there are misgivings about the entry of government tilting the scales to help those who already are the favored ones.

The people who favor the commodity programs have no real response to this argument. Some acknowledge that the programs are biased in favor of the large landholders. Their acceptance of limitations on the amount of payment going to any one farmer (now $45,000) is an effort to cope with this criticism. However, the limitations are set at levels that affect relatively few farmers.

Argument Five: The Programs Involve High Government Cost

A partial accounting of the cost of these programs is supplied by the Department of Agriculture (appendix table 1). From the mid-sixties to the early seventies, these programs, counting only direct payments to farmers, provided from one-fourth to one-third or more of the net income of all agriculture. For individual crops such as wheat and cotton government payments were a much larger share of net income.

Program costs rose with the passage of time. After a sharp drop in cost during the extraordinary time of the mid-seventies, heavy costs were renewed. Government outlays to support farm income quadrupled in two years to an estimated $7.9 billion in fiscal year 1978 (Time, November 6, 1978, p. 102). Added costs to consumers of food were estimated for the period 1964 to 1969 at $4.5 billion a year, 4 percent of the overall retail price of food (Schultze 1971, p. 1). There also are costs in the form of lost efficiency resulting from poor resource allocation, diminution of the overall level of output, and loss of export earnings.

An additional costly feature is the disaster program, which Secretary Bergland characterized as being itself a disaster. It specifies that farmers who cooperate in the commodity programs are eligible for government payments to compensate them for loss in the event of crop failure. This amounts to insurance without payment of premium. It keeps in production areas that are erosive, drought-ridden, or likely to flood and so encourages bad resource use. This program cost $557 million in 1974 and $280 million in 1975 (Miller and Walter 1977).

The transfer of income associated with the commodity programs, say the objective analysts, has accomplished some good things and some bad things. The programs have added some stability to the economy and brought some improvement (at least in the short run) for certain groups in agriculture. On the other hand, they have led to inefficient use of resources, adverse effect on consumers and taxpayers, heavy dependence on government, impairment of export earnings, and a hastening of the trend toward fewer and larger farms. Reckoning up costs and benefits, those who are against the programs come to an adverse judgment.

The program advocates evaluate the commodity programs differently. Suppose the program costs $5 billion a year. What is this against a half-trillion-dollar budget? One percent of the federal budget goes for the farmers, who total 3.6 percent of the people. By this reckoning, agriculture is not yet getting its fair share.

As for the effect on the cost of food, defenders of the programs offer some statistics. The average American family spends about 17 percent of its budget on food. In no other country does so low a percentage of income go for food. What if the programs push up the cost of food by some small increment? Most consumers can afford it. Those who cannot will be taken care of by the food stamp program or by welfare.

Two things trouble consumers: absence of certain food items from the grocery shelves and sharp increases in price. The program reduces these two troublesome hazards in exchange for a continuous slightly higher price. The sugar program essentially worked this way most of the time from 1934 to 1974 and was accepted by the consumers with little complaint. A regulated, stabilized market is a good bargain for both farmers and consumers, say the defenders of the program.

Argument Six: The Programs Involve a Loss of Freedom

Undeniably, the commodity programs substitute government decision-making for individual management. Some look with deep misgiving on the steadily growing role of government and see the freedom of the individual as being in jeopardy. They envision the enticements of government benefits as luring us into a passive state while our freedom withers away. These critics see freedom as a positive value, an end in itself and a proper objective of public policy. This view was eloquently voiced by Ezra Taft Benson, secretary of agriculture during the Eisenhower years.

Those in favor of the programs have a different view of freedom. They view it not as an end, but as one of several alternative means to a number of ends. The ends envisioned are stability, progress, and economic justice. If these ends can be achieved by individual decision-making, well and good, they say. But if these ends can be more readily reached through centralized decision-making, at the sacrifice of freedom, this is a good bargain.

And, as the advocates of the government programs see it, the programs have proved a superior means of reaching the desired ends. The last time we really had individual decision-making we had the Great Depression. Since then, with greater centralized decision-making, catastrophes of that kind have been avoided. As for the great attractiveness freedom is alleged to have, look at the way the farmers clamor to surrender it in exchange for some additional income and stability. So goes the argument.

The clash between the advocates of individual and of centralized decision-making is the greatest argument of the twentieth century, not only in our own land but around the globe. It will not soon be either adjourned or resolved.

POLITICS OF THE BIG COMMODITY PROGRAMS

Agricultural economists have generally considered themselves better qualified to deal with farm policy matters than political scientists and sociologists. Economists have examined the issues with great care, but they may sometimes have imposed economic analysis on phenomena that were more properly political or social.

Bruce Gardner, formerly an agricultural economist on the staff of the President's Council of Economic Advisors, makes this observation: "at some point we have to recognize that the purpose of legislation is better described in political terms. The purpose is to take from those who have less political clout and give to those who have more" (Gardner 1977, p. 64). In this section I shall examine the commodity programs from a political point of view.

Those who support the big commodity programs recite an impressive list of strengths. Farmers enjoy a large measure of goodwill, much more than do the people who merchandise food. Surveys have shown consumer sympathy for farmers and a willingness to pay a bit more for food to help the "poor" farmers. This is an immense political asset. But goodwill, though considerable, is diminishing. Huge payments to individual farmers and especially to farming corporations are undoubtedly the major cause of public dissatisfaction. Commodity program advocates do their best to play down the fact that the programs provide most of their benefits to the large operators.

Though farmers constitute less than 4 percent of the population, they are backstopped politically by large numbers of nonfarm people. From 1930 to 1974, the out-migration from farms totaled 32.8 million, the largest migration in modern times. These are the agricultural alumni. Many of them retain considerable understanding of agriculture and a favorable disposition toward farmers. For these friends of agriculture, the pro-farm attitude continues from father to son, though diminishing somewhat with time. Additional people work at farm-related activities: the service group, the tradesmen, food processors, and the like. They may not be agricultural alumni, but they often root for the team.

Agriculture is represented in the Senate in a manner out of proportion to its numbers. Pennsylvania, an industrial state with 11,793,909 million residents, has two senators. South Dakota, the most "agricultural" state in the Union, has a total population of 665,507, only 6 percent as many as Pennsylvania. But it also has two senators.

Programs that have been in operation for forty-five years obviously have a high degree of continuity. President Eisenhower discovered this during the 1950s when he tried unsuccessfully to abolish a tea-tasting agency that had been established early in the history of the Republic. Momentum may be the greatest thing the programs have going for them.

For nearly half a century the commodity groups have been battling to obtain and then defend these programs. Leaders have learned the techniques of infighting. They are not easily dislodged.

From the Canadian line south to the border states and from the industrial East to the Rocky Mountains lie what are known as the "farm states." Historically, in presidential elections, most of these states were expected to wind up in their longtime home, the Republican camp. This changed during the 1930s. The "farm states" are considered by some people to be "swing states." They were credited with winning the election for Harry Truman in 1948. The "farm vote" is eagerly sought, and the commodity programs are considered to be important in winning that vote. This puts the commodity program advocates in a strong political position.

Liabilities are fewer than the assets, but in some cases they may be decisive for policy issues. When the commodity programs were enacted, farmers totaled

26 percent of the population. In 1978 the figure was less than 4 percent and was steadily working lower. In public life, arithmetic is decisive. With numbers declining both relatively and absolutely, agriculture's political power cannot be other than on the retreat.

With passing time the "farm vote" diminishes in significance. Some years ago John Kenneth Galbraith declared: "the day is not too far distant when farmers will have to go to town to hear the major political candidates—unless they happen to catch them talking on television. The rural vote will be too small to worry about" (Galbraith 1957, p. 10).

Political scientists Talbot and Hadwiger observe, regarding Galbraith's comment: "This judgment seems too harsh. In any state in which the population is more than ten percent on the farm, the farmer still has real power, potentially at least. Where the figure is above five percent he may have negotiating strength as a voter if reasonably well organized and if the two party system in that state is highly competitive. Where the percentage falls below five percent the farmer might just as well go along halfway with Galbraith and turn on his television set—but still vote" (Talbot and Hadwiger 1968, p. 88).

In 1933, when the commodity programs were first enacted, the perceived problem was low and falling prices. During the coming decade the perceived problem, at least so far as the public is concerned, is likely to be high and rising prices. Public support for price-increasing legislation will therefore be difficult to obtain.

One must conclude from this résumé that the farm lobby is still politically powerful despite some erosion of its strength. Now let us look at the positions of the various interests regarding the big commodity programs.

The farm organizations. The largest of the general farm organizations is the American Farm Bureau Federation, with more members than all the others combined: the National Farmers Union, the National Farmers Organization, and the National Grange. The Farm Bureau is organized in every state, but its strength is greatest in the South and the Midwest. The Farm Bureau Federation has long been wary of the big commodity programs, but it has had difficulty reconciling its views with the positions of various of the state Farm Bureaus, particularly in the South, where support for the tobacco, cotton, peanut, and rice programs has been strong. Recently the federation has become somewhat less adamant in its opposition to commodity programs.

The Farmers Union and the National Farmers Organization are strongly in favor of the commodity programs. The Grange, which is a social organization as well as a lobbying group, traditionally takes a position midway between the Farm Bureau and the others.

A newcomer, the American Agriculture Movement, a militant advocate of the big commodity programs, appeared on the scene in 1977. Its survival and ultimate influence are uncertain.

In addition to the general farm organizations there are as many as 120 specialized groups (Hill 1978). Among these are the National Association of Wheat Growers, the National Cotton Council, the American Soybean Association, the National Corn Growers Association, and the National Milk Producers Federation. Their lobbies are active and effective in support of the commodity programs. These organizations have fewer divergent interests to reconcile than do the general farm organizations and therefore can be stronger advocates for their particular interests. Their strength has grown relative to that of the general farm organizations during the past twenty years, just as specialized farming has grown relative to general farming.

One more thing needs to be said about the farm organizations, and it applies to both the general and the specialized groups. Despite their differences, they are alike in one respect: they all reflect, on balance, the views of those who operate large rather than small farms. This they will all deny. But it is inescapably true. Elected leaders are almost invariably the larger farmers, those most financially able to travel and devote time to the organization. No one has yet been able effectively to organize or reflect the felt needs of the small, low-income farmers. The word carried to the legislator, therefore, comes from the larger farm operators.

What can the farm lobbyist offer the congressman or the senator in exchange for the great man's support?

Information about the commodity in question and attitudes thereon—helpful if true, but influential, true or not.

Promises (usually overpromises) to deliver the vote if the desired action is forthcoming.

Warnings (threats?) of political retaliation if the desired support is not given.

Fellowship, hospitality, and camaraderie with the power elite of the commodity group, a valuable item.

Campaign contributions, that most tangible form of legal tender, generally reserved for those of proved performance.

Clearly this kind of input comes disproportionately from the well informed and the well financed.

Congress. Members of Congress with appreciable numbers of farmers among their voters are quite ready to listen to the lobbying efforts of the farm organizations. They tend to be responsive to the organized and vociferous representations of the lobbyists rather than to the rank and file of constituents.

Senators and congressmen concerned with farm policy tend to develop specialized commodity interests. There is a peanut congressman (Mathis, D-Ga.), a rice congressman (Breaux, D-La.), a wheat senator (Dole, R-Kans.), and a sugar senator (Long, D-La.). Eastland (D-Miss.) was for many years a cotton senator. Before he retired, Laird (R-Wis.) was a dairy congressman. Many of these people are chairmen of committees or subcommittees. They are looked to by their colleagues for guidance on commodity program issues. All are supporters of the big commodity programs and all are effective advocates. This separate focus on individual commodities results in fragmentation of the national interest. Congress works by dividing problems and assigning them to separate committees. Roland Young wrote in 1943: "There is no institutional reason which compels a Congressman to have a national point of view."

There is an immense amount of logrolling among the commodity groups, and Congress is the focal point at which this occurs. During the debate on the 1977 farm bill, tobacco and sugar were reported in a voting trade. Congressman James P. Johnson (R-Colo.) had called the federal promotion of "this poison [tobacco] inexcusable." Later he voted for the tobacco subsidy. Congressman William H. Natcher (D-Ky.) said that "last week, when sugar was in trouble . . . about twenty states which produce tobacco marched right down the road [for sugar]" (*Congressional Quarterly Almanac* 1977, p. 430).

The bureaucracy. These officials in the Department of Agriculture who have responsibility for the big commodity programs generally are in-house advocates for them. There is a National Association of County Committeemen who lobby for the programs from the inside. Bureaucrats who work on these programs soon find that life is simpler if they go along with the lobbyists and the congressmen. They develop almost a proprietary interest in the programs they administer. Sometimes, when there is a division of opinion between the executive and the legislative branches, the bureaucracy gets caught in the middle. Which way they go depends on where, in their judgment, lie the power and the political will. Together the commodity interests, the legislative branch, and the bureaucracies make up what John Gardner calls "the Unholy Trinity."

The consumers. Farmers have often considered the consumer the adversary and have thought that consumer resistance would be the main obstacle to the enactment of legislation intended to reduce the supply and increase the price of food products. Consumer boycotts and protests during the rapid retail food price increases of 1973 and 1974 reinforced this belief.

But this resistance never really crystallized. The farm lobby reached out to the consumers, seeking them as allies. By embracing the Food Stamp Program, the farm lobby won many congressional votes. What had been thought to be a shootout developed into a love feast. The stone that the builders rejected became the head of the corner. Consumers were ready to go along with a farm bill that used deficiency payments rather than price supports; this technique promised that the cost would be borne by the citizens as taxpayers rather than by the citizens as food consumers. Deficiency payments are an ingenious device whereby buyers and sellers both get what they want: a high price at the seller's end and a low price for the buyer. The taxpayer picks up the tab. Or, if that is thought too harsh, deficit financing takes care of it and the real cost is borne in the form of inflation.

Presumably the more sedate performance of the retail food price index in 1977, compared with 1973 and 1974, made the consumer groups more amenable to the farm lobby and aided enactment of the 1977 farm bill.

Big labor. Laboring people are wage workers who want to sell their services for a high price and buy their food cheap. Farmers are entrepreneurs who want the exact opposite: a high price for food and a low wage for hired labor. The two appear to be natural adversaries. The farm lobby sought to find a way around this problem. To attract allies from labor in support of the Agricultural Act of 1977, farm congressmen embraced various labor positions: increasing the minimum wage, allowing strikers to have food stamps, and emphasizing the use of deficiency payments rather than price supports. In return, many congressmen with labor constituents supported the farm lobby on the commodity programs. A special minimum wage for workers in the sugar cane and sugar beet fields won labor votes for the Sugar Act. There are various words for such operations—"logrolling" or "accommodation," depending on one's political philosophy. The cynical phrase for it is "rising above principle."

Agribusiness. Among the chief advocates of free enterprise are those who sell production items to farmers, process farm products, and merchandise them at home and abroad. One would expect these people to be in favor of unrestricted production, competitive markets, and individual decision-making.

But for a variety of reasons such advocacy is not forthcoming. Some of them like government to carry the burden of grain storage; it relieves them of this chore. Some like the government to fix the prices; it reduces interfirm competition. Some of them like to be on good terms with their farmer customers and so go along with the commodity programs. Some opposed the commodity programs in the early years, lost repeatedly, and gave up the battle. In addition, they recognize that as industrialists they have a poor public image and their resistance to the commodity programs might have an effect opposite to what was intended. At first thought one might judge the agribusiness people to be stalwarts in fighting for a market-oriented agriculture. But this is not so.

The major political parties. Historically the Democrats favored the big commodity programs. The Republicans opposed them. This lineup persisted, though gradually eroding, for about thirty years. In recent times the agricultural positions of the two parties have been blurred. There is some weariness with the two historic positions. The original gladiators of both camps, who made impassioned speeches in support of the party positions, have passed on or become jaded. Ideology has been in a measure replaced by pragmatism. Significantly, the pragmatist is more susceptible to lobbying influence than is the idealist.

The taxpayers. On June 6, 1978, California voters overwhelmingly passed Proposition 13, cutting by 57 percent the amount of real estate taxes the state can collect. This action sent shock waves through state and national capitals. Warning has been given that the public may no longer be willing to passively pick up the tab for whatever legislation the special interests can crowd through the legislative process. Special interest groups including the farm lobby should take notice.

The White House. Almost alone among politically influential forces, the White House stands in opposition to openhanded commodity programs. This has been true of at least the past three presidents, with no major differences between Republicans Nixon and Ford and Democrat Carter.

Of all the participant groups named, only the White House has responsibility for the entire country—the national interest. This means that any president is inclined to look with disfavor on a farm program that will reduce production, increase food costs, price us out of markets, require interference with international trade, add to the budget. The president wants also, of course, to win or hold the support of farm groups. He therefore is subject to lobby pressure. But his accountability to all the people offsets this lobbying pressure. He seeks to gain control by integrating and coordinating.

The farm lobby, weakened by the decline in farm population and to some degree by the adverse public perception of the big commodity programs, has sought to strengthen its position by seeking allies. The allies have been labor, consumer groups, and to some extent the environmentalists, all politically strong. The alliances have involved the adding together of the objectives of the various groups, with little modification, and joining in their support—logrolling rather than trade-offs.

The question is whether a market-oriented agriculture is politically feasible in such an operation. For an appraisal of that prospect, let us review the political history of the most recent major commodity legislation enacted by the Congress. While this is a review of history and hence backward-looking, it does cast some light on the probable future.

The Food and Agriculture Act of 1977

This is a four-year bill and will expire with the crop grown in 1981. New farm legislation is scheduled for 1981, the year after the presidential election.

The best indicator of the broadening farm policy agenda is the comprehensiveness of the bill. Whereas in earlier days there would likely have been language only on price supports and production controls for the major crops, this time there are fifteen titles. Among them are Rural Development, Food Stamps, Public Law 480, Teaching, Research, Education, and Energy. The bill runs to 181 pages and has something for almost everyone.

The proposals President Carter sent to Congress on March 23, 1977, involved modest increases over the levels of the expiring legislation in target prices for wheat and corn. The legislation sent forward was clearly market oriented. Had it been enacted, the commodity programs would have been rather low in impact and in cost.

Both the lobbyists and Congress had expected much higher loans and price targets. When Secretary of Agriculture Bergland laid the administration's proposals before Congress a great protest arose. Senator Dole (R-Kans.) remarked: "If [former Secretary of Agriculture] Earl Butz had brought this thing up here he'd have needed a bodyguard."

Over the next several weeks the president twice reluctantly revised his proposed target price figures upward, first on the 1978 crops and then retroactively on the 1977 crops, though his proposals were still below the levels being considered in both House and Senate. There were intimations that the president's revised proposal was his final position and that anything more generous would be vetoed. Nevertheless, the Congress passed a bill with higher targets than the president had agreed to.

Originally the president had proposed a commodity program that would involve a calculated budget outlay of $1.4 billion. The bill that was enacted had a cost estimated at the time of passage of $3.8 billion (Penn 1977, p. 92). The actual outlay for fiscal year 1978 was estimated a $7.9 billion (*Time* November 6, 1978, p. 102).

The president signed the bill. In the eyeball-to-eyeball facedown between the president and Congress, it was the president who blinked.

Martin Tolchin asserted that an urban-rural coalition passed the 1977 farm bill (*New York Times* July 29, 1977). Certainly the final vote on the bill in the House and in the Senate testifies to a broad base of support among nonfarm legislators. Charles Hardin commented, "Considering a number of key votes on minimum wage, it seems likely that organized agriculture was giving organized labor more support than one would suspect in the absence of some log rolling'' (Hardin 1978). So the act was passed, with substantial increases in the loans and targets for the big commodity programs. John G. Peters of the University of Nebraska provides an excellent summary of congressional action on this bill (Peters 1978).

A general perception was that the farm lobby demonstrated a surprising amount of strength and that nothing had really changed. A more accurate conclusion would be that the farm lobby recognized its weakness and was astute in making allies, and that the newly created Congressional Budget Committees, which were supposed to hold down costs, were shown to be relatively impotent.

Certain aspects of this bill are of interest. The bill has a new feature: provision for a farmer-owned grain reserve, intended to provide a carryover that would be something more than the chance result of efforts to increase farm prices and farm income. The congressmen hedged their bets. They wrote a two-track bill, and they gave considerable administrative choice to the executive branch. If supplies should become heavy and prices depressed, the stage was set for something like a return to the production controls and price supports of earlier years. If supplies should be short and prices strong, the government supply-management machinery could be shelved; farmers would make their own production decisions and sell their products in competitive markets. We were poised, therefore, to go either way (Johnson 1978; Penn 1977; Spitze 1978).

There were some farmers who had a firm idea about which way we should go. Scarcely was the ink dry on the Food and Agriculture Act of 1977 before a farm protest began. Wheat farmers were especially disappointed with the act of 1977; young farmers who had begun operating during the euphoria of the mid-seventies and then had experienced the down side of the roller coaster were pinched for cash. Drought had hurt farmers in parts of the Midwest and in the Southeast. The Great Plains, the Southeast, and the Gulf Coast were the trouble centers. Protesting farmers demanded 100 percent of parity, an impossible objective, and vowed they would plant no crops until Congress passed legislation giving them what they asked. The protest had considerable spontaneity. The established general farm organizations avoided direct involvement. A loose organization came into being and took the name American Agriculture Movement (AAM). The popular phrase for it was ''the Farm Strike.'' The movement began in the fall of 1977, grew and spread during the winter, and peaked in early spring 1978.

Techniques used were in part an emulation of European farm protests (tractor parades), in part taken from labor (the "strike"), and in part purely original (release of a herd of goats in the nation's capital). In contrast to most earlier farm lobbying efforts, the methods were deliberately abrasive. Farmers broke into the waiting room of the secretary of agriculture and occupied his conference room. They stopped Washington traffic, thronged congressional offices, and jammed hearing rooms. All these things were avidly picked up by television and by the press. These activities certainly got the item on the agenda, which was their purpose. But whether they generated more sympathy or indignation on the part of the public remains unanswered.

The administration sought to placate the movement (or perhaps Congress?) by modest program liberalization. But this had limited effect. In some of the wildest legislative action in memory, the two houses of Congress passed different bills, both openhanded, the Senate's more so than that of the House. The House defeated the conference bill. Thereupon a new more modest bill was passed and signed by the president. Its chief effect was to increase the target price for wheat from $3.00 a bushel to $3.40 and to raise the loan rate for cotton from 44 to 48 cents a pound.

The price increases that emerged during the various stages of this process appear larger than they really are. We were coming off the act of 1973, which had not fully anticipated the rate of inflation. Table 1 shows the various stages by which loans and targets for the crops of 1977 and 1978 were escalated in legislative and administrative maneuverings.

Congress made an additional effort to meet the problem of which the American Agriculture Movement was a reflection. It passed the Agricultural Credit Act of 1978, providing $4 billion of additional credit to farmers facing a shortage of credit from regular sources. This bill provided government-guaranteed loans to eligible farmers at interest rates based on cost of money to the government.

After Congress enacted its restrained response to their demands, the people of the AAM continued their protest. When spring came, however, the striking farmers went home and planted what turned out to be a record crop. But they vowed they would be back the next year. They were; they came to Washington in 1979 and went home empty-handed.

How many people did the AAM represent? The overwhelming number of farmers stayed home, ran their farms, and watched the farm strike on the evening news, with a combination of amusement, amazement, hope, and disgust.

The striking farmers sounded an alarm that may nudge some of the old line farm organizations toward a stronger stance in favor of the programs. They

Table 1. Target Prices and Loan Levels for Major Commodities, 1977 and 1978 Crops, as Affected by Legislative and Administrative Actions

Commodity	Target Price	Loan Level
1. Targets and loan levels for the 1977 crop as specified in the act of 1973		
Wheat, per bu.	$2.47	$2.25
Corn, per bu.	1.70	1.50
Cotton, per lb.	.478	.4258
Soybeans, per bu.	—	2.50
Rice, per cwt.	8.25	6.19
2. Targets and loan levels for the 1977 crop as adjusted by Congress and the Administration		
Wheat, per bu.	$2.90	$2.25
Corn, per bu.	2.00	2.00
Cotton, per lb.	.478	.426
Soybeans, per bu.	—	3.75
Rice, per cwt.	8.25	6.19
3. Targets and loan levels for the 1978 crop as provided by the Food and Agriculture Act of 1977		
Wheat, per bu.	$3.00/3.05	$2.35
Corn, per bu.	2.10	2.00
Cotton, per lb.	.52	.44
Soybeans, per bu.	—	4.50
Rice, per cwt.	8.53	6.40
4. Targets and loan levels for the 1978 crop as established by Congress and the administration in response to the farm strike		
Wheat, per bu.	$3.40	$2.35
Corn, per bu.	2.10	2.00
Cotton, per lb.	.52	.48
Soybeans, per bu.	—	4.50
Rice, per cwt.	8.53	6.40

SOURCE: Data from J. B. Penn, senior staff economist, Council of Economic Advisors.

launched a new lobbying style that may be emulated in the years ahead. In sum, the farm protest of 1977–78 can claim some gains, though they were a small fraction of their demands.

COMMODITY PROGRAMS IN THE 1980s

The big commodity programs will be a continuing issue during the 1980s, perhaps the most important (but by no means the sole) focus of farm and food policy. This is likely to be true for a number of reasons.

The major farm products will experience periodic production problems, weather problems, supply problems, and problems of price and income for which government help will inevitably be sought. Wheat, tobacco, peanuts, sugar, and some of the other commodities have become so reliant on the commodity programs that their abrupt withdrawal would be very difficult. Farm lobbyists will fight hard to avert such an event.

The big commodity programs are classic in the sense that they focus on the major issue of the twentieth century: What mixture of individual decision-making and centralized direction should we have? The programs are also a classic case of counterposing the special against the general interest. Involved is the whole concept of economic justice and its dispensation. All of the acknowledged objectives of public policy—progress, stability, justice, freedom—are central to the future of the big commodity programs.

The antagonists in the fight over the commodity programs are not likely to be the Democrats versus the Republicans, as was once the case. Nor are they likely to be the farmers versus the consumers, as more recently seemed likely. The adversaries will be the executive branch versus the legislative branch, as has been the lineup for at least the past ten years, under both political parties. It was the executive branch that gave birth to these big commodity programs (in totally different circumstances) nearly half a century ago. Now it is likely to try to hold the commodity programs to modest dimensions for reasons that are high in the public interest: to keep costs at reasonable levels, to avoid artificial food shortages, to restrain inflation, to earn the maximum amount of foreign exchange, and to minimize friction with our trading partners.

There will not be many strong supporters to whom the executive branch can turn for help. The two major political parties have become and are likely to be more productive of rhetoric than of resolution on this issue. The agribusiness firms, basically inclined toward the market system, are weary of the battle on the commodity program issue and are not sure whether their participation would be a help or a hindrance. Labor and the consumers appear likely to get involved only to the degree that there is a new surge of inflation in food prices. Will taxpayers focus sharply on a program that takes only 1 percent of the federal budget? This is doubtful.

The legislative branch will continue to be the major focus of the lobbying forces. Because the farm lobby is strong, the legislative branch feels a need to respond to its demands. It is the familiar case involving most issues in which the special interest conflicts with the general interest: the concentration of advocacy and the dispersal of opposition.

There is evidence that the ideological confrontation of earlier years has diminished and has been replaced by a pragmatic standoff. The old advocates of big government programs have come to realize that these programs do not always work and that they are sometimes booby-trapped. The old opponents of these programs generally acknowledge that a greater degree of stability is desirable than is likely to be provided by a completely free market. So, since the late sixties, there has been some de-escalation of arguments concerning commodity programs. From the thirties to the sixties, the agricultural policy course at the typical land grant college had the big commodity programs as almost its exclusive content. During the eighties other topics will be taught—those in the rest of this book.

During the 1980s I expect that the commodity programs will be continued, with a smaller role for government than during the fifties and sixties. There will be greater reliance on competitive pricing, along the lines that emerged in the legislation of the late sixties and seventies, with most of the assistance provided in the form of payments rather than price supports. I expect pricing and merchandising policies that permit us to compete strongly in foreign markets and to escape in part from our former role as residual supplier. There will be continued and intensified attacks on the tobacco program. The public increasingly asks why, when the Department of Health, Education, and Welfare condemns cigarette smoking, the Department of Agriculture should conduct programs on behalf of those who produce the offending product.

Much will depend on unpredictable events. Experience shows that events are more influential in shaping farm policy than are previously stated positions. If supplies should become very burdensome and prices much depressed, there will be considerable willingness to come to the rescue. If program costs should balloon, program benefits will be scaled down. If there should be an upsurge of retail food prices, consumer concern would arise. Program retrenchment would be demanded.

This analysis indicates that the following courses of action may be desirable:

Farmers should not expect these big commodity programs to make farming continuously profitable. They will not. They are more a floor over the pit of disaster than an assurance of profit. Nonfarm people should be cultivated. They buy the products, vote for those who enact these programs, and pay the taxes that underwrite program costs. Abrasive tactics like those used by the American Agriculture Movement are more likely to hurt than to help. The best way to generate goodwill is to scale down the benefits going to the large farms.

There is a point of no return for commodity programs, just as there is in flying. Some commodities (sugar, wheat, peanuts) may have passed this point. Tobacco may think it has passed the point but may nonetheless have to return. Other commodities (feed grains, rice) can reduce their reliance on government programs and may find it in their long-run interest to do so. Still other commodities (soybeans, beef, pork, poultry, fruits, vegetables) have stayed relatively free of commodity programs and can continue on this path.

Relying on government is risky business for people who are losing political strength. The competitive market takes little account of politics. During the next decade, farmers who choose to fight their battles in the legislative halls will be fighting from an eroding base; farmers who elect to compete in the market will experience no such impairment of position.

Researchers and educators should focus on the new issues that are coming over the horizon. Old subject matter may be obsolescent. The academic community should review the research program, reexamine the extension plan, and revise the lecture notes.

The public servant, elected or appointed, should recognize the broadening base of farm and food policy and work up some new speeches. When the president takes a stand that reflects the public interest, he should have as much support as can be given. The new issues should receive attention, both for their own merit and for the broadened base they provide for serving the old clientele.

The rest of this book—far the greater part—will be addressed to the new issues and the new clientele. We will explore the new ground across the farm policy watershed that we passed sometime during the past decade. This watershed was so low in profile that we hardly knew when we crossed it. Nevertheless, like any other watershed, it determines which way the streams flow.

Exploring this new territory should be an exciting adventure. Let us hope the natives will be friendly.

REFERENCES

Benedict, M. R. 1953. *Farm policies of the United States, 1790–1950.* New York: Twentieth Century Fund.

Benedict, M. R., and Stine, O. C. 1956. *The agricultural commodity programs.* New York: Twentieth Century Fund.

Brandow, George E. 1977a. Agricultural production, prices and costs: How have the farmers fared? In *Food and agricultural policy.* Washington, D.C.: American Enterprise Institute for Public Policy Research.

———. 1977*b*. Policy for commercial agriculture. In *Survey of agricultural economics literature,* vol. 1, ed. Lee Martin. Minneapolis: University of Minnesota Press.

Carter, Harold O., and Seevers, Gary L. 1971. Agricultural Act of 1970—New directions or no? *Proceedings of the Western Agricultural Economics Association* 44:175–85.

Cochrane, Willard W. 1947. Farm price gyrations; An aggregative hypothesis. *Journal of Farm Economics* 29:383–408.

Cochrane, Willard W., and Ryan, Mary E. 1976. *American farm policy, 1948–1973.* Minneapolis: University of Minnesota Press.

Congressional Quarterly weekly report almanac. 1977. Washington, D.C.: Congressional Quarterly, Inc.

Findley, Paul. 1969. *Congressional record.* House of Representatives, 91st Cong., 1st sess., May 21, p. 13287. Washington, D.C.: Government Printing Office.

Fuller, Varden. 1964. Wheat, cotton and political arithmetic. *California Monthly,* July–August.

Gafney, M. 1965. The benefits of farm programs: Incidence, shifting and dissipation. *Journal of Farm Economics* 47:1252–63.

Galbraith, John K. 1957. Farm plan with no price is no plan at all. *Co-op Grain Quarterly,* vol. 15, no. 1.

Gardner, Bruce L. 1977. Commentaries. In *Food and agricultural policy.* Washington, D.C.: American Enterprise Institute for Public Policy Research.

Gardner, Bruce L., and Hoover, Dale M. 1975. *U.S. farm commodity programs and the inequality of farm household income, 1969.* Economics Research Report no. 35, Department of Economics and Business. Raleigh: North Carolina State University.

Gray, R. W.; Sorenson, V. L.; and Cochrane, W. W. 1954. *An economic analysis of the impact of government programs on the potato industry.* Technical Bulletin 211. Minneapolis: Minnesota Agricultural Experiment Station.

Hadwiger, Don F., and Browne, William P. 1978. *The new politics of food.* Lexington, Mass.: D. C. Heath.

Halcrow, Harold. 1977. *Food policy for America.* New York: McGraw-Hill.

Hardin, Charles M. 1955. Farm price policy and the farm vote. *Journal of Farm Economics* 37:601–24.

———. 1965. Present and prospective policy problems of U.S. agriculture. *Journal of Farm Economics* 47:1091–1115.

———. 1967. *Food and fiber in the nation's politics.* Technical Paper 3. Washington, D. C.: National Advisory Commission on Food and Fiber.

———. 1978. Agricultural price policy in the United States: The political possibility of a market-oriented policy. Unpublished manuscript.

Heady, E. O.; Mayer, L. V.; and Madsen, H.C. 1972. *Future farm programs.* Ames: Iowa State University Press.

Hill, Frances. 1978. Does it make a difference? Speech given at seminar on agricultural marketing and policy: Can the Family Farm Survive? Columbia, Missouri, November 9.

Hoos, S. 1970. Economic possibilities and limitations of cooperative bargaining associations. In *Cooperative bargaining*. FCS Report 113. Washington, D.C.: USDA.

Hoover, Dale. 1977. Review of W. W. Cochrane and Mary Ryan, *American farm policy, 1948–73*. *American Journal of Agricultural Economics* 59:788–91.

Jacobson, M. A., and Paarlberg, Don. 1966. Parity of net worth. *Journal of Farm Economics* 48:127–39.

Johnson, D. Gale. 1978. The Food and Agriculture Act of 1977: Implications for farmers, consumers and taxpayers. In *Contemporary economic problems,* ed. William Fellner, pp. 167–209. Washington, D.C.: American Enterprise Institute for Public Policy Research.

Johnson, Glenn L. 1952. *Burley tobacco control programs*. Bulletin 580. Lexington: Kentucky Agricultural Experiment Station.

Johnson, Glenn L., and Quance, C. Leroy. 1972. *The overproduction trap in U.S. agriculture*. Baltimore: Johns Hopkins University Press.

Knebel, John A. 1976. 1977 agricultural outlook. In *1977 U.S. agricultural outlook*. Prepared for the Committee on Agriculture and Forestry. U.S. Senate, 94th Cong., 2d sess. Washington, D.C.: Government Printing Office.

Miller, Thomas A., and Walter, Alan S. 1977. An assessment of government programs that protect agricultural producers from natural risks. In *Agricultural food policy review,* pp. 93–103. Washington, D.C.: USDA, Economic Research Service.

Nelson, Frederick J., and Cochrane, Willard W. 1976. Economic consequences of federal farm commodity programs, 1953–72. *USDA Agricultural Economics Research* 28:52–64.

Paarlberg, Don. 1964. *American farm policy*. New York: Wiley.

Penn, J. B. 1977. Some implications of the 1977 food and agricultural legislation. In *Increasing understanding of public problems and policies*. Oak Brook, Ill.: Farm Foundation.

Peters, John G. 1978. The 1977 farm bill: Coalitions in Congress. In *The new politics of food,* ed. Don F. Hadwiger and William P. Browne. Lexington, Mass.: D. C. Heath.

Reinsel, Robert D., and Krenz, Ronald D. 1972. *Capitalization of farm program benefits into land values*. Report 506. Washington, D.C.: USDA, Economic Research Service.

Robinson, K. L. 1960. Possible effects of eliminating direct price support and acreage control programs. *Farm Economics,* vol. 218. Ithaca: Cornell University, Department of Agricultural Economics.

Schuh, G. Edward. 1977. World food production and international trade: Implications of market prospects for the agricultural sector and the trade balance. In *Food and Agricultural policy*. Washington, D.C.: American Enterprise Institute for Public Policy Research.

Schultz, T. W. 1978. Migration: An economist's view. In *Human migration,* ed. William H. McNiell and Ruth Adams. Bloomington: Indiana University Press.

Schulze, Charles L. 1971. *The distribution of farm subsidies: Who gets the benefits?* Staff paper. Washington, D.C.: Brookings Institution.

Spitze, R.G.F. 1978. Food and Agriculture Act of 1977. *American Journal of Agricultural Economics* 60:225–35.

Talbot, Ross B., and Hadwiger, Don F. 1968. *The policy process in American agriculture.* San Francisco: Chandler.

Tolchin, Martin. 1977. Urban-rural coalition successful on farm and food stamp measure. *New York Times,* July 29, p. A19.

Tweeten, Luther G. 1977. Agriculture policy: A review of legislation, programs and policy. In *Food and agricultural policy.* Washington D.C.: American Enterprise Institute for Public Policy Research.

———. 1978. In a letter to Leo Mayer of the Congressional Research Service, Library of Congress, in response to a request to comment on proposals of the American Agriculture Movement. In a report *Evaluations of proposals guaranteeing full parity for farmers in the marketplace.* Prepared for the Committee on Agriculture, House, 95th Cong. 2d sess. Washington, D.C.: Government Printing Office.

Tweeten, L. G.; Heady, E. O.; and Mayer, L. 1963. *Farm program alternatives, farm incomes and public costs under alternative commodity programs for feed grains and wheat.* CAED Rep. 18. Ames: Iowa State University.

U.S. Department of Agriculture. 1977. *Handbook of agricultural charts.* Handbook no. 542. Washington, D.C.: Government Printing Office.

———. 1978. *Farm income statistics.* Statistical Bulletin 609. Washington, D.C.: Government Printing Office.

U.S. Senate. Committee on Agriculture and Forestry. 1960. *Report . . . on farm price and income projections, 1960–65.* 86th Congr., 2d sess. U.S. Senate Doc. 77.

Wilcox, W. W. 1960. Agriculture's income and adjustment problem. In *Economic policies for agriculture in the 1960s.* Joint Economic Committee, 86th congr., 2d sess.

5. The New Agenda

The previous chapter makes it clear that the big commodity programs were designed by and for the operators of the larger farms, particularly the landowners who produced certain favored products. Other groups in the farm community—farm laborers, operators of small farms, renters, and farmers who grew unprotected products—either were little affected by these programs or were actually hurt and had generally come to accept their position in the patient tradition that has so long characterized powerlessness in the American political system.

But in the sixties and seventies there came a surge of unrest and challenge. Urban people who had not previously thought of themselves as being much interested in farm or food policy began to appear in the agricultural forum. The reasons for this movement are not altogether clear. But any or all of a number of causes might have contributed. Agriculture lost much of its uniqueness and entered the mainstream of economic, social, and political life, with consequent erosion of the insulation that had so long surrounded farm people. There came a change in the national mood that challenged almost anything that was long established. The price of food rose, causing difficulties for low-income people. Expectations raised by the civil rights movement, the War on Poverty, and the Great Society all affected the farm community. Mounting evidence appeared that existing farm policies were narrowly based. The agricultural establishment lost some of its political power.

In any case, a very diverse group of people demanded to participate in the development of farm and food policy. They had two things in common: they were nonfarmers and they had not previously been prominent in farm policy issues. Challenges to the long-established makers of the farm policy agenda came in novel form and from unanticipated sources. Most of these challenges came during the late sixties and early seventies.

The Reverend Ralph Abernathy led his Poor People's March on Washington. They set up Resurrection City along the Reflecting Pool and converged on the nearby Department of Agriculture, demanding more generous food programs.

Cesar Chavez organized his United Farm Workers and led a long-drawn-out strike, resulting in violence on California farms, a boycott of grapes throughout the United States, and passage of California's Agricultural Labor Relations Act.

Ralph Nader organized consumer groups, attacking the retail food chains, the food manufacturers, and many others. Among the leaders in this movement were Carol Foreman, Ellen Haas, Ellen Zawal, Susan Sechler, and Jim Turner.

George Wiley, leader of the Welfare Rights Organization, used the White House Conference on Food and Nutrition as a platform from which to agitate for more assistance to the poor.

Jim Hightower of the Agribusiness Accountability Project let loose a series of diatribes attacking the experiment stations and the extension service, charging them with serving the interests of the agribusiness community. The Sierra Club and Friends of the Earth pushed their environmental initiatives, aimed especially at the Forest Service. Clay Cochran led a movement that worked for larger programs in rural development, demanding services that had scarcely been thought of, let alone previously advocated.

The President's Civil Rights Commission, that august body, condemned the Department of Agriculture for its poor record in working with blacks, Mexicans, Indians, and females. The hunger lobby was formed, a coalition of church people, nutritionists, and welfare groups, who worked for bigger food aid programs at home and abroad. Consumers launched a beef boycott in an effort to bring prices down.

Carol Foreman, from her post as assistant secretary of agriculture, proposed that food policy begin at the consuming end, based on nutritional need, and that the production end of the chain accommodate itself to this model. Farmers thought just the opposite—that food policy should begin at the production end, with government assistance to the farmer, and that the consumer should accept without complaint what this system provided.

Lawsuits, many of them class-action suits, multiplied in kind and number. The Legal Defense Fund came into being. There were lawsuits intended to prevent timber cutting in the national forests and to prevent the implementation of the new beef grades. There were lawsuits intended to require the department to supply more services to minority groups and to provide food programs in counties where they were not available. These suits were brought against the secretary of agriculture, Earl Butz, who said, "I suppose I've been named in 1000 suits—from food stamps to forest preserves."

The movement proceeded along both conventional and extraordinary lines. Among conventional efforts were lawsuits, literature, and political support for favored candidates. But the movement was not limited to these. There were boycotts, strikes, protests, demonstrations, and occasional violence. These initiatives were carefully fashioned to appeal to the television networks and to the viewers. The nationwide boycott of grapes, a strained extension of the controversy regarding collective bargaining for hired farm workers, was an ingenious way to get attention, obtain broad involvement, and give the issue a moral tone. It certainly helped get the subject on the agenda.

Once the agricultural defenses had been breached, it seemed that everyone came pouring through. Among the challengers were sister agencies in the federal government. The Food and Drug Administration took over regulatory activities formerly administered by the Department of Agriculture. The Labor Department, pushed by the unions, succeeded in scuttling the bracero programs, by which Mexican farm workers had been made available for farm employment. The Labor Department, responding to union concern about the high price of food, was also instrumental in imposing an embargo on the export of grain.

In an effort to improve working conditions, the Occupational Safety and Health Agency was set up. It issued regulations covering the hundreds of different types of farm jobs. In response to widespread concern about the environment, a new government bureau was formed, the Environmental Protection Administration. It took over some of the functions formerly serviced by the Department of Agriculture. It issued rules that outlawed use of certain farm chemicals, and it restricted runoff from feedlots.

The State Department and the National Security Council virtually took over the programming of international food aid, despite the fact that the Department of Agriculture had responsibility for funding and administering the programs.

The Justice Department and the Federal Trade Commission attacked the farm cooperatives for alleged restraint of trade. The Department of the Interior undertook to enforce a 1902 law limiting the size of farms eligible to receive irrigation water from federal projects.

In 1971 the president of the United States proposed what amounted to the dismemberment of the Department of Agriculture. Also in 1971 the president imposed retail price controls on food, which had the practical effect of holding down prices of crops and livestock at the farm level.

New initiatives, originating in the nonfarm sector, not only reduced the role of the agricultural establishment on its own turf, they pushed agriculture into unsought activities. Congress, wanting to improve service to nonfarm people, expanded the Rural Development Program, an effort embracing the work of half a dozen executive departments. Leadership was given to the Department of Agriculture, a charge not relished by the agricultural establishment.

The list of challenges and challengers could be lengthened. But this truncated account will indicate the diversity and magnitude of the challenge. There was one curious thing about this effort to broaden participation in the farm and food policy agenda: the surge of interest came almost exclusively from the nonfarm sector. Those farm people who had long been outside the decision-making process—the small farmers, the part-time farmers, and the producers of the un-protected crops and livestock—continued passively to accept their nonparti-cipatory role. Many of them associated themselves with the power elite in agri-culture against the nonfarm challengers. Their commitment to agriculture was great enough to generate loyalty to an agricultural establishment that either was not serving or was actually injuring them.

Another attribute of this movement was that it often lacked understanding of agricultural matters. Coming from nonfarm people, this was to be expected. For example, the Water Pollution Control Act was given an impossible goal: that "the discharge of pollutants into navigable waters be eliminated by 1985."

This broad onslaught threatened the farm groups on two counts. Some of the proposals and actions, like certain Environmental Protection Agency rules on farm chemicals, seriously interfered with efficient farm production. But, more important, these proposals from nonfarm people challenged the agenda-making power of the agricultural establishment, which felt a need to resist. It was this more than the substance of the proposals that upset the long-established agricul-tural elite. As they saw it, the real question was whether they were to continue as masters in their own house.

The farm people and the agribusiness groups had been challenged before, though never so strongly. By a variety of strategies and tactics, they had held their ground rather well. It had been possible, for three-quarters of a century, to circumvent the law that limited to 160 acres those farms that received irrigation water from federal projects. Efforts to tax farmer cooperatives as if they were ordinary business firms had been beaten down. Social legislation had been written so as to exclude agriculture. The pure food laws had been enacted, but had been so administered as to pose relatively few problems for the agribusiness community. The Commodity Exchange Authority, which regulated trading on the great futures markets, and the agency that regulated the marketing of live-stock had been tucked into the friendly Department of Agriculture and so defanged. The secretary of agriculture was given the job of monitoring the price behavior of his friends, the farmer cooperatives.

The agricultural community sought to meet the new challenge with tactics that had succeeded before: ridicule proposals that appeared preposterous; ignore those thought to be faddish until they went away; confront the challengers when there was thought to be power to win; and try to co-opt those that could not be overcome. The string of victories won by these tactics had been almost unbroken for a hundred years.

So, at first, the challenges were not thought to pose a grave threat. When the environmentalists opposed locating smelly feedlots close to town, farmers tossed out the old farm quip about feedlot odor: "It smells like money to me!" But this time it wasn't funny. When the use of the feed additive diethylstilbestrol was challenged, farmers pointed out that its elimination would reduce efficiency, and raise the retail price of beef. But they found that efficiency, the touchstone of farm policy for the past hundred years, was no longer the decisive criterion. Some thought it best to wait for the consumer movement and environmental concerns to die down. But during the wait these movements grew stronger. Expansion of the Food Stamp Program was resisted head on during the early seventies. But the strength of the movement was underestimated. Resistance redoubled the zeal of the hunger lobby, and the program expanded geometrically.

The new challenge did not go away, and the old guard reluctantly conceded to the new challengers a place on the farm and food policy agenda.

The architects of the farm and food policy agenda came to comprise three diverse subgroups:

Group 1, dating from 1862: the remnants of the research and education movement.

Group 2, dating from 1933: the New Dealers and their heirs, with their price supports and production controls.

Group 3, dating from the mid-sixties: the new zealous coalition with its food stamps, environmental programs, consumer issues, and rural development.

Some people think the new agenda seems too flimsy and lacking in substance to have a long life. But numerous legislators sensed a ground swell of public concern and quickly stepped forward to give it leadership. Many of the new initiatives were institutionalized with legislation, government agencies, and budgetary support. In public policy, these are certificates of longevity.

Can so diverse a set of interests have enough cohesion to continue as a political force? Multiple conflicts tend to become two-party conflicts. Will leadership of the new coalition gravitate toward one of the company? If so, which one? How will the people of the first, the second, and the third agendas work together in framing the farm and food policies for the next decade? Or will they work together at all?

The changes that produced the research and education agenda and the big commodity programs agenda were changes from within; the new agenda is a change from without. The change during the thirties was abrupt, dramatic, and decisive; the change of the sixties and seventies was so gradual that some establishment people still deny it has occurred. The first farm policy agenda has been on the stage for a hundred years, though reduced from the main event to part of a variety show. The second agenda ran for forty years and still draws a crowd. There is dispute over whether the third agenda will have a long run or will quickly fold. The show is new, and so far the reviews are mixed.

6. Price Control

Inflation, not falling price, will be the dominant price problem of the 1980s, and dealing with it will be an important part of farm and food policy. Inflation is primarily a phenomenon of money and credit, not something caused by farmers or the food industry. Government has a monopoly on the creation of money and creates too much of it. In a way, it cannot help itself; it is caught up in its own indulgence, like a drug addict. For political reasons, government caves in to the PIGs (Particular Interest Groups). It votes increased price supports for farmers, boosts the minimum wage for labor, grants rate increases to regulated industry, writes cost-plus contracts with the military-industrial complex, and provides openhanded welfare benefits to the needy. Government appropriates huge sums of money to fund these outlays but refrains from voting the taxes required to cover the costs. This behavior results at least in part from the correct political judgment that people would rather receive money from the government than pay taxes. The consequence, of course, is a huge deficit. In our banking system the deficit is monetized, providing the base for the creation of yet more money. All of this gives an upward boost to the price level.

Keynesian concepts, wrongly interpreted, give seeming respectability to this inflationary process. As the supply of money increases, the value of each unit decreases, and it takes more units to pay for a pound of meat, a pair of shoes, a month's rent, an automobile, or a suit of clothes. This is inflation. It is on the money side of the equation that the price increase is generated. Inflation is a phenomenon of money and credit, not of shoes or meat or rent or cars or clothes. But the government (which indulges the special interests) and the

65

banking system (which accommodates the government's indulgence) would like to have the public think inflation is a phenomenon of groceries and shoes and many other things. The public, accepting what is called "the money illusion" (the notion that the dollar has a stable value) is ready to believe that the problem lies with the goods and services rather than with the money in which' prices of all goods and services are denominated.

As if this were not enough, there are other inflationary forces at work. There is our adverse balance of payments, the result of various forms of self-indulgence. At present this is running about $25 billion per year. The inevitable result is a weak dollar, declining in value against the sounder currencies. A dollar of declining exchange value means rising relative prices, within the United States, for internationally traded goods, as all experience and every economics textbook will affirm. This additional inflationary force seems to be the prospect for the 1980s.

The United States is not the only country that is caught up by inflation. Inflation is a worldwide phenomenon. Countries import and export inflation with every international transaction, and we cannot wholly isolate ourselves from the inflationary forces rampant in the world.

Inflationary expectations have been built into the economy. The prices of farmland, apartment houses, and virtually all other forms of real property reflect this anticipation. The point is that these expectations tend to become self-fulfilling. For example, suppose a farmer buys land at a high price, on credit, as many have done, with the expectation that inflation will validate the outlay. Then suppose the inflation does not come, and the price of wheat and of land does not rise. The land is then overpriced, and the farmer cannot pay his debt. Inflation will help prevent putting this man through the wringer and so has an advocate. When inflationary expectations have been built strongly into our long-term transactions, price stability is relative deflation, with all its pains.

Government itself has a stake in inflation. Inflation nudges people up the graduated income tax schedule and increases government revenue. The government is like other borrowers; inflation reduces the value of the dollar and makes it easier to retire the bonds as they mature and to roll over the debt.

People have a love-hate relationship with inflation. They hate inflation but they love the things that cause it: government benefits, low taxes, plentiful money, cheap interest rates. People love the idea of a stable price level, but they hate the actions that would be necessary to bring it about: curtailment of their government benefits, higher taxes, tighter money.

In the present state of affairs, with inflation institutionalized, if government gets the "old time religion" and puts a strong brake on appropriations and on the creation of new money, it causes unemployment and recession, as was demonstrated in 1974. At least that much of the Keynesian concept is valid. It is unlikely that any popularly elected government could survive the unemployment and recession that, under conditions likely during the 1980s, would be required to take the inflationary uptilt out of the price level. An economic lesson could be taught—that fiscal and monetary restraints are capable of curbing inflation. But the first principle of education is that the teacher should survive the lesson. The estimate of most government officials, elected and appointed, is that the lesson might be taught but the teacher would be fired.

Difficult as inflation may be, it is judged politically preferable to its alternative under present conditions—unemployment and recession. Thus is the government captured by the process it has created, condoned, and validated.

From all this I conclude that price increases for farm and food products—rather than price declines—are the phenomena with which public policy must deal during the 1980s. This is not to deny that there will be painful price declines for particular commodities at particular times. It is the general price trend that is under consideration here.

What is the effect of inflation on farmers? We have to rethink this question. During earlier times, when an increase in the general price level was likely to be followed shortly by a decrease, we thought we knew the answer. Prices received by farmers were made in competitive open markets, rising sharply when the general price level increased and falling rapidly when it declined. Prices paid by farmers were generally administered and sticky; they rose and fell less than did the general level of prices. So during inflation prices received rose faster than costs and resulted in good times. A falling price level meant hard times. In those earlier, simpler days, farmers did not consider inflation a problem; they considered it the solution to a problem—temporary, perhaps, but effective. This attitude on the part of farm people is evident in their support for the Greenback party after the Civil War, their advocacy of the free coinage of silver in the late nineteenth century, and their push for what was called "reflation" after the falling price levels of the early thirties. All these proposed actions were inflationary.

This view was understandable when prices fluctuated moderately around a fairly stable level and when people expected that kind of performance. It is not suited to our present and prospective circumstances. Now the general price level rises more or less continually, and people expect that this will be true indefinitely.

What is the present and prospective impact of inflation on farmers? I list four effects, welcomed or deplored depending on their incidence.

Windfall gains to landowners. From 1972 to 1976, inflation-induced capital gains on all United States farmland were estimated at $339 billion. This was

more than twice as much as was earned from the production of crops and livestock on that land. During 1978 net farm income was $28.1 billion, while the
inflation-caused increase in farm real estate was $90 billion, more than three
times as much. This enormous windfall gain was conferred without regard to
economic performance or service to society.

Structural changes in landholding. People expect inflation to continue. They
see the windfall gains that accrued to landowners during the past forty-five
years. They bid up the price of land to levels not justified by its present or
prospective earnings. Landownership has become in considerable measure the
pursuit of capital gains and a hedge against inflation. Under these conditions
certain people can afford to buy land while others cannot. An established
farmer who already has substantial equity in a going operation can afford to purchase land. He can borrow and buy, spreading his interest and amortization
over the larger unit. He can enlarge his holdings far beyond the size needed for
efficient operation and wait for inflation to carry his net worth up to gratifying
levels. Nonfarm people with good incomes, like doctors and lawyers, can
follow the same strategy. They can buy farmland, meet the carrying charges
with their nonfarm income, and wait for inflation to make them rich. Foreigners
can buy farmland. Our adverse balance of payments puts enormous numbers of
dollars into their hands. Some of these dollars they logically invest in United
States property, including farmland. Not able to buy are the young men with
limited capital who want to get started farming but cannot pay an inflated price
for land. They cannot afford to pay 10 percent mortgage interest for land that
will earn some small fraction of that amount. If they bought land under these
conditions they would go broke long before they realized the hoped-for capital
gains.

As the message now is heard, inflation is saying: "The price of land is going
up. So go for the capital gains. If you have savings or something you can
mortgage, buy land. The important consideration is not so much the price of
land or what it will earn or the efficiency with which you manage; it's whether
you can meet the carrying charges." It would be difficult to think of a circumstance less consistent with the criterion of efficiency, more likely to freeze out
young farmers, or more potent for disaster if the bubble should burst. Some
years from now we may look back on the present as a time when major undesir-
able changes took place in the pattern of landholding. We are developing a
wealthy hereditary landowning class, which is contrary to American tradition.

Misallocation of resources. When money is invested for speculative gain
rather than for productive enterprises, resources are misallocated. Money spent
enlarging a farm primarily for capital gains reduces efficiency rather than increasing it. Stockpiling for inventory appreciation rather than for physical need

gives out wrong economic signals to suppliers. Tying up capital in title to farmland in the hope of reaping windfall gains diverts investment from productive enterprise.

Inequities. Inflation confers unearned gains on the borrqwer, the speculator, and the owner of real property. It means undeserved losses for the saver, the lender, retired people, and people on fixed incomes. These changes are capricious in their incidence and contentious in their effects. They set person against person and group against group.

Inflation, which was tolerable and even considered desirable by farmers when it meant a brief and modest upward departure from a fairly stable price level, is something quite different when it threatens to become a way of life. It leads to public clamor that the government ''do something.'' The most dramatic thing that can be done is to pass a law or issue an edict that prices should not rise. During the Nixon administration, from 1971 to 1974, the first peacetime price controls in history were imposed. Whether price and wage controls worked for the nonfarm sector is left for others to judge. But in the food sector, where products are perishable and prices are competitive, the experience was adverse. The livestock industry was disrupted, and there were alternate shortages and gluts at the meat counter. Interference with the flow of fruits and vegetables to market meant spoilage losses. Hidden price increases occurred as quality deteriorated. Black markets sprang up and illegal transactions occurred. Burdensome report forms had to be filled out. Disrespect for government grew. Price increases were postponed rather than averted.

I was in the Department of Agriculture during this troubled period. Part of the time I worked within the department, trying to get farm prices up in accordance with legislation passed by Congress. The rest of the time I attended White House meetings, trying to hold prices down as specified by presidential edict. The public deserves more from the expenditure of a tax dollar than that it offset the effect of spending some other tax dollar. But, characteristically, when government initiates a change in policy it continues at least for a time the old practices that are being superseded.

As we learned, when farm prices are long held above competitive levels, production control and surplus disposal are required. This we have demonstrated by forty years of costly experience. Similarly, if farm prices are long held below their competitive levels, rationing and subsidized production become necessary. This has not yet been fully demonstrated, because price ceilings have not been long maintained. Each venture, whether floor or ceiling, means a vast expansion of government bureaucracy. Both are expensive. The difference is that price ceilings result in shortage, which is more objectionable than the surplus caused by price floors.

One of the illusions involved in setting ceiling prices is the view by public officials that inflation has been brought under control so that economic stimulation can be applied without pushing up the price level. In other words, if you tie down the safety valve you can shovel more fuel into the firebox and generate greater horsepower. This was done in 1972 to help win the election; it meant a price explosion later, in 1973 and 1974.

For many years agriculture had the political power to obtain legislation that boosted farm prices. And it had the power to escape legislation that would have held food prices down. This preferred treatment was eroded with President Nixon's Economic Stabilization Program. Quite likely there will be attempts to make future government regulation of farm and food prices symmetrical; that is, there will be efforts to establish price ceilings as well as to legislate price floors. Sometime during the 1980s, when legislation to increase farm price supports is before Congress, it is not unlikely that there will be a consumer-led effort to impose price ceilings as well as floors. Contributing to this likelihood are the following: Public concern regarding inflation is likely to be strong. The political strength of agriculture declines. Competitive pricing decreases in importance, while administered pricing increases. This means that fewer and fewer people understand the open market economy, on which agriculture is heavily reliant. The present generation does not understand how disastrous it would be to our food system if we froze the price structure. The passage of time dims the memory of difficulties experienced during 1971–74. Time is required to erase past disappointments and lay the basis for another attempt at price control. How soon can a nation reinstate price and wage control after having thrown them out? Ten years. Maybe five years. It depends on circumstances.

Farmers and the food industry do not cause inflation. Farmers produce abundantly. Food products, for the greater part, are competitively priced. Farmers and the food trade rightfully resent being held responsible for increases in the price of food that originated elsewhere. Farmers and people in the food trade, who price their products competitively, do not feel guilt about getting together on a price mutually satisfactory to buyer and seller. And they do this with little regard to what is said by the president or by Congress. The farmer's dislike for price controls is one of his soundest instincts. Resistance to price controls will merit whatever political power farm people can marshal.

An intruder has broken into the farm and food policy field. He has burst through the door uninvited, unannounced, and poorly understood. His name is inflation. He will be with us for a while. Farm people will have to decide how to cope with this intruder. He is not the friend farmers once thought he was.

REFERENCES

Dunlop, John T., and Feder, Kenneth J., eds. 1977 *The lessons of wage and price controls: The food sector.* Cambridge: Harvard University Press.

Eckstein, Albert, and Heien, Dale. 1978. The 1973 food price inflation. *American Journal of Agricultural Economics* 60: 186–96.

Goodwin, Craufurd D., ed. 1975. *Exhortation and controls: The search for a wage-price policy, 1945–1971.* Washington, D.C.: Brookings Institution.

Kosters, Marvin H., and Ahalt, J. Dawson. 1975. *Controls and inflation: The economic stabilization program in retrospect.* Washington, D.C.: American Enterprise Institute for Public Policy Research.

Nelson, Glenn. 1974. *Food and agriculture policy in 1971–1974. Reflections on controls and their impact.* Washington, D.C.: U.S. Department of the Treasury, Office of Economic Stabilization.

Weber, Arnold. 1973. In *pursuit of price stability: The wage-price freeze of 1971.* Washington, D.C.: Brookings Institution.

7. The Consumer Movement

Perhaps nothing so clearly depicts the recent change in the farm and food policy agenda as does the consumer movement. Historically we have thought of ourselves as producers—farmers producing food, workingmen selling their labor, manufacturers producing industrial goods, professional people providing services. Relatively little attention was paid, in terms of policy, to consumption. We organized ourselves into groups related to what we produced: farm organizations, trade associations, labor unions. We set up our government agencies on the basis of vocation: Department of Agriculture, Department of Labor, Department of Commerce.

So pervasive was the producer orientation that we organized many of our educational institutions according to vocation: the School of Agriculture, the School of Business, the School of Labor Relations, and so on.

The textbooks in these schools were heavily focused on production. Production economics was and is a major subject in departments of agricultural economics. Until recently, consumption economics scarcely existed as a coherent body of thought; if the subject was taught at all it was likely to be an accounting course in what was then the School of Home Economics. Research was focused on production; consumption was thought to require little special study or attention. Farmer cooperatives deliberately drew a line between themselves and consumer cooperatives.

All of this might seem strange to the uninitiated. Consumption is half of economic activity. The purpose of production is consumption, a fact known to everyone in a subsistence economy. This central fact had somehow got lost in our advanced industrial society. But when one understands the principle and theory that have dominated economic thought for the past two hundred years, the explanation for this one-sidedness becomes apparent.

Our economic thought exalted a principle called "consumer sovereignty." The notion was clear in neoclassical economics, which postulated an open competitive system. According to this concept the consumer was indeed sovereign. By his purchase he expressed preference in the market for this or that good or service. Thus the price was bid up for those items that were high on the consumer's list of priorities. The producers, noting the rise in price, hastened to increase production of the preferred product. and they cut back the output of any good or service that consumers held in low esteem, disfavor being expressed by nonpurchase and hence a falling price. So by this concept the consumer was at the center of the decision-making process; all resources were automatically allocated and reallocated to meet his needs. Consumers needed no advocate; the whole system was set up to serve them. Producers by definition stood in service to consumers, and there could be no real issue between them. What was good for farmers—or laborers or General Motors—was good for the country. A lobbyist could push the case for his particular constituency with a clear conscience. Whatever he did to help his producers was helpful to the consumers as well.

It must be said that this view had much truth to it. In the United States, where it reached its apex of acceptance and performance, it resulted in a high standard of living and great individual freedom. It worked best, of course, when its assumptions were fulfilled: an open market, many firms in competition with one another, and full knowledge of the merits of the merchandise.

But in recent times this whole body of belief has come into question. Is the consumer really sovereign, or are his wants manipulated? Some time ago I attended a Food Manufacturers' meeting in Florida and heard one of the speakers declaim thus: "Let's face it; the consumers don't need any new food products. They already have more products to choose from than they need. The only way we can sell our new product is to create a felt need for it. So: advertise, promote, and get out there and sell!" One likes to think that his needs have been determined by himself rather than programmed by a group of salesmen and advertisers sitting around a conference table.

Are the interests of farmers—or General Motors—really identical with the public interest? Manufactuers and farmers use political and economic power to push up prices and to screen themselves off from competition. Those who buy the products find it hard to reconcile this behavior with consumer sovereignty. Many consumers no longer believe the old theory. They do not consider themselves sovereign. They think they have been deposed or captured. They feel that they are being manipulated, and they resent it. That is the psychology of the consumer movement.

The origins of the consumer movement go back a long way. The radical economist Thorstein Veblen laid its foundation at the beginning of this century. The book *100,000,000 Guinea Pigs,* by Arthur Kallett, and F. J. Schlink appeared in 1933 and shook public faith in the received doctrine of consumer sovereignty. Vance Packard brought out his book *The Hidden Persuaders* in 1957 and further eroded orthodox belief about the markets. The modern philosophical godfather of the consumer movement is undoubtedly John Kenneth Galbraith, who successfully made the point that our economy is not as competitive as it once was or is still thought to be. Ralph Nader, with his attack on auto safety, was in the vanguard of action. In the food area, the consumer movement was led by Esther Peterson, Carol Foreman, and a number of others. In the political arena, leadership was given by Senator George McGovern of South Dakota and Congressman Benjamin S. Rosenthal of New York. All these people were, in greater or lesser degree, antiestablishment types, which of course assured the opposition of the power elite.

The consumer movement is visibly and favorably related to organized labor, thereby giving special offense to agriculture. For example, in 1976 there was a harvesttime strike in California that resulted in the spoilage of farm crops. The wastage of food reduced the supply and increased the retail price. The California Department of Agriculture estimated a loss of $22–24 million a day to the California economy. But consumer advocates, who had raised great protest about rising food prices, voiced no complaint about this labor-related increase in the price of food.

Farmers were highly critical of the leadership that took hold of the consumer movement—its radical leanings, its sometimes unsound positions, its strange alliances, and its abrasive style.

The consumer movement is locked into a power position by legislation, bureaus, and appropriations. There are thirty-three federal agencies with responsibility for consumer activities. These include approximately four hundred bureaus and subagencies operating more than a thousand consumer-oriented programs (Chou and Harmon 1978, p. 24).

How broad is the base of what is called the consumer movement? Is it narrow, led by a few aggressive captains with a following of summer soldiers who will desert with the first snowfall? Or is it a general movement with broad appeal to large numbers of people? In my opinion, dissatisfaction with the producer-oriented economic and political system has long been latent. Leaders discovered it, released it, fanned it into flame, partially organized it, and gave it focus. The gap between the consumer advocates and the rank and file of consumers is probably no greater than the gap between the farm leaders and the rank and file of farmers.

Food is the largest item in the consumer's budget, and it is purchased more often than any other. Food is closely associated with health, tradition, and aesthetics. It has ethical and religious overtones. Furthermore, consumers know much less about food than formerly, and their suspicions therefore are greater. When most people were farmers or only a generation away from agriculture, and when agriculture was simple, there was little difficulty in understanding. Everyone knew a good potato when he saw one. But farmers are fewer, agriculture is more complicated, food products are more highly processed, and our agricultural origins are increasingly remote. Thus the problem of understanding is now much greater.

Consumer concern about food arose from a variety of causes: alarm about chemical residue that can be harmful to health; resentment at being manipulated by advertisers; displeasure with the general inflation that carried up prices of everything including food; suspicion that consumers were being "ripped off" by the food trade; all aggravated by massive misunderstanding regarding the food and agriculture complex. Because of its special economic and emotional attributes, the food area emerged as a prime focus of the consumer movement.

As regards food, the consumer movement took these forms in addition to those already mentioned in chapters 2 and 5:

A drive for a consumer protection agency in the federal government.

An effort to tighten up meat inspection.

Antiagribusiness campaigns, based on the contention that large corporations engage in monopolistic price-increasing practices.

The push for federal grades like United States number 1 instead of proprietor's grades like Swift's Premium Ham.

An effort to have food items labeled with nutritional content and unit-priced to permit ready price comparisons for different-sized packages.

Date labeling, to show the freshness of the food.

Support for food-related campaigns such as the ecology movement, various welfare programs, and commodity reserves.

Insistence on consumer representation on various governmental advisory boards.

Virtually all these initiatives were offensive to farmers. The consumer movement, as the farmers saw it, was blameworthy because it challenged the establishment, especially the agenda-making role of farmers and their associates in the food industry; it was often ill-informed, and sometimes its charges were unfounded; it lacked appreciation for America's bountiful, economical, nutritious, and generally wholesome food supply; it was exploited by personally ambitious individuals in both public and private life.

The difficult but appropriate thing would have been to sort through the consumers' various charges to find what substance they had, if any, and then make the indicated changes. But this was more than the farmers were capable of. They decided that the consumer was the adversary. This was a strategic error of the first magnitude. One should not engage in confrontation with a group of people upon whom one is dependent for his market, and whose strength is greater than one's own. And there was no doubt where the strength lay. Farmers totaled 4 percent of the population and nonfarmers 96 percent. This is the new math of agricultural policy.

Farmer resistance added mightily to the zeal of the consumer advocates. Nothing so arouses the fervor of a movement as victory over a dedicated opponent. The consumers piled up one victory after another: the food programs, price control, and export embargoes, for example.

Is the consumer movement a passing phenomenon or will these issues be of a lasting nature? Defeat of the proposed consumer protection agency was hailed by some as an indication that the consumer movement had crested and was about to collapse. In my opinion it may have crested, but it is not about to collapse. The changes that gave rise to the consumer movement were conceptual and attitudinal, as I indicated earlier. These changes appear to be fundamental and enduring rather than passing. A strategy of waiting for the consumer movement to die seems doomed to fail.

Government, long the producers' accomplice in many schemes against consumers, was perplexed. The consumer movement was of undoubted strength and so had to be reckoned with politically. Programs advocated by the consumers were voted in, often operating alongside programs that were hurtful to them. There was a period during the mid-seventies when it seemed that on Mondays, Tuesdays, and Wednesdays the government strove on behalf of consumers; the rest of the workweek it strove against them. On Sunday the government rested. Simultaneous pursuit of opposing objectives is an understandable form of behavior for a cautious government. Politically, it is then possible to point out to each protagonist that the government is doing something for him. And from the standpoint of substance the new policy venture is not a certain winner. Keeping the old programs going means holding the other option open.

Let us take a brief overview of consumer concerns that appear to be unfounded or exaggerated. What of the allegation that the American diet is generally deteriorating as a result of junk foods, modern processing methods, poor nutritional content, and poverty-related malnutrition? Such hard evidence as exists is to the contrary. Nutrition-related diseases such as rickets, goiter, scurvy, and beri-beri are in a steady decline (Chpu and Harmon 1978, p. 33). The height of children has been exceeding that of their parents for several generations now. Athletic records are steadily being broken. The life-span is lengthening. The greatest nutritional problem in the United States is obesity, for which the individual consumer is responsible, not the farmer or the food industry. The percentage of the consumer's budget that goes for food has been declining irregularly throughout the past half-century. In 1929, the first year of record, it stood at 23.4 percent. The great controversy about food prices during 1974 was evidenced by a blip on the chart, an increase from 16.3 to 16.9 in the percentage of disposable income spent for food, after which the long-term decline was resumed. (The figures given are averages only. Those who earn less than $8,000 a year spend 23 percent to 39 percent of their incomes for food.)

What of the charges that the food industry is not competitive, that it takes excessive profits? Returns on investment, either before or after taxes, show the food trade to be generally in line with other enterprises (Paarlberg 1974, p. 28). The Joint Economic Committee of Congress recently received testimony showing that prices were higher in markets where concentration was high. Other prominent economists disputed these findings at the same hearing (U.S. Congress 1977). The Federal Trade Commission and the Department of Justice keep a sharp watch on the food trade to see that it continues to be competitive.

The consumer drive to impose price controls on food resulted in misallocation of resources and spoilage. The export embargoes for grain and soybeans, which had consumer support, brought little reduction in the consumer price index but gave great offense to farm people and were a disturbing factor in our international affairs. Sales of wheat to the Soviet Union, which consumers strenuously protested, may have increased the consumer price index by 1 or 2 percent.

The hard evidence is that, in substance, most of these consumer causes were shallow and poorly founded. But they had great emotional appeal to large numbers of people and undoubtedly were instrumental in marshaling support for the consumer movement. They got the issue on the agenda, which was their prime purpose. The farmers should have recognized the technique for what it was, having themselves used this method in times past. The power elite in food and agriculture, who were being challenged, rushed from one sector to another, whenever a new attack came, refuting allegations with demonstrable facts, yet still losing the decision.

On other issues the hard evidence supports the consumer position. First is the consumers' misgiving about farm programs that have reduced the supply of farm products and increased the retail price of food. We saw in chapter 4 that this has indeed been the effect of the commodity programs (Schultze 1971, p. 1).

Consumers have a point, too, regarding grades and standards for food. Our grades and standards were largely developed by the people in the food trade, who presumed that they knew what was good for consumers. For example, our grading system provides inducements to produce more animal fat than consumers desire. We still price milk at the farm level so as to encourage butter-fat production; the consumers, mindful of their doctors' admonitions, want low-fat milk or skim milk. So the government buys up the surplus butter and distributes it to needy persons, to the advantage of their palates if not their health.

Some years ago I attended a dinner at the old Stockyards Inn in Chicago honoring Allan Kline, past president of the American Farm Bureau Federation. It was just after the International Livestock Exposition, and I was sitting with a group of commission men who were selling the prizewinning 4-H Club calves. These men were deploring the fact that the blue-ribbon calves were too fat for the trade and had to be sold at a discount. Here was a system of honors, rewards, and grades that was out of touch with consumer preference. The discrepancy was known to farmers and the food trade. But instead of changing practices in the feedlot and the show ring, as should happen if the system reflected consumer sovereignty, the effort was to educate consumers on the alleged merits of high-finished beef. Consumers, worried about cholesterol, less in need of fat as a source of energy than were their forebears, and mindful of the greater cost of high-finished beef, are slow to respond. The farmers and the food trade might well do some listening as well as talking.

There is merit, too, in the consumer claim that agricultural research is oriented toward the felt needs of producers rather than of consumers. Some years ago Dr. Ned Bayley, assistant secretary of agriculture for research and education, proudly brought with him to the secretary's staff meeting a new peach developed by the Agricultural Research Service. Bayley recited the merits of this new peach variety: high yield, good shipping quality, strong disease resistance. "But how does it taste?" asked Secretary Hardin. Bayley's face fell; apparently taste had not been one of the criteria. The idea of the old farm policy agenda that service to producers automatically results in improving things for the consumers has truth, but only partial truth.

If the hard evidence is against some of the consumer causes and for certain others, there are many issues for which the evidence is inconclusive. This should not be surprising. Much of the past research in the food area simply disregarded the concerns now voiced by consumers. In the language of the researchers, these matters were considered "externalities" or "exogenous variables," or they were impounded in "other things equal." Hence little is known. Where much is alleged and little is known, there is need for more facts.

Foremost among the issues in need of further research are questions associated with food additives, adulterants, and chemical residues. Which of these are harmful and to what degree? Is total purity possible, or is this a standard that, if strictly adhered to, would remove from our diets the bulk of our present food supply? How many years or how many generations do we have to wait before we declare that "delayed effects" of certain chemicals are no longer a danger? What do we encounter in terms of cost as we approach absolute purity in our food supply? How much weight should aesthetics have in our food intake, along with considerations of cost, nutrition, and convenience? The tongue does the talking; to what extent is it speaking for the palate, which is concerned with taste, to what extent for the mind, which is concerned with prestige, and to what extent for the other members of the body, which are concerned with nutrition? Most of what we think we know about human nutrition has been learned from our study of animals; to what degree are we justified in imputing to people what we have learned from rats?

Then there are the questions about nutritional labeling, unit-pricing, pull-dating, specification of contents, federal grading, and "truth in advertising." How much of this do consumers really want? How much would it cost? How many people would we have to add to the government payrolls to do all this work? Should these services be forced on all because they are desired by some? At what point would we encounter "information overload"? How much of our effort to improve nutrition should come from education and how much from regulation? Are consumers intent on total veracity in packaging, labeling, and advertising, as consumer advocates contend? As government moves deeper and deeper into regulation of our food supply, what share of the costs should be borne, respectively, by the farmer, the food industry, the consumer, and the taxpayer?

These questions cannot now be answered. The latitude for undisciplined assertion is therefore almost total. When anything can be asserted and nothing can be refuted, the degree of misunderstanding can be very great indeed.

A new kind of logic has developed around the subject of food additives. The old rule said, "He who asserts must prove." By this familiar concept, if a government agency charged that a food was unfit for human consumption, the burden of proof lay with the government. Now this appears to have been reversed; if the government questions whether a food is fit for use, the doubt is resolved against the purveyor unless he removes it with scientific evidence, whose validity is judged by the government. With facts so few and so difficult to ascertain, the burden on the food trade becomes very great. But in the absence of regulation the danger to the consumer can also be great.

The optimists (and I am one) have hope that the issues between farmers and consumers will abate. This hope can be based on certain judgments: that inquiry and research will develop a growing body of undisputed information reducing the range of dispute; that consumer interests, along with the concerns of producers, are becoming accepted subject matter for public policy; that as the consumer movement matures its abrasiveness will diminish; that farmers will become aware that the consumer is the customer and not the adversary; and that confrontation tactics will therefore be replaced to some degree by an effort to achieve accommodation. But these things will not happen by themselves, and they will not happen at all unless attitudes change. Up to now, as seen by the consumer advocates and the farm leaders, the issues have been more valuable than the solutions. When that changes, and only then, this issue will be de-escalated.

REFERENCES

Chou, Marylin, and Harmon, David P., Jr. 1978. *The new political and cultural environment facing the food industry: The preoccupation with food safety* (draft). Croton-on-Hudson, N.Y.: Food, Agriculture and Society Research Program, Hudson Institute.

Kallett, Arthur, and Schlink, F. J. 1933. *100,000,000 guinea pigs: Danger in everyday foods, drugs, and cosmetics.* New York: Vanguard Press.

Paarlberg, Don. 1974. Statement on consumer food costs made before the Consumer Subcommittee, Senate Commerce Committee, U.S. Congress, June 24. Washington, D.C.: USDA.

Packard, Vance. 1957. *The hidden persuaders.* New York: Pocket Books.

Schultze, Charles L. 1971. *The distribution of farm subsidies: Who gets the benefits?* Washington, D.C.: Brookings Institution.

U.S. Congress Joint Economic Committee. 1977. *Prices and profits of leading retail food chains, 1970–74.* Hearings before the Joint Economic Committee, 95th Congr., 1st sess., March 30 and April 5 (pp. 96–514). Washington, D.C.: Government Printing Office. See especially Willard F. Mueller and Bruce W. Marion, pp. 4–58; Kenneth Farrell, pp. 70–77; Ray A. Goldberg, pp. 58–70; Timothy R. Hammonds and Thomas L. Sporleder, pp. 77–103.

8. The Rise of Government Regulation

Until fairly recent times the accepted way of bringing about change in agriculture was to research a question, give the resulting information to the farmers, and rely on their judgment to change or not change their practices, as they saw fit. Voluntary action, guided by research and education, was the essential principle of the first farm policy agenda. This was the dominant setting for a hundred years. The land grant colleges, the experiment stations, the extension service, and the teaching of vocational agriculture were all set up according to this pattern. The force that drove the system was this belief, explicit in classical economics, coming from Adam Smith: "What is prudent in the conduct of every private family can scarce be folly in that of a great kingdom" (Smith 1776, p. 424).

The results of this policy were impressive. Agricultural efficiency increased, to the benefit of consumers. Quality of the diet improved, as witnessed by the decline of nutrition-related diseases. Farmers' level of living advanced, reflecting improved efficiency both on and off the farm. Farmers' social status improved, as befitted their improved real incomes, their educational advances, and their enhanced decision-making role. Real wages of farm labor increased, the result of increased efficiency both on and off the farm.

But criticism arose. The research and education agenda was said to have been captured by agribusiness and by those who operated the large farms. Matters important to other groups in the food system—small farmers, consumers, hired farm labor, and minority groups—were said to be neglected. Critics claimed that the system focused on the individual interest to the neglect of group concerns. The experiment stations and the extension service were accused of approaching problems exclusively from the standpoint of the farm operator. For example, researchers and extension workers sought to reduce the cost of producing cotton, putting aside other things such as the effect on the environment and the effect on hired farm labor. But the things that were put aside became major matters of public concern. When this concern arose, the research and education community, having focused on other questions, lacked the necessary answers. There is truth in these allegations.

Dissatisfaction with research, education, competition, and voluntarism was general; what we experienced in agriculture was only a reflection of a much broader movement. By degrees, we shifted from *education* to *regulation*. We moved from individual to group decision-making, from voluntarism to mandatory change. We became impatient with the slowness of the voluntary system and sought to speed it up. We moved issues out of the marketplace and into the public forum. There arose a new ethic that subordinated the individual to the group. The force that drove these changes was the belief that the interest of the entrepreneur, instead of being compatible with the interest of the group, is opposed to it. Those who embraced the new ethic could also quote Adam Smith: "People of the same trade seldom meet together, but the conversation ends in a conspiracy against the public, or in some diversion to raise prices" (Heilbroner 1953, pp. 61–62). It followed from this line of thought that individual decision-making must be curbed—regulated. So there came regulation of the market, food safety, the environment, working conditions, land and water use, energy, and numerous other matters important to agriculture.

Most of these regulations were resented by farmers, who have a long and strong tradition of independence. Farmers respond more readily to persuasion than to force. Having set up their own institutions based on voluntarism and having seen this system succeed (at least as they measured success), they opposed the regulatory syndrome. Regulations of the Food and Drug Administration, the Environmental Protection Agency, and the Occupational Safety and Health Administration are anathema to most farm people.

One of my vivid recollections is of sitting around a table in Washington with a roomful of government regulators. Their purpose was to get that last molecule of diethylstilbestrol out of beef liver, although scientists could not show that anyone had ever been harmed by consuming residues of this feed additive. The air was thick with cigarette smoke (325,000 deaths a year attributable to smoking). After the discussion we adjourned to cocktails (25,000 deaths a year from drunken driving, many of the victims nondrinkers). The inconsistency of regulating others and indulging oneself went unremarked by these people and, as far as I could see, unobserved. (The statistics on death from smoking are from the government, reported by Jaroslovsky and Sease, 1978, p. 1. Statistics on deaths from drunken driving are from the Department of Transportation.)

Does a group of officials of nonfarm background, sitting in an air-conditioned office, know enough about agriculture to prescribe the length of the hoe handle for California farm workers? Or the exact window space needed for migrant housing? Yet regulations have been issued on such things. What evidence is there that decisions thus produced are superior to those produced by individuals? What evidence is there that farmers will abide by such arbitrary rules?

The change from a voluntary to a regulated system does not come mainly from deterioration of the environment or poorer performance by the private sector; it comes primarily from a change in mood. The change is more in public perception than in what we usually consider to be objective fact. From a political standpoint, however, public perception is an objective fact, reluctant though farmers may be to acknowledge this.

The difficulty is compounded for farmers because they have two adjustments to make. First, as agriculture loses its uniqueness, they lose the shelter of the exclusionary clauses that had long shielded them; they have to enter a society that is more regulated than agriculture has been accustomed to being. Second, the society they are entering is itself becoming more regulated.

The dilemma is between minimal regulation, with resulting abuses of the public interest, and heavy regulation, with the erosion of self-discipline and the possibility that the regulations might be hurtful.

Up to the present, this issue has generally been resolved by issuing more regulations. Eight thousand regulations are proposed annually (Kahn 1978, p. 30). The Office of Management and Budget estimated that at the end of fiscal year 1971 the federal government had about 6,400 different kinds of forms, not counting tax and banking forms (Weidenbaum and DeFina 1978, p. 29). The current costs of federal paperwork in private industry range from $25 to $32 billion a year (U.S. Commission on Federal Paperwork 1977, p. 5).

For some time now those for and against regulation have been shouting epithets and clichés at one another. Rancor is a component of this issue and will continue to be. Zeal prevails over reason. Confrontation strategy dominates. One trouble with confrontation strategy is that it drives the antagonists to polar positions; anything less than total opposition to the other is interpreted as a concession that there is merit to the rival view and so is unacceptable. If one of the two has the power to win, there is the temptation to impose unconditional surrender on the other. This was done to the farmer with the food safety legislation, the Environmental Protection Act, and the act that created the

Occupational Safety and Health Administration. Had they had the clear power to win (which they did not and will not have), the farmers would have totally escaped regulation. Justice Louis Brandeis said it well: ''The greatest dangers to liberty lurk in the insidious encroachment by men of zeal, well meaning but without understanding.''

There is merit on both sides of the regulatory issue. What is needful is to sort out such facts as there are and to approach this question case by case. This will take reason, analysis, patience, compromise, and the acceptance of losses as well as victories. It involves searching out that fruitful middle ground between the zealous reformer and the old guard. This is difficult. But, if farmers want useful results rather than glorious defeat, this is what they shall have to do.

A central point in the controversy over regulation is the fact—we now know it to be a fact—that, contrary to Adam Smith, what is prudent for each individual family may indeed be folly for a great kingdom. It may be prudent for individual families to dump their refuse into the river. But this may not be wise for the people as a group. Private benefits and costs may diverge from benefits and costs for the group. Such cases constitute the legitimate basis for regulation. As the economist says it, marginal social benefits should be equated with marginal social costs when private and social benefits and costs differ. In everyday language, the individual should not be permitted to profit to the injury of the group. The point is to find those cases in which individual and group interests diverge and, in such cases, to use regulatory measures that respect individual as well as group rights.

This is the moderate's approach to regulation. At one extreme (call it the far right) are the rugged individualists who want no interference whatever with individual decision-making. At the other extreme (call it the far left) are those whose intentions are ''not to correct the deficiencies of markets but to transcend markets altogether—which is to say, government regulation is not economic policy but social policy. It is an effort to advance a conception of the public interest apart from, and often opposed to, the outcomes of the market place and, indeed, the entire idea of the market economy'' (Weaver 1978, p. 56).

Sometimes the regulated capture the regulators. This happened with the transportation industry; government rate-making was used as a means to limit competition and assure profit. It happened during the wage and price controls of 1971–74, when big industrial firms used the control effort as a means of blunting interfirm competition. Rules concerning wages on government construction projects were written so as to hold a wage umbrella for the building trades. Powerful Eastern coal interests succeeded in getting EPA emission standards set so as to give them an advantage over their Western competitors. Farmers were successful in having acreage control regulations so written that the government gets only half or two-thirds of the cutback it pays for. The point is that in the practical world of affairs the regulatory programs work out in ways very different from those assumed in the ideological arguments.

We are at an early stage in the regulatory debate, which certainly will be with us at least for the coming decade. The issue is discernible throughout this book. It appears in some form in each of the policy issues we shall examine.

REFERENCES

Heilbroner, Robert L. 1953. *The worldly philosophers.* New York: Simon and Schuster.
Jaroslovsky, Rich, and Sease, Douglas R., 1978. HEW's Califano finds his anticigarette drive burns up many people. *Wall Street Journal,* May 1, pp. 1, 19.
Kahn, Herman. 1978. *Some cultural contradictions of economic growth: The twelve new emphases.* Croton-on-Hudson, N.Y.: Hudson Institute.
Nutter, G. Warren. 1978. *Growth of government in the West.* Washington, D.C.: American Enterprise Institute for Public Policy Research.
Schultze, Charles L. 1977. *The public use of private interest.* Washington, D.C.: Brookings Institution.
Smith, Adam. 1776. *An inquiry into the nature and causes of the wealth of nations.* 1937 edition. New York: Modern Library.
U.S. Commission on Federal Paperwork. 1977. *A report of the Commission on Federal Paperwork: Final summary report.* Washington, D.C.: Government Printing Office.
U.S. Congress. Senate Committee on the Judiciary. Subcommittee on Administrative Practice and Procedure. 1977. *Administrative practice and procedure.* Senate Report no. 95–25. Washington, D.C.: Government Printing Office.
U.S. Department of Transportation. 1968. *1968 alcohol and highway safety report.* Washington, D.C. Government Printing Office.
Weaver, Paul H. 1978. Regulation, social policy and class conflict. *Public Interest* 50: 45–63.
Weidenbaum, Murray L., and DeFina, Robert, 1978. *The cost of federal regulation of economic activity.* Reprint no. 88. Washington, D.C.: American Enterprise Institute for Public Policy Research.

9. Is Zero Tolerance Tolerable?

Around the turn of the century a series of events aroused public concern regarding the safety of the food supply. There was indignation about the use of impure beef to feed the soldiers who were fighting the Spanish-American War. Upton Sinclair's book *The Jungle* revealed scandalous conditions in the meat packing industry; European countries had reached the point of barring imports of American meat. In 1902 the New York City Health Commission tested approximately four thousand milk samples and found that more than 50 percent were adulterated. Milk was diluted as much as 50 percent with water, then adulterated with chalk or plaster of paris to make it look like milk (Beltmann 1974, pp. 114–15).

In the Department of Agriculture at that time was Harvey W. Wiley, chief of the Bureau of Chemistry. He was a strong battler for legislation to regulate the food industry. After a long fight, Congress passed the Federal Food and Drugs Act. This was in 1906; the Meat Inspection Act went into effect the following year. These laws dealt with interstate and foreign commerce in food and drugs. They were a turning point in the fight for wholesome food. Supervisory work began in the Department of Agriculture but in time was transferred to the Department of Health, Education, and Welfare.

The food industry had opposed the passage of these laws for many years. But the tide of public opinion finally prevailed. In time the laws were strengthened and broadened to cover narcotics, cosmetics, and false advertising. The food industry came to accept them and generally to abide by them. On the whole, the legislation worked rather well. The canning industry's record of safety was exemplary in that it produced an estimated 900 billion containers of food with only five known deaths from botulism during the past half-century (Foster 1976). Public confidence in the wholesomeness of the food supply was generally at a rather high level.

But difficulties were coming. Here, in rough chronological order, are events that shook the public's faith in the food supply.

After World War II the chemical revolution hit agriculture. Insecticides and herbicides—known poisons—were used by farmers on a geometrically increasing scale. There was apprehension that residue from these chemicals, especially the insecticide DDT, would be carried with the food to the dinner table.

Food additives were developed by the food trade in an effort to improve the taste, appearance, keeping quality, and nutritional attributes of processed food. Suspicion arose that these chemical agents might be harmful.

Formulated foods and engineered foods made their debut. Protein beverages, grain-protein concentrates, and textured protein foods became widespread after 1950. Synthetic amino acids were incorporated into these mixtures to compensate for deficiencies in their amino acid balance. The food industry thus accomplished an advance in nutrition, but it came at the price of a loss in public confidence. Some people became aware that their food supply was being tampered with and became increasingly uneasy.

Then came the large-scale testing of nuclear bombs, accompanied by the fallout of radioactive strontium 90. Articles appeared in the newspapers reporting that this deadly agent was taken up with grass by dairy cattle and appeared in the milk. The possibility of birth defects and genetic damage became a worry. In Europe children were born deformed because their mothers used the tranquilizer Thalidomide. Science and technology, which had long been thought benign, took on an ominous tone. "Natural" became good. "Processed," "additives," "formulated," "chemical," and "engineered" became bad.

An antiagribusiness mood arose. The big food companies were producing most of the new food technology and so were vulnerable to the charge that they changed our food habits without our knowledge or approval. The idea that "small is beautiful" was a part of the movement.

Public concern about cancer and heart disease grew; there was widespread suspicion that these diseases were associated with food additives and adulterated foods.

Into this troubled setting Rachel Carson introduced her superbly written book *Silent Spring*. She took her title from the danger that agricultural chemicals would kill off the wildlife; that songbirds would disappear. This book, appearing in 1962, was surely one of the influential works of our time. With this book the antichemical movement escalated.

Further weakening public confidence were a series of accidents and disasters. The worst was the chance mixture of a fire retardant, polybrominatedbiphenols (PPB), with livestock feed in Michigan, with resultant loss of livestock and jeopardy to human health. Then came the Kepone case in Virginia; workers in an agricultural chemical factory experienced serious health impairment, and effluent from the factory did undeniable environmental damage.

All of this jolted an essentially urban public that had limited knowledge of agriculture or of the food industry. The chemicals DDT, PPB, and PCB became familiar, and in the public mind they were synonymous with danger to the food supply.

The consumer activists exploited public concern about the wholesomeness of food. Gradually, during this period, elected and appointed public officials took up the refrain. The Senate Select Committee on Nutrition and Human Needs was formed and became a focal point for expression of concern about the whole range of food problems.

So decisions regarding food gradually moved from the marketplace to the public policy forum. Increasingly, food became politicized. The chief concern was the possibility that cancer might be induced through food adulterated by additives or chemical residues. It is not clear what proportion of the public was aware of and involved in the issue. Certainly it was more than the "attentive public," which Cobb and Elder say does not normally exceed 10 percent of the total. The "general public," usually less active, less interested, and less concerned, became involved. The issue was highly generalized and symbolic, which is necessary if the general public is to be aroused (Cobb and Elder 1972, pp. 107–8).

What are the hard facts about the isue—facts known and agreed on in the scientific community? Let the questioner be a kind of ombudsman and the respondent a spokesman for the food scientists, the nutritionists, the technologists, and the medical researchers. Here, as if in court, is the dialogue:

Q. Can you establish whether certain food additives or chemical residues are capable of causing cancer?

A. Yes, but not in absolute terms. We can do it by subjecting test animals to a large intake of these chemicals under controlled conditions.

Q. Can you establish a threshold, a tolerance level, below which human ingestion of these chemicals would be safe?

A. We cannot establish a level in which we have absolute confidence.

Q. Can you answer the question whether ingestion of these chemicals might result in gene modification for human beings, with likely adverse effects for subsequent generations?

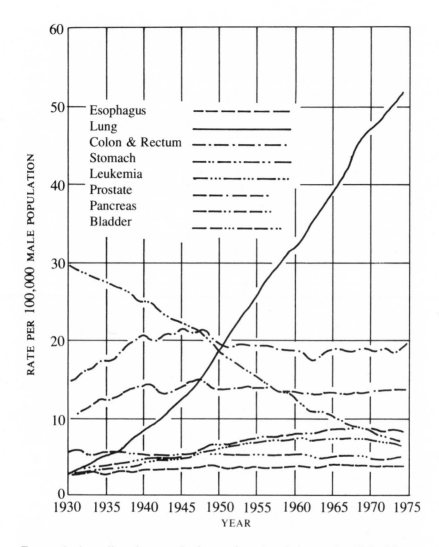

FIGURE 1. Age-adjusted cancer death rates for selected sites, males, United States, 1930–74 (standardized on the age distribution of the 1940 United States census population). Data from U.S. National Center for Health Statistics and U.S. Bureau of the Census.

A. We can prove neither that they will or that they won't. We can only wait and see.

Q. Is there any known case in which cancer has been induced in a human being by the ingestion of foods carrying these chemicals?

A. No. But there have been cases in which a high incidence of cancer has been associated with medical prescription, with long exposure of workers to high concentrations of these chemicals in manufacturing plants, and with exposure of farm workers during field application.

Q. What are the facts regarding the incidence of cancer?

A. Lung cancer is increasing at a phenomenal rate. Stomach cancer is declining. Other forms of the disease have stabilized in recent years. Figure 1 shows the trends.

Q. Can you state with confidence that the incidence of cancer is related to diet?

A. No.

Q. Can you state with confidence that the two are unrelated?

A. No.

Q. What can you do with your scientific skills, regarding the problem before us?

A. We can increase our ability to detect these toxic chemicals.

So we had a very unsatisfactory situation—a concerned citizenry and a scientific community apparently incapable of rendering decisive judgment.

The legislators understandably responded to public concern. In 1958 they passed the Delaney Clause in an amendment to the Federal Food, Drug, and Cosmetic Act of 1938. This clause requires the Food and Drug Administration to establish that all chemical additives be proved safe before being used in food. If a chemical is shown to be capable of producing cancerous tumors in test animals, it is considered unsafe for human beings and its use is prohibited. Responsibility for the safety of a product is placed on the manufacturers, and the responsibility for evaluating the evidence submitted is placed on the Food and Drug Administration.

Since the scientists said they could not identify a safe threshold for the suspected chemical, the law was so written—and interpreted—that the presence of any amount whatever of the agent would result in withdrawal of the contaminated food from the market. The congressmen and the administrators opted for what they thought was total safety. This was the famous "zero tolerance."

The Delaney Clause is thus referenced legally: Food Additives Amendment of 1958, section 409(c)(3)(A)21 U.S.C. section 348(c)(3)(a) 1964. It articulated and made specific a point already in the law, that foods that are unsafe are not to be sold to the public. From a strict legal standpoint, the Delaney Clause changed nothing. But the debate surrounding it raised the issue in public awareness and was seen as mandating vigorous administration. Every law leaves latitude for administrative interpretation. From a narrow legal standpoint, deletion of the Delaney Clause would change little. But deletion would be interpreted as evidence of public displeasure with rigorous enforcement, and the basic law would be administered with less zeal. The issue of zero tolerance has symbolism as well as substance. Though there are of course many other forms of food regulation, the Delaney Clause has become symbolic.

Problems arose when the Food and Drug Administration undertook vigorous enforcement of the Delaney Clause (Whelan and Stare 1975).

1. Detection improved. When the law was passed, laboratory equipment was capable of detecting a suspected chemical if it existed in concentrations measured by parts per million. At present, ability to identify the suspected chemicals has increased so that we can detect parts per trillion (Damon 1973). Strictly interpreted, zero tolerance means that if there is one molecule in a shipload, the entire shipload must be withdrawn from the market. Some idea of the implications of this standard can be seen from the fact that one part per trillion would be equivalent to one grain of sugar in an Olympic-sized swimming pool.

The effect of this advance in technology was to impose a standard a million times more rigorous than when the law was written. What previously would have been measured as zero became detectable, and hence not accepted.

2. Scientists discovered that certain of these troublesome chemicals exist in natural foods. All foods, whether natural or artificial, are made up of chemicals. Some of these chemicals are toxic, and if large quantities of such food are consumed in a short period, harm may result. A dose of 0.33 ounce of caffeine is fatal to humans (Chou et al. 1977, p. 272). Potatoes represent a complex aggregate of about 150 different chemical substances, among them arsenic, nitrates, and solanine alkaloids. Lima beans contain hydrogen cyanide, and bitter almonds contain prussic acid (Whelan 1975, p. 36). Not only is toxicity present in many natural foods, there are other harmful possibilities: the buildup of kidney stones from the oxalic acid in spinach and rhubarb; the induction of goiter by excess consumption of cabbage, cauliflower, turnips, mustard greens, or collard greens; and the induction of anemia by excess consumption of onions (Tannahill 1973, pp. 379–80).

Nitrites and nitrates have been shown capable of causing cancer in test animals, and their use is in question. Nitrates are a natural plant constituent, occurring in spinach, beets, radishes, eggplant, celery, lettuce, collards, and turnip greens. People often consume more nitrates from vegetables than from cured meat products (Ingelfinger 1975, p. 11). These natural chemicals usually occur in very small amounts, so that danger to human health is minimal. But in high concentrations they might cause severe injury or death to test animals, and with modern laboratory equipment some of them might be detected in natural foods. But natural products are not subject to the Delaney Clause and so are not tested. No one can say for sure what would happen if the 7,500 food items on the shelves of the average grocery market were all subjected to the Delaney Clause, but it is likely that many of them would have to be banned.

More scientific knowledge is necessary to help establish tolerance levels in foods. The fact that certain people are allergic to various foods indicates the vast differences in individual metabolism. This greatly complicates the establishing of acceptable levels of residues or additives.

3. Banning certain foods, as required by the Delaney Clause, may be more of a hazard to health than a help. Saccharine, a noncaloric sweetener, is useful for diabetics and for overweight people. Banning it might do more injury than good. Cyclamates, also nonnutritional synthetic sweeteners, are of a similar nature. The withdrawal of nitrates would increase the danger of botulism.

4. Total monitoring of the food system is impossible. The task taken on by the Food and Drug Administration is so great as to be virtually incapable of full accomplishment within any reasonable budgetary allowance. The agency selects certain foods for testing, it uses a limited number of mice or rats; it feeds them prodigious amounts of the suspected chemical for a short period, and so comes to its conclusion, which appears in probabilistic rather than absolute terms. Even if mice were men, this procedure would leave some doubts.

Enforcement is selective. How are foods selected for testing? Consumer complaints? Some estimate of the probable public reaction? The political power wielded by those who produce the food in question? Some advance judgment as to the health hazard? The credibility of the agency? The answer is not clear. The mix of concerns is not divulged. It is possible to obtain a list of items that have been tested and found to be carcinogenic. It has not been possible to obtain a clear-cut list of items that have been tested and approved, or of items that have not been tested. What we have is rigorous enforcement applied to a limited and selected number of foods. Selective enforcement of the law is not the best way to obtain or merit the goodwill and support of the public. But applying the Delaney Clause to all foods that carry additives would take so many foods off the shelves that the law would be revoked. Some opponents of the legislation advocate that very thing.

Here are some celebrated cases of action under the Food Safety Rules:

Aminotriazole. The offending chemical was an herbicide used to control weeds in cranberry bogs. Some of it was picked up by the plants and lodged in the berries. The year was 1959, and the time was just before Thanksgiving. Certain shipments of cranberries had been found to contain aminotriazole, which is capable of causing cancer. Therefore, under the Food Safety Rules, cranberries had to be withdrawn from the market. Arthur S. Flemming, secretary of health, education, and welfare, announced that the sale of cranberries was prohibited, effective immediately. The public reaction was a combination of amazement and panic. Some people who had eaten cranberries in the past began examining themselves for symptoms of cancer. Some who had cranberries in the refrigerator disposed of them stealthily. The turkey made it to the table that Thanksgiving, but not the cranberries. This was a case when concern spread beyond Cobb and Elder's "attentive public" to include many of the "general public."

Prodigious amounts of aminotriazole had been fed to the rats in the testing procedure. Someone figured that to ingest an amount of the chemical equivalent to that consumed by the rats, a man would have to eat eighteen tons of cranberries.

The Food and Drug Administration was astounded at the dimensions of the reaction. Flemming lamely told President Eisenhower's staff, "We thought it best to make the announcement just before Thanksgiving so as to give the agency some added visibility." There was plenty of visibility!

The growers said the weed killer had earlier been approved by the government, which was true. Congress, acting on the basis of a little-used 1935 law, voted ten million dollars in indemnity for the loss farmers had experienced. But it took time for the growers to turn to alternative chemicals and for public confidence in their product to be rebuilt.

Cyclamates. Cyclamates, noncaloric sweeteners that are favorably viewed by diet-conscious consumers, had been widely used in canning fruit. Effective January 1, 1970, cyclamates were banned as agents capable of causing cancer.

Enormous doses had been used in demonstrating their carcinogenic character. The United States Food and Drug Administration (1974) stated: "A twelve-ounce bottle of soft drink may have contained from one-fourth to one gram of sodium cyclamate. An adult would have to drink from 138 to 522 twelve-ounce bottles of soft drink a day to get an amount comparable to that causing cancer in mice and rats."

Public reaction to the cyclamate ban peaked somewhere below the cranberry crest. But the canning industry found itself with much of a season's pack on hand and its sale forbidden. How was the banned fruit to be moved? Government officials mostly looked the other way and did not ask too many questions.

DES. The troublesome agent here was diethylstilbestrol—DES for short—a growth hormone with the well-established capability of improving the conversion of feed into meat. It was used not only in cattle feeding but also in the production of broilers. DES was banned in 1972. Lawsuits arose. The ban was partially lifted and partially reimposed. At present the use of DES in certain forms is legal providing no residues are found.

The Department of Agriculture made a study that estimated that eliminating the use of DES would result in a 4 percent increase in the retail price of beef and, in the short run, would increase the net incomes of cattle feeders. Nevertheless, consumers applauded the ban and cattle feeders protested, illustrating the fact that economic considerations were not the central issue.

Public response to the DES action was somewhat muted, indicating a growing public ennui with these regulations.

Red dye no. 2. This widely used food coloring agent was banned in 1976. In this case the testing techniques were challenged. The Toxicology Advisory Committee, formed in 1975 to evaluate the results of all previous red dye no. 2 studies, concluded that only two of these were of any value, and Food and Drug Administration scientists say that one of these two studies was "botched" or poorly administered (Boffey 1976, p. 50; Chou et al. 1977, p. 272).

Saccharine. Saccharine is a powerful noncaloric sweetener, 300 to 350 times sweeter than sugar, 10 times sweeter than cyclamates. It is widely used in soft drinks and in many food products, particularly by diabetics and weight watchers. It was recommended for banning in 1977, primarily on the basis of tests made in Canada. Public protest arose, and the action was modified.

Nitrates and nitrites. At this time, bacon is suspect because nitrates and nitrites are used as preservatives. These agents form nitrosamines, which have been shown to be carcinogenic.

With nitrites and nitrates a very significant development occurred. The government did not impose an absolute ban; it proposed a staged reduction in use. By a special and much-needed interpretation, the zero tolerance concept was modified. At present the matter is before the courts (Foreman and Kennedy 1978).

The controversy over nitrates and nitrites appears to be largely a battle between government officials and the food industry. The public, though still somewhat concerned, appears to be losing interest. With each new invoking of the Delaney Clause, public skepticism seems to increase. The Food and Drug people, like the boy in Aesop's fable who called "Wolf!" too often, appear to have lost credibility.

The judgment to which I come is that there is indeed a problem, and that the wholesomeness of the food supply is a proper matter for government concern.

But I venture the view that the difficulty has been exaggerated beyond its true importance and that government, by its well-intended intervention, has aggravated the problem rather than alleviating it. The Delaney Clause was a classic case of overreaction.

There is a solution, in my opinion. In the long run it would be what the economist calls a "Pareto-optimal solution," in that it would improve the situation for some and would leave no one worse off. There are few such solutions to public problems; the few there are should be seized enthusiastically. Here is what would be required:

Farmers and the food industry, to a greater degree than before, would have to acknowledge the legitimacy of consumers' concern about the wholesomeness of the food supply.

Scientists would have to indicate, as they do for radiation and as they have begun to do for nitrates and nitrites, a threshold level below which a food would be considered safe. Consumers would have to acknowledge that absolute safety is not for this world. They could be allowed to hope for it in the next. Politicians would have to summon the courage to change the law, setting up some less demanding standard or, what is perhaps simpler, to accept some rule of reason in administering the law.

The components that make this solution possible are coming into place: the gradual replacement of myth by fact, waning public demand for absolute purity, and the increasing difficulty of measuring up to an increasingly difficult standard.

When will the change occur? When the antogonists finally come to realize that more is to be gained by solving the problem than by keeping the issue alive. We already see evidence of a move in this direction in handling the problem on nitrosamines. Were it not for the felt need of the contending parties to adhere to positions previously stated, the problem would have been solved long ago.

An alternative solution, the one I prefer, would be to treat chemical additives in food as we treat cigarettes and movies of questionable quality—with warnings.

This system could work in conjunction with the banning of certain chemicals whose demonstrated effects are so harmful that people should not be expected to make a judgment concerning their use—Thalidomide, for example.

Under this system, each package of the food in question could bear a statement such as this: "WARNING: this food contains so many parts per million of such-and-such a chemical, which has been shown capable of causing cancer when fed to test animals." This step could be accompanied by good public-supported research and education.

The Delaney approach is similar to Prohibition and to censorship. It denies freedom to the individual and places confidence in the judgment of the central decision-maker.

Warning has several advantages over prohibition. It does not require the task—very difficult for scientists—of establishing acceptable levels of risk. A sound food-nutrition-health educational program could be used to make people aware of such facts as are known; then they could make their own choices. This approach would capitalize on the market's ability to function efficiently, once consumers were informed. And, at a time when the public is becoming satiated with regulations, it would be a move toward individual freedom.

William Lowrance defines safety as a judgment of the acceptability of risk. In turn he defines risk as a measure of the probability and severity of harm to human health. A thing is safe if its risks are judged to be acceptable (Lowrance 1976, p. 8). These matters are largely individual and subjective. Thus there is logic in allowing people considerable opportunity to determine for themselves how much safety they want, and how much they are willing to pay for it.

REFERENCES

Beltmann, Otto. 1974. *The good old days—They were terrible!* New York: Random House.
Boffey, Philip M. 1976. Death of a dye. *New York Times,* February 29, section 4, p. 50.
Chou, Marylin; Harmon, David P., Jr.; Kahn, Herman; and Wittwer, Sylvan H. 1977. *World food prospects and agricultural potential.* New York: Praeger, in cooperation with Hudson Institute.
Cobb, Roger E., and Elder, Charles D. 1972. *Participation in American politics: The dynamics of agenda-building.* Boston: Allyn and Bacon.
Damon, G. Edward. 1973. A primer on food additives. FDA *Consumer* 7:10–16.
Foreman, Carol Tucker, and Kennedy, Donald. 1978. Joint statement before the Subcommittee on Agricultural Research and General Legislation. U.S. Senate Committee on Agriculture 7190, 2697–78, September 25.
Foster, E. M. 1976. *The microbiological safety of processed and raw foods.* Paper presented at the Grocery Manufacturers of America, press briefing, October 21–22, Milwaukee, Wisconsin.
Inglefinger, F. J. 1975. A matter of opinion. *Nutrition Today,* vol. 10, no. 4.
Lowrance, William W. 1976. *Of acceptable risk: Science and the determination of safety.* Los Altos, Calif.: William Kaufmann.
Tannahill, Reay. 1973. *Food in history.* New York: Stein and Day.
U.S. Food and Drug Administration. 1974. Letter from the acting commissioner, report on the agriculture-environment and consumer protection appropriation bill. U.S. Congress, House Report no. 93–275 (1973).

Whelan, Elizabeth M., 1975. Healthier than life itself. *New York Times,* July 23, p. 35.
Whelan, Elizabeth, and Stare, Frederick. 1975. *Panic in the pantry.* New York: Atheneum.

10. Domestic Food Programs

People choose particular foods for a variety of reasons: taste, habit, religious precept, convenience, economy, nutrition, appearance, and prestige. It is as wrong to consider food solely from the standpoint of nutrition as it is to consider clothing only from the standpoint of warmth.

Having said this, in the present chapter I shall focus primarily on the nutritional adequacy of the American diet, since we are examining programs whose purported purpose was to overcome poverty-related malnutrition. There is an enormous amount of controversy about the adequacy of the American diet, even among those doing research on the subject. At a congressional hearing or a convention of nutritionists, disagreement seems to dominate. Despite the disagreement, it is my opinion that there is enough accepted information about our diet to support a soundly based food policy.

Questions arise on whether the American diet is improving or deteriorating with the passage of time. The most persuasive answer is that certain nutritional deficiencies have been reduced or eliminated. But we appear, unfortunately, to have continued into our modern sedentary lives some of the food habits that were better suited to an earlier, more active life-style. And we seem, with our modern affluence, to have adopted certain food habits more noteworthy for convenience and taste than for sound nutrition. These matters are important, certainly. But the question that gave rise to the food programs is of another kind: What is the relationship of income to nutrition? Do poor people have enough of the right kinds of things to eat?

Fortunately we have the so-called HANES study of 1971–72, the Health and Nutrition Examination Survey done by the Department of Health, Education, and Welfare. It was a careful survey of 30,000 Americans from one year to seventy-four years of age in sixty-five primary sampling areas of the United States. Findings by race, age, sex, and income are shown in table 2.

The findings of this comprehensive study are interpreted thus by Halcrow:

a high percentage of persons of all ages, both above and below the poverty line, both sexes, and both black and white, had nutrient intakes less than the recommended standard levels for the four most critical nutrients—calcium, iron, and vitamins A and C. . . . in summary, although the surveys of the status of nutrition show that a high proportion of the nation's total population have good to excellent diets, and that the average food intake is perhaps the highest of any nation, signs of malnutrition, hunger, and poor eating habits are evident all around us. [Halcrow 1977, pp. 497–98]

The study showed differences between the diets of the poor and the well-to-do. As I read the evidence, table 2 indicates that, nutritionally, the diets of those in poverty and those above the poverty line were more noteworthy for their similarities than for their differences. Similar findings came from the *Ten-State Nutrition Survey* done by the U.S. Department of Health, Education, and Welfare (1972).

Many studies have shown that the wealthy buy more prestigious, tasty, and expensive foods than do the poor, and that they pay for more service with their food. The weight of the evidence seems to be that they also buy, marginally, more nutrition. But not substantially more.

Two pieces of popular evidence need to be excluded in this search for facts. One is the starving family reported by the television documentary, cited as evidence of widespread malnutrition among the poor. The other is the brawny heavyweight boxing champion coming from a background of poverty, cited as an indication that dietary problems among the poor are a myth. There are such individual cases, but neither is typical. It is human nature to observe and generalize from the unusual.

At least one more thing needs to be said. Individual nutritional requirements vary substantially from the nutritional standards researchers set up. These standards are, after all, based on averages. One may need either more or less than the specified standard, depending on one's age, sex, weight, level of activity, and unique capability of transforming food into energy and growth.

In determining recommended dietary allowances, a safety factor is thrown in. Typically the safety factor is two standard deviations above the average estimated nutritional need, which itself is not precisely known. Thus the recommended dietary allowance is more than is needed by 97.5 percent of the population.

The domestic food programs of the United States had their origin not so much in meeting the food needs of the people as in efforts to dispose of agricultural

Table 2. Comparison of Percentage of Persons with Nutrient Values Less Than the Standards, and Mean Nutrient Intakes as a Percentage of Standard by Race, Age, and Sex for Income Levels, United States, 1971–72.

	White		Black	
Age, Sex, and Nutrient	Percentage of Persons with Intakes Less Than Standard	Mean Intake as Percentage of Standard	Percentage of Persons with Intakes Less Than Standard	Mean Intake as Percentage of Standard
	Income below Poverty Level[a]			
1-5 years, both sexes				
Calcium	14.42	197	35.26	149
Iron	94.46	67	93.61	60
Vitamin A	51.51	160	46.07	187
Vitamin C	58.23	138	48.54	161
18–44 years, female				
Calcium	56.39	110	74.50	80
Iron	94.24	57	94.66	49
Vitamin A	73.54	82	64.42	149
Vitamin C	72.26	108	59.37	132
60 years and over, both sexes				
Calcium	40.43	121	44.67	108
Iron	62.66	95	67.31	93
Vitamin A	61.45	108	62.40	163
Vitamin C	59.16	119	54.65	141
	Income above Poverty Level[a]			
1–5 years, both sexes				
Calcium	12.14	210	24.96	166
Iron	94.88	69	95.29	66
Vitamin A	36.91	157	51.01	199
Vitamin C	42.82	189	52.91	160
18–44 years, female				
Calcium	55.59	110	71.69	77
Iron	91.13	59	94.70	55
Vitamin A	64.90	114	67.36	116
Vitamin C	49.04	150	56.81	127
60 years and over, both sexes				
Calcium	34.41	142	47.71	117
Iron	46.97	114	64.57	109

Age, Sex, and Nutrient	White		Black	
	Percentage of Persons with Intakes Less Than Standard	Mean Intake as Percentage of Standard	Percentage of Persons with Intakes Less Than Standard	Mean Intake as Percentage of Standard
Income above Poverty Level[a]				
Vitamin A	55.56	196	52.24	226
Vitamin C	38.96	174	43.78	165

SOURCE: U.S. Department of Health, Education, and Welfare (1974).

[a]Excludes persons with unknown income.

surpluses. During the Great Depression, surpluses of farm products accumulated in the hands of the government. Simultaneously, there was widespread unemployment and poverty; some people lacked the money to buy the food they needed. The case for matching excess supply with authentic need was compelling. A program to distribute food directly to the poor was set up. In 1939 a Food Stamp Program was inaugurated and continued until March 1943, when it expired, a war casualty. Also in 1939 came the School Lunch Program, followed by the School Milk Program in 1940. Each of these programs was temporarily suspended during World War II (Upchurch 1977, p. 347).

These programs were begun in the Department of Agriculture. All were intended to move farm products that were in surplus, with little regard for nutritive content or the felt needs of the recipients. The prevailing view in the Department of Agriculture in those days was that the major function of American schoolchildren was to ingest surplus food; if they acquired a little knowledge along with the food, so much the better.

There was dissatisfaction among the public with this producer-oriented domestic food program. But the farm bloc was able to cope and maintained control. Year after year, the domestic food programs plodded along, little changed in scope or form. Until the 1960s, that is.

In 1968 a so-called Citizens' Board of Inquiry issued a report, *Hunger, USA*. The authors reported that one-half of all households in the United States had poor diets and that only one-fifth of these, or about five million persons, were reached by food programs. In May 1968 the Columbia Broadcasting System presented an hour-long documentary bearing the same title—*Hunger, USA*. Hunger was portrayed vividly before a nationwide audience. The documentary was a sensation and undoubtedly laid the basis for the subsequent rapid expansion of the food stamp program. I know of no other television documentary that so vividly illustrates the power of the media in influencing public policy.

During May and June 1968 there was a Poor People's March on Washington, demanding food from the Department of Agriculture.

In 1969 Nick Kotz of the *Washington Post* published his book *Let Them Eat Promises: The Politics of Hunger in America,* a strong allegation that both Congress and the administration had defaulted in their responsibility to the poor.

Rapidly then came the 1969 White House Conference on Food, Nutrition, and Health, a platform from which activists demanded more assistance to the needy. The Senate Select Committee on Nutrition and Human Needs was formed, giving political visibility to those who favored expanding the various domestic food programs. The hunger lobby came into existence—a body that rallied church groups and other organizations motivated to help the poor. An alliance came about between those who supported the new domestic food programs and those who were committed to the big farm commodity programs—a marriage of convenience. The farm bloc operated in conformity with the old political admonition "If you can't lick 'em, join 'em."

The result of all this was to escalate the domestic food assistance programs. A new cause had been lifted up—the alleviation of hunger, a cause every voter could understand. From 1969 to 1977 federal expenditures for domestic food assistance programs increased from $250 million to $8,600 million (Hiemstra 1978*b*)—larger than the combined expenditures of the Department of Agriculture on all its historic programs for farm people (research, education, conservation, and commodity programs).

Table 3 shows the various domestic food assistance programs, the amount of federal costs for food, and the total value of food purchased in conjunction with these programs in 1977. The federal costs exclude operating and administrative costs. The total value of food purchased includes payments made by recipients and by state and local governments.

Next I shall present a general description of these various domestic food programs: Direct Donation, School Lunch, and the Food Stamp Program. What is supplied is not an exhaustive examination but rather necessary background for getting at the issues. An excellent overview of these programs is contained in a summary of five USDA food policy seminars (U.S. Department of Agriculture 1978*a*).

DIRECT DONATION

Direct donation of food began during the thirties. Government either donated directly the products it had acquired through price support or went into the mar-

Table 3. Total Value of Food Purchased or Served through USDA Domestic Food Assistance Programs Compared with Federal Costs, Fiscal Year 1977

Program	Federal Cost (millions of dollars)	Total Value of Food Purchased or Served (millions of dollars)
Food Stamp Program	5,058	8,340
National School Lunch Program	2,207	4,457
School Breakfast Program	145	163
Child Care Food Program	127	127
Summer Food Service Program	124	124
Special Milk Program	153	222
WIC Program	259	259
Elderly Feeding Program	19	76
Other food distribution programs	43	43
Total food assistance	8,135	13,811

SOURCE: Hiemstra (1978*b*, p. 7).

ket and purchased farm commodities to be donated (Davis 1959, pp. 681–90). Recipients were people on welfare, charitable agencies, and schoolchildren.

When direct donation was the chief vehicle for our domestic food programs, certain foods were regularly declared to be in surplus and so were eligible for purchase and donation. Prunes were one such food. Pears were another. And they were indeed in surplus; for these specialty crops, government purchases constituted a sufficiently large share of the demand to boost prices significantly and so stimulate production. Government programs, intended to alleviate the surplus, aggravated it instead.

For the more important commodities like beef and pork, government purchases were so small a share of the total supply that they had little real effect on price. But the purchase of some token amount gave the lobbyist, the congressman, and the secretary of agriculture a chance to improve relations with farmer constituents. They could say that the government had entered the market to buy so many million pounds of the product, an impressive quantity reported in this way, even if it amounted to a miniscule share of the total supply. We had almost no leverage on these big commodities. The trick was to buy just as market forces were about to produce a price increase on their own, and then claim credit for the price improvement. It was a charade, and all the principals knew it.

The direct donation program was based on the myth that the donated foods constituted a net increase in consumption—that before the program began the potential recipients had been experiencing a serious shortfall in food intake. There is only fragmentary truth to this belief. When people receive donated food, they reduce their consumption of purchased food. Donated wheat flour and cornmeal tend to replace purchase of these same products. Donated butter tends to replace purchased margarine. Donated meats tend to displace other protein products.

This bundle of myth, self-interest, and goodwill was the process by which Johnny got his hamburger, his applesauce, his prunes, and his peanut butter.

At its height, in 1939, we were providing supplemental food supplies to 13 million Americans. The undertaking was intended to be an agricultural program. Its parentage, upbringing, maturity—and senility—were all within the Department of Agriculture. Practically all the initiative came from the supply side. One must feel some doubt about the degree of need when so much of the volition comes from the donor. The one-sidedness of this program finally became clear, and it was replaced by a greatly expanded Food Stamp Program. At present, direct donation to individuals is serving only about 80,000 persons mainly Indians and people in the Trust Territories. Substantial amounts of food were still being donated in 1976, but the chief recipients were the School Lunch Program and charitable institutions. The cost in that year was $433 million (U.S. Department of Agriculture 1977a, p. 567).

The School Lunch Program

In 1977, 54 percent of our elementary and high school students were eating a noon meal provided under the National School Lunch Program (Gallo and Stucker 1978, p. 25).

The School Lunch Program is a multibillion-dollar operation involving cooperation of federal, state, and local units of government and payments by the children themselves. The federal contribution quadrupled during the Nixon-Ford years (Hiemstra 1976, p. 12). Support in 1976 was as follows:

	Million dollars	Percentage of total
Federal cash and commodities	$1,920	46.2
Children's payments	1,310	31.5
State and local government	826	19.8
Donated goods and services	104	2.5
	$4,160	100.0

The School Lunch Program is really three-dimensional. It is considered a nutritional measure, an educational effort, and a means of increasing the consumption of agricultural commodities. The program offers foods that are in accordance with standards established by the Department of Agriculture. These standards are in terms of broad food groups: protein-rich foods as a main dish, two or more vegetables or fruits, whole-grain or enriched bread, and milk (Hiemstra 1978*a*, p. 70).

In the early years—that is, during the 1930s—the drive for the School Lunch Program came in large degree from a desire to meet the problem of poverty-associated malnutrition among schoolchildren. During the Depression these needs were critical in certain areas. But inability of parents to provide nutritionally adequate diets for their children has now become a subordinate consideration. The program is no longer limited to this purpose or to this criterion of need; it is now intended for all children, rich or poor.

The effect of the program on total food consumption is minor. Undoubtedly it has resulted in some increase in milk consumption. But there is substitution and displacement. A child who eats his school lunch does not eat lunch at home and does not eat out of a lunch box. Certainly not all that he eats within the program is additional. A part of what is supplied publicly is not bought privately. Part of what is paid publicly releases money to be spent privately.

In this brief review we have focused on the parent act, the central thrust of the various child-feeding programs. There are other undertakings of a similar kind: the School Breakfast Program (SBP); the Special Food Service Program for Children (SFSPFC); the Special School Milk Program (SMP); the Program for Women, Infants and Children (WIC), a rapidly growing program that spent more than $300 million in 1978; and the Child Care Food Program (CCFP).

There are few government activities more popular with all parties than the School Lunch Program and its affiliated feeding ventures. Farmers favor its market-expansion effort, which they tend to overestimate. Parents like to have their children receive a warm, nutritious midday meal. School officials say a warm lunch helps students learn. People in the food trade favor the part of the program that is financed by grants and so is spent in the stores and supply houses. Nutritionists are convinced the program improves health. Socially minded people believe the program is of significant help to the poor.

Chief among the critics of the program are those who feel that a part of the proper responsibility for the child has been unwisely shifted from the parents to the public. And there has been growing criticism of abuses in administration of the program, particularly summer feeding in New York. The Department of Agriculture acknowledges that about 15 percent of the average school lunch goes uneaten and ends up in the garbage can (Gallo 1978, p. 36).

THE FOOD STAMP PROGRAM

The Food Stamp Program was born of the belief that poor people, if given the means, could do a better job of meeting their own food needs than could be done for them by the farm interests, intent on unloading surplus crops. This must be acknowledged as a fairly reasonable idea.

The essentials of the program at this time are as follows: To make possible the purchase of a low-cost diet that has been declared adequate, eligible people are given stamps that can be used like cash in food stores. To be eligible, a household must be unable to buy a "nutritionally adequate diet" (as specified by the "thrifty food plan" of the Department of Agriculture) with 30 percent of its monthly net income. It must have less than $1,500 in liquid assets. Recipients of public assistance are automatically eligible and in 1976 constituted a little more than half the total participants. Eligibility standards are uniform across the nation. The Food and Nutrition Service of the USDA estimates that about 59 percent of those eligible in the period of a month and 72 percent of those eligible over the course of a year elect to participate in the program (U.S. Department of Agriculture 1975, p. 66). Reasons for nonparticipation are unawareness of the program, lack of income with which to buy stamps, difficulties of applying for stamps, and desire for self-reliance.

The participating family receives enough stamps to buy the nutritionally adequate diet. Actually, of course, the participants purchase whatever food they please. If a family is at the low end of the income ladder, it receives its total supply of stamps free. These are called "bonus" stamps because they are free. If the family is eligible for stamps but near the "income exclusion point," it receives only a few "bonus" stamps. Between these limits the number of "bonus" stamps received is scaled to income. On the average, recipients pay between forty and forty-five cents for each dollar's worth of food stamps.

Here in simplified form, is the amount of "bonus" food stamps received by a family of four, scaled according to income, effective as of July 1, 1978 (U.S. Department of Agriculture 1978c):

Indicative brackets of monthly income	Bonus food stamps
$0–$ 19.99	$182
100–109.99	157
190– 209.99	129
290– 309.99	99
390– 419.99	69
480– 509.99	42
600– 629.99	24
630 and above	0

Standards of eligibility have changed numerous times, usually being liberalized. In 1975 the Department of Agriculture reported that only 6 percent of all stamp recipients were in households with take-home pay of more than $6,000 a year, and that 87 percent of these families had more than five members.

The most recent legislation further liberalized eligibility requirements. The Food Stamp Act of 1977 eliminated the purchase requirements and removed from eligibility those above the poverty level. It also simplified eligibility criteria. These changes are expected to increase participation by about two million persons, but per person benefits will be lower.

Effect of the Food Programs on Various Groups

We have had these programs in one form or another since before World War II. This should be sufficient time for judging their effect on various groups.

Effect on Participants

The effect of the programs on nutrition is not clear. A study in the state of Washington failed to show significant differences between children whose families participated in the Food Stamp Program and those whose families did not (table 4). Patrick Madden, in his assessment of the dietary effects of the Direct Donation Program and the Food Stamp Program in two counties in Pennsylvania, found some measurable effects of the Food Stamp Program under certain conditions, but they were small. He found no measurable effect of the Direct Donation Program. He also tested for dietary effects associated with income and found no significant association (Madden and Yoder 1972).

Sylvia Lane, in her 1974 dietary study in Kern County, California, found significant effects for the Food Stamp Program but not much effect of Direct Donation (Lane 1974). In 1978 Lane reported that Direct Donation participants in Kern County were receiving more food than they would have purchased with money or with stamps (Lane 1978a, p. 114).

Clinical before-and-after tests, which would be needed to provide definitive answers on the dietary effects of the Food Stamp Program, are not available. This is amazing for a program, rationalized on nutritional need, that costs $5.4 billion a year. One must conclude that such information is not earnestly desired.

A USDA publication (Boehm and Nelson 1978) reviews major economic research on food expenditures by Food Stamp Program participants. The summary paragraph is as follows:

Table 4. Nutrient Intakes of Eight- to Twelve-Year-Old Children from Households Eligible for Food Stamps, State of Washington, 1972–73

	Sample Values (% of RDA)[a]	
	Food Stamp Participants (N = 196)	Eligible Nonparticipants (N = 136)
Energy	77.4	78.5
	(21.2)	(20.6)
Protein	171.4	173.3
	(47.7)	(50.3)
Calcium	92.2	90.0
	(40.1)	(36.3)
Phosphorus	122.8	122.9
	(41.8)	(41.4)
Iron	94.8	94.5
	(40.8)	(39.6)
Vitamin A	123.7	118.1
	(80.0)	(80.9)
Thiamin	101.1	99.1
	(56.7)	(63.6)
Riboflavin	151.0	144.7
	(69.7)	(61.1)
Niacin	93.3	90.2
	(40.0)	(37.3)
Vitamin C	170.7	175.3
	(128.5)	(139.0)

NOTE: Standard deviations of variables are given in parentheses.

SOURCE: West, Price, and Price (1978).

[a]RDA = recommended daily allowance.

Available evidence now indicates that food stamp households allocate their food budgets in about the same way as do other households. There is no evidence that food stamp households spend disproportionate amounts on either non-nutritious foods or relatively expensive convenience foods or cuts of meat. This is not to say, however, that the Food Stamp Plan has not had an influence on the food buying habits of the poor. Quite possibly, the program provides low income Americans with the flexibility to purchase more of the same types of food as does the average customer.

The effect of the programs on the self-reliance of participants goes untested and perhaps could not be researched in quantifiable terms. In the Mariana Islands of the Western Pacific (Trust Territory) the Department of Agriculture distributes free food to 76 percent of the people. Erwin Canham, former resident commissioner of the Northern Marianas, asks: "What would this do to family responsibilities? To the dignity and self respect of people? To agriculture? To the work ethic? Imagine three quarters of the total population on relief, in a lively prosperous island! Is that good?" (Kiener 1978, p. 5).

In Puerto Rico in 1975, islandwide sales of food stamps accounted for 40 percent of the groceries sold (U.S. Department of Agriculture 1977c, p. 29). In the continental United States in 1976, food stamps went to 8 percent of the people (U.S. Department of Agriculture 1976, p. 10).

Why is so large a share of the population on food programs in the Marianas and Puerto Rico? Because the Department of Agriculture dutifully follows the law, which specifies that standards be uniformly applied even in areas where average incomes are not comparable.

Canham's questions are most relevant when participation is at 76 percent of the population. They are pertinent when 40 percent of the groceries are bought with food stamps. They cannot be dismissed when participation stands at 8 percent of the population. Few people question a program that provides food to persons who are truly in need and are unable to help themselves. In my view, the earlier, more modest food stamp program generally measured up to that standard. But the program has been expanded beyond that optimum point.

A major effect of the program is to relieve participants of the stigma of dependency. In former times the needs of the poor were addressed by methods that were voluntary, philanthropic, private—and usually inadequate. The recipient was expected to acknowledge his dependent status, to feel some impairment of his self-esteem, and to be grateful for the help he received.

Now assistance to the poor and near-poor is required by law, tax-supported, openhanded—and politicized. It is considered a matter of right, and everything is done to obscure the dependent status. When public assistance came in, private charity diminished. These changes were not limited to the food programs, of course; the trend was general, in the United States and elsewhere. To many people, these were great social gains. Others, of whom I am one, believe the programs have been carried beyond an optimum point.

Returning to less controversial matters, one effect of the program is clear. There is no requirement that the participants continue their preprogram pattern of cash food purchases after they enter the program. Typically, cash purchase of food diminishes when the stamps are made available. Only about half the value of the stamps goes for additional food expenditures (pers. comm. Stephen

J. Hiemstra, director, Economic Analysis and Program Evaluation Staff, Food and Nutrition Service, USDA., June 8, 1978). The other half of the value of the stamps represents money freed up for rent, health care, clothes, cars, beer, or whatever. This is called "slippage" or "substitution." Subjectively, the participants value these items above additional food. In their own minds, at least, the looseness of the program is an advantage.

The program is loose in another sense. Investigation by the Department of Agriculture, policing its own program, in what may have been a charitable assessment, has shown that about 7 percent of the stamps went to ineligible recipients. Another 7 percent of the benefits went to people who received more stamps than they were entitled to (U.S. Department of Agriculture 1977b). This comes from misrepresentation at the time of filing and from multiple applications. In addition, there are black markets and counterfeiting. It is now possible to cite these flaws without being discredited as a witness. For a long time this program was so popular that those who cited abuse were automatically tabbed as enemies of the program. Attitudes change.

Effect on Farmers

Farmers, on balance, are helped by the programs. But the help is dilute, uneven, and of modest dimensions. The farmer's share of the consumer's dollar is about forty cents. Thus, in the long run, if an additional hundred dollars is spent for food under the Food Stamp Program, about forty dollars can be expected to work its way back to farmers.

In fiscal year 1977, the Food Stamp Program totaled about $5 billion. If slippage was 50 percent, food expenditures were higher by $2.5 billion, of which 40 percent, or $1 billion, may have reached farmers' pockets. In that same year, farmers marketed $96.1 billion worth of crops and livestock. Computed in this fashion, which assumes continuous operation of the program over time, the Food Stamp Program increased gross farm income by 1 percent ($1 ÷ $96 [100] = 1 percent). Halcrow says that in 1977 the Food Stamp Program caused an increase of 1.1 to 1.4 percent in total demand for food (1977, p. 59). Boehm and Nelson say of the program that "it does represent less than one percent of the total personal consumption expenditure for food" (1978, p. 3).

Clearly, the Food Stamp Program and similar food programs are of minor significance as a solution to the problem of excess supplies of farm products. The truth, which emerges whether one studies Direct Donation or the School Lunch Program or the Food Stamp Program, is that these undertakings are more social welfare than agricultural policy. They do, however, have aspects of both. Their dual nature is to their credit rather than to their discredit. But discerning people will recognize that domestic programs of subsidized food consumption are a weak reed for agricultural policy to lean on.

Effect on the Food Trade

People in the food business generally like the Food Stamp Program. It keeps the subsidized food system within private trade channels, it moderately increases the volume of business, and it permits the storekeeper to supply food to the poor at a profit. This he finds better than to say no to the poor, which is both unpleasant and unprofitable.

The growth of the Food Stamp Program has been very rapid. Number of participants and cost of the program, by years, has been as follows:

	Participants, in millions	*Cost, in millions of dollars*
1961	—	1
1962	.1	14
1963	.2	20
1964	.4	30
1965	.4	35
1966	.9	70
1967	1.4	115
1968	2.2	187
1969	2.9	250
1970	4.3	578
1971	9.4	1,576
1972	11.1	1,912
1973	12.2	2,217
1974	12.9	2,865
1975	17.1	4,700
1976	18.5	5,700
1977	17.1	5,400

A biologist might notice that this historical record takes the form of a growth curve, the pattern that characterizes the development of plants and animals (Pearl 1922, p. 250). A mathematician could write an equation for it having three terms: a beginning level, a growth factor, and a limit approached but never reached. At first the increase is rapid in rate of growth, though modest in absolute numbers. Then the increase is great absolutely. The final stage is one of small growth in both absolute and relative terms.

Thinking of the Food Stamp Program in these terms, we can envision a growth factor, the desire to improve the situation for the poor. The growth factor diminishes as we encounter reappraisal of need, awareness of cost, and evidence of abuse. We can think of a limit: providing food for all persons judged by the public to be in need.

Is this model valid for the Food Stamp Program? Perhaps it is. If so, where are we on the curve? In real terms, perhaps somewhere near the upper reaches.

THE ISSUES

What are likely to be the issues surrounding subsidized food consumption during the next decade? I anticipate three, all of them already before us in either implicit or explicit form.

Objectives

What are we trying to do? Following are four goals, sometimes glibly asserted but not thought through. The purpose of listing and examining them is to show that none of the frequently asserted goals is satisfactory as a sole objective.

Improved nutrition. If improved nutrition were the sole desired objective, the procedure would be fairly simple. We would provide a nutritionally adequate diet for those in need. Sylvia Lane reports (1978b, p. 32) that a "nutritionally adequate, palatable but not necessarily enjoyable diet" could be provided at a cost of from 36 percent to 38 percent of the USDA's low-cost family food plan, the basis for the Food Stamp Program. Holding to a standard of adequate nutrition but eliminating palatability and convenience would cut the cost to from 19 percent to 21 percent of the cost of the Food Stamp standard. No one recommends so austere a diet. But the calculations show that dialogues addressed to "nutrition" have considerable overtones of palatability, prestige, and convenience.

Individual choice as a criterion for food policy. Obviously the American people will reject a prescribed diet, however nutritious. So why not see that people have the means to buy an adequate diet and then let them make their own choice? This is the Food Stamp Program. This approach maximizes freedom of choice, but, as we have seen, it does not maximize nutrition.

More for the poor. This has been the force behind the expansion of the domestic food programs. It is the growth factor in the equation referred to earlier. But welfare programs encounter resistance that must be taken into account. There is some necessary ultimate limit to any welfare program.

Reliance on the market. Some people are concerned about the steady decline in individual responsibility and the progressive transfer of activity from the private to the public sector. They assert that the reestablishing of the competitive market should be the objective of food policy. But these people underestimate the public conviction that hunger is a major problem and that the food programs are effective in overcoming it.

Obviously the purpose of food policy is in doubt. We suffer from what social scientists call "goal confusion." The various stated purposes of food policy are not in complete disagreement with one another, and it is the job of the politician to reconcile them so far as he is able. But the area of agreement is not large enough to include all the decisions that need to be made. Some will lie outside it. Offense will have to be given to someone.

What must evolve, then, is a food policy in which there are discernible elements of various objectives with no one of them exclusively important. And obviously we shall fall short of fully achieving any one of them. We shall have to learn to distinguish between the goal as rhetoric and the goal as attainable objective. And while we cannot deprive the advocate of his desire to invoke rhetoric, we can hope that a more attainable goal will emerge than has so far been stated.

Categorical Aid or Cash Grants?

Our food programs have moved from *surplus disposal,* the prime motive for beginning the effort, to an attempt to *overcome poverty-related malnutrition,* to *food assistance,* in which considerations of equity replace concern for nutrition. This is where the programs are at this time. There is yet another phase toward which we are moving, *income supplements,* which would permit participants to make purchases of food and nonfood items in accordance with their own values. The economist can readily demonstrate that income supplements would increase the utility of the program to the recipients. And they might not yield a result that differs greatly from the present system. Recipients now use about 50 percent of their subsidy to buy additional food. Studies show that people in poverty, exercising their preferences freely in the market, typically use about 30 percent of any new income increment to purchase food (Hiemstra, pers. comm., June 8, 1978). So the practical effect of "cashing out" the program (providing cash instead of food stamps) would not be very great; perhaps 30 percent instead of 50 percent of the aid would be spent for food. Substantial administrative costs would be averted.

But there are other considerations. Suppose the program were cashed out. Suppose some family, unskilled in money management, spent its cash grant for frivolous items, as very likely would happen, and the children went hungry. Further, suppose CBS were to zoom in on these hungry children with a television documentary titled *Hunger Update, USA*. We might then have vastly expanded cash grants, or we might reinstate the categorical program and have the two working side by side.

The categorical programs like food programs and rent subsidies are perhaps designed as much for the benefactor's peace of mind as for the recipient's welfare. The responsible official can always point out that a program of categorical aid has been addressed to a specific and recognized need. He can deny that his program accommodates the purchase of liquor and automobiles. Up to now it has been easier to obtain taxpayer support for categorical programs than for cash grants.

The Nixon administration sought, without success, to cash out the Food Stamp Program. But support for cashing out Food Stamps is on the rise, as is shown by recent debates. Additional efforts are sure to come in the next decade.

An interesting fact is that, as we move from the early to the later stages of this progression, consumer choice is widened and farmer benefits, never great, are reduced. Improved nutrition, the rallying call for expansion of the program, fades in importance.

One is reminded of how the big commodity programs began as an effort to save the family farm and how, over a period of forty years, that objective changed. A similar shift in objectives—and similar adherence to earlier rhetoric—characterizes the food programs.

Administration in USDA or in HEW?

Where should the subsidized food programs be administered—in the Department of Agriculture, which gave them birth, or in the Department of Health, Education, and Welfare, which is their natural home from a functional standpoint?

To the beneficiaries and to the economic analyst this question is unimportant, since the programs are likely to be similar wherever administered. But to the politician it is an important matter. Ever since the farm bloc made its peace with the hunger lobby, the domestic food programs have been used as a carrier for the commodity programs. If the programs move over to Health, Education, and Welfare, the agricultural committees of the House and Senate will lose control of them and so lose the leverage needed to enact the big commodity programs. Resistance to the transfer from USDA to HEW is lodged in Congress. Secretaries of Agriculture Hardin and Butz both tried to move the programs but were unable to do so. (There may be other instances of a cabinet officer's trying to give away programs that involved the larger part of his budget, but none comes to mind.) That this issue will arise during the coming decade is highly likely. Transfer of the domestic food programs from USDA to HEW would probably have greater effect on the big commodity programs than on the food programs themselves.

THE PROSPECT

What prognosis comes from all this? I venture four predictions.

1. Growth hereafter will be modest. The programs probably are on the growth path described earlier. Forces of growth are waning, if for no other reason than that the food needs of the poor have been in considerable measure alleviated. Resistance is increasing as costs mount, as needs are reassessed, as the nutritional accomplishments of the programs come into question, and as program abuses become more generally known.

2. A conservative character will emerge. A coalition of bureaucrats, politicians, and special interests will consolidate the gains made by these programs. A new food policy establishment will develop, intent on protecting the new status quo. Members of this establishment will be certain interested groups such as the American School Food Service Association, the National Advisory Council on Child Nutrition, state directors of School Food Services, the American Dietetic Association, and antihunger bodies including church groups and the Children's Foundation. In support of these organizations will be the bureaucracy that runs the programs, the business firms that benefit, and the politicians who find it useful to associate themselves therewith. What was once a liberal movement, promoting change, will become conservative, opposing change and defending the new establishment. So it was with the first farm policy agenda (research and education). So it became with the second (commodity programs). It would be strange if this fundamental pattern were altered for the third agenda.

3. Congress will continue to modify these programs. Except for the possible cashing out of these programs, their pattern seems to have been fairly well established. Incremental growth is probable, retrenchment unlikely. A transfer from one agency to another would, of itself, effect little fundamental change. Even cashing out the Food Stamp Program and the School Lunch Program would alter service to the beneficiaries only in modest degree, as has been shown.

Legislation concerning food remains attractive. Politicians enjoy the opportunity to vote on a food program. So there will no doubt continue to be program adjustments and "perfecting amendments," presented to the public as being more significant than they actually are. Among these will be modification of eligibility standards, changes in the scale of benefits, and so on.

4. The food programs will lose some of their carrying power. In the past, when these programs were in their period of maximum popularity and explosive growth, they were an enormously helpful vehicle to which the big farm commodity programs could be hitched. As the programs mature and stabilize, this attribute will diminish.

But a word of caution is appropriate here. It would be well not to predict these events too soon or with too high a degree of probability. These developments are latent, but they may be a while in appearing. We might take a lesson from experience with the big commodity programs and the parity standard. Years ago, when the commodity programs were at a stage comparable with that of the food programs today, a general prognosis among economic analysts was that parity had had its day and would lose its political clout. "Not so," said a farm-state congressman, "It's good for one more election." He was right. In fact he underestimated the case; it was good for many more.

For many years individual responsibility, a competitive market, nutritional education, and private charity were considered an appropriate set of institutions with which to meet the problems of food and nutrition. The food programs have been added. It will be important to see that the use of this new tool does not detract unduly from the potency of the others.

REFERENCES

Berg, Allen. 1973. *The nutrition factor: Its role in national development*. Washington, D.C.: Brookings Institution.

Boehm, William T. 1978. *The food stamp program: A review of selected economic studies*. USDA, Economics, Statistics, and Cooperatives Service, ESCS-34.

Boehm, William T., and Nelson, Paul E. 1978. *Current economic research on food stamp use*. USDA, Economics, Statistics, and Cooperatives Service, ESCS-37.

Clarkson, Kenneth. 1975. *Food stamps and nutrition*. Washington, D.C.: American Enterprise Institute for Public Policy Research.

Davis, Howard P. 1959. Sharing our bounty. In *Food: The yearbook of agriculture, 1959*, pp. 681–90. Washington, D.C.: USDA.

Gallo, Anthony. 1978. National School Lunch Program: Plate waste and innovative lunches. *National Food Review*, p. 35, NFR-3. USDA, Economics, Statistics, and Cooperatives Service.

Gallo, Anthony, and Stucker, Thomas A. 1978. Federal contributions to the School

Lunch Program. *National Food Review,* NFR-2. USDA, Economics, Statistics, and Cooperatives Service.

Halcrow, Harold. 1977. *Food policy for America.* New York: McGraw-Hill.

Hiemstra, Stephen J. 1976. Economic importance of the National School Lunch Program. *School Foodservice Research Review* 1:11–14.

———. 1978*a*. *Child nutrition review.* Washington, D.C.: USDA, Food and Nutrition Service.

———. 1978*b The impact of USDA food programs on agriculture.* Speech, Arkansas State Farm Bureau, Little Rock.

Hoover, Dale M., and Maddox, James G. 1969. *Food for the hungry: Direct distribution and food stamp programs for low-income families.* Planning Pamphlet 126. Washington, D.C.: National Planning Association.

Kiener, Robert. 1978. Inside glimpses. An editorial in *Glimpses of Micronesia and the Western Pacific* (Guam), vol. 18, no. 2.

Lane, Sylvia. 1974. *Food-aid program effects on food expenditures and levels of nutritional achievement of low-income households.* Paper presented at the annual meetings of the American Agricultural Economic Association, College Station, Texas.

———. 1978*a*. Food distribution and food stamp program effects on food consumption and nutritional "achievement" of low income persons in Kern County, California. *American Journal of Agricultural Economics* 60:108–16.

———. 1978*b*. Poverty, food selection and human nutrition. In *Agricultural-food policy review: Proceedings of five policy seminars.* USDA, Economics, Statistics, and Cooperatives Service, ESCS-AFPR-2.

LeBovit, Corinne, and Clark, Faith. 1959. Are we well fed? In *Food: The yearbook of agriculture, 1959.* Washington, D.C.: USDA.

Madden, J. Patrick, and Yoder, Marion D. 1972. *Program evaluation: Food stamps and commodity distribution in rural areas of central Pennsylvania.* Bulletin 780. State College: Pennsylvania State University.

Martin, Philip, and Lane, Sylvia. 1977. Distributional equity of the Food Stamp Program. *American Journal of Agricultural Economics* 59:1006–11.

Morgan, Agnes Fay, ed. 1959. *Nutritional status, USA.* California Agricultural Experiment Station Bulletin 769. Berkeley: University of California, Division of Agricultural Sciences.

Pearl, R. 1922. *The biology of death.* New York: Lippincott.

Price, David W.; West, Donald A.; Scheier, Genevieve E.; and Price, Dorothy Z. 1978. Food delivery programs and other factors affecting nutrient intake of children. *American Journal of Agricultural Economics* 60:609–18.

U.S. Department of Agriculture. 1969. *Dietary levels of households in the United States, Spring 1965.* Agricultural Research Service. Household Food Consumption Survey 1965, 1966, Report no. 6.

———. 1974. *Comprehensive study of the child nutrition programs, July 1974.*

———. 1975. *Food Stamp Program.* A report in accordance with Senate Resolution

58, prepared by USDA Food and Nutrition Service for the U.S. Senate Committee on Agriculture and Forestry.

———. 1976. *Annual statistical review of food and nutritional programs, fiscal year 1976.* Preliminary Report. Food and Nutrition Service, FNS 161.

———. 1977a. *Agricultural statistics.* Washington, D.C.: USDA.

———. 1977b. *Participation in the Food Stamp Program as shown by quality control reviews, July–December 1976.* Food and Nutrition Service, Food Stamp Division, Performance Reporting System Branch.

———. 1977c. *Program evaluation status reports: Completed studies.* Food and Nutrition Service.

———. 1978a. *Agricultural food policy review: Proceedings of five food policy seminars.* Economics, Statistics, and Cooperatives Service, ESCS-AFPR-2.

———. 1978b. *Food consumption, prices, expenditures.* Economics, Statistics, and Cooperatives Service Supplement for 1976 to Agricultural Economic Report 138.

———. 1978c. Increase in food stamp allotment set for July 1, 1427–78. Press release, May 18.

U.S. Department of Health, Education, and Welfare. 1972. *Ten-state nutrition survey, 1968–70.* Publication no. 72–8134. Atlanta, Georgia.

U.S. Department of Health, Education, and Welfare. 1974. *Preliminary findings of the first health and nutrition examination survey, 1971–72: Biochemical and dietary findings.* Publication no. (HRA) 74–1219–1.

U.S. Senate. Select Committee on Nutrition and Human Needs. 1969. *Poverty, malnutrition and federal food assistance programs: Statistical summary.* Committee print, 91st Congr., 1st sess.

———. 1974. Hearings, June 14, 19–24. 93d Congr. 2d sess., parts 1–7.

Upchurch, M. L. 1977. Developments in agricultural economic data. In *A survey of agricultural economics literature,* vol. 2, ed. George G. Judge et al. Minneapolis: University of Minnesota Press.

Waugh, F. V., and Davis, H. P. 1961. Some economic impacts of the Food Stamp Program. *Agricultural Economic Research,* vol. 13, no. 3.

West, Donald A.; Price, David W.; and Price, Dorothy Z. 1978. Impacts of the food stamp program on value of food consumed and nutrient intake. Review draft; to be published in *Western Journal of Agricultural Economics.*

Wetmore, J. M.; Abel, M. E.; Learn, E. W.; and Cochrane, W. W. 1959. *Policies for expanding the demand for farm food products in the United States. Part 1.* Technical Bulletin 231. Minneapolis: Minnesota Agricultural Experiment Station.

Wunderle, R. E., and Call, D. L. 1971. *An evaluation of the pilot food certificate program in Chicago, Illinois, and Bibb County, Georgia.* Contract Report. Ithaca: Cornell Graduate School of Nutrition.

11. Environmental Protection

For centuries—indeed for millennia—the ethic regarding man's relationship to the environment was the biblical prescription: "Be fruitful, and multiply, and replenish the earth, and subdue it: and have dominion over the fish of the sea, and over the fowl of the air, and over every living thing that moveth upon the earth" (Gen. 1:28).

This charge was in keeping with man's understanding of his relationship to the environment and served to condone his traditional deportment. In accordance with this ethic, man felled the forest, plowed the plains, drained the swamp, slaughtered the buffalo, shot the passenger pigeons, irrigated the desert, and dammed the rivers.

But gradually there came a new ethic. Instead of subduing the earth, treat it gently. Instead of having dominion over every living thing, treat them as fellow creatures (at least some of them—the whooping crane, but not the rat. The snail darter?—a marginal case).

So profound a change in a relationship so basic could not come easily. Farmers have custody of more environment than does any other group. They had been thoroughly in accord with the old ethic. Understandably, the new view caused great consternation among farm people.

The change came slowly. Until the 1960s environmental issues were mostly local or specific. This or that factory was under attack for polluting the air or water. Certain animal species were in danger of extinction and so a cause of public concern. There was sporadic and generally unheeded talk about running out of oil. Soil erosion had been a worry since the thirties, but the predicted disasters had not occurred. Some people were apprehensive about the increased use of farm chemicals, but the advantages of using them were clear and the dangers seemed remote. The conservationists of the day warned about excessive timber-cutting, but the cutting continued. The cities were beginning to choke on automobile exhaust, but we had a love affair with the automobile and were slow to find fault with it. Education, voluntarism, and minimal regulation were the means of coping with environmental concern.

When the environmentalists voiced their worries they were put down with comments such as these:

"If we run out of something, technology will produce a substitute."

"Restraints would increase costs, cause unemployment, and slow the rate of economic growth."

"If we restrict the use of farm chemicals, food supplies would be reduced and millions of people would starve."

"What if the eagle should become extinct? Species have been disappearing since the beginning of time and we're no worse off for it."

"You ecologists forget that human beings are part of the ecology."

The answers and the attitude they portray characterized the American mood. The environmentalist and the ecologist were somewhere out on the fringe. Nice folks, but idealistic and a little odd, like the people who advocated world government.

Then things changed. The environmental movement, once scattered and weak, became unified and strong. Rachel Carson's book *Silent Spring* (1962), both cause and catalyst, had much to do with it.

Perhaps the most important thing was a change in the public mood. Robert Enochian of the Department of Agriculture describes it thus (1977, p. 66):

In the 1960s a new ethic emerged in the United States. The outward signs of this ethic were a changed clothing and lifestyles of the under-thirty population. These changes were the precursors of a changing system of values that is now influencing a growing proportion of Americans. This system of values is characterized by a distrust of our institutions; by the rejection of some aspects of materialism; by a reduction in some kinds of consumption, particularly those which are thought to adversely affect personal health and the environment; and by an anti-technology and anti-waste bias.

The Santa Barbara oil spill occurred in 1969, and the evening television news carried the pictures of pitiful oil-smeared waterfowl, dead or dying.

The environmental cause was powerfully supported, in 1972, by the Club of Rome book *Limits to Growth,* with its Doomsday projections. The following year *Small Is Beautiful* appeared, a book by E. F. Schumacher advocating "intermediate technology," a course somewhere between preindustrial techniques and all-out modern methods. It was well written and highly effective.

The debate over use of the insecticide DDT, which had been a leading environmental issue for some years, came to a decision with the banning of that chemical by William Ruckelshaus, administrator of the Environmental Protection Agency (EPA), effective January 1, 1973. This was the first major successful campaign against agricultural chemicals.

Environmental risks associated with nuclear reactors became a great concern. The planned use of atomic power, once considered a promising replacement for our dwindling supply of petrochemicals, was cut back.

The environmentalists sensed the change in mood and capitalized on it. The ecology movement became the right cause for people who were socially aware. New environmental organizations came into being and existing ones grew stronger. Together they made a formidable list. The Sierra Club, the Environmental Defense Fund, and the Natural Resources Defense Council became familiar names. They formed a coalition. What had been scattered fire became a barrage.

So the environmental issue became a cause. The initiative passed into the hands of the ecologists. The old guard went on the defensive. For the greater part, agriculturalists stood rigid against the environmental initiative. But on a number of issues the farmers joined forces with the environmentalists, opposing such projects as strip mining, use of water for producing energy, and construction of high-voltage transmission lines.

Public-interest law firms undertook the litigation of environmental issues on behalf of persons who could not otherwise afford to take cases to court. Class-action suits multiplied.

The movement was much broader than agriculture. One of the errors of the agricultural leadership was to think of the issue in terms of subject matter only—agricultural subject matter at that—a serious underassessment.

Mightily reinforcing this new antitechnology mood were the PBB, DBCP, and Kepone disasters. With these the old guard lost additional credibility.

To some people these environmental disasters were unfortunate but unrelated and otherwise meaningless events that were seized upon and exploited by self-chosen leaders in search of a cause. But most of those who have studied the matter closely are convinced that the cause for concern is authentic, although grossly overstated by its leaders, as is true of many causes and virtually all leaders.

Some estimate of the longevity of this cause is essential to any appraisal of the policy outlook. The assessment ventured here is that the elements that gave rise to the issue all have a growth factor in them:

Increasing population, which puts pressure on resources.

Increasing technology and the dangers implicit therein if technology plunges heedlessly forward.

A new ethic, perhaps born partly of affluence, that exalts aesthetics relative to material considerations.

If these perceptions are true, agriculturalists will have to accept the new attitude toward the environment. Agriculture is inevitably caught up in this issue and cannot opt out. By intelligent behavior, however, we can—and will—make the needed changes in our actions so as to escape the doomsday fate projected for us by the alarmists. Policy-makers face a great opportunity—to help reshape our technology so it is a blessing rather than a burden. This can be done only if we avoid either condemning technology outright or endorsing it unchanged.

Major legislation affecting agriculture was produced by the environmental movement. (I focus on federal legislation, though many important state laws and local ordinances were passed.)

The Environmental Protection Agency (EPA), which is charged with overall responsibility for the abatement of air, soil, and water pollution, was established under the Presidential Reorganization Plan in December 1970.

The Federal Air Quality Act, intended to reduce air pollution, was passed in 1970. Agriculture, previously excluded from pollution-control laws, lost its exemption.

The Federal Water Pollution Control Act (FWPCA) was amended in 1972 to clean up our rivers and lakes.

The Federal Environmental Pest Control Act (FEPCA) was passed in 1972. It amended and substantially tightened the Federal Insecticide, Fungicide, and Rodenticide Act (FIFRA).

The Toxic Substances Control Act (TOSCA) became effective on January 1, 1977, extending and consolidating federal control over poisonous chemicals.

Other environmental legislation directly affecting culture includes: the Noise Control Act of 1972, the Resource Conservation and Recovery Act of 1976, the Surface Mining and Reclamation Act of 1977, and the Soil and Water Resources Conservation Act of 1977.

With this legislation the federal government was given sweeping power to restrict the pollution of soil, water, and air, the three elements essential to agricultural production. Regulatory authority was established to control the use of agricultural chemicals, to establish permissible amounts of soil erosion, and to prohibit the discharge of air pollutants. Agencies were created, appropriations were made, the regulatory machinery was cranked up, and the control effort began.

In this chapter I shall consider the circumstances to which these regulatory initiatives were addressed. Then I shall look at the regulatory actions taken and evaluate them, to the extent possible. Difficulties of control will next be described. Finally, I shall consider alternatives (or supplements) to the regulatory route.

FERTILIZER

From 1960 to 1975 the use of commercial fertilizer (that is, manufactured chemical fertilizer) on American farms almost doubled. Even so, we fertilize our cereal grain at a lower per acre rate than do the Japanese, the French, and the British.

Fertilizer increases yield per acre. No single estimate of this effect is possible; it varies by crop, by soil type, by geographic region, by rate of application, and by interaction with other cultural practices. For the most important American crop, corn, in the heart of the corn belt, proper fertilization, other things equal, probably doubles the yield per acre over no fertilization (Barber 1976). For the high-yielding varieties of wheat developed by the International Center for the Improvement of Corn and Wheat in Mexico, the use of fertilizer, together with other chemicals, and with good management on irrigated land increases yield perhaps by a multiple of two or three over the levels obtained by traditional methods. In 1943 the national average wheat yield in Mexico was 11.5 bushels to the acre. With the advent of the new wheats, fertilizer, and other improved practices, the national average rose to thirty bushels per acre, almost trebling in twenty years. Few serious students doubt that the use of fertilizer has greatly increased the production and reduced the price of food in the world. Chemical fertilizer has been a major factor in helping food production keep a half-step ahead of poulation growth.

Effect of Fertilizer Use

One of the allegedly hurtful effects attributed to fertilizer—that it reduces the nutritive value of the crop—is refuted almost unanimously by the scientific community (Whelan and Stare 1975, pp. 64–67).

A more valid charge is that leaching and surface runoff of nitrogen fertilizer increase the nitrate content in groundwater and in streams and lakes, causing a hazard to human health. The most frequently cited relevant case is that of fourteen infants in Minnesota whose deaths were caused by nitrates in well water during 1947–50. It is not clear, however, whether the excess nitrates resulted from fertilizer or sewage effluent or livestock operations.

Another legitimate accusation is that leaching and runoff from nitrogen and phosphate fertilizers into lakes and streams destroy the bacterial action that cleans out organic wastes. This is called eutrophication; the water becomes "dead." These charges are considered by some members of the scientific community to be overgeneralizations. However, the consensus among the researchers seems to be that the complaints merit consideration and that precaution is in order (Chou et al. 1977, p. 159; Brubaker 1972, p. 132; Enfield 1970; Bower and Wilcox 1969).

Benefit/cost calculations for fertilizer use are possible for the individual farmer and are clearly positive. Griliches reported that in 1960 the marginal value product from $1 worth of fertilizer was about $3 to $5 (1964, pp. 968–69). As of 1960 and from a microeconomic standpoint, most farmers were using too little fertilizer. A societal benefit/cost computation is not possible with present knowledge; the benefits and costs are not quantifiable. It is clear, however, that the individual farmer-user does not bear all the costs or reap all the benefits from fertilizer use. Clearly, the competitive market does not take into account all the legitimate concerns regarding the use of fertilizer.

One feature of the fertilizer issue that surprises most people is that restricting fertilizer use would reduce crop output, raise prices, and increase farm incomes. Taylor and Frohberg (1977, p. 33) estimate that restricting corn belt farms to one hundred pounds of nitrogen an acre would increase farmers' incomes by $21 million; holding use to fifty pounds an acre would improve farmers' incomes by $2.036 million. Consumers would be correspondingly injured. The difference between the effect of reducing fertilizer use by an individual and reducing fertilizer use by all is the difference between micro- and macroeconomics. A fertilizer restriction program, applied generally, would have a price and income effect similar to that of the acreage limitations of the commodity programs.

Difficulties of Control

Restrictions on the use of fertilizer have been proposed. But how would such restrictions be applied? The alternatives are rationing, a user tax, or a market for pollution rights. A peracre limitation on use, the plan in least disfavor, would be difficult to police because it would require twenty-four-hour checks on the fields. A user tax, making fertilizer more expensive, could be collected at the manufacturer level. A market for pollution rights would make it necessary to determine the basis for the "pollution right" and to monitor the amounts. These alternative methods of control all face stiff opposition from farmers, who prefer to have environmental effects ignored. Farmers have been taught by the extension service, by the agribusiness concerns, and by their own experience to use fertilizer. They have found it profitable and are strong defenders of what they consider to be their own decision-making role. Trying to enforce limitations on fertilizer use would be a nightmare.

An Alternative: Research and Education

There are ways of voluntarily reducing risks from excessive use of fertilizer, ways that would be profitable to farmers, ways that make use of those old and proved means of agricultural betterment: research, education, and enlightened decision-making by farmers. Here are a number, briefly listed:

Voluntary cutbacks in overuse. Some farmers go beyond the point of diminishing returns in fertilizer application; reduced application would be in their own interest. A cutback on use would reduce pollution. The old belief that "if some is good, more is better" does not apply to fertilizer. The relationship of application rate to yield is curvilinear, not linear. This could be made clear by a good extension program. When there was a sharp price increase in fertilizer in 1974, many farmers reduced fertilizer application and found that yields were not seriously cut (Chou et al. 1977, p. 161).

Improved timing and placement. By placing fertilizer properly and applying it at the right times, total use could be reduced. This is the most important way to keep fertilizer out of the water supply.

"Slow release" fertilizer. Pelleted fertilizer is well along in the process of research and development. It is made so that it becomes available by increments as the growing season progresses, thus avoiding the periods of excessive availability and subsequent dearth that characterize present fertilizers and lead to heavy application. With "slow release" fertilizer the total amount used could be reduced. "Nitrification inhibitors" constitute another form of slow release, potentially a great economizer in nitrogen use.

Nitrifying bacteria. Research is under way in an effort to modify non-leguminous plants like cereal grains so they would host nitrogen-fixing bacteria, as leguminous crops now do. This would cut the need for nitrogen, the most environmentally troublesome of the chemical elements in fertilizer.

Use of manure and crop rotation. These practices, which were common before cheap chemical fertilizer led us to junk the manure spreader and continually grow corn, merit reexamination. We could again recycle the manure instead of piling it up unused. Maybe we were oversold on chemical agriculture. Recent research indicates that we need more study of these questions (Klepper et al. 1977, pp. 1–12).

Good updated programs of research and education, appealing to enlightened self-interest, could be an attractive alternative to the regulatory route. Very likely the Environmental Protection Agency and the state regulatory bodies, faced with the near impossibility of regulating fertilizer use, will be inclined to give the voluntary approach a chance to work. They have thus far. The issue of possible efforts to control fertilizer use is a cloud on the horizon, too far off at this time to tell whether it is advancing or retreating.

PESTICIDES

The word "pesticide" is a blanket term to describe various chemical agents used to control insects, fungi, nematodes, weeds, rodents, and predators. Crop yields are reduced by some 10,000 different insect species, 8,000 species of fungi, and 2,000 weed species (Brown et al. 1975, p. 275). Since 1950, in an effort to combat this horde, the use of insecticides and herbicides has increased ten times and use of herbicides twenty times (1975, p. 30). Ridgeway and associates estimate that "the use of modern organic synthetic pesticides has increased about forty-fold" (1978, p. 1).

A 1964 study indicated that outright elimination of pesticides would probably reduce the United States corn crop and livestock and forest production by 25 percent (Upchurch and Heisig 1964). Despite the use of pesticides, estimates of annual worldwide grain losses owing to diseases, insects, weeds, rodents, and poor storage run as high as 400 million tons (Chou et al. 1977, p. 137), an amount equal to 30 percent of total cereal production. Losses are particularly severe in the poorest countries. Tests run by the Department of Agriculture show dramatic yield increases resulting from the use of pesticides (table 5).

Table 5. USDA Test Plots: Effects of Pesticides on Yields

Crop	Percentage Increase in Yield
Cotton	50
Corn	20–100; 60 average
Oats	
Wheat	24–1,000
Barley	
Potatoes	70
Alfalfa	49–90
Apples	100

Source: Adapted from Headley and Lewis, (1976 p. 62, as cited in Brubaker 1972, p. 84).

The profitability of pesticides to the farmer is clear. One prominent estimate indicates that the average (not marginal) return to the farmer for every dollar spent on pesticides is four dollars (Brubaker 1972, p. 85). This is of course computed on the basis of *individual* farmer behavior. If *all* farmers gave up the use of pesticides, food supplies would be sharply reduced, farm prices would shoot up, and farm incomes would increase.

Pesticides not only are useful in combating the enemies of plants and animals, they are also useful in protecting human health. Sri Lanka undertook a program of malaria control during the 1950s and early 1960s, using DDT. By 1963 the disease had been virtually eradicated (seventeen cases in a population of about twelve million). In 1964, the use of DDT in Sri Lanka was prohibited, leading to the following increases in malaria cases (from Beatty 1973, cited in Chou et al. 1977, p. 12):

Year	Number of cases
1965	308
1967	3,466
1968	about 1,000,000

A balanced account of the controversy over DDT is given by Lowrance (1976). While recognizing the widespread dissemination of DDT and its potential danger, Lowrance states: "The banning of DDT occurred despite the fact that massive occupational exposures, or accidental ingestions, even by children, have not been known to cause a single death anywhere in the world in the thirty-five years of DDT history" (p. 172).

Harmful Effects

The first thing to realize is that pesticides are poisons. They are intended to kill weeds, insects, fungus growth, rodents, predators, and bacteria. The problem is to keep them from killing man and his friends. They are different from other chemicals. Lumping the pesticides with other agricultural chemicals is like lumping shotguns with other hardware, or gasoline with other liquids.

The number of synthetic organic chemicals has tripled in the last decade. More than 35,000 different name-brand pesticide formulations are currently registered with the Environmental Protection Agency (Lowrance 1976, p. 107). According to the council on Environmental Quality, 1 percent of the newly synthesized chemicals are believed to be latently toxic to man and possibly carcinogenic, mutagenic, or teratogenic (monster-producing). The remarkable fact is that these poisons have in general caused so little apparent harm to those who consume food grown with their use. This is a tribute to farmers, to the extension service, to the chemical firms, and to the regulatory agencies.

The major threat to man in using pesticides is the danger of accidental poisoning during application. The Public Health Department of the state of California reported 2,704 cases of systemic poisoning between 1956 and 1968 from organophosphate chemicals (Chou et al. 1977, p. 41). Sterling Brubaker of Resources for the Future states: "While deaths can be attributed to improper handling of pesticides, none have been known to result from their residuals in the environment" (1972, pp. 82–83). It could be argued, on the basis of the available facts, that the Occupational Safety and Health Agency (concerned with safety of farm workers) has a more important role in surveillance of agricultural chemicals than does either the Environmental Protection Agency (concerned with pollution) or the Food and Drug Administration (concerned with food safety).

Major causes of anxiety are the wide and growing dissemination of pesticides, the persistence of certain of them in the biosphere, their lethal effect on wildlife, and the carcinogenic (cancer-causing) nature of some of them. The public has limited knowledge regarding these chemicals. Knowing little, people suspect much.

At this time the Environmental Protection Agency has canceled twenty-one agricultural chemicals, and ten have been voluntarily withdrawn (table 6). Approximately eighty compounds or groups of compounds are being reviewed and are required to meet certain tests before they can be reregistered. This is under a process called Rebuttable Presumption against Reregistration (RPAR) (Eichers 1978, p. 11).

Cancellation of chemicals aroused cries of concern in the farm community; there were warnings that crop production would be adversely affected. But there is little evidence that cancellation had much overall effect on crop production. In 1977, despite these cancellations, farmers produced what was then the largest crop in history. The 1978 crop established a new record. Substitute chemicals were used, chemicals that were not carcinogenic and were less persistent (though generally less effective, more costly, and more dangerous to apply).

Withdrawal of chemicals, though of limited overall effect, nevertheless worked hardship on particular farmers and ranchers. For example, the chemical known as ''1080'' was used to kill the coyotes that preyed on the sheep and lambs of Western ranchers. Eagles and other valued species were sometimes killed by eating the poisoned bait or eating coyotes poisoned with this chemical. Ecologists protested. The regulators banned 1080 for use on the range but

Table 6. Agricultural Chemicals Canceled and Voluntarily Withdrawn to Date

Canceled	Voluntarily Withdrawn
Aldrin*	Aramite
Bithionol*	Arsenic trioxide
Chloranil	BHC
Chlordane*	Chloranil
DDD	Copper arsenate
DDT*	Kepone
Dieldrin*	OMPA
Endrin	Phenorasazine chloride
Heptachlor*	Safrole
Kepone	Strobane
Lindane	
Mercury*	
OMPA	
PCB	
Polychlorinated terphenyls	
Sodium cyanide*	
Strobane	
2,4,5,T*	
Thallium sulphate	
Toxaphene*	
Vinyl chloride	

SOURCE: Harmon (1977, p. 15).
*Except for certain very specific uses.

allowed it for urban use. There was some difficulty in explaining this to ranchers.

With pesticides, as with fertilizer, stiff limitations on use would reduce the food supply and increase the price of groceries. A 1964 estimate showed that outright elimination of pesticides (mostly herbicides and insecticides) would increase prices of farm products by 50 percent (Upchurch and Heisig 1967, cited in Ennis, Dowler, and Klassen 1975, p. 595).

Benefit/cost computations, though possible for the individual farmer, are not feasible as an overall guide to public policy. Long-run consequences of chemical use are not measurable. Who can tell whether birth defects might in time occur, or whether cancer might ultimately result? No agreed dollar figure can be assigned to the value of human life or to the alleviation of fear. Signals given out by the marketplace cannot be used to measure, regulate, or equate social costs and benefits. Public officials must weigh these things subjectively. The important point, which often gets lost in the shuffle, is that absolute safety, though promised, cannot be delivered.

Alternatives

Government regulation is necessary, but it cannot do the whole job. Research, education, and enlightened decision-making by farmers have a role to play in pesticide use.

Reduced rates of application. Overuse of pesticides is common. Getting those last few bugs is enormously costly to the farmer, to the environment, and to the society. "Bomb the bugs" is a poor policy. The Environmental Protection Agency shows that in the production of sorghum, increasing the application by a multiple of five raised the degree of control only a few percentage points (adapted from Van Rumker et al. 1974, p. 109).

Pound of active ingredient (parathion) per acre	Control (percentage)	Yield: Pounds of Sorghum seed per acre
0.5	98	4,400
0.1	94	4,500

Good research could drive home to farmers the danger and high cost of excessive dosage. One might say that pesticides have been too cheap, encouraging their overuse.

Integrated pest management. The goal of integrated pest management is to maintain potential pest populations below the level at which they cause health hazards or economic damage. Careful monitoring of insect pests makes it possible to use chemicals only when trouble looms and to avoid the "pesticide syndrome," the heavy routine preventive applications that are so costly, so often unneeded, and so damaging to the environment (Turpin and York 1978, p. 5).

Biological controls. Use of predators and insect pathogens, breeding for insect- and disease-resistance, sterilization to break the reproductive cycle (as has been successfully done in controlling screw worms), use of attractants and repellents—all of these have promise and all have the potential of reducing the need for pesticides.

Better cultural practices. Crop rotation to reduce the buildup of crop-specific weeds, pests, and pesticides, timely application of better materials with improved equipment, making control possible with lighter applications—all these have promise.

These commonsense techniques lessen reliance on pesticides. All require research and education. None of them can quickly or generally meet the problem. So if any are to be effective, patience will be necessary. The hope is that the Environmental Protection Agency will so administer the law as not to substitute regulation for what the farmers, with good research and education, could do on their own.

NONPOINT POLLUTION: CONTROL OF EROSION

Concern about soil erosion had been, ever since the thirties, high on the agenda of the Department of Agriculture. From 1935 through 1976 the department made an outlay of more than $20 billion for cost-sharing, technical assistance, resource management, loans, and research and education (U.S. Department of Agriculture 1977, p. vi). The Soil Conservation Service, begun during that time, has an annual budget of a quarter of a billion dollars.

But Congress, in its concern about the environment, decided to take a different tack. Regulation supplemented (some would say supplanted) the more voluntary earlier methods. The Federal Water Pollution Control Act mandated the development and implementation of controls over agricultural nonpoint sources of pollution.

"Nonpoint pollution" means pollution that enters the environment in a diffuse manner such as by water runoff from a field or a feedlot. This is distinct from discharge of effluent by a pipe or smokestack, which enters the environment at a particular point. The distinction is highly relevant. The discharge from a smokestack or a pipe can readily be detected and measured, and the offender can be held to a standard. This is much more difficult with nonpoint pollution. Sediment is the chief nonpoint pollutant. "Nonpoint pollution" and "sedimentation" are EPA labels for what farmers have long known as erosion.

Farmers are worried about erosion; they rightly consider the loss of topsoil to draw down their production potential. But the Water Pollution Control Act was written by people with a greater passion for clean water than for productive land. It reverses the traditional view and looks on erosion as a water pollutant. The loss of soil from the field worries the EPA only as sediment gets into the stream (Hildreth 1978, p. 4). Farmers have difficulty comprehending this approach; it seems to them like worrying about a high death rate because of the burden on undertakers.

Erosion and stream sedimentation are as old as the earth. They date from the time, some billions of years ago, when rain first fell on the steaming rocks of the primordial world. Stream sedimentation built the Mississippi delta, from Memphis to the Gulf, long before any land was cultivated—indeed, before any human beings appeared in North America. But Congress passed a law that decrees that sedimentation must come to an end. Stream sedimentation is declared to be a pollutant. The goal of the act is that "the discharge of pollutants into the navigable waters be eliminated by 1985" (Taylor and Frohberg 1977, p. 25).

Sediment in streams is the most abundant of all United States water pollutants, resulting in pollutant damages estimated to be as high as one billion dollars annually (Wade and Heady, 1977, p. 13; Holt, Johnson, and McDowell 1973, pp. 141–56; Stall 1972, pp. 353–60). The Department of the Interior estimates that the average annual sediment load for the United States during the 1960s was 432 million tons (Wade and Heady 1977, p. 19), greater than the total tonnage of cereal grains produced.

Part of the difficulty comes from the fact that land in the United States long was abundant and cheap, so that it was possible to use erosive tillage practices, ruin a farm, and move west to a new one. There is the old story about the man who lectured his younger neighbor on how to farm, citing as evidence of his superior experience that he "had already worn out three farms." The story may be apocryphal, but it illustrates an embarrassing aspect of our agricultural history. What we are trying to do now is to change these wasteful old practices.

It is possible, by good tillage, to conserve the soil and reduce stream sedimentation. This is done in various parts of the world. In Italy, between Rome and Naples, there is rolling land that has been in continuous tillage for three thousand years and is now more productive than ever. It has often been said that the thin layer of topsoil is all that stands between man and oblivion. While there is some poetic license in such statements, there is also much truth.

Benefits from reducing erosion and sedimentation have an aesthetic as well as an economic dimension. Water recreation and improved environment for fish and wildlife were the motivating forces in passage of the Water Pollution Control Act. Social benefits of water pollution abatement cannot be quantified. The economist with his "nicely measured less and more" can make only a limited contribution here. He can do a better job of estimating costs than benefits. So we turn now to costs.

Costs of Limiting Sedimentation

First of all, only about 30 percent of the sediment load comes from cropland, where changed tillage practices can reduce sediment loss (Wade and Heady

1977, p. 19). The greater part of the sediment load comes from noncropland—that is, grazing land and wasteland, chiefly in the southwestern United States, where sedimentation cannot be controlled by changing cropland use. The dream of every conservationist, indeed every person, to "see the rivers running clear" as allegedly they once did cannot possibly be fulfilled. The name of the great river, Missouri, comes from an Indian word meaning "big muddy," a name conferred long before the plow broke the plains.

Wade and Heady, using a model that is admittedly imprecise, estimate the costs of tillage practices that would "minimize the national sediment load" (1977, p. 23). They put the annual cost of such control at $13.4 billion. This extreme environmental control provides only a 23 percent reduction in the total sediment load. It would reduce the sediment load from cropland by 90 percent. But erosion from range and wasteland, which produces the great bulk of the load, would be unaffected.

Limiting sediment load would require taking some marginal cropland out of use and would necessitate less intensive use of other cropland. So it would reduce crop production, with the consequences of increased farm prices, enhanced farm income, and higher consumer food costs. The effect would be similar to the effect of a massive acreage limitation program. This price increase would occur only if the changed tillage practices were general. If an individual farmer were to change practices by himself his costs would increase and the price he received would not, so he would be worse off. Everyone wants to believe that conservation tillage is in the individual farmer's interest, so that the extension service could appeal to him, on the basis of self-interest, to engage in good conservation practices. This is true in a measure, for certain practices. But on the scale necessary to achieve major reduction in sedimentation it can be true only if the farmer takes a very long-run view or if he counts as psychic income the satisfaction of being a good steward. The short-run self-interest of the individual and the long-run interest of society are not congruent. In macro terms, farmers should be enthusiastic supporters of EPA efforts to limit sedimentation. It would preserve their assets and increase their incomes. But the individual case is quite different. This is the crux of the problem.

Difficulties of Control

So far as agriculture is concerned, the Water Pollution Control Act is unenforceable. There are understandable reasons for this. The first one is that the standard—no sedimentation by 1985—is physically unattainable, no matter how great the effort. The next is that measuring the amount of sediment originating from a particular farm is, at this time, not technically possible.

Another reason is that the cost of subsidy necessary to induce farmers to change their practices fundamentally would be very great, as has been shown. Yet another is that food costs would rise sharply, a circumstance not likely to be tolerated by the public. Finally, the great bulk of sedimentation comes from lands that are not cropped, for which improved soil management is a severely limited option.

Alternative Methods of Control

Alternative methods by which control might be attempted are these:

A cost-sharing plan, as in the Agricultural Conservation Program of the Department of Agriculture and various programs of the Soil Conservation Service. These programs would be attractive to farmers but would prove enormously expensive if major changes in tillage practices were sought.

A tax on poor land use, the least costly but, to farmers, the most repulsive method. Poor land use is difficult to define, measure, and penalize.

Prohibiting certain practices, such as straight-row cultivation and fall plowing. Farmers would very likely resist this; they would consider it an invasion of their decision-making role.

Section 208 of the Water Pollution Control Act gives primary responsibility for carrying out the act to the state governments, with the Environmental Protection Agency seeing that this is done in a satisfactory manner. Iowa is one of the states that has taken leadership. The Iowa Conservancy Law was initiated to control erosion. The law is designed to be administered by conservancy boards who hear complaints from adversely affected parties and make judgments on improvements required to reduce damage to cropland and to the interests of individuals. The law is to be implemented only if state funds are appropriated to finance it; very limited funds have so far been made available. The question is whether state legislation of this kind is a serious effort to check nonpoint pollution or whether it is intended to build a backfire against federal action.

The Environmental Protection Agency has exercised considerable forebearance in administering this well-intended but unenforceable law. Our brief look at benefits, costs, and enforcement problems reveals sound reasons for cautious administration.

Voluntary Action

Much is known about soil conserving (sediment-reducing) practices. More is known than is practiced. The extension service could push these practices, with the factual and persuasive argument that their implementation "might hold off the feds."

Reduced tillage. On hilly land, minimum tillage reduces soil loss by as much as 80 percent (Griffith, Mannering, and Moldenauer 1977, pp. 20–28). But if conventional plowing and cultivation are to be foregone, more herbicides will be needed.

Contour farming. Under Iowa conditions, straight-row cultivation results in five times as much erosion as does contour farming on terraced fields. The need for improved soil management practices is greatest on hilly, fragile soils. An EPA study showed that two-thirds of the erosion occurred on one-third of the land.

Forgoing fall plowing. By laying the soil open to wind and water erosion for a longer period, fall plowing increases soil loss approximately 10 percent compared with spring plowing (Taylor and Frohberg 1977, p. 30). For many years we held plowing contests, giving the prize to the man who plowed the straightest furrow and turned under all the residue from the previous crop. How wrong we were! Now we know that we should leave trash on the surface, and if we plow at all we should plow on the contour. The moldboard plow itself, some years from now, may be a museum piece. We have so much to unlearn. And some formidable incentives must be reversed.

Other water pollutants besides sediment are of agricultural origin. I have already mentioned fertilizer and pesticides, which enter the water system through runoff and leaching. Another is runoff from feedlots. For some of the larger feedlots this is a major problem. But it affects fewer people and the problem is more tractable.

AIR POLLUTION

The Clean Air Act of 1970 gives EPA responsibility for cleaning up the atmosphere. Agriculture gives off three general kinds of air pollutants.

Soil—dust storms that result from high winds in areas that are dry and lack ground cover.

Smoke—from the burning of crop residues, such as ryegrass straw in the Willamette Valley in Oregon, and rice, wheat, and barley straw in the Central Valley of California.

Smell—the malodorous character of certain livestock farms and feedlots, particularly troublesome if they are close to populated areas.

In addition to federal legislation regarding air pollutants, there are various state laws and local ordinances (Huemoeller et al. 1976, p. 74–90).

Dust storms are the worst of these three air pollutants, and the most difficult to deal with. The loess soils on the eastern sides of the Mississippi, the Mis-

souri, and the Wabash were deposited by the prevailing westerly winds of past
millennia, which picked up dry soil from the floodplains of these great rivers,
carried it some distance, and dropped it. Dust storms predated the plow.

Cropping only land suited for tillage, leaving crop residues on the surface,
and chiseling to roughen the soil and break the sweep of the wind give some degree of control. But the problem is as far from solution as is that of sedimentation. Wind and water are alike in their unresponsiveness to the congressional
mandate "Cease and desist!"

Smoke and smell are considerable problems to a few areas and to a limited
number of farmers and city people. But as threats to the environment they are
not in the same league with pesticides, sedimentation, and dust storms.

As regards air pollution, agriculture may be more sinned against than sin-
ning. Certainly agriculture creates significant air pollution in limited situations,
as indicated. But the more important question in the long run may well be the
potential threat to agricultural productivity from air pollution by nonagricultural sources. Destruction of agricultural productivity owing to auto and industrial air pollutants is very difficult to assess. There has been some indication that forest destruction in California is attributable to air pollution. There
have also been experimental studies indicating significant reduction in crop
yields under polluted air conditions. It is quite possible that agriculture generally stands to benefit more from air pollution cleanup than the cost to it of
complying with goals or rules.

SUMMARY

With all the courage of a government official newly out of office, I offer the
following suggestions:

A Suggested Position for Farmers

Do not fight the Environmental Protection Agency. It has both law and public
opinion on its side. The officials of that agency have a set of laws to administer,
whose faithful enforcement they pledged when they took the oath of office. Up
to now they appear to have exercised considerable restraint. Nothing is to be
gained by antagonizing them.

Sort out the issues case by case. Farmers lack the strength for a successful
stonewalling strategy, resisting all of EPA's environmental initiatives. Some
should be accepted in the farmers' own interests, as, for example, withdrawal
of certain pesticides. Others may be successfully contested, such as efforts to

restrict fertilizer use. Selective rather than blanket resistance increases the credibility of the farm position.

Accept changes in USDA cost-sharing programs. The Department of Agriculture has long had programs for conservation of land and water. From 1935 to 1976 these programs, on both federal and nonfederal lands, involved the following outlay (U.S. Department of Agriculture 1977, p. vi):

Cost-sharing	$13,700 million
Technical assistance	3,300 million
Resource management	2,300 million
Loans for conservation purposes	640 million
Research support	445 million
Education	73 million
Total	$20,458 million

Because of lobby pressure, much of this outlay had only limited conservation effect. The programs shared costs for practices, like the spreading of limestone, that were primarily production-oriented. The department, under both Democratic and Republican administrations, sought to shift the emphasis toward genuine conservation. It is in the farmers' interests to acquiesce in these changes. By so doing, the case for strong EPA action is weakened.

Support a stronger environmental effort on the part of the land grant colleges. The experiment stations and the extension service have found greater farmer interest in crop and livestock production than in soil conservation. Research and education programs reflect this bias. In part this is a reason the regulators have moved in. If this imbalance is redressed, there is a better chance for agriculture to retain custody of matters about which it has the greatest competence.

A Suggested Position for Environmentalists

Years back, we are told, Indian warriors of the Great Plains were more interested in "counting coup" (taking a scalp, stealing a horse, touching an enemy in battle) than in total victory over the rival tribe. This may be a good strategy for the environmentalists and the ecologists. They have taken their share of scalps: laws enacted, agencies established, funds appropriated, pesticides banned, noteworthy environmental improvement. It might be well to ease up somewhere short of an effort to impose unconditional surrender on farmers. It might be better to look occasionally to gains made rather than to think always of the remaining distance between the present condition and that idealized perfect environment, which is in any case unattainable. Costs, in budgets and in public resistance, increase geometrically as the goal of an ideal environment is approached. The environmentalists, who have had many victories, might contemplate President Eisenhower's advice to his staff on how to deal with people: "When you have an adversary, give him a way to retreat with honor. Otherwise you leave him no choice but to fight you with every weapon at his command."

There is no doubt about it; environmental and ecological issues will be a major farm policy concern during the 1980s. The assessment that emerges from this chapter is that farmers and environmentalists have their deep differences, but they also have some things in common. There are signs that the environmental movement has gained somewhat in wisdom and has experienced some diminution in zeal. Farmers, for their part, have come a long way toward greater appreciation for things beyond the line fence and beyond the present generation. What had earlier seemed a collision course may turn out to be converging paths.

The nature of the debate during the next decade will depend on whether the farm and environmental leaders exploit their differences or try to find common ground. Common ground is there if they want to find it. The question for both sides to consider is whether a less-than-perfect solution is worth more than a continuing argument.

REFERENCES

Barber, Stanley. 1976. *Report to industrial agronomists.* Lafayette, Ind.: Purdue University.

Beatty, Rita Gray. 1973. *The DDT myth.* New York: John Day.

Bower, C. A., and Wilcox, L. V. 1969. Nitrate content of the upper Rio Grande as influenced by nitrogen fertilization of adjacent irrigated lands. *Soil Science Society of America, Proceedings* 33: 971–72.

Brown, A. W. A., et al., eds. 1975. *Crop productivity: Research Imperatives.* East Lansing, Mich.: Michigan Agricultural Experiment Station.

Brubaker, Sterling. 1972. *To live on earth.* Baltimore: Johns Hopkins University Press.

Carson, Rachael. 1962. *Silent spring.* Boston: Houghton Mifflin.

Chou, Marylin; Harmon, David P., Jr.; Kahn, Herman; and Wittwer, Sylvan H. 1977. *World food prospects and agricultural potential.* New York: Praeger, in cooperation with Hudson Institute.

Curtis, W.F.; Culbertson, J. K.; and Chase, E. G. 1973. *Fluvial sediment discharge to the oceans from the conterminous United States.* Geological Survey Circular no. 670. Washington, D.C.: U.S. Department of the Interior.

Eichers, Theodore A., and Andrilenas, Paul A. 1978. *Evaluation of pesticide supplies and demands for 1978.* Agricultural Economic Report 399. USDA, Economics, Statistics, and Cooperatives Service.

Enfield, George. 1970. *Water quality in Midwest streams.* Paper presented at the Midwest Fertilizer Conference, February 17, Chicago.

Ennis, W. B.; Dowler, J. W. M.; and Klassen, W. 1975. Crop production to increase food supplies. *Science* 188:595.

Enochian, Robert V. 1977. Food prices, consumer beliefs and values. In *Research issues facing agriculture and rural America.* Washington, D.C.: USDA, Economic Research Service.

Fritsch, Conrad F., and Zimmer, John. 1976. *Factors influencing occupational and non-occupational farm injuries, illnesses and fatalities.* Working Paper no. 7605. Washington, D.C.: USDA, Economic Research Service, Economic Development Division.

Griffith, D.R.; Mannering, J. V.; and Moldenauer, W. C. 1977. Conservation tillage in the Eastern corn belt. *Journal of Soil and Water Conservation,* vol. 32, no. 1.

Griliches, Zvi. 1964. Research expenditures, education and the aggregate agricultural production function. *American Economic Review* 54: 961–74.

Groth, Edward. 1975. Increasing the harvest. *Environment,* vol. 17, no. 1.

Harmon, David P., Jr. 1977. *Agricultural chemicals: Pertinent issues and regulation* (draft). HI–2727–CC, Hudson Institute.

Headley, J. C., and Lewis, J. N. 1976. *The pesticide problem: An economic approach to public policy.* Washington, D.C.: Resources for the Future.

Hildreth, R. J. 1978. *Public policy and regulation.* Paper presented at the Northeast Agricultural Economics Council annual meeting.

Holt, R. F.; Johnson, H. P.; and McDowell, L. L. 1973. Surface water quality. In *Proceedings, National Conservation Tillage Conference,* ed. Max Schnepf, pp. 141–56. Des Moines, Iowa: Soil Conservation Society of America.

Huemoeller, William A.; Nichol, Kenneth J.; Heady, Earl O.; and Spaulding, Brent W. 1976. *Land use: Ongoing developments in the North Central region.* Ames, Iowa: Iowa State University Center for Agricultural and Rural Development.

Klepper, Robert; Lockeretz, William; Commoner, Barry; Gertler, Michael; Fast, Sarah; O'Leary, Daniel; and Blobaum, Roger. 1977. Economic performance and energy intensiveness on organic and conventional farms in the corn belt: A preliminary comparison. *American Journal of Agricultural Economics* 59: 1–12.

Lowrance, William W. 1976. *Of acceptable risk: Science and the determination of safety.* Los Altos, Calif.: William Kaufmann.

Ridgeway, R. L.; Tinney, J.C.; MacGregor, J.T.; and Starler, N.H. 1978. Pesticide use in agriculture. For publication in *Environmental health perspectives,* proceedings of a workshop on Higher Plant Systems as Monitors of Environmental Mutagens, sponsored by the National Institute of Environmental Health Service. Marineland, Florida, January 1978.

Smith, Leslie Whitner, and Rowe, Gene. 1978. *The hired farm working force of 1976.* Agricultural Economic Report 405. Washington, D.C.: USDA, Economics, Statistics, and Cooperatives Service.

Stall, John B. 1972. Effects of sediment on water quality. *Journal of Environmental Quality* 1: 353–59.

Taylor, C. Robert, and Frohberg, Klaus K. 1977. The welfare effects of erosion controls, banning pesticides, and limiting fertilizer application in the corn belt. *American Journal of Agricultural Economics* 59:25–36.

Turpin, F.T., and York, A.C. 1978. Insect management and the pesticide syndrome. Unpublished manuscript, Purdue University Department of Entomology.

U.S. Department of Agriculture. 1977. *Initial report on the land and water conservation program of the U.S. Department of Agriculture.* Prepared by the initial report team for the Land and Water Conservation Task Force, Washington, D.C.

Upchurch, L. M., and Heisig, C. P. 1964. *The economic importance of pesticides to the U.S. consumer.* Washington, D.C.: USDA, Economic Research Service.

Van Rumker, R.; Lawless, E. W.; and Meiners, A. F. 1974. *Production, distribution, use and environmental impact potential of selected pesticides.* Washington, D.C.: Environmental Protection Agency.

Wade, James C., and Heady, Earl O. 1977. Controlling nonpoint sediment sources with cropland management: A national economic assessment. *American Journal of Agricultural Economics* 59:13–24.

Whelan, Elizabeth, and Stare, Frederick. 1975. *Panic in the pantry.* New York: Atheneum.

12. Occupational Safety and Health

Agriculture is a dangerous occupation, ranking third after mining and construction in number killed per 100,000 workers. More than 2,200 agricultural workers die in farm accidents each year, and another 200,000 are disabled. (Compare this with the hazards to consumers from food additives and chemical residues, to which no deaths have been attributed.) Department of Labor statistics show that production agriculture makes up 4.4 percent of the nation's work force but accounts for 16 percent of the job-connected fatalities in the United States (Aherin 1976, p. 3). Upward of 108 million working hours are lost to agriculture each year from occupationally related injuries or illnesses (Fritsch and Zimmer 1976, p. 21).

Tractors upset and crush their drivers. Machines harvest human arms as well as ears of corn. Toxic chemicals kill people along with the bugs. Saws, axes, and other hand tools turn against those who wield them. Ladders, hoists, and conveyers, seeming servants of man, can be deadly to him. Bulls, cows, horses, and hogs are as yet imperfectly domesticated; they turn on those who tend them, causing injury and death. Frequently at farm meetings one sees farmers without fingers, hands, or arms, vivid testimony that farming is dangerous business.

There have been efforts to cope with farm safety problems through legislation. Thirty-three states have some specific coverage of agriculture under workmen's compensation laws. California probably has the toughest set of farm labor laws.

But in many states farmers have been able to obtain exclusionary clauses for agriculture, keeping hired farm workers from enjoying the protection provided to other workers.

141

From 1942 to about 1954, extension farm safety specialists were named in ten states, primarily in the region from Ohio to Nebraska. They began educational programs, working with both young people and adults, teaching farm people how to reduce risk, generating pressure on state law-making bodies for improved legislation, and working with equipment manufacturers for better machine design. But for more than twenty years the number of states with full-time extension safety specialists remained almost constant. Research relating to farm safety received little attention.

During the ten years from 1968 through 1977 agriculture work deaths per year fell from 2,600 to 1,800, a decrease of 31 percent. During the same years the death rate (per 100,000 workers) fell from 65 to 53. Nebraska, with a strong safety education program, reduced accidental deaths by 35 percent between 1971–73 and 1974–76. Ohio, which also had a farm safety program, cut farm fatalities from 194 to 141 during the years from 1972 to 1976. Puerto Rico initiated an extension farm safety program and reduced compensation payments by 25 percent (Tofany 1978). How much of this progress resulted respectively from safety education, better medical service, stronger state and federal legislation, improved machine design, and various other causes cannot be ascertained. Although progress was being made, the educational effort and the state legislation were judged insufficient. Late in December 1970 Congress passed the Occupational Safety and Health Act creating OSHA. Organized labor was the force behind this law. The desire was to make legislation regarding health and safety identical in the various states; some employers had been setting up plants in states with the weakest laws.

Agriculture was included in this legislation, since it ranked among the most dangerous of all occupations. The farm organizations were preoccupied at that time with the forty-year-old legislative battle on farm price supports and production controls. The inclusion of agriculture in OSHA legislation aroused only limited agricultural concern. That is, until the regulations were written and the effect on agriculture came into focus.

Responsibility for administering the act was given to the Department of Labor, the Department of Health, Education, and Welfare, and the Occupational Safety and Health Review Commission. Leadership was with Labor. None of these agencies knew much about agriculture.

When the responsible officials began examining hired farm labor, the new candidate for federal regulation, they found what were to them surprising facts: Three-fourths of farm labor is supplied by the farmer and his family and so is beyond the scope of OSHA regulations. The labor load is not uniform throughout the year; 33 percent of hired farm labor is seasonal. Of hired farm labor, 7 percent is migratory. Jobs are enormously varied, and work locations are dispersed. Many work singly; others work in gangs. The pattern of hired farm labor in California differs almost totally from that in Iowa. The range runs from straight manual labor to skills as great as those found in any industry. Relatively few farm workers are organized. Employers are tough-minded and fiercely independent, with a thorough dislike for regulation.

Despite this, the bureaucrats set out to write uniform regulations covering hired labor under all these conditions. For their general standards, not specific to agriculture, they wrote thirty-five pages of instructions on the design of exit signs alone (National Safety Council 1977, p. 1). They produced proposed regulations such as these: "(2) Location (i) Toilet facilities shall be located within a five-minute walk of each employee's place of work in the field where access to toilet facilities is not limited. Where specific work breaks are provided for employee access to toilet facilities, the facilities shall be immediately available at the time and location of work break."

They set up a Standards Advisory Committee on Agriculture (SACA) with seventeen subcommittees. Regulations were issued on slow-moving vehicle emblems, storage and handling of anhydrous ammonia, pulpwood logging, temporary labor camp housing, roll-over protective structures for tractors, and guarding of farm, field, and farmstead equipment. Plans were laid for regulations on agricultural noise, walking and working surfaces, portable power and hand tools, field sanitation, electricity, nuisance dust, housing as a condition of employment, ladders, personal protective equipment, and transportation of agricultural workers. Employers were required to keep records and to be ready for inspection.

OSHA put out a series of leaflets intended to educate farm workers on hazardous work conditions. The original version was written for the average farm worker. Several were also written in Spanish, and some were written in simplest English for use by farm workers with a low educational level. One of these (U.S. Department of Labor 1976) pronounced these uncontestable truths: "Hazards are one of the main causes of accidents." "When floors are wet and slippery with manure you could have a bad fall."

With its plethora of regulations and the inept statements in its publications, OSHA laid itself open to ridicule, the agricultural tactic that had been used successfully so often in the past. Ridicule had failed to check those recent initiatives the consumer movement and the environmental thrust, but it did check OSHA. Virtually every farm organization joined in the attack. On no other issue could they so readily make common cause. Farmer opposition to OSHA, which had been weak when the act was in the legislative process, became robust when attempts were made to administer the law. The bureaucratic regulations and the unfortunate publications were weak spots in the OSHA armor, through which the adversaries drove with lethal effect.

The degree of public disaffection with the OSHA work rules for agriculture was measured by the 1976 senatorial election in Wyoming. Gale McGee, the incumbent, was considered to have a safe seat. But Malcolm Wallop defeated him by pointing out that McGee had been in the Senate when these offensive rules were promulgated. The message got through to Congress—and to OSHA.

When the clamor of protest arose, defenders of OSHA were few. Farm workers were poorly organized and put up no effective resistance. The big labor unions had other fish to fry; they were concerned mostly with industrial labor. Agriculture had been included in OSHA as somewhat of an accident and was dropped like a hot potato.

So OSHA backed down. Congress revised the rules so as to exempt farms employing no more than ten workers; this eliminated 95 percent of all farms. In 1978 Wendall Glaiser, OSHA's agricultural safety officer, told Richard Pfister of Michigan State University that "nothing was being done in the area of farm safety standards" (National Safety Council 1978). The farmers had won. They relished the victory. It was one of the few.

The food marketing sector remains subject to controls. Grain elevators, meat packing plants, canning factories, and like agribusiness concerns continue under OSHA rules. The state laws remain in effect.

Advocates of federal regulation for health and safety of hired farm labor, badly beaten and lacking in organized support, are not likely soon to launch a new initiative. But the problem remains. Farming continues to be one of the most hazardous of all occupations. Farm workers generally have less protection, in terms of safety and health, than do other workers.

A fair guess is that the farm policy issue surrounding the OSHA initiative is closed for the coming decade. This is especially likely to be true if the forces of voluntarism take responsibility. There are signs that this may be happening. At this time, OSHA has taken a new tack. Contracts have been awarded in Missouri and Michigan to study the effect of education on farm safety (F. R. Willsey, pers. comm.). A voluntary educational program has this advantage: it can relate to the whole agricultural labor force, whereas OSHA is limited to one-fourth of it—hired labor. Even if OSHA should be completely successful and reduce occupation-related accidents and illness of hired farm workers to zero, and accomplish nothing else, the overall safety and health record in agriculture would be improved by only 25 percent.

So far as protecting the health and safety of hired farm workers is concerned,

OSHA appears to be dead. But it would be both wise and gracious to wait a decent interval before burying the body or writing the epitaph.

REFERENCES

Aherin, Robert. 1976. *The Occupational Safety and Health Act (OSHA) and agriculture*. Extension Bulletin 398. Minneapolis: Agricultural Extension Service, University of Minnesota.

Fritsch, Conrad F., and Zimmer, John M. 1976. *Factors influencing occupational and non-occupational farm injuries, illnesses and fatalities*. Working Paper 7605. Washington, D.C.: USDA, Economic Research Service, Economic Development Division.

National Safety Council. 1977. *OSHA up to date,* vol. 6, no. 10. Chicago: NSC. 3M. 1978. *Report of the winter meeting farm conference,* Phoenix, Arizona. Miscellaneous Publication. Chicago: NSC.

Skubitz, Joe. 1976. *Congressional record.* 94th Cong., 2nd sess., House H6603. Vol. 122, no. 99.

Smith, Leslie Whitener, and Rowe, Gene. 1978. *The hired farm working force of 1976*. Agricultural Economic Report no. 405. Washington, D.C.: USDA, Economics, Statistics, and Cooperatives Service.

Tofany, Vincent (president of the National Safety Council). 1978. Statement before the Appropriations Subcommittee on Agriculture, House, March 22.

U.S. Department of Labor. 1976. *Safety with beef cattle.* Report 2286. Washington, D.C.: Occupational Safety and Health Administration.

13. Prime Agricultural Land

We are in the process of redefining the public interest in privately held land. This will be an important farm policy issue during the eighties. One form this issue takes is the concern that prime agricultural land might be swallowed up by urban development, jeopardizing our food supply. An associated issue is the scramble between various units of government for the dominant role in determining land-use policy.

Land policy issues are as old as America: Indians versus settlers, squatters versus government, sheep versus cattle, fences versus range, plantation versus family farms. But by the latter part of the nineteenth century it was thought that the central issues had generally been settled; we had a fairly well-agreed land policy.

What was that policy? It had these main components:

1. Get as much of the public domain as possible into private hands, preferably for agricultural use. Family farms were thought to be the proper way of relating the individual to the land.

2. Individual property rights were thought to have priority. The public purpose would be well served, it was believed, if individual property holders pursued their own self-interest.

3. Decisions regarding land use should be made through the market. To sell or not to sell, to buy or not to buy, involving whom and for what price and purpose—these were matters for the market.

This was a policy, though it has become fashionable to characterize it as the absence of one. But a deliberate determination to rely on individual decisions and to respect the market as a worthy institution certainly constitutes a policy. And the policy produced remarkable results. It settled the continent. It got the various farm crops produced in the areas best suited to them. It located the cities with due regard to markets and transportation. It produced a thriving agriculture and helped achieve rapid economic development. With the help of these institutions, we lifted the individual to a level of freedom and status not enjoyed elsewhere, and we quickly rose from a fledgling nation to a world power.

As the population increased, as shortcomings of the market system became more apparent, and as economic planning became more popular, there were complaints that our historic land policy encouraged exploitation rather than stewardship, thus jeopardizing the future, and that it favored individual interests over the interests of the group.

A strong point of the market as a means of deciding land-use questions is that in a competitive situation it allocates the land to the most efficient user. A weak point is that the market does not automatically allow for the creation of open space or environmental amenities. As the economist would put it, the market does not necessarily equate social benefits with social costs. In the absence of intervention the market sometimes permits the individual landowner to gain at the expense of the group and lets group needs go unmet. The disputes center on the frequency and gravity of such occasions.

CONFRONTATIONS

The charges against our historic land-use policies are broad and general. Perhaps the issues can be sharpened if they are cast in current and confrontational terms.

Conservationists versus users. Many who speak for the future charge that our land policies have been wasteful, jeopardizing the food supply. Urban sprawl gobbles up prime farmland. Unwise tillage of fragile land leads to erosion and loss of topsoil. Surface mining destroys the land. Reservoirs inundate fertile valleys. If we do not mend our ways—and soon—starvation looms.

Defenders of our historic land-use practices point out that the average person is better fed than ever, that predicted disasters have not occurred, and that advancing technology has more than offset whatever damage has resulted from bad land use.

Farm versus city. Farmers list these charges against city people: the cities, growing and spilling out into the countryside, require services that result in unbearably high taxes on farmland. A farmer does not know when his farm will be swallowed up by urban development; he cannot plan ahead. As the cities move out, they dilute the rural culture. As farms are gobbled up there comes a time when their numbers fall below critical mass; they become so few that farm service establishments fold up. This is the point below which farming is no longer viable.

The city people counter with a barrage of charges against farmers. Livestock operations are smelly. Runoff from fields and feedlots pollutes the streams. Suburbanites are kept awake during planting time by the roar of tractors in adjoining fields. Slow-moving farm implements are a highway hazard. Farm people vote against the sewers and schools that city people want.

But not all is controversial between farm and city. Farm people, especially those in or approaching retirement, may welcome the chance to sell the farm to city developers at a substantial premium over its agricultural value. At the same time, some city people look with favor on agriculture. It provides open space in what otherwise might be a wall-to-wall urban area. Agriculture provides a spot of green to offset the city grayness. It nourishes the nostalgia for an earlier, simpler life. City people, one or two generations removed from farming, like to be reminded of their heritage.

Farm versus industry. In the Western Great Plains, surface mining for coal competes with farmers and ranchers for land and water. In various locations, nuclear and coal-fired power plants are planned for rural areas, a disturbance to the status quo. The siting of industrial plants in the countryside has its own mixture of costs and benefits. It provides jobs but competes with farmer-employers for labor. It develops the area but displaces farms. It increases opportunities but changes life-styles. It lifts living levels but may jeopardize the environment.

Farm versus farm. Farmers who want to continue farming complain when their farmer neighbors sell to the developers. Downstream farmers complain about the water and sediment dumped on them by their upstream neighbors. Downwind farmers complain about toxic spray and dust that drift onto them from upwind. Operators of small farms allege that wide-open land-use policies result in huge corporate operations, a threat to traditional family farms.

The settler on the American frontier, very likely an immigrant and a landowner for the first time, tended to think of landownership as an absolute right. This was the historical meaning of landownership to the feudal lords of Europe, where the immigrants came from. But, clearly, landownership in modern society cannot mean total autonomy with regard to land use. Every good professor of land economics tells his students that the ownership of land relates to a bundle of rights, specified by the process of public policy. Some of the sticks in the bundle are right to use, right of access and egress, right to buy and sell, right to tax, right of condemnation, right to inherit and to bequeath, and right to redress from nuisance. These rights are not given by God; they are specified by the society. Almost nowhere in today's world does the society confer this entire bundle of rights on the occupant of a tract of land. What is now being sought, one hopes with proper attention to due process of law, is a redefinition of these rights in accordance with the needs of the times.

This issue is a deeply troublesome one, as any student of history knows. Proposals for change in the institutions surrounding ownership of land are a challenge to property owners, often the power elite. The last time landholding institutions were called into question was during the New Deal of the 1930s. The Resettlement Administration experimented with cooperative rather than individual ownership of farmland. Some twenty thousand families were resettled. Land acquisition totaled twenty million acres (Baldwin 1968, pp. 105–8). The challenge was thrown back, leaving some scar tissue and little gain to either adversary. Policy-makers are understandably wary of issues regarding changes in ownership and use of land. The subject is more conducive to making speeches than to casting votes.

Farmland Preservation

The charge is made that we are using our land in a prodigal manner, paving over our farms with concrete and asphalt, reducing our future food-producing capability and jeopardizing our grandchildren's food supply. Let us examine the facts. More than half the land in our fifty states is used for agriculture (table 7). The total amount of cropland has been relatively stable for the past half-century. Between 1969 and 1974, intensive nonagricultural land use (urban area, highways, railroads, airports) increased from 2.5 to 2.7 percent of the total area. Extensive nonfarm uses (parks, primitive areas, wildlife reserves, defense and industrial areas, and state institutional lands) increased from 4.8 to 5.1 percent of our land surface (table 8).

Prime agricultural land as defined by the Department of Agriculture is "land that has the best combination of physical and chemical characteristics for producing food, feed, forage, fiber, and oilseed crops, and is also available for these" (U.S. Department of Agriculture 1978, appendix, p. 1). Of the 384 million acres classed as prime farmland, 250 million are now in crops (Brubaker 1977, p. 1039). As a result of urban development and farmers' decisions to take land out of crop production, the cropland base shrinks by about 1.4 million acres a year, or about 0.4 percent (Cotner 1976, abstract).

The Soil Conservation Service says there are something like 100 million

Table 7. Agricultural and Nonagricultural Uses of Land, United States, 1974

Major Land Use	Acreage (million acres)	Percentage of Total
Agricultural		
Cropland	467	20.6
Cropland used for crops	(363)	(16.0)
Soil improvement crops and idle cropland	(20)	(.9)
Cropland pasture	(84)	(3.7)
Grassland pasture and range	598	26.4
Forest land grazed	179	7.9
Farmsteads, farm roads	8	.4
Total agricultural land	1,252	55.3
Nonagricultural		
Forest land not grazed	539	23.8
Special uses	176	7.8
Urban and other built-up areas	(62)	(2.7)
Primarily for recreation and wildlife	(87)	(3.9)
Public installations and facilities	(27)	(1.2)
Miscellaneous land	297	13.1
Total nonagricultural land	1,012	44.7
Total land area	2,264	100.0

SOURCE: Frey (1977, p. 4).

acres, not now tilled, that could be converted to cropland, if prices were attractive, within one or two decades (Cotner 1976, p. 3). These acres would be less productive and more erosive than those now in use.

Now, in 1978, our agricultural capability is sufficiently great that we are paying farmers to hold nineteen million acres out of production under our commodity programs, 5 percent of our cropland. The consensus of those reputable researchers who have studied the matter closely is that between now and the year

Table 8. Changes in Special Uses of Land, United States 1969–74 (millions of acres)

Special Use Area	1974	1969	Change
Total land area	2,264.0	2,264.0	
Intensive uses			
Urban area	34.9	31.0	3.9
Highways and roads	21.6	21.0	.6
Railroads	3.1	3.2	− .1
Airports	2.0	1.8	.2
Total	61.6	57.0	4.6
Percentage of total area	2.7	2.5	
Extensive uses			
National and state parks	36.8	35.0	1.8
Wilderness and primitive areas	14.8	14.3	.5
Federal and state wildlife areas	35.8	32.0	3.8
National defense and industrial areas	25.0	25.6	− .6
State institutional and other uses	2.0	1.9	.1
Total	114.4	108.8	5.6
Percentage of total area	5.1	4.8	
Total special uses	176.0	165.8	10.2

SOURCE: Frey (1977, p. 11).

2000 (as distant a date as economic visibility permits) the world will be able to provide, on the average, a modest improvement in the per capita food supply for the growing numbers of people.

There is no doubt that urbanization is wiping out agriculture in certain areas and creating problems of local adjustment. But the alleged threat to the nation's food supply appears not to be well-founded. That we should be good stewards of our land and use land-sparing rather than land-destroying policies is clear enough.

The chief concern of farmers is that urban sprawl results in higher taxes, increased uncertainty about the future, an unwanted change in life-style, and possibly sale of the beloved old farmstead. A concern of city people is that urbanization may become nearly total, wiping out open space altogether and destroying the desired balance between city and country. For some counties and even for some states (Connecticut, New Jersey) farming as a meaningful enterprise may disappear by the end of the century. These concerns find convincing rationale in an alleged threat to the food supply. The issue is morally upgraded if it is cast in terms of future welfare rather than current self-interest.

If this analysis is correct, the loss of prime agricultural land is reduced from a national issue, involving the nation's food supply, to a series of local issues involving the differing interests of farm and city people. Let us now examine briefly the alternative methods for dealing with the limited case.

Real estate taxes based on farm value rather than market value. Between 1956 and early 1976, forty-two states authorized assessments of farmland on the basis of its current or recent capacity to generate income from agriculture rather than on the basis of its apparent market value (Barlowe and Alter 1976, pp. 3–4). Market value may reflect the income expected when the land is eventually converted to residential, industrial, or commercial use. The difference between market value and value for agricultural purposes can be very large. In rapidly suburbanizing Du Page County, Illinois (near Chicago), property taxes based on market value were as high as $210 an acre. The per acre tax under farm-value assessment would have been $25 (Esseks 1977, p. 4).

Farm-value assessment has plausibility. If real estate taxes are based on market value, many farmers will be "literally unable to pay them and would be involved in a forced sale of farmland or serious deficit financing" (Spencer Volpp, Illinois Agricultural Association legislative representative, quoted in the *De Kalb Daily Chronicle).*

The stated purpose of farm-value assessment is to permit urban-fringe farmers to continue operating their farms. But farm-value assessment may not hold the land in farming, particularly if spectacular prices are offered by developers. A 1975 study in New Jersey showed farm-value assessment to be an inadequate preservation toll (Kolesar and Scholl 1975, pp. 28–29). A 1976 study in Illinois came to a similar conclusion (Vogeler 1976, pp. 74–76). A nationwide study concluded: "differential assessment, by itself, is likely to be an ineffective deterrent to conversion of farmland" (Regional Science Research Institute 1976, p. 63).

Farmers, of course, favor taxing their land at its farm value rather than its market value; this substantially lowers their costs. Farmers and their organizations have lobbied powerfully and successfully on this issue. Taxing farmland at farm value is a point on which virtually all farm organizations agree. The attractiveness is somewhat reduced if there is a provision for mandatory repayment of back taxes if the property is sold, as is the case in twenty-two states (Esseks 1977, p. 8).

The major political opposition to farm-value assessment comes from local governments, especially from tax officials. They complain of greater administrative cost, of revenue lost, and of the increase in the tax burden of nonfarmland owners (Esseks 1977, p. 7). Following farm-value assessment in New Jersey, "in some heavily agricultural municipalities, the tax rates were inflated as much as sixty percent because of the loss in farm ratables" (Kolesar and Scholl 1975, p. 11). In California, for the year 1974–75, eight counties lost revenue or experienced tax burden shifts amounting to 4–10 percent of total revenues. In three counties the tax difference (loss or shift) totaled 10 percent, and in one it was 22 percent (Gustafson and Wallace 1975, p. 381).

Farm-value assessment sometimes miscarries. A study of 1973 recipients of farm-value assessments in the Chicago metropolitan area showed that 40 percent were nonfarmers (Vogeler 1976, p. 67). Most nonfarm owners of farmland near or in metropolitan areas will eventually either develop the land themselves or sell it at a profit to other nonfarmers. In the meantime they can lease the land to farmers and charge rents that cover the taxes. If farm-value assessment keeps these taxes low, the rent may cover part or all of the interest cost as well. In effect, farm-value assessment may encourage speculation by reducing carrying costs on the land (Esseks 1977, p. 8).

If a city increases in population, it needs more space. There is no acceptable institutional device that will make it possible to pen up a growing city population within some specified perimeter. There are two ways to persuade farmers to sell their land to accommodate this needed growth. One, the carrot, is to offer a high price per acre. The other, the stick, is to increase taxes. Typically the two are used together. It is difficult for me to think of a more equitable or more voluntary way of acquiring the needed land.

It is possible to be only moderately troubled by the problems of a farmer on the urban fringe who can sell two hundred acres of land for enough money to buy four hundred acres of equally good land some distance off. The problem has been exaggerated beyond its true importance.

Agricultural districts. "Agricultural Districts are areas of 500 acres or more voluntarily formed by landowners, who commit their land to farming for eight-year periods" (McKinney 1972). If the district is approved by county authorities or a state review agency, the land qualifies for a number of benefits: property taxes can be based on farm-value assessment; the land is protected from "nuisance ordinances" that might interfere with normal farming practices such as driving slow-moving farm vehicles on public roads; protection is provided against non-farm-related construction such as road building; protection is assured against special tax assessment for streetlights and sewer or water lines; and moderation of regulations is promised, such as those aimed at reducing farm-derived air and water pollution.

In short, the agricultural districts give promise of income-enhancing benefits that may help farmers resist purchase offers by speculators. Benefits to the farmers—and costs to nonfarmers—are greater than is the case with simple farm value assessment. The land's higher relative earnings tend to push the farmers' reservation prices beyond or closer to the speculators' offers.

New York State passed districting legislation in 1971. As of October 1976, New York had 320 districts, making up about 4.4 million acres, or close to half of New York's total land in farms. A districting bill, patterned after the New York statute, was introduced into Vermont's legislature in 1973 (Lesher 1975b, p. 32). An Illinois bill, which was first introduced in 1975 and was reintroduced in 1977, also owes much to the New York example.

The emphasis on farmland preservation appeals to many environmentalists in the urban areas and contributes to the attractiveness of agricultural districts. They provide substantial benefits to farmers and so win strong farm support.

But there is opposition. There is the loss of tax revenues. In addition, local government officials may oppose the agricultural districts because they limit freedom to guide the city's growth. Similar opposition comes from community leaders who favor unrestrained suburban development.

Agricultural districts are too new for us to judge whether, in addition to providing attractive benefits to farmers, they are an effective deterrent to urban sprawl. They are, at this time, an innovative but as yet unproved effort to find common ground—the farmers wanting to continue farming with as little molestation as possible and the city people wanting visible confirmation of their belief that the world consists of something more than concrete and asphalt.

Purchase of development rights. Landownership, as I have said, involves a bundle of rights. Long Island and New Jersey have split up this bundle. The idea: have the government buy development rights from the farmer and impound them on a long-term basis. The farmer, having sold the development rights for an amount roughly equal to the difference between the market value and the value for farming, continues to farm, assured that the city will not reach out and gobble him up. He bequeaths to his heirs the farming but not the development rights to his land. He pays taxes on a farm-value basis.

In September 1976, Suffolk County, New York, on Long Island, approved a $21 million bond issue for the first phase of a three-part purchasing program that in total is expected to transfer to the county government the development rights for nearly 14,000 acres or about 25 percent of the county's remaining farmland (Lesher 1975a, p. 43).

On the one hand, farmers like the payment, the reduced tax burden, and the assurance of continuing a chosen occupation in a preferred location. On the other hand, if development rights are sold, the possibility of substantial future windfall gain is foregone. The premium of market value over farm value might increase if urbanization goes forward more rapidly than was anticipated or if inflation continues, or both.

City people likewise have mixed reactions. Attractive to them are: preserving open space, an orderly pattern of urban growth, maintaining local agribusiness, and having continued access to nearby supplies of farm products. Supporting the purchase of development rights in Suffolk County was a "Save Our Farms" coalition of twenty-seven environmental organizations, six local government bodies, and twenty-nine civic associations.

Negative reactions arise from the high cost. In New Jersey the estimated average cost of development rights came to $1,000 per acre (New Jersey Department of Agriculture 1977). For the Suffolk County program on Long Island, the cost of development rights was expected to average $6,000 per acre (Esseks 1977, quoting from Lesher 1975a, p. 16). There is also opposition from realtors and builders who envision curtailment of their activities. In addition, there is disquiet about the development rights that have been purchased but are impounded; their use cannot be exercised in conjunction with the right to farm, which is in other hands.

The New Jersey initiative was opposed by the New Jersey Farm Bureau on the grounds that it lacked complementary measures, such as relaxation of state regulations affecting agriculture, that would make farming viable. The Farm Bureau said the program might preserve farmland but fail to preserve farming. Other opposition came from the New Jersey Association of Realtors and the State Builders' Association.

Purchase of development rights is still too new and too novel for evaluation. How much is it worth to a city person to have farmers and farmland within driving distance? How much development-induced appreciation in land value will a farmer forego in order to continue farming? These, as of now, are unanswered questions.

Restrictive zoning. With the purchase of development rights, the action is voluntary and farmers receive compensation. Restrictive zoning is mandatory, and no compensation is paid. Government sometimes attempts to achieve by *compulsion* (at low financial outlay) what it might better obtain by *inducement* (at higher cost). But to compel people one must have power, and the public must accept the use of it.

Some farmers favor zoning as a way of keeping city people out. Against it are farmers who maintain that they are being deprived of property (the market value of development opportunities) without due process of law. Also against it are people who are opposed on ideological grounds. "If you're going to tell me what to do with my land then you should buy it!" So said a farmer at a 1977 meeting in Elburn, Illinois, discussing preservation of farmland (Esseks 1977, p. 21).

Zoning is often discussed on an idealized basis, lifting up the logic of optimal resource use. Practically, zoning is imposed by those who have more political power on those who have less. The tactic of the central planners is to compare the market, with its known defects, to a Utopian zoning system. On this basis planning will always look better. The only fair way to compare the market system and the central planning system is to consider the two on the same basis. Either consider both in their ideal form or consider both in their actual operation.

Rezoning petitions and requests for variances are likely to be heard by board members with reference to personal friendship and past favors. Marion Clawson and other students of land conversion warn against expecting local governments to resist such pressures (Esseks 1977, p. 15).

Land purchase. The farmer who told the zoning officials to buy the land if they wanted it used in a particular way may have been expressing a piece of deep wisdom. If the cities want open space (a legitimate and laudable desire), it might be best to go out and buy it, using eminent domain if need be—a legal, effective, and accepted instrument. This might be better than alleging that this space is needed for farming to avoid starvation; or pretending that the cities are getting open space by farm-value assessment, which they are not; or getting open space for a time with agricultural districts; or paying for open space but not controlling it, as with buying development rights; or trying to get it without cost by restrictive zoning.

Buying property is expensive, as are many other good things. But it remains true, as it has always been, that a good measure of the desire for the continued use of property is willingness to pay for it. If the cities buy the land outright they can lease it out for farming if that is their wish. Or if they want to convert the land to public parks, that is possible.

All the foregoing ways of attempting to preserve prime farmland—farm-value assessment, agricultural districts, purchase of development rights, restrictive zoning, and outright land purchase—are possible without new federal legislation.

JURISDICTIONAL BATTLES

To the degree that government involves itself in the dispute over use of prime agricultural land, should this be done at the local or state or federal level? Or at all three? If the federal government is to participate, with which agency should leadership lie? Clearly, the Department of Agriculture is reaching for a decisive role (Gardner 1977, p. 1028). Assistant Secretary of Agriculture Rupert M. Cutler has set up a USDA Land Use Committee that "will be busy looking at an appropriate mix of tools for preserving prime farm land and other values, such as land use controls, easements, tax and other incentives" (Cutler 1977, p. 6).

At least four federal agencies are interested in land use: the Department of Agriculture (interested in farming and forestry), the Department of Housing and Urban Development (interested in city problems), the Department of the Interior (responsible for the national parks and the Bureau of Land Management), and the Environmental Protection Agency (concerned about pollution). These jurisdictional rivalries can result in unjustified ventures, more on the basis of preempting the turf than on authentic need.

Congress has shown initiative of its own with regard to land-use legislation. Jurisdictional and substantive issues are reflected in the legislative as well as the executive branch. Proposed legislation generally includes grants to the states to help them develop land-use plans and to assist in carrying out these plans. Draft bills thus far drawn up at the federal level typically reflect limited faith in the market as a means of determining land use.

Meanwhile, states are administering or drawing up land-use laws, and local governments such as counties and cities are likewise active, developing and carrying out ordinances they deem appropriate. It is at the local and state levels that most of the action has thus far taken place.

Land cannot be moved. All the other agricultural input and output items— crops, livestock, machinery, labor—are mobile and so are subject to forces of a wider market area. But land is fixed in location and thus essentially local in nature, that being its prime attribute. It follows that legislation concerning land must accommodate local needs.

THE ANTAGONISTS

The contenders in this issue (with much overlap) are the conservers, the ecologists, and the planners on one hand and the users, the developers, and the enterprisers on the other. Farmers are found on both sides of the issue, depending on the individual case.

Permeating the issue is fervor of various kinds, ranging from commitment to an old-fashioned belief in the sanctity of property to the newer idea that the interest of the group should take precedence over that of the individual. All these deep convictions are likely to be voiced, though the immediate question may be no more profound than whether a farmer on the urban fringe should be allowed to run his tractor at night.

De-escalation, common ground, and trade-offs are the ingredients of good policy decisions. What have these three good friends to offer in this case? First of all, the issue can be de-escalated by demonstrating that it has little or nothing to do with our capability to feed ourselves. It can be further de-escalated by our recognizing that most farmers are far enough from the cities so that they are not affected, and that to most city people it is not an issue. Then there is the common ground that many farmers on the urban fringe want to continue farming and many city people want them to do so. Finally, there are possible trade-offs of the kind that good neighbors have long employed; for example, abatement of farm nuisances like smelly feedlots on the one hand and acceptance of most standard farm practices on the other. In some cases, where open space is desired the necessary land might be purchased for value received.

Need we make a major issue of whether and how we might preserve prime agricultural land? Do we need federal legislation? One may hope that this issue would be left for the states and the local communities.

REFERENCES

Alampi, Phillip. 1977*a*. *The New Jersey Agricultural Preserve Demonstration Program Act*. Paper delivered at the National Land Use Symposium, sponsored by the Soil Conservation Society of America. Omaha, Nebraska.

————. 1977*b*. *Report of the Blueprint Commission on the Future of New Jersey Agriculture*. Trenton: State of New Jersey.

Baldwin, Sidney. 1968. *Poverty and politics: The rise and decline of the Farm Security Administration*. Raleigh: University of North Carolina Press.

Barlowe, Raleigh, and Alter, Theodore R. 1976. *Use-value assessment of farm and open space lands*. East Lansing: Michigan State University Agricultural Experiment Station.

Barrows, Richard L., and Prenguber, Bruce A. 1975. Transfer of development rights: An analysis of a new land use policy tool. *American Journal of Agricultural Economics* 57:549–57.

Brubaker, Sterling. 1977. Land: The far horizon. *American Journal of Agricultural Economics* 59: 1037–44.

Chumney, Richard D. 1976. Farmland preservation: The New Jersey experience. *Journal of Soil and Water Conservation,* vol. 31.

Clawson, Marion. N.d. *Suburban land conversion in the United States*. Washington, D.C.: Resources for the Future.

Conklin, Howard E. 1975. Agricultural districts in New York State: Where and why they work. In *Proceedings of the Conference on Rural Land-Use Policy in the Northeast,* October 2–4, 1974. Ithaca: Northeast Regional Center for Rural Development.

Conklin, Howard E., and Bryant, W. R. 1974. Agricultural districts: A compromise approach to agricultural preservation. *American Journal of Agricultural Economics* 56: 609.

Cotner, Melvin L. 1976. *Land use policy and agriculture: A national perspective.* ERS–630. Washington, D.C.: USDA, Economic Research Service.

———. 1977. *Land use policy and agriculture: A state and local perspective.* ERS–650. Washington, D.C.: USDA, Economic Research Service.

Cutler, Rupert M. 1977. How the Department of Agriculture views the land-use issue. Paper presented at the chapter meeting of the Soil Conservation Society of America, June 9, Washington, D.C.

Esseks, J.D. 1977. The politics of farmland preservation. Paper delivered at the Agricultural Policy Seminar, USDA and the Farm Foundation, July 26, Washington, D.C.

———. 1978. The politics of farmland preservation. In *The new politics of food,* ed. Hadwiger and Browne. Lexington: D. C. Heath.

Frey, H. Thomas. 1977. *Major uses of land in the United States.* Working Paper 34. Washington, D.C.: USDA, Economic Research Service, National Resource Economics.

Gardner, B. Delworth. 1977. The economics of agricultural land preservation. *American Journal of Agricultural Economics* 59: 1025–36.

Gustafson, Gregory C., and Wallace, L.T. 1975. Differential assessment as land use policy: The California case. *Journal of the American Institute of Planners* 41: 381–82.

Kolesar, John, and Scholl, Jaye. 1975. *Saving farmland.* Princeton: Center for Analysis of Public Issues.

Lesher, William G. 1975a. *Land use legislation in the Northeast: New York.* Ithaca: Northeast Regional Center for Rural Development.

———. 1975b. *Land use legislation in the Northeast: Vermont.* Ithaca: Northeast Regional Center for Rural Development.

McKinney. 1972. *McKinney's consolidated laws of New York.* Annotated. Book 2B. St. Paul, Minn.: West Publishing Company. See article 25–AA—Agricultural Districts, Agriculture and Markets Law.

New Jersey Department of Agriculture. 1977. Farmland preservation demonstration project. Press release, October 14.

Regional Science Research Institute. 1976. *Untaxed open space: An evaluation of the effectiveness of differential assessment of farms and open space.* Washington, D.C.: Council on Environmental Quality.

U.S. Department of Agriculture. 1978. *Statement on land use policy* (draft). Secretary's Memorandum no. 1827, rev. Washington, D.C.: USDA, Land Use Executive Committee.

Vogeler, Ingolf. 1976. *The effectiveness of differential assessment of farmland in the Chicago metropolitan area.* Springfield, Ill.: Department of Local Government Affairs.

14. The Great Thirst

This chapter will consider the struggle between farm and non-farm interests for control of water, the lifeblood of the West. There is a great thirst in the land. That thirst is greatest in the arid West. I shall focus on the water problems of the seventeen Western states, the states generally west of the ninety-fifth meridian, from the Dakotas, Nebraska, Kansas, Oklahoma, and Texas on west to the Pacific Coast, where water policy issues are most pressing.

This chapter concentrates on supply of and demand for water for agriculture rather than on water quality, which was considered in chapter 11. It omits flood control, navigation, hydropower, Indian water rights, recreation, wildlife, and management of wetlands—all water-related subjects. So we have before us essentially a regional problem, and a limited version of that. But what is left is big enough.

Farm versus Nonfarm Use Water

Water issues are in large measure agricultural. In Arizona in 1967, agricultural use of surface water plus groundwater totaled 6.4 million acre-feet, more than ten times as much as all nonagricultural uses combined (Kelso, Martin, and Mack 1973, pp. 31–32). In California in 1975, the total statewide agricultural, municipal, and industrial applied water usage was approximately 38.6 million acre-feet. About 85 percent of this figure represented applied agricultural water (Robie 1977, p. 938). In the seventeen Western states, 90 percent of the water used is for irrigation (White House 1978, p. 12).

The West was settled with the idea that development meant agricultural development. And it was clear that in many cases agricultural development could occur only with irrigation. So dams were built and streams were diverted. The arid land, well supplied with plant nutrients that had accumulated through the ages, produced abundantly once water was applied. First came small individual irrigation projects, then private group action through irrigation districts, then federal assistance and state projects. In 1902 came the major effort, the Reclamation Act and the Bureau of Reclamation.

With the advent of state and federal funds, water projects were pushed beyond the level that would have prevailed if economic considerations had been decisive. The Interior Department estimates the subsidy in the Westlands Project in California to be $1,540 an acre, approximating the market price of land in the district (U.S. Department of Agriculture 1978, p. i).

In many cases benefit/cost studies are slanted in favor of new projects. Low interest rates are often used in such studies. Benefits are overestimated or double-counted (President of the United States 1978, p. 3). Adverse effects are not charged against the projects. As in many undertakings, particularly at times of rising prices, cost overruns are common.

The drive and momentum for water development is enormous. There are twenty-five federal agencies spending a total of $5 billion a year on water-related planning, construction, maintenance, and grant and loan programs (White House 1978, p. 1). Typically, the federal government picks up 80 to 90 percent of the cost of irrigation projects. The states pick up the rest (White House 1978, p. 10). Water recipients are obligated for less than 20 percent of the investment in structures and conveyance systems, including imputed interest on that investment over the normal repayment period (North and Neely 1977, pp. 995–1007).

There is a large backlog of federal water projects in various stages of construction and planning, distributed as follows (White House 1978, p. 6):

	Number of projects	Estimated cost (billions)
Construction already under way	783	$20.0
Unstarted separable units of larger projects on which some construction has begun	30	2.1
Projects that are authorized, but construction of which has not yet begun	497	13.2
Projects that are inactive, though approved	271	not determined
Projects currently being planned	612	not determined

We are pushing closer to physical limits with these projects. President Carter's Water Policy Message carries this passage (President of the United States 1978, p. 2): "Of 106 watershed subregions in the country, 21 already have severe water shortages. By the year 2000, this number could increase to 39 subregions. The nation's cities are also beginning to experience water shortage problems which can be solved only at very high cost."

With surface water supplies so near full development and with the thirst so great, attention turns to groundwater. Much of the West consists of valleys with deep beds of soil, sand, and gravel. In this porous storehouse lie vast supplies of water, the accumulation of runoff from adjoining upland and of percolation down from the surface. Sometimes the water is trapped, as in mountain pockets, and has been in place for thousands of years. Sometimes it seeps slowly along below the surface, following the course of a river valley, as with the Platte.

There came a conjunction of events: greater awareness of this underground water, the development of better well-drilling machinery, more efficient pumps, the advent of lightweight aluminum pipe, the invention of center-pivot sprinkling systems, and the availability (before 1973) of cheap fuel. So water is now pumped from this underground storehouse and used for irrigation. In most cases the rate of pumping exceeds the rate of replenishment. In Arizona the imposed draft on these underground supplies has been about three times the annual recharge, gradually depleting the stock on which the economy depends (Kelso, Martin, and Mack 1973, p. 12). Water is being mined, like coal and petroleum. To some people this is prodigal use of a vital resource; to others it has the same rationale as mining for coal or for copper, lead, or zinc.

Groundwater provides an appreciable share of the total water applied to crops. In Arizona since 1953, a little less than half the water used was from underground sources (Kelso, Martin, and Mack 1973, p. 12). In California, groundwater has provided about 40 percent of the state's total applied water use (Robie 1977, p. 938).

With this heavy pumping, the water table drops. How great the underground supply is and how long it will last no one dares estimate with any real claim for accuracy. Significantly, the falling water table means rising costs for pump irrigation. This squeezes out marginal users, particularly as a result of increased fuel costs since 1973.

Agriculture's primacy with respect to water is confirmed legally. Water rights in the West are divided into two different but related categories: *surface water* rights and *groundwater* rights. In the Western states generally the governing principle with respect to surface water is prior appropriation, "first in time, first in right." For the greater part, agriculture was first in time.

The principle is weakening. Texas, California, and Hawaii recognize certain riparian rights explicitly (Dewsnup and Jensen 1973, p. 5). The guiding principle of the riparian rights concept is that the owner of land contiguous to a stream has the right to use the water in that stream (Richard 1978, p. 217). In the California water code the legislature declared that water for domestic purposes has the highest priority and that irrigation is the next highest use. The right of a municipality to its reasonable water needs for existing and future uses is also protected (Hutchins 1956, p. 12). Nevertheless, the principle of prior appropriation is still powerful, at least in the minds of those who have enjoyed prior use.

These rights are manifest in a series of laws, rulings, and precedents, the product of numerous federal, state, and local agencies. In 1955 the Hoover Commission found forty-three national agencies directly or indirectly involved in management and development of water resources (U.S. Commission on Organization . . . 1955, pp. 59–61). Professor Richard of the University of Wyoming reports that his state has sixteen agencies and seven advisory boards involved in water policy. At the local level, there are ninety municipalities with water departments. Special purpose districts in Wyoming include: irrigation, drainage, water conservancy, soil and water conservation, and water and sewer (1977, p. 9).

To a large extent, agricultural users of water powerfully influence the agencies that are responsible for water allocation. In Wyoming, a survey of administrators involved with water showed that 55 percent were from agricultural backgrounds (Richard 1978, p. 219).

Agricultural inputs are generally said to consist of land, labor, and capital. Management is sometimes included. This formulation was laid down two hundred years ago in a humid area, England, where and when water was thought to be a free good. This powerfully influenced our thought. I studied economics in the humid East; water was used as a classroom illustration of a free good. Had the framework of economics been laid down in recent years, in the West, the utility of water would very likely have been better recognized. Part of the problem in the arid West is the acceptance there of attitudes originating in the humid East.

We have been treating water as an appurtenance to land and have sought to govern its use through a system of rules and regulations applied to land. Supplies of and demands for surface water are not determined primarily in the market like most other factors of production. Water rights are mostly determined in the public forum, in the courts, and by administrative ruling. This means that, as with almost all institutionalized decision-making, changes come slowly. For surface water, decision-making is administratively determined. As we shall see, this can result in a pattern of resource allocation that departs in major degree from what would occur through the interaction of market forces.

Charges for surface irrigation water are usually far below cost. Municipalities and industrial users, being able to pay more than irrigators, are usually required to do so (Brewer 1964, p. 232). The California Department of Water Resources has calculated that state water delivery to the Westlands Project would cost an average of $21 an acre-foot, compared with the current price of $7.50 (U.S. Department of Agriculture 1978, p. i).

Priced at approximately one-third of cost, water is treated as if it were abundant when in fact it is scarce. Furthermore, the rules generally provide that if water rights go unused for a length of time they revert to the allocating agency, to be reapportioned. As a result, water is sometimes used not so much for production as to keep the other fellow from getting it. Incentives are thus tilted in the direction of overuse.

For groundwater the situation is different. It varies by state. In Arizona groundwater is, at least nominally, subject to the common-law rule that each owner of overlying land has title not only to the surface of his tract but to everything beneath the surface (Kelso, Martin, and Mack 1973, p. 62). Rights in groundwater are restrained by the rule of reasonable use. The owner of overlying land may extract from beneath his land all the water he needs, but he may not be wasteful.

For groundwater the cost pattern thus far is primarily individual, depending on the particularized expense of raising and distributing the water. There may be some tendency to overuse groundwater, arising from the desire to obtain one's share before the neighbors pump out much of the supply and drop the water table below the depth from which it can economically be lifted. This is the principle that resulted in preemptive pumping of petroleum in Texas and ultimately led to centralized decision-making on pumping rates.

Farm and ranch people own most of the privately held land in the West and thus have title to most of the groundwater supplies. So farmers have legal right to most of the surface water and most of the groundwater as well.

The drawdown of groundwater increases. During the dry year 1977, three thousand new wells were drilled in the San Joaquin Valley of California (Robie 1977, p. 941).

It is in this setting that agriculture contends with other users for scarce water supplies. Agriculture has a strong hold on these supplies, surface and underground, rooted in both law and practice. This hold is being challenged by those interested in mining, industry, urban residence, and recreation.

While agriculture's position is strong in terms of law and tradition, its economic position is weak. Compared with its rivals, agriculture is not an efficient user of water. In Arizona in 1970, farming produced 3 percent of the state's personal income while using 90 percent of its water (Kelso, Martin, and Mack 1973 pp. 15, 176). Table 9 indicates, for various enterprises, the acre-feet of water required to produce a thousand dollars worth of output. The comparisons are crude in that figures indicate average rather than marginal relationships, but the picture nonetheless comes through clearly. The disadvantage of agriculture as compared with virtually all other users is apparent. Roughly one hundred times as much water is required to produce a given value of agricultural products as is required to produce that same value of nonagricultural goods and services. Among agricultural products, the most thirsty users of water are grain and forage. Livestock production is next. Least thirsty are the fruits and vegetables. None of these enterprises could compete with the nonagricultural water users for new increments of water if the market were free.

Those who manage water resources for the West can follow various strategies. They can conserve water, get more water, forego economic development, or transfer water from agricultural to nonagricultural uses. Very likely they will pursue these strategies simultaneously. Let us consider each of them.

Water is overused, as we have seen. There have been times when water was scarce and less of it was used without serious reduction of yield. Conservation is the primary focus of the president's new water policy. The difficulty is that with water priced far below its cost and its utility, there is little incentive to conserve it. By exhortation the farmers are told to use it sparingly; by the pricing system they are told to use it lavishly. The evidence is that they hear the admonition of price more clearly than they hear the counsel of conservation.

The most popular proposal is to obtain more water. This could retain for agriculture the primacy in law and in use that it has long enjoyed. This has been the historic (and up to now, from the standpoint of the farmers, generally successful) strategy. There are proposals to extend this strategy further, to divert water from the Columbia River to southern California, and somehow to get water from the Mississippi system to the High Plains of Texas. The costs of such projects have not been estimated. Water development sometimes suffers from what can be called "the engineering syndrome," the idea that anything that can be done should be done, regardless of cost. But with surface water near "full"

Table 9. In-State Raw Water Requirements, in Acre-Feet, per $1,000 of Output and per $1,000 of Final Demand

Producing Sector	Direct Requirement per $1,000 of Output	Direct and Indirect Requirement per $1,000 of Final Demand
Meat animals and products	0.407	9.337
Poultry and eggs	0.008	15.803
Farm dairy products	0.252	17.655
Food and feed grains	42.087	43.630
Cotton	12.551	14.896
Vegetables	6.413	6.582
Fruit and tree nuts	9.950	10.227
Citrus fruits	11.154	11.841
Forage crops	46.938	47.103
Miscellaneous agriculture	6.408	10.307
Grain mill products	0.019	13.365
Meat and poultry processing	0.012	5.758
Dairy products	0.010	9.052
Canning, preserving, and freezing	0.043	1.016
Miscellaneous agricultural processing	0.020	2.140
Chemicals and fertilizers	0.030	0.564
Petroleum	0.020	0.064
Fabricated metals and machinery	0.003	0.131
Aircraft and parts	0.004	0.086
Primary metals	0.187	0.387
Other manufacturing	0.009	0.283
Mining	0.147	0.282
Utilities	0.210	0.277
Selected services	0.010	0.082
Trade and transportation	0.010	0.052
Unallocated services	0.010	0.122
Construction	0.010	0.120

SOURCE: Derived from Tijoriwala et al (1968). Direct requirements are identical with their estimates. Direct plus indirect requirements are modified to reflect total requirements if Arizona did not import products. In Kelso, Martin, and Mack (1973, p. 184).

development and with groundwater falling below the levels at which it could economically be raised for agricultural purposes, this strategy is losing feasibility. Hitherto the effort has been to solve water problems from the supply side. Henceforward they will have to be solved, increasingly, from the demand side.

There are groups of people who dislike development, who look askance on increasing population growth and industrial expansion, achieved through a drawdown of resources. Some people like the idea of an agriculturally based no-growth economy. So there are those who accept something like the present pattern of water use and the present mix of economic activity. Some would like to go further. They would like to curtail the present level of economic activity and reduce or eliminate the drawdown of underground water supplies. But the preponderance of opinion favors growth over no growth.

If economic growth is desired (higher real income, more jobs, growing population) and if water supplies cannot be appreciably increased, then water must be taken from agriculture and transferred to nonagricultural use. This is the crux of the matter. The transfer can be accomplished either by price or by law. The issue is in its infancy.

THE ANTAGONISTS

In one camp, in effect defending the status quo, are very diverse groups: farmers, agribusiness people, administrators, traditionalists, some ecologists, opponents of economic growth, and those who worry about the adequacy of the food supply. Tradition and much of the law are on the farmers' side. Farmers have the water, and, as Colley Cibber put it several centuries ago, "Possession is eleven points in the law."

In the other camp, pushing for increased use of water for nonfarm purposes, are municipal groups, mining interests (especially coal, potentially oil shale), industrial users, and developers. Economics is on their side in overwhelming measure.

Where will this issue be adjudicated? The status quo people will try to keep it in the administrative agencies where they have the edge. The advocates of growth will attempt, in effect, to get a change of venue. They will try to shift the issue to the legislative halls where growing nonfarm representation affords the possibility of legal change, to the courts where past administration decisions can be reversed, and to the market where they can clearly win.

Groundwater is already in the market to a considerable degree. Industry, mining, and municipal agencies can afford to lift water from greater depths than can farmers. As the water level subsides, farmers will be squeezed out. They will sell their land, with underground water rights, to nonfarm interests who can afford to lift the water.

Where individual decision-making is possible, the change in resource use can occur. This change will be painful and protracted. Farmers will resist it, except some who will be happy to sell out at a good price. Most farmers will try to hang on. They will ask for higher price supports for their crops to match their increased water costs. But the change will occur, at the margin, as is already happening. Where the market can function the change will take place. The impersonal nature of the market makes acceptable, albeit with pain, changes that would otherwise be next to impossible.

Kelso, Martin, and Mack (1973, p. 27) say the solution to the problem lies in "creating a water market or establishing an allocative agency charged with facilitating water transfers from uses of lower value productivity to uses of higher value productivity." Thus, they say, "the Arizona economy can continue to grow without significant restraint stemming from 'water shortage.' " The solution to the problem in Arizona, they say, can be achieved "more cheaply for many years to come if it is approached through institutional (policy) reform relating to water transfer rather than through development and/or importation of additional water supplies. The water problem in Arizona is a 'man-problem' rather than a 'nature-problem.' "

Changes are taking place. There is already an impressive list of transfers out of agricultural use to a variety of nonfarm uses, achieved through the courts, through administrative rulings, and through changes in law (Richard 1977, pp. 14–16).

In the West, rights to land and water were transferred from the Indians to the ranchers. Rights were then transferred for a part of this land and water from the ranchers to the irrigators. Now the prospect is that some of the irrigators' land and water are to be transferred to nonfarm users.

That water use in the West will be a major public policy issue in the decade ahead is a certainty. And that agriculture will lose relative to nonfarm users also seems certain.

Farmers and nonfarmers are on what seems to be a collision course over the use of water in the West. Only if agriculture is willing to accept some modification of tradition and received doctrine, or if the West settles for no growth, can collision be avoided. And if collision does come it seems likely to me that agriculture will be the loser.

THE 160-ACRE LIMITATION

Many of the issues discussed in this chapter are brought into sharp focus by the fight over water in the Imperial Valley of California and in the Westlands District of that same state. The catch phrase for this issue is "the 160-acre limita-tion." The question concerns administration of a 1902 law limiting to 160 acres farms that use water from federal reclamation projects. Farms receiving such water now average much larger than 160 acres. The courts have found present procedures to be inconsistent with the law and have required the Department of the Interior to take corrective action. Supporting the present pattern of land-holding and water use are the concerned farmers, their friends, and their organi-zations. Opposing are a variety of activists and antiestablishment people. The issue is heavy with symbolism. Where one stands on this matter is the acid test for his position on the water question. This issue is likely to be with us at least for the decade of the 1980s, the time horizon considered in this book. Let us look at it both on its own merits and as a case study.

The 1902 Reclamation Act contained the following provision: "No right to the use of water for land and private ownership shall be sold for a tract exceed-ing 160 acres to any one individual landowner, and no such sale shall be made to any landowner unless he be an actual bonafide resident on the land, or occu-pant thereof residing in the neighborhood" (Act of June 17, 1902, ch. 1093§5. 3.2 Stat. 389,43. USC 431).

As has been shown, irrigation water is priced to the user at some fraction of its cost. Seckler and Young say that water recipients are obligated for less than 20 percent of the investment in irrigation projects (1978, p. 577). The Depart-ment of Agriculture says federal water in California is priced at about one-third as much as state delivery would cost (U.S. Department of Agriculture 1978, p. i). So the land, with its irrigation rights, became very valuable. The desire of the farmer-irrigator to own more of this valuable asset than the allowed 160 acres is quite understandable. In response to this desire, the Reclamation Act was administratively interpreted, long ago, so as to entitle a man, his wife, and two children to 160 acres each. Understandably, questions have been raised about the appropriateness of a substantial water subsidy to farms of such size.

In 1933 Secretary of the Interior Ray Lyman Wilbur ruled that the 160-acre limitation did not apply to the Imperial Valley of California (U.S. Department of Agriculture 1978, p. 3). Farms using federal water in the valley are therefore uninhibited as to size. Some are very large. There are 150 farm operations in the Imperial Valley having an average of 1,767 acres (Seckler and Young 1978, p. 580). In Westlands, the Southern Pacific Land Company has 80,000 acres of land under recordable contract; the Boston Ranch Company has 26,000 acres; Westhaven Farms has 11,000 acres. Much of the land is leased. There are 199 farm operations in Westlands, farming an average of 2,889 acres (Seckler and Young 1978, p. 580). The average farm size is nine times the average size in the United States and eighteen times the 160-acre limit.

This pattern of landownership and operation began to totter in August 1975, with a court ruling on a suit brought by National Land for the People, an activist group. The plaintiffs challenged Bureau of Reclamation procedures employed in the disposal of excess lands in the Westlands Irrigation District in the San Joaquin Valley. The court ruled that the United States Bureau of Reclamation should "forthwith promulgate rules and regulations on procedures and criteria to be used in the disposal of excess land" (Hinds 1977, p. 3).

In August 1977 a three-judge panel from the Ninth Circuit Court in San Francisco ruled that the 160-acre limitation *does* apply to the Imperial Valley, thus reversing Secretary Wilbur's decision of forty-four years earlier (U.S. Department of Agriculture 1978, p. 3).

Secretary of the Interior Andrus, in response to these court actions, issued proposed regulations for enforcing the 160-acre limit and the residency requirement. Proposed rules specified the manner in which acreage over the 160-acre limit should be disposed of. These proposed rules allow 160 acres each to a man and his wife. They require the owner to live within fifty miles of his land. They specify that excess land is to be disposed of at the predevelopment price, $750 per acre, by lottery (Seckler and Young 1978, p. 580). Whether these proposals will be acceptable to the courts remains unclear at this time.

Many affected landowners consider the new Interior Department rules a disaster. The existing rules had been in effect for three-quarters of a century. Land had been bought and sold in good faith, farms had become established and families had come to accept the rules of the game as if they were permanent. A certain amount of equity (as well as inequity) comes into being for any institution that has been long in existence. How far back do you go in an effort to establish the status quo ante? On the other hand, some observers believe that the procedures outlined by Interior only make modest adjustments in historic methods of administering the 160-acre limitation (Seckler and Young 1978, p. 575).

Of the "excess land" slated for disposal, about 265,000 acres are in the Imperial Valley Irrigation District and 302,000 are in the Westlands Water District. The focus is on California, which has 89 percent of the "excess lands." Nevertheless, the issue has repercussions in other states. All together, 1,165,875 acres are involved. There are, in all, about 150 Bureau of Reclamation Projects providing water services in the seventeen Western states (U.S. Department of Agriculture 1978, p. v).

When the court decisions and the secretary's actions upset what had been considered a settled situation, the affected landowners looked for help to the Department of Agriculture and the land grant colleges. But such help was not forthcoming.

The 160-acre limitation is a deep and an old issue. President Theodore Roosevelt spoke thus in defense of the limitation in 1912, before the Commonwealth Club of San Francisco:

I wish to save the very wealthy men of this country and their advocates and upholders from the ruin that they would bring upon themselves if they were permitted to have their way. It is because I am against revolution, it is because I am against the doctrine of the Extremists, of the Socialists; it is because I wish to secure this country against ever seeing a time when the "have-nots" shall rise against the "haves"; it is because I wish to secure for our children and for our grandchildren and for their children's children the same freedom of opportunity, the same peace and order and justice we have had in the past. [Taylor 1971, p. 262]

Roosevelt's threat of revolution from the left is countered by implication of revolution from the right. A spokesman for this view was Robert W. Long, senior vice-president of the Bank of America. In 1969 he called the 160-acre limitation a "ridiculous law, fostered by provincialism and Eastern political jealousy . . . subjugating economic realism to petty political tyranny. . . . Maybe this is what causes the seeds of civil war" (Taylor 1971, p. 253).

It would be difficult to think of an issue involving more adversary relationships:

The development issue, taken up earlier in this chapter: agricultural versus nonagricultural use of water.

The social issue: the establishment versus the challengers, the "haves" versus the "have-nots."

The efficiency issue: large farms versus small farms.

The legal issue: the use of administrative discretion versus strict interpretation of the law.

The economic issue: how resources are to be allocated and rewards bestowed.

The subsidy question: who gets how much from the federal treasury.

The political issue, embracing all the above.

The controversy over the 160-acre limitation is of far greater importance than would appear from considering only the number of people directly involved or the number of dollars at stake.

Various areas of the world have been able to achieve economic development despite limited water supplies. Israel is a notable example. The problem is not above solution. But treating scarce water as if it were a free good does not appear to be a solution.

Possible courses of action for dealing with the 160-acre limitation include the following: New legislation increasing the acreage limit from 160 to 320 acres and removing the residency requirement. This is the initiative taken by the affected landowners (Farm/Water 1978). Strict enforcement of the 160-acre limit, the position taken by the challengers. A compromise position, the strategy of the Interior Department. Fundamental changes in the system, advocated by various people. Interesting changes are proposed by Seckler and Young (1978, pp. 585–88). They propose that the government control the water, not the land. Hitherto the idea has been to control the water indirectly through controlling the land. There would be a two-tier water pricing system. There would be a base price (below cost) for water up to a certain limited amount. Beyond that amount, the price of water would be market-determined. The base price would be higher than the present price, reducing the subsidy and the windfall gains accruing to new owners of land and water rights. Base water rights would be limited to bona fide farmers. The person who receives the water rights would have to live on the farm, manage it, and not sell his base water rights. Cost of water for leased land would be the market price, not the base price. If the land were sold, it would be sold at the preproject price.

This approach would give each farmer a choice. If he wanted to play by the rules of the market, he could buy himself out of governmental regulation by paying the market price for water. If he wanted to benefit from the lower price for base water, then he would have to play by the rules of the administrators.

If past experience is a guide, there is not likely to be a clear-cut or settled choice of one of these alternatives over the others during the decade of the eighties.

Earlier in this book I made the point that agriculture is losing its uniqueness. This change has profound significance for water and for the West. Preference in water use was given to farmers on the basis of agriculture's uniqueness. As agriculture loses its uniqueness and enters the mainstream of economic life, to that same degree the case for preferred agricultural access to water is eroded. We saw in the previous chapter that economic and political forces weaken agriculture's ability to compete nationwide with nonfarm people for the use of land. In the West these forces weaken the farmer's hold on water as well.

REFERENCES

Bergland, Bob (Secretary of Agriculture). 1978. Letter to Cecil B. Andrus, Secretary of the Interior, January 25. Released to the public.

Brewer, Michael F. 1964. Economics of public water pricing: The California case. In *Economics and public policy in water resource development,* ed. Stephen C. Smith and Emery N. Castle, pp. 222–47. Ames: Iowa State University Press.

Cutler, Rupert M. 1978. *Water resources: New initiatives.* Address before the 25th annual National Watershed Congress, June 26. Toronto, Canada.

Dewsnup, Richard L., and Jensen, Dallin W., eds. 1973. A summary. In *Digest of state water laws.* Washington, D.C.: National Water Commission.

Farm/Water. 1978. *The Farm Water Act of 1978: Summary of S2818.* Washington, D.C.: National Alliance to Modernize the 1902 Water Law (L'Enfant Plaza).

Hibbard, B. H. 1939. *A history of public land policies.* New York: Peter Smith Company.

Hinds, Eugene. 1977. The acreage limitation provisions of reclamation law. Paper delivered to American Farm Bureau Federation Conference on Federal Acreage Limitation, Denver, Colorado.

Hutchins, Wells A. 1956. *The California law of water rights.* Sacramento: USDA, Agricultural Research Service.

Kelso, Maurice M.; Martin, William E.; and Mack, Lawrence E. 1973. *Water supplies and economic growth in an arid environment: An Arizona case study.* Tucson: University of Arizona Press.

North, R. M., and Neely, W. P. 1977. *A model for achieving consistency for cost-sharing in water resource programs.* Water Resource Bulletin 13 (pp. 945–1007).

President of the United States. 1978. Water policy message, June 6.

Richard, John B. 1977. The scramble for water: Agriculture versus other interests in Wyoming. Paper presented at the Agricultural Policy Symposium, Washington Policy Studies Organization, USDA, and the Farm Foundation.

————. 1978. The scramble for water: Agriculture versus other interests in Wyoming. In *The new politics of food,* ed. Don H. Hadwiger and William P. Browne. Lexington: D. C. Heath.

Robie, Ronald B. 1977. Pressures created by a severe drought on water institutions. *American Journal of Agricultural Economics* 59:938–42.

Seckler, David, and Young, Robert A. 1978. Economic and policy implications of the 160 acre limitation in federal reclamation law. *American Journal of Agricultural Economics,* vol. 60, no. 4.

Smith, Stephen C., and Castle, Emery N., eds. 1964. *Economics and public policy in water resource development.* Ames: Iowa State University Press.

Taylor, Paul S. 1971. The 160 acre law. In *California water,* ed. David Seckler, pp. 251–62. Berkeley: University of California Press.

Tijoriwala, Anilkumar G.; Martin, William E.; and Bower, Leonard G. 1968. *The structure of the Arizona economy: Output interrelationships and their effects on water and labor requirements.* Part 1. *The input-output model and its interpretation.* Arizona Experiment Station Technical Bulletin 180. Part 2. *Statistical supplement.* Department of Agricultural Economics File Report 68–1. Tucson: University of Arizona.

U.S. Commission on Organization of the Executive Branch of the Government. 1955. *Task force report on water resources and power,* vol. 1. Washington, D.C.: Government Printing Office.

U.S. Department of Agriculture. 1978. *The U.S. Department of the Interior's proposed rules for enforcement of the Reclamation Act of 1902: An economic impact analysis.* ESCS–04. Washington, D.C.: Economics, Statistics, and Cooperatives Service.

White House. 1978. *Water policy message: Detailed background.* Press release, June 6.

15. Energy and Food

Beginning in 1973 came a series of events that together produced what became known as "the energy crisis": the oil embargo, the sharp increase in the price of fuel, the growing realization that the supply of fossil fuels is finite, increases in oil imports, and a worsening balance of payments. There came a widespread belief that the market for fuel, as we had long known it, could not cope with events of this magnitude. In the absence of government intervention, actual and prospective windfall profits to the oil companies would exceed what the public would consider tolerable levels. So began the search for "an energy policy."

Agriculture is affected by these events, as is every sector of the economy. In this chapter I shall examine the possible effect on agriculture of the new and prospective energy situation. I shall consider what policy issues are likely to arise, what alternatives are available, and what might be the consequences of pursuing the various alternatives. The probable lineup of the respective antagonists will be indicated and, if courage permits, some prognoses will be offered. The analysis will be limited to agriculture; there will be no effort to address overall energy policy.

The assessment of the fuel situation that underlies this chapter is a fairly conventional one.

For the next ten years there is unlikely to be a major breakthrough in fuel technology. While there may be significant scientific advances and an increase in the use of nuclear power, these initiatives are not likely to produce such a volume of new fuel, within the decade, as to greatly relieve our dependence on conventional fuels. We are likely to rely, during the 1980s, on much the same

Table 10. Direct and Indirect Energy Use in the Food System, 1974

Activity	Percentage of Total U.S. Use
Production	2.9
Processing	4.8
Marketing	1.3
Consumption level preservation and preparation in home	4.3
Consumption level preservation and preparation away from home	2.8
Transportation across the system	2.5[a]
Total	16.5

SOURCE: Federal Energy Administration.

[a]Some of this amount is included in the earlier activities; so the column will sum to more than 16.5.

fuels as we now use. The United States will be so heavily dependent on imported fuel as to make us highly vulnerable to an interruption of supplies.

Prices of fuel will be higher than they were before the events of 1973. They are likely to increase both absolutely and relatively from 1978 levels.

Table 10 shows that food uses 16.5 percent of the nation's energy. Food uses about 17 percent of the consumer's income. The two numbers are nearly the same; compared with the rest of the economy, the food system is neither fuel-intensive nor fuel-sparing.

Within the food system, the big fuel users are processing, transportation, and preparation of food for the table. Farmers receive 40 percent of the consumer's food dollar, but they use only 18 percent of the energy that goes into a dollar's worth of food. Obviously, if big fuel savings are to be made in the food system they will have to be made after the product leaves the farmer's gate.

Farmers rely on the various fuels as follows:

Gasoline and diesel	58 percent
Electricity	24 percent
Liquefied petroleum and natural gas	18 percent

Of the energy used in agricultural production, 31 percent goes for making nitrogen fertilizer, and 13 percent is for irrigation fuel. These are the two biggest uses. Other substantial uses are fuel for drying crops and motor fuel. All together, farmers' direct expenditures for fuel equal 5 percent of the value of the products they sell.

The most vulnerable farm practice, from the standpoint of rising fuel cost, is pump irrigation, especially as water tables decline. As fuel prices increase, some acres, previously irrigated, will shift to dryland farming. This is already occurring. Nitrogen fertilizer, for which natural gas is the feedstock, is also vulnerable. But farmers showed, during 1974, that they could and would pay high prices for nitrogen.

PROPOSALS

Let us examine four proposals that have been offered, intended to deal with the prospective energy situation as it relates to agriculture.

Favorable Pricing and Allocation of Farm Inputs

There are proposals that fuel be allocated to farmers in amounts and at prices based on the past, thus protecting farm people from the need for adjusting to the new fuel situation. In support of these proposals, agriculture's alleged uniqueness is asserted. The critical importance of assuring an adequate food supply is attested. The familiar goal, maintaining net farm income, is invoked. A new goal is set up—averting regional decline. The attractiveness of preferential treatment is very great. A pertinent comment comes from Otto Doering (1977, p. 1069): "if the agricultural sector is effectively shielded from energy price increases and shortages it will be a technological dinosaur by the time the rest of the economy finally insists that it rejoin the real world."

We have seen in the preceding chapter how far from efficient resource use we can get when we seal ourselves off from the competitive discipline. All the problems of black marketing and all the inequities of rationing are implicit in a system involving allocation and price control.

Low-Energy Agriculture

Various studies have been made of the energy balance in agriculture—that is, the calories of energy produced in relation to the calories of energy used in the production process. While these studies vary in method and in findings, they are alike in one respect; they show that agriculture in the aggregate consumes more energy than it produces (Pimentel et al. 1973, pp. 443–48; Perelman 1977). The studies show that the energy balance for modern scientific farming is poorer than for low-technology agriculture, and that the energy balance for American agriculture today is worse than it was a quarter-century ago. This has led to proposals that we move away from energy-intensive agriculture, that we use less fertilizer, fewer pesticides, less mechanical power. The Agency for International Development has been urged to advocate low-energy-using forms of agriculture in its overseas technical assistance programs.

The error in these proposals comes from failing to put proper price tags on all the various inputs and outputs of energy used and produced in agriculture. Agriculture takes low-value calories (petroleum) and converts them to high-value calories (food). To compare inputs with outputs while ignoring value differences is, as Job says, to "darken counsel by words without knowledge" (38:2). Another error comes from failing to take account of all the inputs. The radiant energy of the sun is left out of these calculations. Modern agriculture produces abundant leaf surface and thus catches enormous amounts of radiant energy, provided at zero cost. It minimizes the use of human energy, which is inefficient and expensive. Premodern agriculture has opposite attributes.

Pesticides come in for special criticism because their manufacture requires large amounts of fossil fuel. But these products are basically energy-efficient inputs in terms of the resources they replace (Berry 1978, p. 4). Using non-mechanized farming, an acre of Maine potatoes could be produced with ninety-six hours of labor. But labor costs would exceed the value of the potatoes (Council for Agricultural Science and Technology 1977). One study indicated that controlling weeds by hand in corn production increased the energy yield by 0.2 million kilocalories per acre. However, at 1976 costs of labor and herbicides, the net profit on the plots with weeds controlled by herbicides was seventy-eight dollars an acre; on the hand-weeded plots there was a net loss of sixty-six dollars an acre (Green and McCullock 1976, pp. 95–100).

If we were really intent on saving energy in the food system and having a low-energy form of agriculture, we could accomplish this by changing our diets. We could consume grain directly rather than feeding these crops to livestock and then eating the resulting meat, milk, and eggs. This would reduce agriculture's energy needs to a fraction of the present level. But so great a change in diet is unacceptable to the public. Low-energy agriculture based on dietary change, like low-energy agriculture based on premodern methods, is a computational curiosity. Both proposals lack policy potential.

Fuel from Farm Crops

The sun is and has always been the source of all energy. Millions of years ago it produced the plant growth that became our supply of petrochemicals. The proposal is made to produce a continuing supply of organic matter and extract fuel from it. We would then be obtaining fuel from a renewable resource rather than from a dwindling asset. Corn, an efficient converter of solar energy into biomass, is proposed as the candidate crop. If corn could be converted into fuel, we might simultaneously solve the agricultural surplus and help meet the energy problem. The idea is attractive to farmers, ecologists, agribusiness firms, and politicians.

The technical feasibility of getting fuel from farm crops is one of the few things on which everyone is agreed. Alcohol from farm crops makes an excellent fuel. It was used during the Great Depression, when corn was cheap. It was used during World War II, when fuel was scarce. It has long been used in Brazil, as a supply-management device, when sugar is in excess supply. It is now being used in that country as a continuing program.

The most common proposal is to mix 10 percent grain alcohol with 90 percent gasoline to produce a fuel called "gasohol." For advocacy of gasohol, see Fricke 1977; Scheller and Mohr 1976; Scheller 1977; and Long-Rock 1975.

While most advocates of gasohol concede that the product is not now economically feasible, they cite arguments for introducing considerations other than current cost-benefit analysis: Fuel prices will rise, putting the product in the black. Technology will advance, lowering production costs and making it pay. We have excess agricultural capacity. In 1978 we idled nineteen million acres and incurred costs and loans totaling $7.9 billion. If a subsidy is needed to support the gasohol program, the cost should be judged against the cost of paying farmers to immobilize part of our farm plant.

Opponents of gasohol advance a series of strong arguments. For opposition to gasohol see Kendrick and Murray 1978; Illinois Farm Bureau 1978; and Schruben 1978.

Argument one: The energy balance is adverse. More energy is used up in making a gallon of alcohol than there is in the gallon after it is made. The only man who finds a positive energy balance is Dr. Scheller of the University of Nebraska, and his anlysis is subject to question (Illinois Farm Bureau 1978, p. i). Thus says Peter J. Reilly, associate professor in the Department of Agricultural Engineering at Iowa State University (1978): "The total amount of fossil fuel necessary to produce 2.6 gallons of ethanol from a bushel of corn is between 339,000 and 394,000 BTUs. Burning the ethanol yields only 218,000 BTUs. Therefore it cannot be claimed that producing ethanol by fermentation of corn produces energy. The opposite is instead true. This process, if used on a large scale, will worsen the U.S. energy situation."

The point is relevant. But simple energy-balance computations are misleading. Price tags must be attached to the different forms of energy. A thousand

BTUs in the form of fuel alcohol to run a car are worth more than a thousand BTUs in the form of the coal used in the fermentation process.

Farm people should beware of relying on simple energy-balance computations as a basis for policy decisions. Agriculture itself, in the aggregate, has an adverse energy balance; we use up more energy than we produce. Human beings have an adverse energy balance. If energy balance were the sole criterion of policy decisions, human beings would be consigned to the dustbin of history. *Argument two: A sizable subsidy would be necessary.* Kendrick and Murray estimate that a subsidy of nine cents a gallon would be required to promote sales of gasohol (1978, p. 36). Tyner and Okos of Purdue University say the pump price of gasohol would be 10 percent higher than that of gasoline (1978, p. 6). The Republican Conference of the United States Senate puts the required subsidy at four to nine cents a gallon (1977, p. 50). Other studies report other numbers. Clearly, under present conditions substantial subsidy would be required. The price of grain alcohol at distilleries in the fall of 1977 was $1.40 per gallon (U.S. Senate, Republican Conference 1977, p. 44), two and a half to three times the refinery price of gasoline. Gordon Leith, vice-president of Farmland Industries, says, "Blending alcohol with gasoline is like stretching hamburger with filet mignon." Tyner and Okos say that for a grain alcohol program to operate economically, corn would have to be priced at seventy-five cents a bushel, one-third of its 1977 price. They summarize thus: "About 7.1 million barrels of gasoline are being consumed each day in the United States. This amounts to 108.8 billion gallons of gasoline each year. If six cents of tax is exempted from each gallon of gasohol, the total value of the subsidy would be $6.5 billion each year, or thirty dollars for every man, woman, and child in this country" (1978, p. 7).

What of the prognosis that fuel costs are going to increase and that therefore the size of the subsidy needed will in time diminish? The change would not be as great as many people think. If the price of energy goes up, production cost for gasohol also goes up; fuel is a substantial part of production costs. Rising prices of energy would appear on the debit as well as the credit side of the ledger.

Argument three: The proposal is no solution to the energy problem. The volume of gasoline we consume is so great that only a small part of it could be replaced by grain alcohol. It would take half the nation's corn crop to produce the 10.9 billion gallons of ethanol required to make the 10 percent blend (Tyner and Okos 1978, p. 7). To supply gasohol and feed the nation as well, a sharp increase in agricultural production would be required. This would bring into use fragile, erosive land and jeopardize our land resource. Topsoil washed down the Mississippi and discharged into the Gulf of Mexico is no more renewable than oil pumped out of the ground and burned.

Gasohol has more potency as an income-boosting program for farmers and agribusiness than it does as a solution to the energy problem. Significantly, the support for it comes from the farm and agribusiness sectors rather than from those responsible for energy policy. It has some of the attributes of a solution in search of a problem.

Argument four: Excess agricultural capacity is not assured. Only a few years ago many people thought agriculture would be unable to feed the world's people. Now the thought is that it can supply not only food but a part of our energy as well. The one view may be as wrong as the other. A huge fuel alcohol complex is difficult to turn off and on, with varying market conditions.

Argument five: Substantial changes in farm and food prices would result. A gasohol program capable of producing a 10 percent blend any time in the foreseeable future is inconceivable. It would skyrocket retail food prices to an unacceptable level. Even a modest program, involving 132 million bushels instead of the 4,270 million required for a 10 percent blend, nationwide, might increase the price of corn by twenty-five cents a bushel and increase gross farm income of corn producers by $1.5 billion (Kendrick and Murray 1978, pp. 43–44). But the by-products (distillers' dried grains) would depress prices of other protein feeds such as wheat-mill feeds and soybean meal. The farm community is not of one mind on the gasohol issue.

Fuel from Farm Wastes

Some people advocate producing fuel alcohol from cornstalks and other by-products of the farm enterprise. Technically this can be done. Recent discoveries at Purdue University improve the feasibility of extracting alcohol from cellulosic material. At this time, pilot operations are being launched in Florida, using bagasse, the residue from sugarcane processing. Costs and benefits are not now known. According to Stephens and Heichel (1974), we produce 800 million tons of residues each year, dry weight basis (Price 1978, p. 13). If all this biomass could somehow be collected and converted to energy, the yield would be equivalent to about a billion barrels of oil annually. But there are complications: gathering, storing, technical problems of conversion, huge amounts of energy required in the process, removing organic matter that should go back into the land, and exposing the soil to erosion.

What are the chances that the market for energy in agriculture will be allowed to function in something like its historic pattern during the 1980s? To me, the chances seem good. There will be difficulties, as with the pricing of any dwindling resource. Except in a few areas and for a few commodities, energy for agricultural production is so valuable and so efficient that farmers can afford to bid for it against other enterprises. Fuel for lifting irrigation water is an exception to this generalization.

Large-scale use of fuel from renewable resources seems an unlikely prospect in the United States, at least in the foreseeable future. The fossil fuels were grown free of charge millions of years ago and stored underground at zero cost. There they are, waiting for us to pump or dig them out. They are so efficient that we will probably continue to rely on them until they are much nearer exhaustion than they will become during the decade of the 1980s.

Ill-considered energy proposals are full of danger. In combination, diverting a substantial share of our agricultural resources to gasohol production and restricting the use of energy-intensive inputs could place our food supply in real jeopardy.

Energy savings can be made in high-yield modern agriculture. This can be done by reduced tillage and by judicious use rather than overuse of farm chemicals. This modest and undramatic response to the energy situation is perhaps the most realistic objective for the decade ahead.

REFERENCES

Berry, John H. 1978. Pesticides and energy utilization. Paper presented at the American Association for the Advancement of Science, Washington, D.C.

Council for Agricultural Science and Technology. 1977. *Energy conservation in agriculture*. Report 68. Washington, D.C.

Doering, Otto C., III. 1977. Agriculture and energy use in the year 2000. *American Journal of Agricultural Economics* 59: 1066–70.

Fricke, Charles R. 1977. Gasohol defended. Letter to the editor. *Lincoln* (Neb.) *Star*, November 7.

Green, Maurice B., and McCullock, Archie. 1976. Energy considerations in the use of herbicides. *Journal of Science Food Agriculture* 27:95–100.

Illinois Farm Bureau. 1978. *Gasohol: Current status and potential for the future*. Bloomington: Commodities Division Research Report.

Kendrick, James G., and Murry, Pamela J. 1978. *Grain alcohol in motor fuels: An evaluation*. Report no. 81. Lincoln: Nebraska Agricultural Experiment Station.

Long-Rock J.V. Study Group. 1975. Grain alcohol study summary. Prepared for Indiana Department of Commerce, Indianapolis, Indiana.

Peart, Robert M. 1978. *Process gas from organic residues: Corn cobs*. I Seminario Sobre Energia de Biomassas no Nordeste, Universidade Federal do Ceara, August 15–18, Fortaleza, Brasil.

Perelman, Michael. 1977. *Farming for profit in a hungry world: Capital and the crisis in agriculture.* New York: Universe Books; Montclair, N.J.: Allenheld, Osmun.

Pimentel, David; Hurd, L. E.; Bellotti, A. C.; Forster, M. J.; Oka. I. N.; Sholes, A. D.; and Whitman, R. J. 1973. Food production and the energy crisis. *Science* 182:443–48.

Price, D. R. 1978. *Fuel, food, and the future.* Ithaca: Cornell University.

Reilly, Peter J. 1978. Gasohol remains energy guzzler. *Iowa Stater,* February.

Scheller, William A. 1977. The use of ethanol-gasoline mixtures for automotive fuel. Paper presented at the Symposium on Clean Fuels from Biomass and Wastes. Orlando, Fla.: Institute of Gas Technology.

Scheller, William A., and Mohr, Brian J. 1976. Net energy analysis of ethanol production. Paper presented at the 171st national meeting, American Chemical Society, Division of Fuel Chemistry, New York, New York.

Schruben, Leonard W. 1978. Evaluation of Kansas Senate bills 591 and 592 as related to agricultural ethyl alcohol as a motor fuel. Statement before the Committee on Transportation and Utilities, Kansas Legislature, Topeka, Kansas.

Stephens, G. R., and Heichel, G. H. 1974. *Proceedings, NSFS Special Seminar on Cellulose as a Chemical and Energy Resource.* Berkeley: University of California.

Tyner, Wallace, and Okos, Martin. 1978. *Alcohol production from agricultural products: Facts and issues.* CES Paper 29. West Lafayette, Ind.: Purdue University.

U.S. Department of Agriculture. 1978. *Gasohol from grain: The economic issues.* ESCS 11. Washington, D.C.: USDA, Economics, Statistics, and Cooperatives Service.

———. 1978. Residues: A valuable commodity. In *Agricultural research.* Washington, D.C.: USDA, Economic Research Service.

U.S. Senate. 1977. *Economic feasibility of gasohol.* Hearings of the Subcommittee on Agricultural Research and General Legislation, Committee on Agriculture, Nutrition, and Forestry. Indianapolis, Indiana, December 22. Washington, D.C.: Government Printing Office.

U.S. Senate. Republican Conference. 1977. *Alcohol: The renewable fuel from our nation's resources.* Staff report. Washington, D.C.: Government Printing Office.

16. The Future of the Family Farm

In 1910, 35 percent of our population lived on farms—farms that were mostly small in terms of acreage and capital invested. In 1979, fewer than 4 percent of Americans live on farms, and these farms average nearly three times as much acreage and use six times as much mechanized power and machinery (in real terms) as in 1910 (Carter and Johnston 1978, p. 742).

Is the family farm an endangered species, like the blue whale and the California condor? The answer depends on how you define family farm. If you define it in historical terms—the operator and his family supplying all the factors of production (land, labor, capital, and management)—it is indeed in danger. But if you define it as a farm on which the farmer and his family supply most of the labor, then the family farm is doing fairly well. Thus defined, family farms constitute 95 percent of all farms and produce about two-thirds of all farm products for sale. These percentages have not changed appreciably for decades (Nikolitch 1972, p. 4).

Family farms, however defined, are fewer in number, of course. A corn belt farmer with modern equipment can cultivate many times the number of acres his grandfather, farming with horses, could handle. Mechanization led to farms' being consolidated.

A modern farm, big enough to supply a labor return equivalent to what a person of equivalent ability could earn in town, might involve an investment of half a million dollars or more. Hottel and Barry (1978) report capital requirements needed to generate gross farm sales of $40,000 to $60,000 a year, based on 1976 asset values: livestock ranches, $573,000; fruits and nuts, $285,000. Net returns would be some fraction of the gross. These are farms of moderate

184

size: if the operator of such a farm had little equity in the land and was without off-farm income, he would not be doing very well.

Not only have the capital requirements of modern agriculture increased; the managerial skill needed to operate a modern farm is also very great. Not every farm-raised young man can qualify. So a new idea has come into agriculture—or, rather, an old idea, long used in industry, is being applied. Capital, land, and labor are now obtained separately and, under good management, combined in optimum fashion. This is the idea that transformed the hand loom into the textile factory and the ironmonger's shop into the steel plant. It is transforming agriculture, and some people do not like the result.

Some sectors of agriculture already have been remade along industrial lines—poultry for one. The broiler industry now probably bears a closer organizational resemblance to the automobile industry than to the traditional farm. Is this case unique or does it foreshadow the future? Is it prototype or aberration? Ask this question of any group of farmers, and you are assured of a heated argument.

Alarmists see all kinds of dire events impending if the family farm is replaced by the large-scale corporate farm (Berry 1977). A valuable way of life would be lost. they say. The family farm represents, in the minds of many, an idealized form of preindustrial living, the son apprenticed to the father, living close to nature and producing the most needed product of all, the older people spending their lives in usefulness and dignity. The basic idea comes from John Locke. It was articulated clearly by the French physiocrats, particularly Quesnay. It was powerfully advocated in this country by Thomas Jefferson. It is discernible, in modified form, in the rural communes that were set up some years ago by young people in various parts of the country. Those who hold this agrarian belief fear that agricultural production might become dominated by a few huge agribusiness firms, which would then use their monopoly power to extort high prices from the American public. They fear any system that involves absentee owners holding land in large tracts. They are apprehensive about a hereditary landowning elite. This concern is not unique to our country. "Land to the tiller" has been a rallying call in much of the world for most of the twentieth century. The family farm, it is said, is not just a way of producing crops and livestock; it is a way of producing people—good people. Oliver Goldsmith said it well many years ago in *The Deserted Village:*

> Princes and lords may flourish or may fade;
> A breath can make them, as a breath has made;
> But a bold peasantry, their country's pride,
> When once destroy'd, can never be supplied.

"Romantic nonsense," say those who believe in modern agriculture. What is unique about agriculture? Why should agriculture be organized on a family basis when practically everything else is industrialized? If a large-scale corporate farm can produce food and fiber at a lower cost than a family farm, it should be free to do so. So goes the argument. Such industrialization of agriculture as has already occurred has reduced the price of food, not increased it. Witness broilers and turkeys. Besides, say these advocates of an industrialized agriculture, the merit of the family farm was a myth in the first place. Farmers exploited their children and deprived them of education. Are people of family farm background really superior citizens? The evidence is in dispute, and the contention is denied by some (Griswold 1948). How frail democracy would be if it depended on an agricultural base! In 1969, agriculture as a proportion of the labor force was 4.5 percent in the United States, 2.9 percent in the United Kingdom, 9.5 percent in West Germany, and 14.7 percent in France (Beer et al. 1973, p. 752). Many of those who praise the family farm do so from their air-conditioned downtown offices, having long ago left its drudgery and deprivation. Their advocacy of the family farm is the result of selective memory.

Can the family farm compete? Or is it doomed to lose out to the corporate farm? Is there enough merit in the family farm so that we should try to keep it, even if there is some penalty in the form of higher food costs? What is needed in the way of adjustments if it is to succeed? Who will control agriculture? These are the public policy questions.

FIRST, THE FACTS

Much of the discussion regarding the family farm is like the old kerosene lamp—more noteworthy for heat than for light. In accordance with the belief that more facts mean fewer factions, I shall quantify and analyze some of the major trends affecting the family farm.

Trends in Size and Number

Figure 2 shows, dramatically, what has been happening to the size and number of farms in the United States. The chart needs little elaboration. In 1976 there were only 43 percent as many farms as in 1910, and acreage per farm had gone from 139 acres to 393. The big change occurred during World War II and the postwar period.

In political circles, rhetorically at least, these trends are almost universally

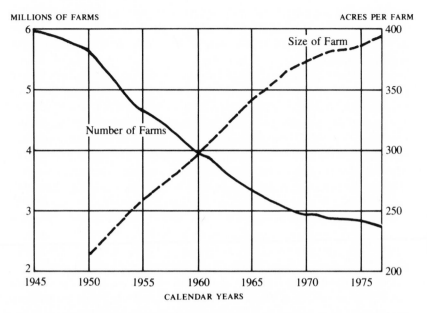

MILLIONS OF FARMS   ACRES PER FARM

FIGURE 2. The changing United States farm sector, 1945–77; number of farms and number of acres per farm. From U.S. Department of Agriculture (1977, p. 422).

deplored. At the same time, there is political support for the programs that have helped produce them.

The trend toward larger and fewer firms is not restricted to agriculture. Automobile firms, airlines, food processors, schools, churches, and retail groceries are all becoming larger and fewer. The same is true of government. In the Midwest, the townships, the smallest units, have almost disappeared, their functions absorbed by the next larger units, the counties, and even by the states and in some cases by the federal government. The reasons for the trends in the nonfarm sector appear to be similar to those that have been operative in agriculture. In non-agricultural enterprises, the trends were a cause of some apprehension, true enough. Concern led, for example, to restraints in the form of limitations on mergers. But, for the greater part, structural changes outside of agriculture were accepted, either as the evidence of progress or as the price thereof. "Bigger is better" has had considerable standing as an ethic in the nonfarm sector. In agriculture, however, the trends appear to be viewed with greater misgiving. This is largely because of the agrarian tradition, the mystique of the family farm and the residual degree of agriculture's uniqueness.

In any case, it is ironic that, in agriculture, public policy inadvertently helped produce the technology responsible for the trends. Modernization and technology were the key, though various other causes are alleged. The corporations, the government, agribusiness, foreign investors, and city buyers of farmland are among the alleged villains.

A very important thing needs to be said at this point. Had farm numbers not declined, farm income would necessarily have been divided among larger numbers of people, and the share per farmer would have been smaller. When we lament the reduction in the number of farmers, we should compare our pain with the alternative: low per capita farm incomes and the limited economic growth that would have been associated with pinning down a larger share of our population in food production.

What has been the effect of public policy on the size and number of farms? Despite the speeches in favor of the small farmer and occasional widely publicized preferential legislation on his behalf, the net effect of public policy has been to speed up the trend toward fewer and larger farms.

Publicly supported research and extension. This generates new technology, which generally requires large farms for its efficient use. The technology is offered to all farmers, cafeteria style, and is picked up most avidly by the larger operators. This speeds up the trend toward larger and fewer farms. Up to a point this is desirable.

The commodity programs. These provide income support on a per bushel basis, thereby putting thousands of dollars into the pockets of those already well off and giving limited help to those with little to sell. One percent of the farmers, those with large farms, receive 29 percent of all the government program payments (General Accounting Office 1978, p. iii). The commodity programs have helped the big operators take over the small ones (Cochrane and Ryan 1976, p. 52). The effect of the commodity program on farm enlargement has been marginal, not major. Farms increased in size whether they were in the programs or not. Nevertheless, the directional tendency of the commodity programs has been to put additional pressure on the small farms.

Features of federal tax laws. Various institutional arrangements combine to give added purchasing power to prospective land buyers in high income brackets. These include: the privilege of using cash-basis accounting, preferential taxation of any prospective capital gains, deductibility of interest on borrowed funds as a business expense in computing income tax liability, investment tax credit, and several methods of computing accelerated depreciation (Raup 1978, p. 304). These taxing provisions favor the large farmer over the small one. For example, a prosperous farmer with a combined federal and state marginal income tax rate of 33 percent and a seven-year depreciation schedule can obtain a present-valued tax saving over seven years equivalent to approximately 40 percent of the cost of a new item of equipment. If his marginal rate is 10 percent, the saving is only 18 percent. If he is really poor and has no net taxable income, he must pay full price for the equipment (Fuller 1977). Another form of tax preference is a recent change in federal taxation that makes it easier to keep a large farm in the family when the owner dies (Harl 1978). What might result is something like a hereditary landowning class, not really compatible with an agriculture open to young farmers.

Size and Efficiency

There is much talk about farms having to be large to be efficient. This argument is put forward by those who operate superlarge farms. There is a blend of truth, propaganda, and self-deception in this contention.

The true measure of efficiency is cost per unit of output. The evidence is that most of the efficiency of size, thus measured, has been achieved, in the irrigated cotton area of California, with farms of 320 acres (U.S. Department of Agriculture 1978*d*, pp. 53–54). Beyond that, added size means mostly added income from having more acres, and only to a minor extent added income from increased efficiency per unit of production. The average size of farm in the Westlands of California is 2,889 acres. The Department of Agriculture reports that in the corn belt, most of the efficiencies can be achieved on a one-man farm provided it has modern equipment (Bailey 1973).

Usually the larger farm attracts the more skilled manager; larger farms tend to be better managed than small ones. Thus a part of the seeming advantage of size is a reflection of better management rather than of size as such (Seckler and Young 1978, p. 576).

Of course, if the farm is larger the farmer gets the return from more acres and more capital investment. If he is objective, the operator of a superlarger farm should say he likes the big operation for a number of understandable reasons: it provides more income, it means greater net worth, it gives him more power and prestige, and it conforms to the American ethic that any successful business should grow. He should not claim that it is appreciably more efficient. *He* has an interest in having a superlarge farm. But *society* will not get its food much, if any, cheaper as a result.

The operator of a superlarge farm can legitimately say of any proposal to discriminate against the larger farms that such action would place a ceiling on individual opportunity. And he can ask this very tough question: "Why should there be a limit on individual opportunity in agriculture and not elsewhere?"

Clearly, if a limit is placed on individual opportunity in agriculture, some superior managers will turn their backs on farming and make their commitment elsewhere.

The relationship of size to efficiency is one of the oldest issues in agricultural economics. The subject has been treated recently and capably by Stanton (1978), Carter and Johnston (1978), Seckler and Young (1978), and U.S. Department of Agriculture (1978d).

Public concern about size of farm focuses not so much on efficiency as on the community effect. Many years ago a controversial study contrasted two California communities: Arvin, surrounded by large-scale agriculture, and Dinuba, in an area of small farms. The comparison showed the small-farm community to be superior as measured by commonly accepted criteria (Goldschmidt 1947).

More recently, a task force in California cautiously stated that: "There is some evidence that communities surrounded by small farms offer a higher quality of life (a larger local business community, more diversified and stable employment opportunities, more schools, parks and playgrounds, and more social and civic organizations) than towns with very large farms nearby" (Community Services Task Force Report 1977). The Department of Agriculture endorsed that conclusion by quoting it in its report (1978d, p. viii).

Those who oppose the trend toward larger and fewer farms can claim, with some legitimacy, that such farms endanger what is called the "quality of life." They cannot legitimately say that these trends mean higher food costs.

There are few very large farms and many very small farms (a skewed distribution, a statistician would say). The degree of concentration is increasing. In 1950, 103,000 of the country's biggest farms produced 26 percent of United States agriculture's cash receipts. Today, the largest 155,000 operators account for nearly 60 percent of agricultural sales (Beale 1978, p. 1). If present policies persist, concentration will increase further. The legitimate public policy question is whether this should be allowed to occur. The landholding pattern in much of the United States was developed as a protest against the landed estates of feudal Europe. There is apprehension lest we drift back toward the institutions from which we escaped. Efficiency is not the decisive consideration in this public policy issue, though the economist thinks it is.

Trends in Tenure and Debt

In 1900, 55.8 percent of the farmers held title, sometimes encumbered by debt, to all the land they operated. By 1974 this percentage had risen to 63.5 percent (U.S. Department of Agriculture 1977, p. 424). If a farmer holds title to part of the acreage he operates and rents additional land, he is called a part-owner. This is the typical route to farm enlargement. Part-owners aspire to become full owners, and many of them make it. Between 1900 and 1974 part-owners increased from 7.9 to 26.5 percent of all operators. Meanwhile, covering this same span of years, the percentage of tenants decreased from 35.3 to 10.9. In the South, share-cropping, once a major form of tenure, had diminished until it included only 7.4 percent of the farms. Clearly, absentee ownership is not now a dominant attribute of American agriculture.

Farm real estate debt rose between 1968 and 1978 from $25.1 billion to $64.2 billion (U.S. Department of Agriculture 1976, p. 426). But equity in farm real estate rose much faster, from $175 billion to $461.6 billion (U.S. Department of Agriculture 1978*b*, pp. 6, 18). The ratio of farm real estate debt to the value of farm real estate was virtually unchanged during this ten-year period, at about 12 to 13 percent. In aggregate terms, agriculture at this time is in strong financial condition. But some individual farmers are heavily in debt and are experiencing a serious cash-flow problem. Many of these were involved in the American Agriculture Movement of 1977–79.

Trends in Income

Since 1940, per capita disposable income of farm people has been below the corresponding figure for nonfarm people. But it has been closing the gap (U.S. Department of Agriculture 1978*c*, p. 37).

Year	Per capita disposable income, farm, as a percentage of nonfarm
1940	36.7
1950	58.1
1960	53.8
1970	74.1
1975	88.4
1977	81.8
1978	90.7

Had farms remained constant in size and had there been no diminution in their number, the per capita income figure for agriculture would have been much less than it is and the ratio drastically lower. Individual decisions by farm people to adjust farm size and farm numbers helped to keep the ratio from being worse than it is.

The differential income is the force that expedited migration off the farms, which in turn resulted from the industrialization of agriculture. The migration was voluntary, and so acceptable. Differential incomes, though deplored, were the least difficult way of achieving the necessary adjustment.

Trends in Contracting, Integrating, and Specialization

Years ago farms were distinct units. Most farmers bought their fuel and fertilizer from farm supply firms, produced a wide variety of products, and sold their crops in an open competitive market. All these things are changing. More and more farms are specialized rather than diversified. Increasingly (though still to a relatively small degree) they are part of a food system under single management, from manufacture of input items through production, processing, and merchandising. Tenneco, a conglomerate with an agricultural component, said in 1970: "Our goal in agriculture is integration from the seedling to the supermarket" (Robbins 1974, p. 64). When this happens some markets cease to function; title is not transferred as the product moves from stage to stage. When sale occurs, this increasingly is accomplished by contract rather than by competitive bidding in a central market. It gets more difficult to decide what is and what is not a farm, and what is the price of farm products.

How far has this gone? In 1970, about 22 percent of United States agricultural production was under contract or vertical integration (Mighell and Hoofnagle 1972, p. 4). Many of these arrangements involved no real impairment of farmers' decision-making, as, for example, a contract between a farmer cooperative and a milk distributor assuring a continued market. A few involved highly centralized management, such as a canning factory growing fruit for its own account. The incidence of contracting or vertical integration varied widely by commodity:

Crops	14 percent overall
Sugarcane and sugar beets	100 percent
Vegetables for processing	95 percent
Citrus fruits	85 percent
Livestock products	36 percent overall
Milk for drinking	98 percent
Broilers	97 percent
Turkeys	54 percent
Eggs	40 percent
Fed cattle	22 percent
Hogs	2 percent

Many of the percentages have since increased. Most of the specialization, contracting, and integrating have occurred with the willing acquiescence of the farm people involved. Concern about it comes primarily from farmers and non-farmers who view it from the outside. The trends worry some people on several counts. Farmers lose their unique and valued character; they become unidentified components of industrial firms. Farmers give up part of their decision-making role. Markets become thin in volume of commodity traded and more susceptible to manipulation.

But those who defend these trends offer counterarguments. Farmers who sell by contract rather than through central markets do not lose their freedom; the right to contract is one of the rights of a free man. Vertical integration, with production planning under a single well-informed management, results in a better allocation of resources, with fewer gluts and shortages. Risk can be shared throughout the system rather than being borne almost totally by the farmer-producer.

Specialization, vertical integration, and contract farming seem to have caught on most rapidly where certain conditions prevail. One is the existence of a large body of unused scientific knowledge that traditional family farmers are unwilling or unable to adopt. This was the case in broiler production. Another is the opportunity to link production directly with marketing, as with a new product like frozen concentrated orange juice.

Trends in Incorporation

No issue concerning the structure of agriculture is more contentious than corporate farming. The number of corporate farms rose from 8,200 in 1957 to 28,090 in 1974 (U.S. Congress 1978, p. 19). The 28,000 incorporated farms constituted 1 percent of all farms (Coffman 1973, p. 10). Most of the increase since 1957 came from the incorporation of family farms. Of the 21,500 farm corporations operating in 1969, 90 percent were family corporations, formed primarily for tax purposes, for managerial advantages, for better access to credit, and for easing transfer of the farm between generations (Coffman 1973, p. 4). These corporations are closely held; that is, they have ten or fewer shareholders. In most respects other than legal form, these farms are indistinguishable from ordinary large family farms.

The public concept of corporate farms is that they are large "factories in the field," owned and run by people outside the farming tradition. The nearest quantification available regarding the numbers of such units is given by statistics on farming corporations with more than ten stockholders. In 1969 there were 1,797 such corporations. They totaled about 0.06 percent of the total number of farms and produced 2.9 percent of total farm sales (U.S. Congress 1978, p. 20). Most of these corporate farms were in California, Texas, Hawaii, and Florida.

There is no indication that these corporations are going to take over agriculture. In recent years a number of large-scale farming corporations have failed, including Black Watch, Gates Rubber, CBK Agronomics, Multiphonics, and Great Western Land Company. Ralston Purina withdrew from its broiler operation.

There are good reasons for this poor record. For one thing, farmers have traditionally bid against one another to push the price of land up so high that it will provide—in current returns, over the years, and on the average—considerably less than the mortgage rate of interest. A farmer bids up the price of land because he looks on a farm not just as an income-earning enterprise but also as a place to live and as an assured way of continuing to do the work he prefers. Pride of ownership enters into it, and anticipation of inflation. The farmer would like to get a larger income from his investment but finds it hard to do so on land prices into which he has bid intangible wealth. Reluctantly he reconciles himself to a low return.

A farming corporation, however, has investors who get few of the fringe benefits that accrue to the owner-operator of the family farm. If the farming corporation had to buy into farm ownership at the going price of land and were equally as efficient as a family farmer, it could, over time and on the average, return to its shareholders less than they could get from nonfarm enterprises. Stated in another fashion, if the corporation went to the bankers to borrow, or to the market to sell bonds, it would have to pay more for its money than it could earn thereon. The family farmer, with his demonstrated (though grudging) willingness to accept a low return on his capital, is a very tough competitor.

For another thing, the family farmer has incentive beyond that of a hired manager. He is self-employed and self-supervised. He works long hours at planting time and during harvest as the need arises. He naturally directs his efforts wherever the payoff is greatest. He is always alert to the health of his herd or the condition of his crop; he will stay up all night, if need be, at lambing time. Contrast this with "the hireling, whose own the sheep are not." If times are hard the family farmer takes in his belt, pays himself a lower wage, and is there, ready to go, when things improve. Compare this with the handicaps of corporate farming: unionized wages, harvesttime strikes, limited working hours, prescribed working conditions, unmotivated labor, and the need for detailed supervision.

To all this, add that the large corporate farm (more than ten stockholders) must pay 48 percent of its net income to the federal government in taxes. The family farm pays no such tax.

The surest prediction in this book is that the 1980s will see no takeover of agriculture by corporate farms. The political campaign against the corporate farm has twin attractions: it is popular with the voters, and it is assured of success. These two things, rather than any real danger from corporate farming, account for the vigor of the campaign. Nothing is more attractive politically than to carry a popular banner in a sure victory.

Trends in Cooperation

Small and moderate-sized operations can better compete with large-scale farms and can improve their terms of trade by joining together in cooperatives. In 1973, about 31 percent of farm marketing was through cooperatives, and 26 percent of farm supplies were thus acquired (U.S. Department of Agriculture 1977). There are farm supply cooperatives, marketing cooperatives, and cooperative credit associations, irrigation companies, mutual insurance companies, rural telephone and electric companies, and breeding associations. From 1959 to 1972, gross business done by farmers' marketing cooperatives increased from $11.7 billion to $25.6 billion. Gross farm supply business increased during this same span of years from $3.6 billion to $8.8 billion (U.S. Department of Agriculture 1976, p. 494). Farmer cooperatives are used effectively in redressing what would otherwise be an economic disadvantage for small family farmers.

Trends in Part-time Farming

Here is an astounding fact: for those people categorized by the USDA as farmers (that is, they receive $250 or more annually from the sale of farm products or have more than ten acres and sell at least $50 worth), money earned off the farm averages a greater source of income than does the sale of farm products. Table 11 indicates that in 1977 only 39 percent of the income of farm people came from marketing of crops and livestock.

Part-time farming was formerly viewed as a temporary condition, leading eventually either to full-time employment off the farm or to full-time farming. But it is emerging as a stable form. Breimyer puts it well: ''Paradoxically, the farming likely to show the most staying power may be the part-time or retirement farm that does not need to depend solely on farm income for its viability'' (1977, p. 22). Increasingly, people on small farms continue to live in the country, among friends and relatives, enjoying a culture they know and appreciate. More and more they have the amenities of modern life: good schools, roads, electricity, telephone, water, sewer, television, and health services. They drive five or ten or twenty or forty miles to a job in town, taking off some time in the spring to plant and some time in the fall to harvest. They have the best of both

Table 11. Distribution of Farms, Cash Receipts, and Income per Farm by Value of Sales Class, 1977

Value of Sales Class (dollars)	Number of Farms (thousands)	Percentage of Farms	Percentage of Cash Receipts from Farming	Income per Farm[a] (dollars)	Percentage of Average Income from Farming
100,000 and over	162	6.0	52.6	47,946	80
40,000–99,999	348	12.9	25.6	24,513	75
20,000–39,999	321	11.9	11.1	16,949	59
10,000–19,999	311	11.5	5.4	14,453	35
5,000–9,999	302	11.2	2.7	14,875	18
2,500–4,999	304	11.2	1.4	16,067	9
Less than 2,500	958	35.3	1.2	16,595	9
Total	2,706	100.0	100.0	19,059	39

SOURCE: U.S. Department of Agriculture (1978c, pp. 53, 54, 60).

[a]Net income from farming plus off-farm income divided by number of farms.

worlds. For many, off-farm work has eliminated the one handicap of small-scale farming: low income. Increasingly, farm women are comporting themselves like urban women; they take jobs and add to family income.

This combination of farm and off-farm income has occurred throughout the entire profile of agriculture. Based on 1977 data, for small farms with sales less than $2,500, off-farm income brings in 91 percent of the average family's resources. For large farms with sales of more than $100,000, off-farm income accounts for 20 percent of the average dollar inflow (U.S. Department of Agriculture 1978c, p. 60).

Nonfarm income has grown in importance with the passage of time. From 1934 to 1975, nonfarm income per farm increased, in real terms, more than five times. The progression was fairly steady. From 1934 to 1960 the increase had an annual value of about 3.5 percent. From 1960 to 1974, the trend rate of growth was about 7 percent (Gardner 1976, pp. 15–16).

One would think this trend would warm the hearts of those who are concerned about the incomes of farm people. Think how advantageous this is: it provides most of its benefits to just that group in greatest need of augmented income; it has to it a steadiness not found in an agriculture unstable in both yield and price; and it provides the labor for our modern economy without either depopulating the countryside or thronging the overcrowded cities. Certainly a dollar earned off the farm will buy as much education or food or health and will pay as much tax as a dollar earned from farming. But among most farm lobby groups, part-time farming is deplored. It is cited às evidence that income from agriculture is so low that farmers are driven to these supplemental income sources. Probably the pain arises in part from this further evidence of agriculture's relative retreat. Besides, acknowledgment of nonfarm incomes of farm people as a major and growing component of their well-being would detract from the alleged importance of commodity programs. How can one argue that commodity programs are needed to help the small farmers if one acknowledges that on the average they get 91 percent of their income from nonfarm sources, and that many of them are not really poor?

Trends in Foreign Ownership of American Farmland

Japanese, German, Italian, and other foreign buyers have been purchasing farmland in the United States. The reasons seem to be several. First, there is the rise in American farmland prices and the expectation that the rise will continue; the desire to hedge against inflation is worldwide. Additionally, the adverse balance of payments and the resulting accumulation of American dollars in the hands of foreign investors leads to their investing these dollars in the country from which they came. The declining exchange value of the dollar is also a factor. It improves the relative attractiveness of the United States as a place to invest. Much concern has arisen regarding these investments. Various fears are expressed (Atkinson 1978, p. 11). There is concern that national sovereignty is threatened, that the land may be poorly managed and a national asset impaired, that foreign ownership might change the structure of local communities, and that the price of land will be bid up, putting it out of reach of young Americans who want to start farming.

What are the facts? In 1975 the Department of Commerce surveyed all foreign firms and individuals with direct investments in the United States. The study was difficult to make, and the results, though indicative, were not conclusive. According to that study, 4.9 million acres of United States land were owned by foreigners (U.S. Department of Commerce 1976). Adjusting this figure for holdings of nonfarm land and for small tracts that went unreported, Wunderlich tentatively concludes that this would still have been less than 1 percent of our 1.3 billion acres of privately owned land (1978, p. 1). The United States General Accounting Office, in a 1978 spot check of landownership in twenty-five counties of five states, found only 0.3 percent of the land owned by nonresident aliens (U.S. Department of Agriculture 1978a, p. 16). Hjort estimates that the annual value of farmland sold to foreign investors would amount to about $120 million. Even if that amount were doubled, foreign purchases would represent only about 1 percent of the annual value of sales of farmland in the United States (1978, p. 3–4). USDA statistics for 1976 show that 65 percent of the land transferred went to active farmers. The remainder went to local non-farmers, noncounty residents, and "others." By far the largest percentage of land sold was to expand the acreage of existing farms; in 1976 farm enlargement accounted for 63 percent of all farm purchases (Hjort 1978, p. 3).

Americans have very large investments abroad, both agricultural and other. There is illogic in denying to others investment privileges that we ourselves enjoy. Foreign buyers seem to be a minor force in the land market. But the issue has considerable political potential and will be before us, in some form, during the decade ahead.

These are the trends in size, numbers, institutional setting, legal form, source of income, and transactions in land, domestic and foreign. Can the family farm survive in such a transforming time? The answer one must give, based on the evidence, is that if the concept of the family farm is held in the mold of the past, it is doomed. But if it is given flexibility and the opportunity to adapt, it can survive. "The family farms of today are radically different from those of four decades ago—so much so that in philosophical, social, and political terms the concept of the family farm has lost much of the meaning implicit in that term throughout the nineteenth century" (Dorner 1977, p. 20).

With the family farm defined as a farm on which the farmer and his family supply the majority of the labor, family farmers will continue to fare well if allowed to continue making their own decisions.

PROPOSALS AND CONSEQUENCES

What to do? One alternative, always, is to do nothing; to continue as at present. The consequences of such a decision are reasonably predictable—fewer and larger farms, more specialization, more integration and contracting, more part-time farming, and more nonfarm income. The farmer will increasingly rely on nonfarm sources of capital. More land will be rented, more money will be borrowed, more specialized services will be hired. As it becomes increasingly difficult for the farmer to supply all the factors of production, he will gradually slough off providing the capital, owning the land, and even supplying the labor. He will retain to the last that most precious role of all, entrepreneurship—the decision-making function.

If that prospect is acceptable, there is no need to change public policy. If it is not, if the trends need to be slowed down or reversed, then various alternative actions should be considered. Very few people contend that these trends should be speeded up, and so I do not focus on that public policy alternative. Proposals for slowing down the trends may be grouped into two categories: those of substance and those unlikely to be effective.

Programs of Substance

Certain policy actions would probably be effective in slowing down or reversing the observed trends if they could be enacted. The attribute common to these proposals is that all are resisted by the power elite and so are unlikely to be adopted.

A progressive tax on farm real estate could quickly remove the attractiveness of superlarge farms. It would relate to accumulated wealth in land much as the progressive income tax relates to the annual flow of wealth. Very likely it would be validated legally in the same fashion as was the income tax. Virtually every established farm lobby group would resist this proposal.

Tough inheritance laws could be written. Instead of making it easier to pass large farms intact from one generation to another, as was the purpose and effect of recent legislation, the objective could be to force the breakup of such farms by tough inheritance tax laws. This would require sale of part of the land to pay the federal tax and would give young men a chance to buy land and start farming. Proposals of this kind run 180 degrees counter to the prevailing mood. This and other tough alternatives are listed simply to show that if the concern about larger and fewer farms is authentic there are ways of checking the trend.

Limitations on government payments could be tightened. If we had a low limit on government payments to farmers, large farms would be less able to take over small ones. But in the Agricultural Act of 1977, payment limits were increased from $20,000 to $45,000, evidence that this policy tool for helping small farmers is not likely to suffer from overuse.

Rural development could be pushed. Rural development means more nonfarm jobs in rural areas. It means that the rural labor supply will have attractive off-farm job opportunities and so will be less readily available for farm work. It means acknowledged status for part-time farming, and it means that part of the resources now devoted to research and extension for production agriculture would be diverted to this new clientele. With rural development to increase the flow of nonfarm income, small part-time farms would become more viable. But these developments are looked on with disfavor by the full-time large-scale farmers. The big operators want an abundant supply of labor, and they do not want research and extension workers to be spending time with part-time farmers. The big operators look on part-time farmers as unfair competition. "A part-time farmer can operate his farm for nothing if he is earning $10,000 a year in an off-farm job.'' So rural development wins little support from the farm lobby.

An interesting fact regarding the large farm–small farm controversy is this: the small farms have been to a degree co-opted by the large farms, where the real farm policy leadership lies (Raup 1978, p. 305). Most of the policy proposals outlined above, though they would slow and might even reverse the decline in the number of small farms, would in all likelihood be opposed by the small farmers as well as the large ones. The conclusion must be that strong actions to reverse the trend toward fewer and larger farms are unlikely to be seriously considered, to say nothing of being enacted.

Programs Likely to Be Ineffective

Following are half a dozen proposals that have been put forward as ways of slowing the trend toward fewer and larger farms; all of them, however, deal with the form of the problem rather than with its substance.

Increased farm price supports are often proposed as a means of saving the small farmer. Enough has been said in this and previous chapters to indicate that action of this kind, if it remains in the general form of the past forty-five years, is more likely to hasten the demise of the small farm than to lengthen its life. There are proposals to have a two-tier system of commodity programs, with larger benefits for the small farmers. This is based on the supposition that small farmers are poor. Some of them are. But many have substantial off-farm income and are in reasonably good circumstances. This would have to be taken into account.

Prohibiting farming corporations is popular counsel in many areas. North Dakota, Kansas, Minnesota, Oklahoma, and South Dakota all have anticorporate farm laws of various kinds (U.S. Congress 1978, pp. 20–21). But, as has been shown, corporate farming is not a major threat to family farming. Furthermore, flat prohibition of farming corporations would mean that family farms could not incorporate. This would deprive them of a useful means of dealing with the business problems of modern agriculture.

Prohibiting contract farming is the prescription of some. There are proposals to pass laws to forbid sale by advance contract. Much of the advocacy comes, covertly, from those with vested interests in the older types of markets. To outlaw contract farming would deprive farmers of an assured home for the product, with known terms of sale. Contracts reduce risk. Allegedly, contracts are a way of exploiting farmers, but this is difficult to evaluate. Farmers have more bargaining power before the production period than they do at the time of sale. A tomato grower can deal more effectively on price and delivery terms before he plants than he can if he comes to the unloading dock with his perishable crop and asks "What will you give me?"

Prohibiting purchase of land by nonfarmers is a proposal that has grown in popularity. The fact is that with farms becoming fewer and larger, the amount of money needed for farm ownership becomes so great that farmers themselves can no longer supply all of it. A 1966 study showed net worth per family in agriculture to be four times as much as net worth per nonfarm family. If farmers were to retain ownership of all farmland and farms were to become larger and fewer, this ratio would grow to an intolerable degree. There is some acceptable level that this ratio cannot exceed. Ownership of farmland by nonfarmers and its intelligent leasing to farm operators is a means of preserving the family farm, not endangering it. Closing the economic border between farm and nonfarm sectors ill becomes farm people, who have crossed the border freely in the other direction, to take jobs and make investments. But prohibiting the purchase of farmland by nonfarmers holds considerable surface popularity. No doubt there will be many such proposals during the 1980s.

Cheap credit is proposed to help young farmers get started and to save the family farm. Indeed, the Farmers' Home Administration has thus helped establish a limited number of farmers. But this is very expensive. Furthermore, subsidized credit inflates land values, making purchase more difficult for those who are not covered by the subsidy. Subsidized credit can be helpful to the recipients (the "right" ones, one hopes, who have a good chance of success but cannot meet commercial credit standards). But it can do no more than contribute in small measure to preserving the family farm. Government guarantee of farm mortgage loans taken out by young farmers is another proposal. This too would be helpful in individual cases but would further inflate land values and injure those who were not included in the program. If we go very far with cheap or guaranteed credit, government will be deciding who does and who does not get credit and consequently who will and who will not farm.

Government purchase and lease of farmland is proposed. Government could purchase farmland and lease it to young farmers. This would permit government control of farm size, but not without complications. Through ownership, government would be able to prescribe not only the institutional character of agriculture but also the form of land use and participation in various government programs. It would be able to select those to whom farming opportunities were granted and determine from whom such opportunities were withheld. To adopt this approach in the United States would be to reverse the land policies of most of our national history, when the drive was to get land out of the public domain and into private hands. It is doubtful whether we are ready for so major a change in land policy. The government sold land for $1.25 an acre to help young men get started in farming; should government now buy it back, at $2,000 an acre, for the same purpose? This would be grotesque even for government. Congress is unlikely to vote such a program.

SUMMARY

No doubt the 1980s will see much debate on the future of the family farm. There will be general hand-wringing regarding the trends toward larger and fewer farms, farming corporations, vertical integration, and contract farming. Increased off-farm earnings will be cited as evidence that farmers are in financial difficulty. Public policy will continue to put pressure on the family farm, and politicians will continue to deplore the results.

Faced with alternative policies which on the one hand would check the trends they lament, and on the other hand escalate what they allege to be the problem, Congress will choose the latter course. It may appear inconsistent for the politician to take actions helpful to the large farmers and at the same time to speak out in favor of the small farmers. But from the politician's standpoint these two actions are consistent; they consistently contribute to his reelection. The important thing is that the observer not take the rhetoric at face value.

Perhaps this debate is unnecessarily heated. Agriculture need not be, nor is it likely to become, monolithic. We are a pluralistic nation, socially, politically, and economically. That the trend has been in the direction of the large-scale units does not mean it will automatically extend itself until it embraces all of agriculture. Nor does it mean that large-scale farming should be abolished.

New England has the tradition of the smallholder. In the Midwest we have the heritage of the Homestead Act. In the South there is the legacy of the plantation system. The Southwest reflects the history of the Spanish hacienda. In the Northwest there is family farming, brought by covered wagon over the Oregon Trail. Why try to obiterate all these differences and homogenize this heritage? Perhaps our present mix of large farms, small farms, and part-time farms has considerable justification. Those who believe in market competition should also believe in the appropriateness of competing institutional forms.

There is little need to worry about trends in the pattern of farm organization so long as we have a reasonably open and effective representative government and policy alternatives are available to change these trends. If the alternatives are there and go unusued, it must be that the existing situation is not all that bad.

As for the family farm, it can continue as a major organizational form:

If it is permitted the flexibility that will allow efficient use of modern technology and management.

If it is provided with good research, education, and credit.

If it makes wise use of the principles of cooperation.

If it has ready access to the market.

If there is opportunity to supplement farm income with income from off the farm.

If it continues to enjoy the goodwill of the public.

A summary prognosis on this issue for the decade of the 1980s is that there will be much discussion regarding the future of the family farm, numerous proposals offered, and relatively little policy change. Because, in the last analysis, the decisive consideration will be that old and wise political maxim, "If it ain't broke, don't fix it." The family farm, understood in its context, is far from broken. It has survived war, depression, natural disaster, and a technological revolution, and with a little luck it can survive a political debate as well.

REFERENCES

Atkinson, J. H. 1978. Should foreigners own our land? *Purdue Farm Management Report* (August). Agricultural Economics Department, Cooperative Extension Service. West Lafayette, Ind.: Purdue University.

Bailey, Warren R. 1973. *The one-man farm.* ERS Report no. 519. Washington, D.C.: USDA.

Beale, Calvin. 1978. Small-farm issue. Unpublished document, USDA.

Beer, Samuel H., et al. 1973. *Patterns of government: The major political systems of Europe.* New York: Random House.

Berry, Wendell. 1977. *The unsettling of America.* San Francisco: Sierra Club.

Bock, C. Allen, and Neumann, Lorena, eds. 1978. *Effects of high farm land prices.* AE 4461. Urbana: University of Illinois, College of Agriculture.

Breimyer, Harold F. 1977. The changing American farm. *Annals of the American Academy of Political and Social Science* 429:12–22.

Carter, H. O., and Johnston, Warren E. 1978. Some forces affecting the changing structure, organization and control of American agriculture. *American Journal of Agricultural Economics* 60 (August): 738–48.

Cochrane, Willard W., and Ryan, Mary E. 1976. *American farm policy, 1948–1973.* Minneapolis: University of Minnesota Press.

Coffman, George. 1973. Agriculture unincorporated. *Farm Index* 12: 4–6. Washington, D.C.: USDA.

Community Services Task Force Report. 1977. *The family farm in California.* Sacramento: State of California.

Dorner, Peter. 1977. *Transformation of U.S. agriculture: The past forty years.* Agricultural Economics Staff Paper Series no. 116. Madison: University of Wisconsin.

Dorow, Norbert. 1972. Policies affecting capital accumulation and organizational structure. In *Who will control U.S. agriculture?* pp. 44–52. North Central Regional Extension Publication 32. Special Publication 27. Urbana: University of Illinois.

Fuller, Earl I. 1977. *Income tax management for Minnesota farmers.* FM 205. Minneapolis: University of Minnesota, Agricultural Extension Service.

Gardner, Bruce L. 1976. The effects of recession on the rural farm economy. *Southern Journal of Agricultural Economics* 8:13–22.

General Accounting Office. 1978. *Changing character and structure of American agriculture: An overview.* Staff Study. Washington, D.C.: USDA.

Goldschmidt, Walter. 1947. *As you sow.* New York: Harcourt Brace.

Gray, R. W.; Sorenson, V. L.; and Cochrane, W. W. 1954. *An economic analysis of the impact of government programs on the potato industry.* Technical Bulletin 211. Minneapolis: Minnesota Agricultural Experiment Station.

Griswold, A. Whitney. 1948. *Farming and democracy.* New York: Harcourt and Brace.

Guither, Harold D.; Krause, Kenneth R.; and Bottum, J. Carroll. 1972. Effects of access to technical knowledge and commercial inputs. *Who will control U.S. agriculture?* North Central Regional Extension Publication 33. Urbana: University of Illinois.

Harl, Neil E. 1978. Public policy and the control of agricultural production: Review and discussion. Paper presented at the annual meeting of the American Agricultural Economics Association, Blacksburg, Virginia.

Hjort, Howard H. 1978. Statement before the House Agricultural Committee, Subcommittee on Family Farms, June 20, pp. 1755–78. USDA, Rural Development and Special Studies.

Hottel, J. Bruce, and Barry, Peter J. 1978. Issues related to entry of young people into farming. *Agricultural Finance Review* 38:6–12.

Kyle, Leonard R.; Sundquist, W. B.; and Guither, Harold D. 1972. Who controls agriculture now? The trends underway. In *Who will control U.S. agriculture?* North Central Regional Extension Publication 32. Urbana: University of Illinois.

Mighell, Ronald L., and Hoofnagle, William S. 1972. *Contract production and vertical integration in farming, 1960 and 1970.* ERS Report 479. Washington, D.C.: USDA, Economic Research Service.

Moore, Charles V. 1977. *Effects of federal farm programs and policies on the structure of agriculture.* Working Paper, Economic Research Service, National Economic Analysis Division. Washington, D.C.: USDA.

Nelson, Frederick J., and Cochrane, Willard W. 1976. Economic consequences of federal farm commodity programs. 1953–72. *Agricultural Economics Research,* vol. 28, no. 2. Washington, D.C.: USDA, Economic Research Service.

Nikolitch, Radoje. 1972. *Family size farms in U.S. agriculture.* ERS Report 499. Washington, D.C.: USDA, Economic Research Service.

Paarlberg, Don. 1978. Agriculture loses its uniqueness. *American Journal of Agricultural Economics* 60:769–76.

Penn, J. B., and Boehm, William T. 1978. Research issues re-emphasized by 1977 food policy legislation. *Agricultural Research* 30:1–14. Washington, D.C.: USDA.

Quance, Leroy, and Tweeten, Luther G. 1972. Policies, 1930–1970. In *Size, structure and future of farms,* ed. A. G. Ball and E. O. Heady. Ames: Iowa State University Press.

Raup, Philip M. 1978. Some questions of value and scale in American agriculture. *American Journal of Agricultural Economics* 60:303–8.

Robbins, William. 1974. *The American food scandal: Why you can't eat well on what you earn.* New York: William Morrow.

Scott, John T., Jr. 1977. Returns on corn-soybean farms by size of unit and implications for land values. In *Returns to land in the corn belt, government crop price guarantees based on cost of production, and land values.* AE 4448. Urbana: University of Illinois, Department of Agricultural Economics.

Seckler, David, and Young, Robert A. 1978. Economic and policy implications of the 160 acre limitation in federal reclamation law. *American Journal of Agricultural Economics* 60:575–600.

Stanton, B. F. 1978. Perspectives on farm size. *American Journal of Agricultural Economics* 60:727–37.

U.S. Congress. 1978. *Public policy and the changing structure of American agriculture.* Background paper, Congressional Budget Office. Washington, D.C.: Government Printing Office.

U.S. Department of Agriculture. 1976. *Agricultural statistics.* Washington, D.C.: Government Printing Office.

———. 1977. *Agricultural statistics.* Washington, D.C.: Government Printing Office.

———. 1978*a*. American real estate: The overseas link. *Farm Index* 17:16–17. Washington, D.C.: Economics, Statistics, and Cooperatives Service.

———. 1978*b*. *Balance sheet of the farming sector, 1978.* Agricultural Information Bulletin 416. Washington, D.C.: Economics, Statistics, and Cooperatives Service.

———. 1978*c*. *Farm income statistics.* Statistical Bulletin 609. Washington, D.C.: Economics, Statistics, and Cooperatives Service.

———. 1978*d*. *The U.S. Department of Interior's proposed rules for enforcement of the Reclamation Act of 1902: An economic assessment.* Staff Report ESCS–04. Washington, D.C.: Economics, Statistics, and Cooperatives Service.

U.S. Department of Commerce. 1976. *Foreign direct investment in the United States.* Especially vol. 8, appendix L, Foreign investment in land. Washington, D.C.

University of Illinois Cooperative Extension Service. 1973. *Who will control U.S. agriculture?* North Central Regional Extension Publications 32–1 through 32–6. Special Publication 28. Urbana: University of Illinois.

Wunderlich. Gene L. 1978. *Foreign ownership of U.S. real estate in perspective.* ESCS-24. Washington, D.C.: USDA, Economics, Statistics, and Cooperatives Service.

17. Agribusiness and the Restraint of Trade

Agribusiness is a catchall word used to describe commercial activities related to the food industry. The word was given prominence in 1957 in a book titled *A Concept of Agribusiness,* written by John H. Davis and Ray Goldberg of Harvard University.

When agricultural economists use the term they mean everything from input items (fuel, feed, fertilizer) through farm production and on, including financing, transporting, processing, and retailing. This is the definition I shall use here. When farmers talk about agribusiness they generally omit their own sector, production at the farm level. To them agribusiness refers to the business firms from whom they buy and to whom they sell. Consumers rarely use the word; when they do they usually mean food processors and retailers.

We considered agribusiness from the consumer viewpoint in chapter 7. We looked at it with respect to the family farm in,chapter 16. In this chapter we shall look at agribusiness primarily with regard to allegations that it is engaged in the restraint of trade. The charge is that agribusiness firms often violate antitrust laws that govern business conduct. They are accused of engaging in unethical as well as illegal practices, to the injury of both farmers and consumers. These charges are made by farmers, consumers, labor leaders, politicians, and firms claiming injury. The newspapers pick up the charges and repeat them. Agribusiness has a bad press. Let us consider four interrelated allegations regarding agribusiness firms: that they manipulate prices, squeeze out competing firms, engage in market sharing, and, as a result, extract exorbitant profits.

206

Pricing

The accusation is that the big firms establish prices in a noncompetitive fashion, putting pressure on the smaller firms. Once the small rivals are eliminated, so it is said, the big firms set prices favorable to themselves, both in buying and in selling. Where there are several large firms, they allegedly collude, establishing prices at levels that assure profit. Many Indiana hog producers believe that the big meat packers get together on the telephone each morning and agree on the price of hogs for the day. Many consumers think the price of groceries is similarly determined.

Agribusiness firms respond to these charges, often with an air of injured innocence. These firms generally claim to be operating according to the competitive model, in which no individual firm can exercise appreciable influence over price. They say the food business is one of the most competitive sectors of the American economy. They contend that in terms of public perception they cannot win. If they price *below* someone else, they say, they are charged with engaging in cutthroat competition. If they price *above* their competition, they are said to be profiteering. If they price *the same,* they are said to be guilty of collusion.

A list of court decisions indicates that agribusiness firms have sometimes acted in restraint of trade and have violated the antitrust laws. In most of these cases some aspect of pricing was at issue.

A landmark case was the finding of the court against the American Tobacco Company in 1911 for attempting to monopolize the tobacco business (Areeda 1974, pp. 135–36).

Another significant case was the one against the meat-packers, who were charged with attempted monopoly and restraint of trade. A solution was negotiated. In the famous consent decree of 1920, Swift, Armour, Morris, Wilson, and Cudahy agreed to dispose of their holdings in public stockyards, railroad terminals, public cold-storage warehouses, and retail meat stores, and to quit the wholesale distribution of nonperishable groceries. Swift and Company was forced to divest itself of Libby, McNeill and Libby (Horst 1974, p. 12).

In 1975 a Federal Trade Commission administrative law judge ruled that the Central California Lettuce Producers Cooperative fixed prices illegally and should be disbanded *(The Packer,* April 1, 1975). In that same year, mint-growers of the Northwest won a total of $13,580,000 in an out-of-court settlement with William Wrigley and other buyers of mint oil. The suit, brought in 1970, charged the six major users of mint with fixing prices paid to farmers for mint oil, allocating supplies among themselves, and engaging in other practices in violation of the Sherman Act (Scofield 1978a, p. 192). In 1973 the Federal Trade Commission had an action against Southland Corporation, the nation's largest operator and enfranchiser of self-service convenience food stores, alleging that the company had used the purchasing leverage of its stores and dairy division to obtain sales for its chemical division. Southland consented to refrain from such acts (Southland Set . . . 1973, p. 9). In 1975, Safeway Stores signed a consent decree agreeing to avoid certain antitrust practices and to pay a \$40,000 settlement (Scofield 1978*b,* p. 63). At this time, a six-and-a-half-year-old case against General Mills, Kellogg Company, and General Foods Corporation is still unresolved. The government charged the companies with operating a "shared monopoly" in breakfast cereals, alleging that they practiced "follow-the-leader" pricing (Antitrust suit . . . 1978, p. E5).

Many such antitrust cases have been brought against agribusiness firms. In some of these, the court's findings went against the firm in question. In others the defendent was exonerated. Some cases were dismissed. Sometimes the accused firm pleaded nolo contendere, declining to defend itself. In such cases a solution to the problem was negotiated. Robbins, with more wit than accuracy, interprets a consent decree and a negotiated solution as an "anomalous settlement of a legal action under which a corporation denies it ever did any of the bad things charged and promises never to do them again" (1974, p. 96).

For a time I had responsibility for the Commodity Exchange Authority, the agency that supervised trading of agribusiness firms on the Chicago Board of Trade. Later I had responsibility for the Farmer Cooperative Service and so learned about the operations of the big milk cooperatives. My experience leads me to some skepticism regarding the "Who, me?" attitude often affected by agribusiness firms accused of manipulating prices and acting in restraint of trade.

CONCENTRATION

The change is that the big agribusiness firms buy up rival firms. They merge with one another, increasing the degree of concentration. Huge conglomerate firms are formed; the allegation is that this makes it possible for an agribusiness enterprise, as a component of a conglomerate, to establish artificial prices and maintain a loss position over a period of years, putting extreme pressure on competitors. Advertising and product differentiation, techniques well-suited to large, established firms, make it difficult for new firms to enter the business.

In their defense, agribusiness firms point out that trends toward fewer and larger firms are to be found throughout the entire economy, not just in agribusiness. Farms, the automobile business, schools, newspapers—all are becoming

Table 12. Concentration in Food Processing and Merchandising

	1947	1954	1958	1963	1966	1970	1972
Selected concentration ratios[a] (%)							
Meatpacking plants	41	NA	34	31	27	23	20
Canned fruits and vegetables	NA	NA	NA	24	24	21	20
Frozen fruits and vegetables	NA	NA	NA	24	24	26	29
Cereal preparation	79	NA	83	86	87	90	90
Bread, cake, and related products	16	NA	22	23	25	29	29
Average weighted concentrated ration[b] (%)	37.7	38.0	37.2	37.9	38.6	39.3	NA
Total retail stores (thousands)	NA	NA	359.5	319.4	294.2	267.4	NA
Market share of large grocery chains[c] (%)	NA	29.4	NA	NA	36.1[d]	NA	38.9
Food processing establishments (thousands)	NA	NA	23	20	17	NA	13

SOURCE: Carter and Johnston (1978, pp. 742–43).

NOTE: NA = not available.

[a]Value of industry shipments accounted for by four largest companies.
[b]Average weighted four firm concentration in thirty-one food and related industries (Mueller 1973).
[c]More than 101 stores.
[d]1967.

fewer in number and larger in size. The trend toward large agribusiness firms is said to be a response to the greater efficiency of the large firms rather than the result of a drive for market power.

Mueller (1973) shows that the concentration ratios (value of shipments accounted for by the four largest companies as a percentage of the industry total) for food processing and merchandising, combined on a weighted basis, stood at 37.7 percent in 1947 and increased slightly to 39.3 percent in 1970.

For cereal preparations, concentration in 1970 was high—90 percent—and increasing. For meat-packing plants, on the other hand, the concentration was relatively low—20 percent—and falling. From 1958 to 1970 the number of retail food stores fell 26 percent. From 1958 to 1972 the number of food processing establishments fell 43 percent. Details are shown in table 12.

Connor (1978, p. 19) shows that the food processing industry is part of the conglomerate movement. In 1950, fourteen of the twenty-five leading food processing companies included from one to five grocery product industries. None had as many as twenty. By 1975, none of the twenty-five leading food processing companies had as few as five grocery product industries, and three had more than twenty.

The picture that emerges shows agribusiness reflecting the trend toward larger and fewer firms that characterizes most sectors of American business. Conglomerates are on the increase. But the trends are selective and gradual.

MARKET SHARING

Big agribusiness firms are charged with dividing the business and setting up trade zones; by informal understanding they are said to respect one another's turf. Thus, it is alleged, they preserve the appearance of competition, though in fact competition is blunted.

The firms deny this charge outright. There is no point in going into an area already serviced by another firm, they say. It is not collusive action that accounts for the predominance of one firm in a particular area and the differing geographic orientation of another firm. It is a matter of logistics, not market power.

The Federal Trade Commission shows that food retailers do best in cities in which they have a large share of the sales (table 13). The motivation for wanting a large market share and limited competition from other firms is quite clear.

Table 13. Market Share and Net Profits of a Large Food Chain in 304 Cities

Share of Sales (percentage)	Number of Cities	Contribution to Warehouse Profits[a] (cents per dollar of sales)
4.9 and under	25	0.2
5.0–9.9	68	2.1
10.0–14.9	70	4.3
15.0–19.9	41	4.9
20.0–24.9	40	5.9
25.0–34.9	34	6.0
35.0 and over	26	6.9

SOURCE: Federal Trade Commission (1966).

[a]These are the profits at the retail level exclusive of warehouse overhead expenses.

PROFITS

The accusation is that by illegal and unethical practices the agribusiness firms force down prices to farmers, jack up prices to consumers, and make excessive profit. The accused firms counter by saying that their earnings are not excessive. Agribusiness firms report that earnings are generally below the levels that prevail in other enterprises. One of the repeated affirmations of the trade is that the food business is a highly competitive, low-profit activity. If they really had the market power attributed to them, they say, their profits would be much larger than they are.

Agribusiness firms make the assertion, supported by fact, that they have greatly increased the services associated with food: built-in maid service, convenience foods, table-ready meats, year-around availability of foods that formerly were seasonal, frozen foods, cake mixes, and all the rest. They have provided these added services without appreciably increasing the percentage of the consumer's food dollar that goes for marketing. To do this, they say, efficiencies have been achieved. This is hardly the behavior one would expect from an industry of monopolistic character, making exorbitant profits.

Table 14. Annual Profit Ratios (after Federal Income Taxes) of All Manufacturing, Manufacturers of Food, Textiles, Apparel, and Fifteen Retail Food Chains, 1960–73

| Year | Food Manufacturers | | | | Textile Mill Products | Apparel and Other Finished Products | All Manufacturing Industries | Fifteen Retail Food Chains[b] |
	Total[a]	Dairy	Bakery	Meat-packers[b]				
	Profits as a Percentage of Stockholder Equity							
1960	9.2	—	—	—	5.8	7.7	9.3	13.0
1961	9.4	—	—	—	5.0	7.3	8.9	12.0
1962	9.2	—	9.2	—	6.2	9.3	9.8	11.7
1963	9.3	8.6	9.4	—	6.1	7.7	10.3	11.4
1964	10.4	9.5	9.1	—	8.6	11.9	11.7	11.5
1965	11.0	10.7	9.2	—	10.9	12.8	13.1	11.3
1966	11.5	11.4	10.9	7.1	10.3	13.8	13.6	11.4
1967	11.1	10.3	12.2	11.5	7.6	12.2	11.8	10.3
1968	10.9	9.8	11.9	10.2	8.8	13.0	12.2	10.3
1969	11.0	10.1	8.6	8.8	7.9	11.9	11.5	10.4
1970	10.9	10.2	8.8	8.7	5.1	9.3	9.3	10.6
1971	11.1	11.1	10.7	10.8	6.7	11.2	9.7	10.1
1972	11.3	10.1	10.6	9.1	7.5	12.0	10.6	5.1
1973	12.8	10.8	5.8	11.2	9.0	10.8	12.6	7.6
	Profits as a Percentage of Sales							
1960	2.2	—	—	—	2.5	1.4	4.4	1.3
1961	2.2	—	—	—	2.1	1.3	4.3	1.2
1962	2.2	—	2.3	—	2.4	1.6	4.5	1.2
1963	2.2	1.9	2.2	—	2.3	1.4	4.7	1.2
1964	2.5	2.3	2.2	—	3.1	2.1	5.2	1.3
1965	2.6	2.5	2.1	—	3.8	2.3	5.6	1.2
1966	2.5	2.5	2.3	.9	3.6	2.4	5.6	1.2
1967	2.4	2.4	2.6	1.4	2.9	2.3	5.0	1.1
1968	2.4	2.3	2.6	1.2	3.1	2.4	5.1	1.1
1969	2.4	2.2	1.9	1.2	2.9	2.3	4.8	1.1
1970	2.3	2.1	1.9	.9	1.9	1.9	4.0	1.1
1971	2.4	2.3	2.3	1.3	2.4	2.4	4.1	.9
1972	2.4	2.0	2.2	1.0	2.6	2.4	4.3	.5
1973	2.5	2.0	1.1	1.1	2.8	2.0	4.7	.7

SOURCE: Compiled from *Quarterly Financial Report for Manufacturing Corporations,* published by the Federal Trade Commission and the Securities and Exchange Commission.

[a]Food and kindred products excluding alcoholic beverages.

[b]Compiled from *Moody's Industrial Manual.* Data for 1973 are preliminary.

Table 14 shows profits as a percentage of equity for various sectors of the agribusiness community from 1960 through 1972. For comparison, data are shown for all manufacturing industries. Returns to agribusiness firms appear to be comparable to returns elsewhere. The table shows that profits as a percentage of sales are low for retail food chains and for most other agribusiness firms. This is because of rapid turnover. Returns were low during the period of price control. They have since recovered.

Recent figures support the picture shown in table 14. According to the Federal Trade Commission (1978, p. 14), the after-tax return on equity early in 1978 for firms that manufactured food and kindred products was 11.4 percent, somewhat lower than returns of 12.4 percent on other enterprises. The Quarterly Financial Report of the Federal Trade Commission says that in 1977 the food manufacturer, on the average, received an after-tax profit equal to a little over 3 percent on sales. In other words, if the food manufacturers provided all their present services and gave up all their profit, other things equal, the consumer could buy groceries for about 3 percent less. If the meat-packer gave up all his profit in 1977, the consumer would have paid $1.26 per pound for choice beef (an aggregate of all cuts) instead of the $1.37 actually paid. Clearly, profits of the meat-packers and the food manufactuers are a small part of what the consumer pays for food. And without the profit the services would not be supplied.

PERSECUTION

Are the agribusiness firms accurate in their contention that they are subjected to an extraordinary amount of inquiry and criticism? In my view they are. There are 3.7 million farm families producing food, more than 50 million families consuming food, and only a handful of agribusiness firms. Attacking agribusiness gives gratification to the many and offense to the few. Many politicians, farm leaders, and consumer advocates find this arithmetic irresistible. In fact, the only way farmers and consumers have been able to make common cause is around their shared mistrust of "the middleman." Agribusiness is to many farmers what the employer is to many laboring people: adversary and scapegoat—and utter necessity.

The National Commission on Food Marketing, which reported in 1966, examined agribusiness in great detail, looking for evidence of monopoly and other practices that might increase the price of food. Labor, by far the largest component of the food marketing bill, making up 48 percent of the total marketing costs in 1977 (U.S. Department of Agriculture 1978, p. 12), was ignored. This was in spite of the fact that organized labor is known to have work rules that increase marketing costs and thus retail food prices. I asked George

Brandow, director of the National Commission on Food Marketing, why the commission had not looked at labor. The enigmatic reply: "It would have been a can of worms."

During the mid-seventies there was a move, initiated in Congress, to launch another Commission on Food Marketing. The cooperation of the Department of Agriculture was sought, since USDA had many of the people and much of the information needed to conduct such a study. The department said it would co-operate if—and only if—the study were truly comprehensive, inquiring into all aspects of the food industry, including labor practices. Thereupon the proposal was dropped. This raises the question whether the proposed study was an authentic effort to get the facts regarding food marketing or whether it was a witch hunt, with the witch selected in advance.

MULTINATIONAL AGRIBUSINESS FIRMS

"Multinational" is a word that has recently come into prominence. The briefest and most understandable definition of a multinational firm is that it is an enterprise doing business in several countries. The number of such firms and the volume of business done have expanded tremendously in the last two decades. In recent years more than a fifth of American corporate profits have been earned abroad, and a fourth of all new corporate investment has been made in foreign countries (Bergsten, Horst, and Moran 1978, p. vii).

Agribusiness firms have been part of this movement. A total of 114 United States firms have been identified as having foreign manufacturing plants or significant financial interest in the food systems of foreign countries (Scofield 1978c, p. 15). Of the 114 firms identified, 32 were classified as primarily manufacturers of farm inputs, 60 were primarily involved in food processing, and 22 were in retail food distribution. Geographically, their foreign operations were concentrated in Western Europe, Japan, Australia, and a few of the more developed Central and South American countries. There was little such activity in the less developed countries. Some familiar American-based multinational agribusiness firms are: Anderson-Clayton, Central Soya, Continental Grain, CPC International, Deere and Company, General Foods, General Mills, W. R. Grace, Heinz, Heublein, Kellogg Company, Kraftco, Ralston-Purina, Safeway, and Tenneco.

Japanese and European food firms have shown interest in the United States food industry in recent years, either through acquisitions or through establishment of new production facilities. With the growing accumulation of United States dollars in the hands of foreigners, such investments are likely to increase. One effect will be to help us better understand the attitudes of other countries toward American agribusiness firms.

Multinational firms bring capital, technology, management, and marketing skills to countries that need them. Jobs are created, government tax revenues are increased, and economic development occurs. American multinational companies speed the development of our trading partners and propagate the capitalist way of life.

Recently, opposition to the multinationals has arisen both at home and abroad. This has put questions regarding multinational firms on the policy agenda. Within the United States, the multinationals are accused of exporting American jobs, becoming excessively involved in the internal politics of other countries, taking bribes, dictating the course of United States foreign policy, and having the ability to cause chaos in the international exchange markets. In the developing countries, the multinationals are alleged to be a form of neo-colonialism. They are said to distort economic development with capital-intensive enterprises. They are charged with influencing consumption patterns in a fashion that clashes with traditional values.

Agribusiness firms come in for their share of criticism. American consumers accused the multinational grain firms of draining the United States of its food supplies by sales of wheat to the Soviet Union during 1972–75. Anderson-Clayton was charged with setting up our rival, Mexico, in cotton production. Outside the United States, agribusiness multinationals are similarly subject to attack. United Fruit was charged with dominating the governments of Central America and was pressured into reducing its acreage of bananas. American-based multinationals that produce machinery and chemicals are accused of promoting high-capital-using and high-energy-using forms of agricultural production in countries where labor is superabundant while fuel and capital are scarce. Agribusiness multinationals are faulted for distorting consumption patterns. A favorite accusation is that they have pushed formula-feeding rather than breast-feeding of infants, with the result that child health has been impaired rather than improved.

Political and economic changes affecting multinationals have come so rapidly as to call for reconsideration of existing policies (and nonpolicies). Some agreed international code of conduct seems needed. Agribusiness firms will be affected by whatever decisions emerge. The issue is in its early stages. The only prediction I venture here is that the multinational movement is likely to become reciprocal, with the United States on the receiving end as well as the investing end.

SOME REFLECTIONS

The facts, so far as they are ascertainable, appear to refute many (but not all) of the charges made against agribusiness. But the facts are not decisive so far as public policy is concerned. When the will to think evil is so widespread, facts lose much of their relevance.

What are the reasons agribusiness has so bad an image? Part of the problem no doubt results from the natural antipathy between buyer and seller. Part of it results from dislike for the large firm; agribusiness firms are large and have been growing. Part of it relates to the major economic issue of the twentieth century—the legitimacy of the capitalistic system. Part of it results from agribusiness attitudes that are a carryover from earlier times—the presumption that business knows best. Part of it results from actual cases of price-fixing, collusion, and trade restraint documented by the regulatory agencies. Part of it is simply poor public relations. And part of it is both cause and consequence of political attack.

What concerns the public and the government is inequality of market power. There is a deep feeling that buyer and seller should operate from comparable power bases. Sometimes this equivalence of market power is sought by *curbing* monopoly, as with agribusiness. Sometimes it is sought by *conferring* monopoly, as with labor and some of the commodity programs in agriculture. Countervailing power is built up to redress the disadvantage of the weak; antitrust action is imposed to restrain the concentrated economic power of the strong. Curbing monopoly is not a sustainable explanation of government action. Government *requires* monopoly for farmers (tobacco program), *condones* it for labor (union shop), and *prohibits* it for agribusiness (antitrust). These seemingly inconsistent actions make sense only if understood as part of the pursuit of an equivalence of market power for the various parties.

Whether the government accurately perceives the locus of weakness and strength is another question. And whether the effort to redress the imbalance is properly accomplished is yet another. When, through government action, the power of the weak has been built up to equivalence with that of the strong, it does not automatically stabilize itself at that level. The hunger for power is not thus satisfied. Instead, the appetite is whetted. The behavior of agriculture and labor, two sectors originally "weak," amply supports this generalization.

At the heart of the adverse reaction to agribusiness is the widespread but erroneous belief that trade is a "zero-sun game." The myth is that if two people engage in a transaction and one of them is seen to gain thereby, it must follow that the other has lost. Put simply, the concept is that utility (usefulness), like energy, can be neither created nor destroyed; it can only be passed from hand to hand. Thus if someone gets more, someone else has less.

The theory of trade, as agreed to by virtually all economists of the Western world, is that if two people engage in voluntary trade, both gain. Total utility has increased. Each parts with something in exchange for something else that for him has greater utility. If the consumer voluntarily gives up twenty-five dollars for a supply of groceries, which to him has greater utility than the money, he is a net gainer. If the retailer parts with the groceries in exchange for the twenty-five dollars, which to him has greater utility than the groceries, he is better off. This is the force that drives the market system, the exchange economy.

Once a person embraces the myth that trade is a zero-sum game, many things follow. All profits become evil because they have been taken away from someone else. Wealth is, on its face, evidence of exploitation. Any nation that accepts the myth of the zero-sum game is likely to inject government deeply into the marketing and pricing process and will substitute centralized decision-making for the operation of free markets. As with most myths, the zero-sum game concept has enough truth to make it credible. There are some business transactions in which one person's gain is indeed the other person's loss. The job of the antitrust people is to keep the number of such transactions to a minimum.

The attack on agribusiness, from the farmer's side, has come chiefly from the Farmers Union and the National Farmers Organization, as well as from a number of commodity groups. From the consumer's side, the attack has been led by Ralph Nader and by Carol Foreman. Jim Hightower of the Agribusiness Accountability Project has joined the attack. Church groups dislike agribusiness. Politicians are generally critical.

Defense has come from agribusiness itself. Some help has been given by the Farm Bureau, which has long defended the free enterprise system as a matter of principle. There are few defenders of agribusiness among politicians. Former Secretary of Agriculture Earl Butz is a noteworthy exception; he was almost denied confirmation as secretary of agriculture because of his known support for agribusiness. If there are defenders among consumers, they have not come to my attention.

What do farmers want from agribusiness, and what do consumers want? So far as the subject matter of this chapter is concerned, farmers and consumers are in substantial agreement. They want vigorous enforcement of the antitrust laws, to assure that agribusiness will be competitive.

There is one reservation with respect to this position, and it relates to farmer cooperatives. Under the Capper-Volstead Act of 1922, the secretary of agriculture is given responsibility for seeing that prices are not ''unduly enhanced'' as a result of cooperative action (Bergland 1978, p. 4). Farmer cooperatives market 31 percent of our farm products. Despite the vigorous efforts of the cooperatives to get better prices for their members, in fifty-six years no secretary of agriculture has ever found that prices were "unduly enhanced." The farmers like it that way.

Summary

Will regulation of agribusiness be an issue of farm and food policy during the next decade? The present legal and regulatory structure seems well established. The legislative and executive branches of government have considered the institutions, the law, and the performance with diligence and concern over a long period. Legislative and administrative changes have been relatively few. Issues are ill defined. Objectively measured, the problems are not great.

To the activist—farmer, consumer, or politician—the agribusiness firm is a useful whipping boy. The issues are worth more alive than dead. So "solutions," if indeed there are any, will not be avidly sought.

During the 1980s the "middleman" will no doubt be a target of political attack, as he has been from the day he first undertook to supply a marketing service. The wise agribusiness man will decide to run his company as best he can and forego the desire to be loved. That is unlikely to happen, no matter how he conducts himself.

References

Antitrust suit against U.S. cereal industry at a standstill. 1978. *Lafayette* (2nd.) *Journal and Courier,* November 12, p. E5.

Areeda, Phillip. 1974. *Antitrust analysis: Problems, text, cases.* Boston: Little, Brown.

Bergland, Bob (Secretary of Agriculture). 1978. Testimony submitted to the National Commission for the Review of Anti-Trust Laws and Procedures, July 27. Washington, D.C.

Bergsten, C. Fred; Horst, Thomas; and Moran, Theodore H. 1978. *American multinationals and American interests.* Washington, D.C.: Brookings Institution.

The billion dollar farm co-op nobody knows. 1977. *Business Week,* February 7, pp. 54–64.

Carter, H. O., and Johnston, Warren E. 1978. Some forces affecting the changing structure, organization and control of American agriculture. *American Journal of Agricultural Economics* 60:738–48.

Connor, John M. 1978. The conglomerate firm in food processing: An overview. *National Food Review,* vol. 3. Washington, D.C.: USDA, Economics, Statistics, and Cooperatives Service.

Cook, Hugh L.; Blakley, Leo; and Berry, Calvin. 1976. *Review of Philip Eisenstat, Robert Masson and David Roddy.* Research Bulletin R2790. Madison: University of Wisconsin.

Davis, John H., and Goldberg, Ray A. 1957. *A concept of agribusiness.* Boston: Harvard University, Division of Research, Graduate School of Business Administration.

Eisenstat, Philip; Masson, Robert T.; and Roddy, David. *An economic analysis of the Associated Milk Producers, Inc. monopoly.*

Federal Trade Commission. 1966. *Staff report on food retailing.* Washington, D.C.
———. 1978. *Quarterly report,* p. 14.

French, Ben C. 1977. The analysis of productive efficiency in agricultural marketing: Models, methods and progress. Part 2 of *Survey of agricultural economics literature,* vol. 1, ed. Lee Martin, pp. 94–206. Minneapolis: University of Minnesota.

Hightower, Jim. 1972. Hard tomatoes, hard times: The failure of the land grant college complex. Preliminary report. Task Force on the Land Grant College Complex, Agribusiness Accountability Project.

Horst, Thomas. 1974. *At home abroad.* Cambridge, Mass.: Ballinger.

Mueller, Willard F. 1970. *A primer on monopoly and competition.* New York: Random House.

———. 1973. Testimony and statement presented before the Judiciary Subcommittee on Monopolies and Commercial Law of the House of Representatives Committee on the Judiciary, 93 Cong., 1st sess., July. In *Food price investigation.* Serial no. 15, pp. 313–44. Washington, D.C.: Government Printing Office.

National Commission on Food Marketing. 1966*a. Organization and competition in food retailing.* Technical Study 7. Washington, D.C.: Superintendent of Documents.

———. 1966*b. The structure of food manufacturing.* Technical Study 8. A report by the staff of the Federal Trade Commission. Washington, D.C.: Superintendent of Documents.

———. 1966*c. Studies of organization and competition in grocery manufacturing.* Technical Study 6. Washington, D.C.: Superintendent of Documents.

Robbins, William. 1974. *The American food scandal.* New York: William Morrow.

Scofield, William H. 1978*a. Agribusiness notes, part I: Manufactured production inputs and agricultural production.* Prepared for Economics, Statistics, and Cooperatives Service. Washington, D.C.: USDA.

———. 1978*b. Agribusiness notes, part II: Food processing and distribution.* Prepared for Economics, Statistics, and Cooperatives Service. Washington, D.C.: USDA.

———. 1978*c. Agribusiness notes, part III: International aspects of the food industry.* Prepared for Economics, Statistics, and Cooperatives Service. Washington, D.C.: USDA.

Southland set to end buying, selling practice that FCC challenged. 1973. *Wall Street Journal,* August 16, p. 9.

Soybean broker pleads guilty to bucketing Board of Trade orders. 1978. *Wall Street Journal,* October 12, p. 30.

U.S. Department of Agriculture. 1975. *USDA comments on FTC staff report relating to marketing orders.* Washington D.C.: USDA.

———. 1976. *The question of undue price enhancement by milk cooperatives.* Capper-Volstead Committee. Washington D.C.: USDA.

———. 1977. *USDA comments on the Department of Justice report on milk marketing.* Washington D.C.: USDA.

———. 1978. *National Food Review,* vol. 3. Washington, D.C.: USDA, Economics, Statistics, and Cooperatives Service.

U.S. Department of Agriculture. Interagency Task Force. 1975. *Price impacts of federal market order programs.* Agricultural Marketing Service—Farmer Cooperative Service Special Report 12. Washington, D.C.: USDA.

18. People on the Fringe

Up to now I have focused on the farm and food policy issues of interest to those who have had the political power to get their concerns before the public. In the farm sector, these have been the issues originated by what we have called "the agricultural establishment"—that is, the farm organizations, committees of Congress, the Department of Agriculture, and the land grant colleges.

But there are other people in the farm sector who are not a part of the establishment: small farmers, hired farm workers, nonwhites, and women. They have long been on the fringe in terms of formulating farm policy. Especially since the middle 1960s, certain of these groups have made efforts, or others have done so on their behalf, to penetrate the power complex. In this chapter I shall consider the characteristics of these people. I shall examine the matters that appear to be important to them and review the strategies and tactics they have hitherto used. Finally, I shall speculate whether these people are likely to be involved in farm and food policy issues during the 1980s and, if so, what subjects they might raise.

SMALL FARMERS

So much depends on how you look at agriculture. If you think of farming as *crops and livestock,* you can get more than half of it by looking at only 162,000 farms, 6 percent of the total, those with annual sales of $100,000 or more. But if you think of farming as *people,* almost half are found in the small-farm category

221

with annual sales of less than $5,000. They operate 46 percent of the nation's farms but produce less than 3 percent of the output (U.S. Department of Agriculture 1978, pp. 53, 54, 60). The public would generally agree that men and women are more important than corn and cattle. But farm policy reflects commodities more than it does people. More accurately, it reflects the interests of those people who control the bulk of the commodities.

Most of those who are in the bottom economic bracket in farm income are there because their farms are small or because they lack managerial skills. (By the way, they do not like to be called "small farmers," or "low-income farmers," or "part-time farmers"; most of them want to be considered farmers without modifying adjectives.) Many of these farms were large enough to support a farmer and his family a generation or two ago. But modern agriculture has grown away from them.

Small farmers are an exceedingly varied group. A few of these farms have the sale of farm products as their major if not sole source of income; the operators are really in poverty. Some farms are the homes of retired people with little income but Social Security; they get into the farm category by selling a few dollars worth of eggs or garden produce. There are a few essentially subsistence farmers, largely outside the exchange economy, in the tradition of the old frontier. Most of them are part-time farmers and rural residents who live in the country and work in town. Their off-farm incomes may be substantial.

As a group, small farmers get only 9 percent of their income from agriculture. But their average income, combining farm and nonfarm sources, is close to the average of all farmers, similarly calculated. Though some of them thus do very well, the farm policy mind set insists on seeing only the farm side of their existence and so generally considers them to be in poverty.

Small farmers are numerous, both in absolute numbers and as a proportion of the farm population, in Appalachia, in the Southeast, in the cutover region of the Great Lakes, in the Ozarks, and in scattered intermountain areas. They are least numerous in the Great Plains and in the corn belt. But there are some in every county and in virtually every neighborhood.

"Get big or get out!" That was the advice given to small farmers when the technological revolution struck some decades ago. A number of them stayed in agriculture and got big; a few of John Steinbeck's Okies are today's big California farmers. Most of them got out; Theodore W. Schultz puts the actual out-migration between 1930 and 1974 at 32.8 million people, the largest migration of modern times. Some of them neither got big nor got out; they stayed in, added nonfarm income, and got well-off. Some stayed in, made no adjustments, and stayed poor.

In connection with the off-farm migration, it is well to note a hidden subsidy provided to the urban areas by the farm sector. The people who migrated from farm to city were mostly young, on the threshold of their productive years. Tweeten and Brinkman (1976, p. 92) estimate the rearing costs of such young people, including schooling paid from local taxes, at $10,000 per net migrant, in 1970 dollars. They estimate the investment in human resources transferred from farm to city during the period from 1930 to 1970 at $400 billion. Much has been said about the subsidy that went to agriculture from the cities in connection with the commodity programs; little has been said about the much larger subsidy in human resources that went the other way.

Had there been no migration, farms would today be numerous, tiny, and inefficient. Income per farm would be at the poverty level. Food would be higher priced. We would have lacked the manpower that has improved our education, health services, housing, transportation, and other good things of life. Adjustments took place through individual decisions in accordance with individual circumstances. There were a few government programs to resettle people, but they were of minor importance compared with the out-migration that occurred. The posture of the average public official was to deplore the adjustment; had he known how to do so, he would in all likelihood have prevented it.

What we see in the small farm sector is the unresolved residual of what was an enormous adjustment task, the overwhelming part of which has already been accomplished by the people themselves. We should spend more time celebrating the adjustments that have been made and less time deploring the problems that remain. But it would be callous to ignore the people whose problems are still unsolved.

Insofar as the small farms have been involved in farm policy, this has come about through their being co-opted by the large farmers. Practically all of these people spend more money for food than they receive from the sale of farm products; their unperceived interest is in a low rather than a high food price policy. Yet they support the big farmers in the effort to get prices up. They usually support the farm organization position on hired farm labor, which is to keep available an abundant labor supply at low wages. This makes tougher competition for the small farmers, who are self-employed. Such political power as small farmers have, they willingly supply to those whom they like to think of as their peers. There is a poorly understood degree of self-flattery in thinking that one's few acres of cotton put him on the same policy plane with the man who has a thousand acres. Some nourish the hope that they also may in time farm a thousand acres. Throwing in with the big farmers seems to them better than associating themselves with some group that is "against agriculture" or foregoing use of their political power altogether.

What is the likelihood that these people, constituting half the farm vote, will become a potent force in food and agricultural policy during the 1980s? Very little. They have been inclined to solve their problems by individual action, as they did by finding nonfarm employment. The agricultural establishment, with its commodity programs and its big-farmer orientation, has taken for granted the support of the small farmers. So far this has worked, as very likely it will for some while to come.

But these people have begun to feel less allegiance to agriculture, from which they get one dollar in eleven, and more allegiance to those who supply them with the other ten dollars and with social services. Rural development, which provides some such services and helps generate such income, is a means by which the agricultural establishment night "put its arm around these people," in the phrase coined by True Morse, undersecretary of agriculture during the Eisenhower years, who conceived the Rural Development Program. But the agricultural establishment, which sometimes seems caught up in a death wish, is apathetic regarding rural development. Either consciously or unknowingly, the agricultural establishment runs the risk of reducing by half its already diminished numbers.

HIRED FARM LABOR

Hired farm workers are an exceedingly diverse group. At one extreme is the highly skilled year-round worker who may have responsibility for care of half a million dollars worth of livestock and may operate machinery fully as sophisticated as is found in industry. He may be on the first rung of the old agricultural ladder that leads eventually to farm ownership, the ladder that still works for a few. At the other extreme is the illegal alien from Mexico who has only manual skills, no education to speak of, and little competence in the English language, and who lives in constant fear that he may be caught and deported. He has virtually no bargaining power. Between these extremes are migrant worker gangs, many of them with their families. These may be Appalachian whites, Florida blacks, Texas Mexicans, or crews from the Caribbean. During harvest, casual labor comes into the work force: housewives, older people, and children below legal working age. During summer vacation high school youths work on farms, some of them willingly, to earn spending money, and some of them urged into the fields by their parents to "learn the value of a dollar." At the peak of the season derelicts may enter the labor force, rounded up from the city slums by some farmer desperate for harvest help. Food stamps, unemployment insurance, and various welfare programs reduce the availability of such labor, to the consternation of the farmers.

Nationwide, approximately three-fourths of the labor in American agriculture is supplied by the farmer and his family; only one-fourth is hired. This has not changed in any substantial degree for many years. The farm labor force in 1976 is thus described by Smith and Row (1978):

The work force numbered 2.8 million persons age fourteen and over, but those who did twenty-five days or more of farm work numbered only 1.6 million.

Most were young (median age was twenty-three, and 60 percent were under twenty-five), white (74 percent), and male (75 percent).

Only 24 percent were engaged chiefly in farm wage work. About 54 percent (primarily housewives and students) were not in the labor force most of the year. Farm wage work averaged eighty-six days per worker.

Most (81 percent) had nonfarm residence, compared with a 35 percent average for 1948–49.

Only 213,000, or 8 percent of the total, were migratory workers. This represents a decrease of about 50 percent since 1960.

Casual workers (less than twenty-five days) accounted for 41 percent of all farm workers, but accounted for only 5 percent of the man-days completed.

Most were not well paid. Average earnings were $19.25 a day for eighty-six days of farm work. The 333,000 year-round workers averaged 305 days of farm wage work and earned $6,392.

For all hired farm workers, average daily earnings were $15.36 in the Northeast, $18.04 in the North Central region, $18.04 in the South, and $23.13 in the West.

Eleven percent were Hispanics; 14 percent were blacks and other minorities.

Hired farm workers twenty-five years of ago and over had a median education of 10.1 years compared with 12.4 years for all people of like age. Median years of education were: whites, 12.1; Hispanics, 5.4; blacks and other, 7.9.

California, Texas, and Florida have the largest numbers of hired farm workers. Nearly a fourth of the hired work force is in the Southeastern United States, where large fruit and vegetable farms have high peak labor loads. In these states the hired hands typically work in crews, under contract with the farmer through a crew leader. Much of the work is "stoop labor," which many people dislike. Farm laborers are at the bottom of the male occupational hierarchy in terms of education, income, and status and are largely excluded from labor standards and social insurance programs. Farm workers generally are not covered by unemployment insurance. Only a few states provide workmen's compensation for hired farm laborers. In 1976 United States legislation extended workmen's compensation and unemployment insurance to those working in establishments employing more than ten workers, a small minority of the total hired labor force. Minimum wage standards apply to larger farms only, and in 1971 they covered 535,000 of the 2,6000,000 people who worked on farms for wages that year. Collective bargaining rights are provided for hired farm labor in Hawaii and California but not in other states. Federal legislation excludes hired farm labor from bargaining collectively on the terms of employment.

Providing social services to hired farm labor is very difficult. Except in California, Arizona, Texas, and Florida, much farm labor is dispersed, a man or two to a farm, with most farms operated by family labor only. Employment is highly seasonal. Much employment is casual, and some workers migrate, following the season north. These unique features of farm labor have been cited as the basis for excluding hired farm labor from most of the social legislation enacted since 1933.

Farms produce more young people than are needed to replace farmers who retire. The combination of a high rural birthrate and a decline in the number of farms means that on the average only one of each six farm-reared boys reaching age twenty will find a job as a farm operator (Horne 1972). There is therefore a continuing off-farm movement of young men and women. The farm sector has long provided the labor pool from which nonfarm employers obtained the increased help when times were good. When times were bad, the off-farm migration slackened and labor backed up in the rural areas, largely in the form of underemployment. As the farm population declines, the surplus labor pool function of the rural areas is diminished but not abolished.

The competitive position of the farm wage worker is adverse because rural areas have surplus labor, because entrance into the farm labor force requires no special skill, and because there are no artificial barriers to entry. These facts, rather than greed or conspiracy on the part of farmer employers, are the prime reasons a farm worker earns only about half as much as a worker in the city.

Farmers do not consider farm wage rates to be low. Growers of fruits and vegetables in the Southwest look at their competition across the border in Mexico, where a man can be hired for a week at the cost of a day's pay in the United States. Already Mexico and other countries with farm wages lower than those in the United States have beaten us out of much of our production of tomatoes, strawberries, and other labor-intensive crops.

Farmers try to economize on the use of hired labor because of its increasing real cost, its unreliability, and the trouble associated with recruiting, housing, and supervision. In addition, there is the difficulty of complying with government regulations. So farmers use machines in every way they can, even for some operations that long seemed incapable of mechanization: harvesting tomatoes, picking blueberries, gathering cherries and grapes. Largely as a result, employment of hired farm workers fell from 4,342,000 to 2,767,000 during the twenty-six-year period from 1950 to 1976 (Smith and Row 1978, p. 2). Since 1960 the number of migratory workers has declined almost by half. Research done at the state experiment stations has speeded up the rate of mechanization and drawn the fire of those sympathetic to hired farm workers.

Farmers rightly say that increasing the wages of hired farm labor would, in effect, increase the rate of farm mechanization, drive labor-intensive crops across the border to Mexico, and reduce employment in rural areas.

Most farm labor is unorganized. The exception is Cesar Chavez's United Farm Workers of America, AFL-CIO, which in 1973 had 53,000 members (Ortiz 1978, p. 186). By midsummer 1977, the UFW reportedly had 101,000 workers under contract with 424 farms in the West (Ledbetter 1977, p. 18).

Farmers fear unionism, primarily because of their vulnerability to harvest-time strikes. For some crops the harvest season lasts only a few weeks. To be deprived of labor during that period is to lose the income of an entire year. So there is bad blood between farmers and organized farm labor. It is the old fight between bourgeoisie and proletariat, between employer and employee, between the person with power and the person who lacks it, between those who are established and those who challenge. During the 1973 strike, two members of the United Farm Workers were killed (Ortiz 1977, p. 3).

Other than the United Farm Workers and a branch of the Teamsters, farm labor has virtually no organization. The big urban-based unions will give organized farm workers some limited help in a secondary boycott on grapes or lettuce, but they are mostly baffled about how to organize a labor force that is dispersed, seasonal, migratory, enormously diverse in tasks, largely apolitical, and short on leadership.

Several times there have been efforts to provide federal legislation extending collective bargaining rights to hired farm labor. During the seventies, Secretary of Agriculture Earl Butz, not a strong advocate of labor unions, visited California and was appalled at the violence and animosity then prevailing between the growers and the United Farm Workers. He became convinced that collective bargaining might bring some order out of chaos, and he worked with the secretary of labor to get federal legislation. But, to the surprise of many, the farm workers did not want federal legislation; it would have denied them the use of the secondary boycott, their chief weapon. They preferred state legislation, which left them some opportunity to use the secondary boycott in states other than California. So nothing happened at the federal level.

By themselves, hired farm workers are not able to get their problems on the agenda. It is only when powerful sympathizers take up their cause that their case can get before the public. That happened during the 1960s, when President Johnson's Great Society and War on Poverty took up the problems of farm workers, along with the problems of many other people. Church groups, idealistic young people, union workers, and most of the liberal establishment rallied to the farm workers' cause. This coincided with the coming to power of Cesar Chavez, charismatic leader of the United Farm Workers. The results were a strike against the California growers, a widely supported secondary boycott against the purchase of grapes, recognition of the union by a number of growers, some gains in wages and working conditions, and enactment of California's law authorizing collective bargaining for farm labor. Perhaps most important was the sensitizing of the public to farm labor problems.

But being sensitized to the problems is one thing, and finding solutions is something else. The influential and well-meaning friends of farm labor do not always perceive what the farm workers desire or what would really help them. This is understandable, since the concern is vicarious. People of goodwill are not necessarily the best judges of what will work. A weak group that finds a powerful and well-motivated but uninformed ally runs a considerable risk—that the action that ensues may not be helpful. Boosting the wages of farm workers, with its predictable consequences—speeding up the rate of farm mechanization and encouraging the flight of farm production across the border into Mexico—might not be helpful to farm workers.

What might be done? Providing collective bargaining rights, which are enjoyed by most other workers and are desired by many hired farm workers, seems a reasonable thing despite its dangers. Whether this should be sought through state or through federal law is perhaps best left to the workers themselves.

Workmen's compensation, now available for farm labor only on large farms, could be made more generally available. Health services, education, and other amenities are needed and appropriate. Whether unemployment insurance would have significant effect on the total diverse, dispersed, and seasonal work force is doubtful.

Perhaps the thing these people need most is something that cannot be legislated: the respect of the people in the community where they work. Efforts to satisfy the demands of disadvantaged groups by supplying economic benefits while withholding personal respect have never succeeded.

The argument that agriculture is unique is breaking down, and with it there is erosion of the exclusionary clauses that keep farm labor from participating in the gains achieved by labor elsewhere in the economy. Just as farm people are entering the mainstream of economic, political, and social life, so is farm labor. Both changes bring a combination of satisfactions and disappointments.

Will farm labor issues be on the public policy agenda during the 1980s? Very likely. If the issues come up they will not arise as part of farm and food policy; they will arise as labor policy. They will not be heard by the agricultural committees of Congress, where the attitude is hostile; they will come up in the Committee on Labor, where the attitude is friendly.

THE MINORITY GROUPS

Agriculture has a strong white tradition. The land was taken from the Indians so that white men might farm it. Negroes were enslaved for the purpose of working the white man's plantations. The United States borders were extended to include the Spanish American Southwest because the "Anglos" wanted the farm and ranchlands there. So to the Indian, the black, and the Spanish American, the white, especially the white farmer, has a bad connotation.

There are other minority groups in agriculture—Orientals, religious cults, and European ethnics. But the big three, in terms of numbers, are those first named. The 1970 census of population shows numbers of all rural-farm persons in households as follows:

White	7,724,000
Spanish	113,000
Negro and other	446,000
Total	8,283,000

The nonwhites are on the fringe of political and economic power. We shall consider their circumstances, their aspirations, their strategies, and their prospective involvement in farm policy. The most striking thing about the ethnic and racial minorities is their exodus from agriculture. For the Indian it was not an exodus; it was nonentry. An excellent survey of rural ethnic minorities is given by Durant and Knowlton (1978, pp. 145–67).

The Blacks

There is an inclination to think of the southern black as a farmer, in the sharecropping tradition that was instituted after the Civil War. In 1920 there were 900,000 nonwhite farm operators in the South. The indication is that by 1974 this number had declined to fewer than 50,000, about 5 percent of what it had been fifty-four years earlier (Payne 1978, p. 173). In 1910, blacks owned fifteen million acres of land. By 1969 this figure had shrunk to about one-third of that.

The reasons for the exodus of black people from farm operation are not difficult to find. Agriculture became capital-intensive, and the black farmers lacked capital. The economic opportunities for them lay off the farm, not in farming. Agriculture was the occupation that had enslaved their forefathers, and so the connotations of agriculture were generally adverse.

There were limited efforts to help black people get started as farm operators. Agricultural education in the black land grant colleges of 1890 was one such effort. But the black young men and women of farm background looked on education not as a way of getting started in farming, but as a way of getting out.

The American black is now overwhelmingly urban, more so than the American white. In 1976, 4.1 percent of the white population was on farms. The corresponding number for black people was then half as much, 1.9 percent (Calvin Beale, pers. comm.).

The blacks who gave up farm operation did not, in any large numbers, become hired farm workers; the number of black farm laborers also declined. The transition was not down the status ladder within agriculture; it was out of agriculture and to the city.

Hispanics

The Spanish American role in agriculture has been not so much farm operation as hired worker. Numbers of people in the migrant crews have diminished sharply, as has been shown. Some found nonfarm jobs that paid better. Some settled in the more congenial of the locations visited during migration and became established citizens.

Illegal Aliens

Illegal aliens in the United States have been variously estimated to number from two to twelve million (Chiswick 1978, p. 308). Numbers are difficult to estimate; to allow oneself to be counted is to run the risk of deportation. Illegal alien apprehensions have increased sharply since the early 1960s:

1960	71,000
1965	110,000
1970	345,000
1975	767,000
1977	more than a million

Overwhelmingly, these people are from Mexico. Of those apprehended and deported in 1975, nearly 90 percent were from Mexico (U.S. Department of Justice 1975, table 27B). The surge of illegal aliens from Mexico began with the termination of the bracero (contract farm labor) program that was in effect from 1942 to 1964.

Formerly, the great majority of illegal aliens from Mexico took farm jobs in the United States. This is no longer true. They now try mostly for urban jobs—in restaurants, hotels, service stations, and industry. In 1970 only 27 percent of the employed foreign-born males and apprehended illegal aliens were farm workers (North and Houstoun 1976, p. 108). The United Farm Workers, whose members are largely Spanish American, want to keep out the Mexican illegals. Chavez has complained to the Immigration Service about the lack of enforcement (Severe 1974, p. 81).

There are no promising solutions to the problem of illegal aliens. The American wage standard is so high relative to that of Mexico that no acceptable border patrol system seems capable of stopping the movement. How can you police a two-thousand-mile border? The problem of illegal aliens will clearly be a policy issue during the 1980s. The agricultural role in this issue diminishes as the farm labor force shrinks and as these people turn increasingly to nonfarm jobs.

Indians

A considerable effort was made to help the Indians get established as farm operators. Sheepherding was traditional with the Navajos, and some success was achieved with this enterprise. But for most of the tribes the male occupations had been hunting and fighting; when the game was gone and the tribes were pacified, the Indian male encountered what we might call technological unemployment. He did not readily convert to agriculture. Two of the most difficult transitions to make, anthropologists tell us, are the change from nomadic to settled life and the shift from a subsistence to an exchange economy. We asked the Indians to make the two simultaneously, and for the greater part they were unsuccessful.

Today, despite all the talk about racial integration, production agriculture is probably more white than it has been since colonial times.

WOMEN'S RIGHTS

There is another group of people in agriculture who lack status. They are not a minority because they are a bit more numerous than the prestige group. They are the women. They also have long been on the fringe rather than at the center of public policy formation. They may be in the majority in numbers, but they are in the minority in policy-making. The agricultural tradition not only is white, it is white male. Traditionally, in this country farming has been a man's job. The men were not above accepting help in the fields from their wives during the busy season (Wiser 1975). But decision-making was a male prerogative, at least in its visible form. The woman's place was in the home. She was honored and loved, but she had her assigned role. If a young woman went to college—a rare event—she was expected to study home economics or nursing. She could work and earn money, before she was married, in any of three eligible occupations: teaching, nursing, and later "stenography." She was expected to get married, and when she did she was expected to give up working and raise babies while her husband raised crops.

These things are changing. Women are becoming active participants in decisions concerning the farm business. They are working outside the home. They are developing interests apart from the family and the farm. They appear on committees and on boards of directors of farm organizations and agribusiness concerns. The content of the extension program for farm women has been modernized.

Women's involvement in farm policy matters appears to be on the increase. In 1977 the American Agri-Women, a group of farm wives, claimed three thousand members (Robbins 1977). They supported the American Agriculture Movement. A similar group, Women Involved in Farm Economics (WIFE), held a convention in Nebraska. Up to this point the farm women have supported established policy positions and have advocated few new things of their own.

This was not the first women's venture into the farm policy field. In the late nineteenth century there was Mrs. Mary Elizabeth Lease of Kansas, "a tall, slender, good-looking woman of thirty-seven years," Irish by birth and endowed with the talents attributed to her people. She was a Populist and the mother of four. She had studied law and been admitted to the bar. In the campaign of 1890, as a speaker for the Farmers' Alliance and Union Labor candidates, she made 160 speeches. She was sufficiently eloquent to be called "the Patrick Henry in petticoats." The burden of her message: "What you farmers need to do is to raise less corn and more Hell!" (Hicks 1961, pp. 159–60).

Whether raising hell or corn or consciousness, women are in for a bigger role in agriculture. A good survey of the changing role of rural women is given by Flora and Johnson (1978, pp. 168–81).

SUMMARY

How did these various minority groups conduct themselves within their traditional assigned roles? The prevalent white male view was that their roles were generally accepted with good grace. Indeed, the minority groups were expected to appreciate their good fortune in that responsibility lay with those wise, beneficent people, the white males. But we know that there was much smoldering dissatisfaction with the assigned roles. It came to light with the civil rights movement and with women's liberation during the sixties and seventies. These initiatives did not originate in the farm sector. They began mostly in the urban areas and spread to the minorities in agriculture.

The small farmers, as a generalization, did not seek a strong policy-making role. They chose to meet their problems mostly by individual decision-making: out-migration, adding nonfarm income, or, in some cases, settling passively for low-income status.

A nucleus of hired farm workers in California, with their own leadership, sought to enlarge their policy-making role by seeking and winning the support of influential people outside their group.

The blacks, who were at the core of the civil rights movement, relied primarily on their own leaders. They developed their own goals and strategy. They sought and won support from the outside, but the strength of the movement came from within.

Women's liberation appears to have had more breadth and more spontaneity than is true of the other three disadvantaged groups and appears to have been powered almost wholly from within.

These different strategies no doubt reflect the differing settings within which these disadvantaged groups operated. The direct effect of these movements on agriculture has not been great. The chief effect has been to change, in some degree, the farm mind-set on these matters. The most visible consequence was—and will be—through services supplied to farmers by government. Some white farmers who had long been served by a white extension man may now be served by a black one. Some black farmers may get more service than formerly. County Agricultural Stabilization and Conservation Committees may now have minority as well as white members. The 4-H clubs are now integrated. Food programs of the Department of Agriculture have been broadened to serve a higher proportion of minority people than formerly. Women will appear increasingly in decision-making rather than supportive roles.

Will the agricultural fringe people participate more fully in the formulation of farm and food policy in the years ahead? The answer, as I see it, is almost certainly yes. This role is more likely to be exercised in agribusiness, education, and government programs than in farm production.

Indians are finding that the courts can be an effective forum within which to pursue their land claims. If the courts generally find that treaties reserving land for the Indians have been violated, the consequences for agriculture could be immense.

Blacks will continue to work for stricter compliance with the Civil Rights Law of 1964. The colleges of agriculture and the USDA will feel the pressure.

Spanish Americans will emulate the tactics used successfully by the blacks.

Women on the farm and on the job will increasingly reject the restricted role traditionally assigned to them.

The problem of illegal aliens will be on the policy agenda during the 1980s, put there not by farm people but by labor.

Most important, these fringe people will insist that they receive respect as individuals. This, the most important thing of all, costs the white male nothing more than the relinquishing of tradition and prejudice. But as history shows, these are among the most prized of all possessions, among the last to be given up.

REFERENCES

Chiswick, Barry R. 1978. Immigrants and immigration policy. In *Contemporary economic problems,* ed. William Fellner, pp. 285–325. Washington, D.C.: American Enterprise Institute for Public Policy Research.

Cutler, Rupert M. 1978. Breathe life into our cold statistics. Remarks at Small Farms Conference. Albuquerque, New Mexico.

Durant, Thomas J., Jr., and Knowlton, Clark S. 1978. Rural ethnic minorities: Adaptive response to inequality. In *Rural USA: Persistence and change,* ed. Thomas R. Ford, pp. 145–67. Ames: Iowa State College Press.

Economic report of the president. 1978. Washington, D.C.: Government Printing Office.

Flora, Cornelia B., and Johnson, Sue. 1978. Discarding the distaff: new roles for rural women. In *Rural USA: Persistence and change,* ed. Thomas R. Ford, pp. 168–82. Ames: Iowa State College Press.

Ford, Thomas R., ed. 1978. *Rural USA: Persistence and change.* Ames: Iowa State College Press.

Fuller, Varden. 1973. The struggle for public policy on farm-labor management relations. Mimeographed. Davis: University of California.

Fuller, Varden, and Van Vuren, William. 1972. Farm labor and labor markets. In *Size, structure and future of farms,* ed. A. Gordon Ball and Earl Heady, pp. 144–70. Ames: Iowa State College Press.

Graham, Frank P., and Randolph, A. Philip. 1967. *Farm labor organizing 1905–67.* New York: National Advisory Committee on Farm Labor.

Hadwiger, Don F., and Browne, William P. 1978. *The new politics of food.* Lexington: D.C. Heath.

Hardin, Charles M. 1967. *Food and fiber in the nation's politics.* National Advisory Commission of Food and Fiber Technical Paper 3.

Hawley, Ellis W. 1966. The politics of the Mexican labor issue, 1950–1965. *Agricultural History* 40:157–76.

Hicks, John D. 1961. *The Populist revolt: A history of the Farmer's Alliance and the People's party*. Lincoln: University of Nebraska Press.

Horne, James. 1972. Farming opportunities for vocational agriculture students and rural farm boys. M.S. thesis, Oklahoma State University.

Larson, Donald K., and Lewis, James A. N.d. *Small farms profile*. Washington, D.C.: USDA, Economics, Statistics, and Cooperatives Service.

Ledbetter, Les. 1977. Farm workers celebrate the past and plan expansion at convention. *New York Times,* August 29, p. 18.

McConnell, Grant. 1959. *The decline of agrarian democracy*. Berkeley: University of California Press.

McElroy, Robert. 1972. *The hired farm work force of 1971*. Agricultural Economic Report 222. Washington, D.C.: USDA, Economic Research Service.

McWilliams, Carey. 1940. *Factories in the field*. Boston: Little, Brown.

North, David, and Houstoun, Marion T. 1976. The characteristics and role of illegal aliens in the United States labor market: an exploratory study. Mimeographed. Washington, D.C.: Linton.

Ortiz, Isidro D. 1977. Governor Brown, the farmworkers, and collective bargaining. Paper presented at the Symposium on Agricultural Policy, July 5, Washington, D.C.

———. 1978. The politics of collective bargaining in agriculture. In *The new politics of food,* ed. Don F. Hadwiger and William P. Browne, pp. 185–98. Lexington: D.C. Heath.

Payne, William C., Jr. 1977. Implementing federal nondiscriminatory policies in the Department of Agriculture, 1964–76. Paper presented at the Agricultural Policy Studies Organization, July 27, Washington, D.C.

———. 1978. Implementing federal nondiscriminatory policies in the Department of Agriculture. In *The new politics of food,* ed. Don F. Hadwiger and William P. Browne, pp. 173–84. Lexington: D.C. Heath.

President's National Advisory Commission on Rural Poverty. 1967. *The people left behind*. Washington, D.C.: Government Printing Office.

President's Task Force on Rural Development. 1970. *A new life for the country*. Washington, D.C.: Government Printing Office.

Robbins, William. 1977. Women in agriculture fight for their families and their farms. *New York Times,* November 14, p. 44.

Severe, Richard. 1974. The flight of the wetbacks. *New York Times Magazine,* March 10, pp. 17, 77–83.

Smith, Leslie Whitener, and Row, Gene. 1978. *The hired farm working force of 1976*. Agricultural Economic Report 405. Washington, D.C.: USDA, Economics, Statistics, and Cooperatives Service.

Soth, Lauren. 1970. Shameful bias prevails in Dixie ag education. *Des Moines Register,* November 4.

Tweeten, Luther, and Brinkman, George L. 1976. *Micropolitan development: Theory and practice of greater rural economic development*. Ames: Iowa State University Press.

U.S. Congress. 1978. *Public policy and the changing structure of American agriculture*. Congressional Budget Office. Washington, D.C.: Government Printing Office.

―――. 1978. *Farm income statistics*. Statistical Bulletin 609. Washington, D.C.: USDA, Economics, Statistics, and Cooperatives Service.

―――. 1977. *Agricultural statistics, 1977*. Washington, D.C.: Government Printing Office.

U.S. Department of Agriculture. 1976. *Agricultural statistics, 1976*. Washington, D.C.: Government Printing Office.

U.S. Department of Justice. 1975. *1975 annual report*. Table 27B. Washington, D.C.

Wiser, Vivian. 1975. Women in American agriculture. Talk given at the Auditorium of Freer Gallery, Washington, D.C., November 18.

19. The USDA under Fire

For several decades the Department of Agriculture has been on the defensive. This has resulted in part from its changing status and in part from changing organizational concepts. Both of these hazards will be present during the 1980s.

REORGANIZATION

There are various ways to organize an undertaking. One way is to organize by academic discipline as the universities do: a Mathematics Department, a Biology Department, an Economics Department, and so on. Another way is to organize by function, as business does: Research and Development, Production, Sales, and the like. The federal government follows neither of these patterns. Reflecting its political nature, it organizes primarily by clientele: a Department of Agriculture, a Department of Labor, a Department of Commerce—thirteen departments in all.

This pattern of organization results in much confusion. In 1971 the president reported to Congress as follows (Nixon 1971, p. 6).

Nine different federal departments and twenty independent agencies are now involved in education matters. Seven departments and eight independent agencies are involved in health. In many major cities there are at least twenty or thirty separate manpower programs, funded by a variety of federal offices. Three departments help develop our water resources and four agencies in two departments are involved in the management of pub-

237

lic lands. Federal recreation areas are administered by six different agencies in three departments of the government. Seven agencies provide assistance for water and sewer systems. Six departments of the government collect similar economic information—often from the same sources—and at least seven departments are concerned with international trade.

Whenever the federal government takes on an important new assignment or identifies a new clientele, the chances are good that a new organizational entity will be established to deal with it. Unfortunately, as each new office is set up, little attention is given to how it will fit in with the old ones. Sometimes there are direct conflicts; one agency will set out to drain a swamp and another will try to preserve it. One program increases farm production; another curtails it. One agency tries to get prices up; another tries to hold them down.

The president—any president—feels frustration in attempting to direct such an operation. Strenuous efforts are made to achieve coordination. In 1970 there were 850 interagency committees. But those present at such sessions typically were more intent on protecting their own turf than on solving problems. During the mid-seventies the Department of Commerce had a "meeting-goer," name mercifully withheld, whose instructions reportedly were to attend interagency meetings on a wide range of subjects, keep his mouth shut, listen to what was said, and report back to his principal if, and only if, Commerce turf were threatened. He performed these tasks with such skill that he was nominated by his agency for the superior service award.

If the president or Congress wants to launch a program or change a program or even learn how a program is working, it often becomes necessary to consult with half a dozen or more authorities, each of whom can blame the others when something goes wrong.

President Nixon set up a council headed by Roy Ash of Litton Industries, charged with developing a plan for streamlining the organization of the executive branch. The council's report was released in February 1971 and formed the basis for the president's proposed governmental reorganization.

Reflecting the business orientation of its chairman, the council proposed a reorganization based on function or mission rather than on clientele, the existing form (Superintendent of Documents 1971, pp. 29–34). The proposal was to retain four of the departments, the historic ones that had been set up long ago on a mission basis: State, Treasury, Defense, and Justice. All other departments, including Agriculture, were to be abolished. Their operations were to be desaggregated, regrouped, and transferred to four new departments: Natural Resources, Human Resources, Economic Affairs, and Community Development. Activities of the Department of Agriculture were to be dispersed to all of these.

For example:

Forest Service and Soil Conservation: to the Department of Natural Resources.

Farmers Home Administration: to the Department of Community Development.

Food and Nutrition Service: to the Department of Human Resources.

Stabilization and Conservation Service: to the Department of Economic Affairs.

Economic Research Service: This agency would be split three ways, parts going to each of the new departments except Community Development.

Supporting the proposal were the president, his official family, and a number of professors of business and of public administration who declined to take a public position.

Opposing it were the government employees, the lobbyists, the congressional committees, and many of the more articulate citizens. The bureaucrats attacked it from within, the lobbyists attacked it from without, and the congressional committees attacked it from above and below. The bureaucrats opposed it because it involved major change, which they constitutionally resist. The lobbyists were opposed; they had sunk the mine shaft down to the mother lode and wanted no disputes regarding title to the claim. The congressional committees were opposed; each had secured its little fiefdom and wanted no disturbance. The various patrons of the various departments felt they had direct relationship with government under the old system; they saw the proposed change as a deliberate affront. And so it was defeated.

Abolishing an agency by which the citizen feels favorably linked to his government has a bad effect. This had not been properly assessed. In government, symbolism is more important than service.

When Congress refused to act, the president proceeded on his own. He retained the existing departments but set up four counselors along lines recommended by the Ash report: counselor for economic affairs (and secretary of the treasury), George Shultz; counselor for community development (and secretary of HUD), James Lynn; counselor for natural resources (and secretary of agriculture), Earl Butz; counselor for human affairs (and secretary of HEW), Caspar Weinberger.

But this venture never really got off the ground. There was limited support for it, even among the newly appointed counselors. Increasingly, Watergate absorbed the president's attention and the system folded.

Old-timers say that for a governmental reorganization plan, defeat is not death. Over time, by bits and pieces, changes occur in accordance with the pattern outlined in the proposed plan. So it was with the Hoover Commission, set up to reorganize the federal government. The Hoover Commission made 273 proposals of which "116 had been carried into effect by 1954, thirty-five more had been mostly accomplished, and forty-five partially put into effect" (Millett 1959, p. 128).

When President Carter came in he undertook to reorganize the executive branch. But his was largely a gathering together and renaming of agencies within existing departments. It resulted in some turmoil among the civil servants but received little notice out in the country. At this time, additional reorganization appears to be in the offing, probably by increments rather than on a grand scale.

ATTRITION

We have been considering the hazard that the Department of Agriculture might be reorganized out of existence. More likely is the possibility that various parts of it might be peeled away and given to other agencies, leaving only a shadow of its once larger self. Many departmental missions have already been stripped away and have gone to other agencies: weather to Commerce, work on the environment to the Environmental Protection Agency, food and drugs to Health, Education, and Welfare, regulation of the commodity exchanges to an independent agency.

As agriculture's political strength weakens, these raids are likely to continue. At this time such is the case. There are efforts to take away from Agriculture its various regulatory activities and transfer these to a central agency. The proposal to take consumer-related activities out of the various departments and transfer them to a Consumer Protection Agency has been defeated, but the idea is not dead. The Department of Interior has long tried to take over the Forest Service. Commerce, with its Small Business Loans, is encroaching on the turf of the Farmers Home Administration. The proposed Department of Education would like to take over the Child Nutrition Programs and the USDA Graduate School. The National Security Council and the State Department have virtually taken over Public Law 480, leaving the Department of Agriculture with little more than the job of picking up the tab.

Some people in agriculture encourage slimming down the department. They want to slough off everything except the historical clientele. They want to prune off everything we have called "the new agenda." They want to give the Food Stamp Program to the Department of Health, Education, and Welfare and Rural Development to anyone who will take it. They say that if this is done "the USDA budget will be smaller and agriculture won't look so costly."

If the clientele of the USDA were limited to commercial farmers, the Secretary of Agriculture would have as his constituents something less than 2 percent of the population. His departmental budget would be approximately 1 percent of federal expenditures. In size, his operation would be exceeded by a number of independent agencies that do not have departmental status (U.S. Congress 1978, pp. 82–83). This is the new math that farm people will have to learn. In such circumstances Agriculture might be unable to retain its departmental status.

In politics numbers are decisive. The most serious political defect—and one of the most common—is inability to count. Some of agriculture's most dedicated friends suffer from an impaired sense of numbers.

Most farm people feel that there must be a government department representing them, headed by a secretary who is equal with the other cabinet members, maybe a little more equal. How can this be if the secretary's constituency and his share of the government operation shrinks toward the vanishing point? Those who want to purge everything but the historical clientele unknowingly suffer from a death wish.

SUMMARY

It may be true that the most efficient way of organizing the federal government would be set it up along functional lines, as the Ash Report recommended. Elsewhere than in government, form usually follows function.

But government is primarily a political activity. It is primarily neither a business venture nor a scientific undertaking. Nor is it an educational institution. Efficiency is important and should be an objective. But governments do not stand or fall on their efficiency or the lack thereof. The critical question is whether the citizen identifies with his government. Politicians are aware of this. Businessmen are fond of saying that government is just another business and should be run in business fashion. If he has his wits about him, any businessman coming into government will learn in his first month of service that this is not true.

Possibly a government organized along functional lines would be more efficient. Probably service to the people would be better and the cost would be less. But if this comes through giving serious offense to important constituencies, it is a bad bargain. It may be that the politicians know more about how to organize the federal government than do the efficiency experts. And it may be that the bureau chiefs in the Department of Agriculture, battling for their turf against raids by other departments, are operating from basically sound instinct.

The Department of Agriculture will be on the defensive during the 1980s, though none of us in the agricultural establishment likes to admit it. Two things a captain should not do if he is on the defensive. One is to capitulate; the other is to pretend he has the initiative and launch an attack he cannot sustain. Both of these options should be stricken from the agricultural policy strategist's plans for the decade ahead.

The Department of Agriculture is on its way toward becoming, in fact if not in name, a Ministry of Food. Its prospect for longevity depends in considerable measure on whether it accepts or rejects this new role.

The Department of Agriculture is like a congressman who had a secure seat, with constituents whose needs he understood and served well, but who has been redistricted. New constituents have been added, whom he does not know so well and for whom he has less empathy. But if he is going to continue serving his old beloved constituents he will have to pay attention to his new ones so he can continue in office.

REFERENCES

Harvey, Ray; Koenig, Louis W.; and Somit, Albert. 1955. *Achievements in federal organizing*. New York: Citizens Committee for the Hoover Report.

Millett, John D. 1959. *Government and public administration*. New York: McGraw-Hill.

Nixon, Richard. 1971. Message to the Congress, March 25. In *Papers relating to the president's departmental reorganization program: A reference compilation*. Washington, D.C.: Government Printing Office.

Rasmussen, Wayne, and Baker, Gladys L. 1972. *The Department of Agriculture*. New York: Praeger.

Superintendent of Documents. 1971. *Papers relating to the president's departmental reorganization program: A reference compilation*. Washington, D.C.: Government Printing Office.

U.S. Congress. 1978. *1979 congressional budget scorekeeping report*. No. 4. Washington, D.C.: Congressional Budget Office.

20. The Foreign Dimension

For our purposes, international agricultural policy divides itself into three more or less distinct categories: commercial trade in farm products (subject of chapter 21), food aid (chapter 22), and agricultural development (chapter 23).

A New Setting

All these matters are conditioned by circumstances and perceptions that have arisen in recent years. Our comparative advantage in farm production has been rediscovered. The adverse balance of trade amplifies the urgency to export farm products. A protectionist mood has arisen, which may make exports more difficult. The Third World has launched a drive for a New International Economic Order that may affect our agricultural trade in various ways. I shall consider each of these and then examine several additional international policy matters that affect agriculture. The present chapter is an umbrella for the three that follow.

Agriculture in World Markets

Events of the mid-seventies drove home the point that American agriculture was increasingly part of the world food economy. Earlier thoughts that we could or should insulate ourselves from world market forces receded. The economic storms of 1973–76 made clear the international role of American agriculture.

Our growing reliance on foreign markets has been thus described (Hjort 1978): From 1960–64 to 1978, United States agricultural exports increased from $5.4 to $27.3 billion. Roughly one-fourth of the cash receipts of agriculture came from exports. During the 1972–76 period the following percentages of production of our major crops went into export:

wheat	59 percent
soybeans	51 percent
cotton	36 percent
tobacco	36 percent
grain sorghum	25 percent
corn	21 percent

The United States share of world agricultural exports increased from 12.3 percent in the early fifties to 16.5 percent in 1976–77. The trade balance in the agricultural sector increased thus during the last quarter-century:

Years	Billions of dollars
1951–55	−1.16
1956–60	0.10
1961–65	1.58
1966–70	1.62
1971–75	7.06
1975–76	12.25
1976–77	10.63
1977–78	13.4

What happened was that we capitalized on our comparative advantage in agriculture. This will bear importantly on trade policy during the decade ahead.

The Adverse Balance of Trade

Gradually, and then with a rush, the overall balance of trade turned against the United States. The 1978 *Economic Report of the President* reports these figures (p. 377):

Year	Balance in billions of U.S. dollars
1965	4.3
1970	.8
1973	−2.2
1974	−9.5
1975	4.2
1976	−14.6
1977	−36.4

Whatever the causes of this shift may have been, one result was to increase the importance of utilizing our comparative advantage in agriculture so as to earn as much foreign exchange as possible. This gives public policy endorsement to the natural interest of farm commodity groups in maximizing agricultural exports.

The Rise of Protectionism

The high tariff rates enacted by Congress in 1930 were charged with having contributed to the severity of the Great Depression that followed. In 1934 President Franklin D. Roosevelt and Secretary of State Cordell Hull pushed through Congress a piece of legislation that became known as the Reciprocal Trade Agreements Act. This act transferred certain tariff-making authority from Congress to the president. The General Agreement on Tariffs and Trade (GATT) came into existence, an institutional invention of the first order. This is a forum within which the various nations negotiate multilaterally to adjust trade relations. In all, six ''rounds'' of tariff negotiations have been carried out. In 1934, before beginning these negotiations, tariff revenues equaled 18 percent of the value of imports. By 1977 tariff revenues equaled only 5 percent of the value of imports, about one-fourth as much as forty-three years earlier. This astounding reduction in tariff barriers was accompanied by a fourfold increase in the real volume of world trade in agricultural products and by a phenomenal rise in the standards of living in virtually all trading nations.

But, by the late seventies, almost the only tariff-protected items were products that were either so economically vulnerable, so politically powerful, or so strategically important that further tariff reductions were exceedingly difficult. Increasingly, as tariff reductions were forced through for items that were economically vulnerable or politically powerful, nontariff barriers such as quotas were substituted. This happened with steel, textiles, cotton, sugar, certain dairy products, and peanuts. It is hardly a gain for liberal trade to substitute the more discriminatory instrument, quotas, for the less discriminatory one, tariffs.

There has come a weakening of the forces that supported liberal trade. The labor unions, fearing for their jobs, sought to keep out foreign goods. The South, historically in favor of liberal trade, became industrialized and took on more of a protectionist character. The technological lead long enjoyed by American industry diminished, exposing more enterprises to foreign competition. The oil embargo demonstrated how vulnerable nations can be if they are deeply dependent on foreign sources for strategic supplies. The worsening trade balance gave credibility to those who sought to keep out foreign goods. Not only in the United States but also in other countries, protectionist forces gained strength. After nearly half a century during which liberal trade policy had been effective in reducing trade barriers, the initiative now appears to have passed into the hands of the protectionists.

This poses a hazard for the expansion of trade in all forms, including agriculture. Unfortunately, this development comes at a time when American agriculture is poised to utilize its comparative advantage by increasing farm exports.

The New International Economic Order

A convenient grouping of the world's more than 160 countries puts the developed nations of the Western world in one bloc and the communist countries of the Eastern world in another. The remaining countries—"the South," the "Less Developed Countries"—now number 114 and have 1.75 billion people. They are not clearly either among the constitutionally democratic or the authoritarian nations. They are the Third World, mostly new, mostly agricultural, and mostly poor.

The Third World nations attribute some share of their problems to the established economic order, which reflects the dominance of the developed nations. They allege that the developed countries exploit those that are less developed and accomplish this in part through trade. The Third World therefore proposes a New International Economic Order, the purpose of which is to redistribute wealth. The main components of this proposed new order are: assured markets for them in the developed countries; price increases (and protection against price declines) for their export commodities, to be achieved by the use of indexation and buffer stocks; protection against sharp price increases for commodities they import; a fund, underwritten by the developed nations, to provide the financial backing necessary for the stabilization plan; and large-scale grants for economic development, unrestricted as to use, provided by the developed nations.

The Third World has neither the economic nor the military power to put these proposals into effect. But politically, in the international organizations, with one country–one vote, the Third World can be effective. In 1973 nations contributing less than 5 percent of the United Nations budget and having only 10 percent of the world's population nevertheless had the necessary two-thirds vote to apportion the budget in any way they liked (Alden 1973, p. 8). The desire of the United States to be on as good terms as possible with these countries, plus their voting strength in the United Nations, requires that their proposals be given consideration rather than dismissed out of hand. Additionally and importantly, the Organization of Petroleum Exporting Countries (OPEC) has taken diplomatic and political leadership on behalf of the developing countries. American dependence on oil imports is so great as to require a certain respect for this leadership and hence more attentiveness to demands of the New International Economic Order than would otherwise be the case.

Agricultural products are a fairly important part of the international trade of the Third World, both imports and exports. Deference to Third World proposals would influence our international trade in farm products during the decade ahead. On the one hand, to the degree that their proposals might increase their rate of economic growth, our agricultural exports would be increased. On the other hand, concessions to them might result in increased imports into the United States of beef, sugar, oilseeds, and specialty products. Their enhanced ability to produce tobacco, rice, and cotton might cut into our exports of these products (Warley 1978).

Of the four trade developments described, the first two (our comparative advantage and the need to export) indicate an increase in our agricultural export volume. The third (protectionism) will probably be an inhibitor. The effect of the fourth (the proposed New International Economic Order) is unclear. In any case, agricultural trade policy parameters are changing.

THE NEED FOR CONCORDANT POLICIES

At this point it is well to indicate several major respects in which some rough harmony of trade policies is needed. One is that international trade policy must bear some kinship to internal trade policy. If we pursue protectionist policies internally, this will require some degree of protection externally. A second respect in which similar policies are needed is in the relationship of international trade in agricultural products to nonagricultural trade. Some divergence of policy between these two sectors is possible, of course, and indeed commonly exists. But there are limits to the degree of divergence. A third area calling for policy compatibility is exports and imports. The old axiom, quoted so many times that it seems banal, is indisputably true: trade is a two-way street. We should not expect to export, continuously and in volume, unless we are willing to accept imports. And, conversely, we cannot continue indefinitely to import huge amounts of petroleum and industrial goods unless we export something to pay the bill with. Fourth, trading nations must accommodate one another. For example, to do business with the state-trading Soviet Union the United States has had to make some modification of its private trading institutions.

The consequence of the foregoing generalizations is that trade in agricultural products is disciplined by a number of factors outside agriculture. The notion that American agriculture can develop its own trade policy independently of policy in other sectors is popular with many farmers, but it is not valid.

WHAT ROLE RESPECTIVELY FOR UNILATERAL, BILATERAL, AND MULTILATERAL POLICIES?

Zealots for internationalism are prone to apply global solutions to almost any problem. If some national effort has failed, the inclination is to elevate it to the multinational level, with the assumption that a solution will then be automatic. Other people, nationalistic in their views, look with misgiving on any venture that bears the international label. Between these polar positions are thoughtful people who consider which undertakings are amenable to international initiatives and which are not.

Some matters of importance to agriculture are clearly global. Weather systems are global; the World Meteorological Organization does useful work in monitoring the world's weather, to the advantage of all cooperating countries. The food trading system is increasingly global; crop reporting is therefore a logical candidate for being internationalized and is well on its way. Agreements on grades and health standards for internationally traded food products are useful to all trading nations; Codex Alimentarius is an operative expression of this mutual interest. Exchange of information on national policies with respect to the major crops is helpful to all. The International Cotton Advisory Committee and the International Wheat Council reflect this interest.

Other areas that may appear to be appropriate objects for multilateral control seem not yet ready to be internationalized. Formal international agreement on carrying a grain reserve was proposed by Sir John Boyd Orr (World Food Bank) soon after the formation of the Food and Agriculture Organization (FAO) but was not accepted. The FAO proposal for Buffer Stocks during the 1950s had a similar fate. More recently, in 1974, the World Food Conference proposed an International Grain Reserve, but at this time this initiative has not been accepted. The evidence is that the various countries are unwilling to turn over to an international body the disposition of nationally owned grain stocks.

International commodity agreements have had a spotty experience. An International Wheat Agreement worked fairly well for the decade or so after its establishment in 1949. This success was due in large measure to the wide latitude for competitive price discovery and to the fact that economic conditions were fairly stable during that period. A subsequent International Wheat Agreement failed when it prescribed a price range less compatible with market conditions. After many years of trial and error there existed in 1977 only five commodity agreements (coffee, cocoa, sugar, wheat, and tin), and these were rather ineffective in regulating world markets. I would judge that international arrangements that involve major departures from competitive conditions have no better than a marginal prospect for success.

Up to now the United States has not been willing to surrender its sovereignty regarding domestic agricultural policy to any international body. Pronouncements of the Food and Agriculture Organization regarding United States domestic farm policies simply go unheeded. Efforts in international trade negotiations to get the Europeans to change their Common Agricultural Policy or to get the United States to change its dairy program have thus far been ineffective.

The evidence is that international undertakings whose major attribute is mutual gain are likely to be accepted. Those whose dominant feature is transfer of control over real assets or the major subordination of market forces to centralized decision-making are marginal. Those that require outright and visible sacrifice of national sovereignty are likely to be rejected.

Some initiatives that are not amenable to full-scale internationalization can be handled on a bilateral basis. Thus we have bilateral grain agreements with the Soviet Union, with Poland, and with several other countries. These are state-trading nations; we have modified our trading practices to accommodate them. But we have been unwilling to generalize this pattern.

What we come out with, then, is a series of undertakings, adapted to the respective economic, political, and diplomatic settings. Unilaterally we develop our domestic commodity programs, having some awareness of their international significance. Bilaterally we work out trade agreements with certain countries, based on unique circumstances. Multilaterally we deal with tariffs and other issues that involve minimal impairment of national sovereignty. Some undertakings such as food aid and agricultural development we administer simultaneously on a bilateral and a multilateral basis.

The point is that neither the advocates nor the opponents of internationalism can hope to carry the day. The international sector is not for ideologues. The decade of the eighties will find us feeling—and fumbling—to find those international undertakings that promise some degree of success and to reject those that do not. The principle is similar to the one by which we deal with certain issues at the state level and others nationally. Even though we have been working at this for nearly two centuries, we are not sure in which setting some issues belong.

TO WHAT EXTENT WILL AGRICULTURE BE A TOOL OF DIPLOMACY?

During the global food concern of the mid-seventies there came increased awareness of the strong role the United States played in the international food trade. At that time the United States had suffered a series of setbacks: militarily in Vietnam, economically at the hands of the OPEC countries, and diplomatically in the United Nations. The thought arose that some of our lost influence might be recaptured through the use of food. Objectives proposed for this strategy were achievement of United States foreign policy goals and increased export earnings. The columnist Eliot Janeway was among the first to propose the use of food power. Secretary of Agriculture Butz gave support (1974). Lester Brown developed the thought (1975). The idea was cogently set forth in *Business Week* in an article titled "Food Power: The Ultimate Weapon in World Politics?" (1975, pp. 54–60). The concept grew and then languished. It was revived by Senator McGovern during the summer of 1978. It remains the hope of certain people and may have some effect on the food and agricultural policies of the 1980s. Let us give it a brief examination. The question takes several related but different forms.

Is Food Power Comparable to OPEC's Oil Power?

The answer to this question appears to be negative. Critical differences are cited (R. Paarlberg 1978, pp. 539–40). The United States' share of world grain exports, ranging in the neighborhood of 50 percent, is substantially less than OPEC's share in petroleum exports, 85 percent. World trade in food is less critical to total consumption than is world trade in oil; more than half of the world's oil consumption is satisfied through imports, but only about one-eighth of world grain consumption depends on world trade. Efforts to wield food power can have the pernicious effect of inflicting more pain upon the government of the initiating nation than on the government of the target nation. Oil can be more easily withheld from the market than can food. Using food as a weapon would require action abhorrent to farmers. A government embargo would be required when pressure was being applied. It would require a greatly expanded role for government in international trade and would have an unsettling effect on the market both at home and abroad.

Sober deliberation by responsible American officials has resulted, up to now, in the nonuse of this nonweapon.

Do Food Exports Give Us Influence over Communist Countries?

During the past several decades we have vacillated on agricultural trade with the communist nations. At various times we have vigorously rejected such trade, undertaken it apologetically, interrupted it reluctantly, and embraced it enthusiastically. There is no assurance that our latest policy, that of active trade promotion for many though not all commodities, will be permanent.

The arguments for such trade, in capsule form, are that what the communist countries spend on food they cannot spend on arms; that food trade dependence on the United States will make them more cautious diplomatically; and that we need the markets.

There are several arguments opposing such trade. First, the communist countries have declared themselves our adversaries. They gain by trade with us, obviously, or they would not undertake it. We should not strengthen them. In addition, the communist countries move in and out of the market in abrupt fashion. Trade with them destabilizes domestic prices.

The dispute over trade with the communist nations, including agricultural trade, is likely to be an issue during the 1980s. With a growing population and rising real income, food needs in the USSR are certain to increase. Agriculture is the Achilles' heel of the Soviet Union. That country is likely to need the United States as a supplier. Increased agricultural trade with the People's Republic of China is a likelihood.

One thing is clear. By refusing to trade with the communist nations we do not deprive them of access to commodities. If we refused to supply them, there would simply be a shift in world trade. Other countries would withdraw from certain markets they now supply in order to ship to the communist world, perhaps at an improved price. We would move our products into the markets vacated by the other exporters. The change would be more of form than of substance. There are precedents that validate this view. When we stopped trading with Cuba the pattern of world trade shifted to accommodate the change.

Should We Use Food to Support Diplomatic Initiatives?

Experience with using food to support diplomatic purposes is mixed. Food aid was successfully used by Secretary Kissinger in 1974 in support of our efforts to promote Arab-Israeli military disengagement in the Middle East. During 1965–68 we sought unsuccessfully to use food aid in persuading India to support our policies in Southeast Asia (Bjorkman 1975, pp. 192–209).

Experience is varied, as with every other form of support for diplomatic initiatives. To rule out the use of food altogether would be unwise. To proclaim it as an all-purpose tool would be equally in error.

It seems probable that the 1980s will see food sufficiently abundant so that we will be looking for places to put it rather than withholding it as a diplomatic lever. The importing nations may consider that they do us a favor by accepting it. Access to American food supplies is unlikely to be the valuable consideration it was from 1972 to 1976.

Summary

Very likely there will be policy battles on these matters during the 1980s. The basic face-off will be between those whom we might call the internationalists and those who might be called nationalists. On particular issues, some groups will find it within themselves to "rise above principle" and support positions that reflect their economic situation rather than their stated ideology.

As I view it, there has been substantial disillusionment with the mood of internationalism that followed World War II, the era that produced the United Nations and its family of specialized agencies. International conferences, motivated by high hopes, have not always produced the desired results. These meetings have been turned into political theaters within which the communists and the Third World belabor the United States and its friends. How long the developed countries will pay the bill for the abuse to which they are subjected in these meetings remains to be seen. At this time the United States has pulled out of the International Labor Organization.

Whatever may be the international issues during the 1980s, the influence of the United States in resolving them is likely to be less than it was during the early postwar years, and the consequences for agriculture are likely to be greater.

References

Alden, Robert. 1973. Small nation interests dominate U.N. *New York Times,* September 11, pp. 1, 8.

Bjorkman, James W. 1975. Public Law 480 and the policies of self-help and short tether: Indo-American relations, 1965–68. In *Report of Commission on the Organization of the Government for the Conduct of Foreign Policy.* June 1975. Appendixes in seven volumes, Case Studies: Economic Policy, pp. 192–209.

Brown, Lester R. 1975. *The politics and responsibility of the North American breadbasket.* Worldwatch Paper 2. Washington, D.C.: Worldwatch Institute.

Butz, Earl L. 1974. *Food power: A major weapon.* Washington, D.C.: Department of Agriculture.

Food power: The ultimate weapon in world politics? 1975. *Business Week,* December 15, pp. 54–60.

Hjort, Howard. 1978. Foreign demand and export potential for U.S. farm products. Remarks at the Symposium on World Agricultural Trade, sponsored by the Federal Reserve Bank of Kansas City, May 18, Kansas City, Missouri.

Lewis, W. Arthur. 1977. *The Evolution of the International Economic Order.* Princeton: Princeton University Press.

Paarlberg, Robert L. 1978. The failure of food power. *Policy Studies Journal* 6:537–41.

Thompson, W. Scott, ed. 1978. *The Third World: Premises of U.S. policy.* San Francisco: Institute for Contemporary Studies.

U.S. Council of Economic Advisers. 1978. *Economic report of the president.* Washington, D.C.: Government Printing Office.

Uri, Pierre, ed. 1975. *North-South: Developing a new relationship.* Atlantic Papers, Paris: Atlantic Institute for International Affairs.

Warley, T. K. 1978. Implications of alternative trading institutions. Paper presented at Farm Foundation 1978 National Policy Conference, September. Burr Oak State Park, Ohio.

21. Commercial International Trade

In this chapter I shall frankly make the case that the United States has the best agricultural capability of any country in the world and is well able to supply a growing overseas market. I shall then consider whether farm and food policies are likely to permit us to capitalize on our great natural advantages.

Certain parts of the earth's surface are especially well suited to agricultural production. They have that favored combination of soil, topography, and climate that makes them garden spots. In this list must be included Northern Europe, the Danube Basin, the Ukraine, the valleys of the Ganges and of the Nile, the Pampas of the Argentine, and choice areas in the People's Republic of China.

But none of these favored farming areas approaches in its natural endowment the size and quality of the American heartland stretching from the Appalachians on the east to the Rockies on the west and from Mexico to the Canadian border. Over the eons, this land surface rose and fell, the seas came and went, the glaciers advanced and receded, sculpting and molding a terrain well suited to modern agriculture, laying down a fertile, responsive soil.

There are other superb agricultural areas in the United States, though of lesser size: the Central Valley of California, parts of the Pacific Northwest, scattered spots in the intermontane area, productive locations in the Southeast, and some good farming sections in the Northeast. When we think of American agriculture we think of the total. But for sheer magnificence, nothing in the world matches the areas between Columbus, Ohio, and Denver, Colorado; between Brownsville, Texas, and Grand Forks, North Dakota, a thousand miles or more in each direction.

Consider briefly how good this area is. The topography on the whole is level enough for modern tillage, the soil so deep the plow seldom strikes stone, the natural fertility approached but not equaled elsewhere in the world. Population per square mile permits farms large enough to be efficient. The area is well watered in the east though drier in the west, relieved in part by supplemental irrigation. Being in the middle latitudes, its growing season is long enough to produce a good crop, and the winter is sufficiently severe to reduce the disease and insect problems that beset tropical areas.

The area is penetrated by great waterways. The Saint Lawrence–Great Lakes system reaches more than a thousand miles inland; oceangoing vessels load at Duluth. The Mississippi system has more than six thousand miles of river transport, reaching as far inland as Minneapolis to the north, up the Missouri into the corn and soybean country, up the Ohio to Pittsburgh and beyond, up the Illinois to connect with the Great Lakes, up the Arkansas toward the wheat area, and deep into the middle South with the Kentucky and the Tennessee.

The frontiersmen who penetrated the American midland had the vision to foresee its possibilities. They insisted that it be settled in a pattern of private individual ownership rather than in the feudal forms of Europe, from which they had fled. They set apart one section of every township, the proceeds from whose sale were to go for an elementary school. They set up a land grant college system to give status as well as knowledge to the farm operator. They began experiment stations, so that farmers might develop the new knowledge required to best use the land, and an extension service to bring the new fund of knowledge directly to the farm operator. They crisscrossed the area with roads, railroads, and, in time, airlines. They improved the rivers. They fought for and got Rural Free Delivery, rural electrification, and rural telephones. They worked and saved and invested in tile ditches, drainage districts, irrigation projects, better buildings, and modern equipment. They set up markets, elevators and warehouses. They built stockyards, processing plants, and distributing plants. A whole new set of agricultural input industries was created: farm machinery, fertilizer, motor fuel, and agricultural chemicals among them. They set up private credit institutions to tap the Eastern money markets and so bring needed investment capital into the new area. In managerial capacity the people who farmed this agricultural empire were and are among the most capable in the world. Good basic education, good agricultural research, good adult education programs, plus the incentives latent in entrepreneurship—all these they had.

The American agricultural plant was capable of producing much more food, feed, and fiber than the United States needed. The system was fashioned for competition in world markets, and there was little doubt in the minds of those early leaders that the United States could compete. We did so. In 1925 agricultural exports were 41 percent of United States' total exports (U.S. Department of Agriculture 1953). By the time the United States was two decades into the twentieth century, most of this infrastructure was either in place or in progress. What this country had, then, was the best natural agricultural endowment in the world, supported by the best infrastructure men could devise.

And this agricultural plant fit well with national objectives. With its expanding agriculture the United States fed its growing population, including some thirty million new immigrants. Agriculture was earning an export balance; with this help we imported the capital equipment with which the nation industrialized. Thus the growing nation combined natural endowment, entrepreneurial activity, and enlightened government action to produce the greatest agricultural success story in the world up to that time.

Then, as was described in chapter 4, came a period of forty years when the United States turned away from the international market. Laws were written setting up a price structure largely independent of competition in the rest of the world. We priced ourselves out of markets and reduced production, conceding export market growth to other countries.

During the mid-seventies the international market was rediscovered. The two pertinent dimensions of that market—its probable magnitude and our ability to supply it—will be examined next.

SIZE OF THE WORLD MARKET

In forthcoming pages the focus will be primarily on the food grains and feed grains and on the oilseeds, of which soybeans are the major one. The food grains, the feed grains, and the vegetable oils provide most of the protein, carbohydrate, and fat consumed by man and so are the backbone of the world's food supply.

The world's population stood at 3.6 billion in 1970 and by 1978 had reached 4.2 billion. The United Nations median variant projects a population of 4.8 billion by 1985 (U.S. Department of Agriculture 1978a, p. 11). The big increase will be in Asia, but all parts of the world will grow. Not only will population grow, but per capita real incomes are expected to increase as well. As real incomes rise, people wish to improve their diets. This means, usually, more livestock products, which in turn call for more feed grains and soybeans, two types of farm commodities that the United States is superbly qualified to supply.

The world food market is expected to grow at an annual rate of from 2.3 to 3.0 percent during the next seven years, depending on the assumptions made in the various studies (U.S. Department of Agriculture 1974, p. 36; United Nations 1974). The increase is expected to come both from population growth and from an increase in real income. Sector by sector, where might United States agricultural export opportunities lie?

Historic Markets

Our chief historic agricultural export market has been Western Europe. In 1977 the European Economic Community took close to $7 billion worth of our agricultural exports. But growth of our agricultural market in Western Europe is inhibited by a number of factors. The Common Agricultural Policy stimulates farm production on the Continent and so limits the growth of our export opportunities. European protectionism is both cause and consequence of the Common Agricultural Policy. Basic to that policy are special devices for keeping out the products of other temperate countries like the United States. There is a tapering off in both the rate of population increase and in economic growth among the European countries.

To those who limit their vision to our historic markets (and so largely to Western Europe), export prospects are not particularly promising. This is the pessimistic analytical syndrome from which we suffered for so many years before 1972.

Recently Developed Market Economies

When one looks at the opportunities in newer markets, the picture becomes more optimistic. Chief among the new markets is Japan. In fiscal year 1977 Japan took $3.8 billion worth of our agricultural exports, an increase of four and a half times in eight years. After correcting for inflation this is still a sharp increase. Japan has grown in population and in real income. She has little tillable land of her own. She earns enormous amounts of foreign exchange from her exports of industrial goods; she is capable of buying more farm products from us. Her people consume less meat, milk, and eggs per capita than do other people of comparable income. The chances for increasing agricultural exports to Japan are good. But Japan's understandable desire for a greater degree of self-sufficiency and for diversity in sources of supply are limiting factors. To some degree the Japanese situation is repeated for other countries such as South Korea, Taiwan, and Malaysia.

The Oil-Rich Countries

The OPEC countries have the foreign exchange with which to buy food. Many of them are poor in agricultural resources and are using their new wealth to import food and improve their diets. In 1970 American agricultural exports to the OPEC countries totaled $362 million. In 1977 they stood at $1.7 billion, more than a fourfold increase. In the future the United States should have an opportunity to increase its agricultural exports to the OPEC countries: Nigeria, Indonesia, Saudi Arabia, Iran, Iraq, Kuwait, and Venezuela as well as to non-OPEC oil exporters like Mexico.

The Centrally Planned Countries

Here is real opportunity for growth. Ideological differences with the Soviet Union and with the People's Republic of China long kept the United States from considering them seriously as major potential partners in agricultural trade and no doubt kept them from thinking of this country as a supplier. Trading with them does pose substantial problems. They are state traders. In buying, they behave like the monopsonists they are. They can move in and out of the market abruptly, on a large scale, and so can be an unsettling influence. But they are populous countries, they are making real gains in per capita income, and they are intent on upgrading their diets. Our agricultural exports to the centrally planned countries, which stood virtually at zero in 1970, were more than $2.7 billion in 1976. The ideological controversy over trade with the centrally planned countries has subsided in recent years.

The difficulties of dealing with a state-trading nation are not insuperable. The five-year trade agreement with the Soviet Union, ending in 1980, is an example of successful coping with this problem. The USSR agreed to take from us, annually, from six to eight million tons of grain, with escape clauses for each country in the event of unforseeable events in crop production. Specific terms were left open. If there is sincere intent to trade, trading can take place.

The Developing Market Economy Countries

By "developing countries" we mean mostly the Third World countries of Asia, Africa, and Latin America. The developing market countries in 1977 took about 30 percent of our agricultural exports. The great bulk of this was for dollars.

The International Food Policy Research Institute of Washington, D.C., published a report (1976) addressed to the food needs of developing countries to the year 1990. In estimating food needs, production in these countries was assumed to continue to grow at the 1960–75 rates, and population growth was projected at the United Nations median rate. Growth in real income was expected to increase food needs. Under these assumed conditions, production of staple food crops in these countries would fall short of meeting needs in 1990 by 120 to 145 million metric tons. This is more than three times the total of 37 million metric tons of grain imported by these countries during the relatively good production of 1975.

It is difficult to conceive of international food movements at such very high levels. Perhaps these countries will expand food production more rapidly than was projected. If they do, the import need would be less than the indicated amount. But almost certainly it would still be substantial.

Would the developing market countries be able to buy such enormous amounts of food? In the past the assessment has been pessimistic. But reappraisal is in order; these countries may be able to do better than we have been assuming. They are, to an increasing degree, exporting manufactured products into world markets and using the revenues to buy food. During 1960–74, the volume of food imports into developing countries grew 4.4 percent each year. During the last four years of that period, at a time of rising prices, their food imports grew 6.2 percent annually. Thus, food's share of the import bill rose substantially during 1970–74 (Valdes and Huddleston 1977, p. 1).

When PL 480 food was available in large quantities (concessionary sales or donation) the United States often pushed this food out, based on the judgment that the countries could not pay. When the PL 480 tether was shortened, repayment capability became evident.

If the developing countries are to import food and pay for it, they will have to export goods or services of some kind. What can they export? Here the conventional wisdom will also have to be reexamined. These developing countries have long been considered primarily agricultural; they have not been thought of as having early or significant potential as exporters of industrial products. But with capital internationally mobile and with managerial skills reasonably transferable, this is changing. Labor is the big cost in industrial production; these countries generally have abundant labor at relatively low wages. It may well be that their comparative advantage lies more with industry and less with agriculture.

Fred Sanderson of the Brookings Institution has done an interesting study of the export performance and export potential of the developing countries (1978). He finds that exports of the non-oil-exporting countries have been growing, in real terms, at an annual rate of 7 percent during the last two decades. He projects the grain deficit of these countries at $5.5 billion by 1985 and concludes: "The foreign exchange cost of grain imports amounts to only three percent of projected export receipts of non-oil exporting developing countries—about the same percentage as at present" (p. 69).

If economic development and world trade are to take the directions indicated in this analysis, the case for liberal trade will have to be asserted and defended.

Food Aid

The foregoing export markets are commercial. In addition, there is need for food aid. In 1976 United States food aid was $1.2 billion. This constituted 5 percent of United States agricultural exports. It was 64 percent of total world food aid (Libbin 1977, p. 16). The World Food Council established a food aid target of ten million tons a year, substantially above recent levels. Food aid is now, and will be, a legitimate claimant on our agricultural production and exports. If there was any doubt about this point, it should have been dispelled during the 1973–76 period of short food supplies and high prices. The United States continued supplying international food aid, though at a reduced level.

All together, export prospects come to a considerable increment above the expanded levels of the mid-seventies, not just in dollars but in tons. The directional inference is clear. The surge of the mid-seventies was not a one-time thing. The value of United States agricultural exports, by countries, for the year 1977 is shown in appendix table 2. The value of our agricultural exports by commodity groups for that same year is shown in appendix table 3.

UNITED STATES AGRICULTURAL POTENTIAL

Is American agriculture capable of meeting the needs of an expanded export market? In 1973 the USDA issued a report on America's capacity to produce (Culver 1973, pp. 8–18). For the major crops, certain volumes were deemed likely by 1985, if land resources were not withheld and if prices were reasonably remunerative. In the brief listing below these projected volumes are set forth, compared with actual output of 1973 and of 1977. We seem to be on our way toward the projected totals.

Crop	1973	1977	1985
corn, billion bushels	5.8	6.4	9.1
wheat, billion bushels	1.7	2.0	2.3
soybeans, billion bushels	1.5	1.7	2.3
cotton, million bales	12.9	14.5	16.4

Of one thing there is no doubt. There is great need for the United States to earn large amounts of foreign exchange for at least the next decade in order to pay for the huge volume of petroleum and other products that will be imported. This will be true almost regardless of any conceivable developments in energy policy, environmental issues, or discovery of new energy sources.

OTHER EXPORTERS

Among the developed countries, traditional competitors of the United States are Canada, Australia, and South Africa. These countries have potential for expanded agricultural production. To the degree that the United States restricts production in an effort to increase price, room is made in the market for them to expand export sales.

At least four developing countries have major capabilities for expanding production. The prime example of an awakening agricultural giant is Brazil, which has shifted from exporting two cash crops (coffee, sugar) to being a multicrop exporter. From 1970 to 1977, Brazil expanded soybean production from one million to more than twelve million tons (U.S. Department of Agriculture 1978*b*, p. 5). Argentina, which for many years unintentionally discouraged agriculture with its pricing system, appears to be moving toward more enlightened farm policies and better use of its great potential. Thailand, a newcomer in grain production, can increase its yields substantially. The Sudan has capability for expansion and with substantial Arab investments may become a breadbasket for the Middle East (U.S. Department of Agriculture 1978*b*, p. 6). The likelihood is that other countries will not wait passively for us to exploit the growing world market.

OTHER VIEWS

Other researchers offer modifications of the foregoing analysis and emphasize particular aspects of it. A report of the National Research Council titled *World Food and Nutrition Study* is inconclusive on the prospect for market growth. It finds that yield increases in the developing countries will need to average 2.5 percent a year during the remainder of the century, and that this will not be easy to achieve and sustain (1977, p. 2). Nathan Koffsky, former director of the International Food Policy Research Institute, foresees, for the developing countries, the prospects of "large and increasing food deficits over time, although the food crisis of 1974 has receded" (1978, p. 21). A 1978 economic study by the Department of Agriculture projects, to 1985, foreign demand for grain from the developed countries as a group. This combines the United States, Canada, Australia, and like countries. The base year is 1970. The finding is that foreign demand for their grain is likely "to increase at least seventy-five percent and possibly as high as 125 percent, as a result of both stronger feed demand in the richer importing countries and stronger food demand in the developing countries" (U.S. Department of Agriculture 1978a, p. viii).

The appraisal of the market potential offered in this chapter is bracketed above and below by prestigious estimates. The estimate of United States production potential offered here is viewed as too high by some people in the American agricultural research establishment, who contend that we are lagging in the discovery of new knowledge. On the other hand, some farm groups, with their inborn fear of surplus, view our potential as greater than the USDA projection. I expect that American agriculture will be capable of meeting such commercial export demand as is likely to develop during the decade of the 1980s.

DOUBTS AND DANGERS

How likely is it that exports will grow at something like the amounts based on importers' needs and exporters' capabilities? This prospect could be aborted by any of several developments.

War

War, that great destroyer, severs trade lanes, doing damage to importer and exporter. The expansion of trade increases both the costs and the consequences of war. A growing volume of trade, therefore, makes the outbreak of war less likely, and, if war does occur, makes its results more fearful. Twice during the memory of living persons, during World Wars I and II, Western Europe was almost brought to its knees by its dependence on foreign food supplies. Japan was similarly affected during World War II. These memories are not easily erased. Vulnerability to wartime disruption of trade will lead to a greater degree of self-sufficiency than would result from comparative advantage alone.

Trade Restrictions

Trade restrictions are another kind of war—economic war—varying in intensity according to the nature and degree of restriction. A worldwide return to protectionism could convert American agricultural capability from an asset to a liability. After production had been expanded, markets would be shrunk. The United States would be burdened with surplus and importers would be deprived of needed food.

United States Government Restrictions on Output

The United States might again boost prices above the competitive level and so price itself out of world markets, requiring cutbacks in production. Growth in export markets would thus be conceded to countries less well endowed.

Many years ago Cornell Professor Frank A. Pearson told his class about three classic failures of agricultural policy. One, he said, was the Stevenson Plan of the 1920s, which reduced the supply and raised the price of rubber in the Malay States and stimulated rubber production in a rival country, Java. Another, he said, was the Brazilian plan to restrict the supply and raise the price of coffee, which put a competitor, Africa, into the coffee business. A third, he stated, would prove to be the American program, then in its early stages, to reduce the supply and raise the price of cotton. It would, he said, increase cotton production in various rival exporting countries around the world. He was correct.

Having succeeded, during 1973–77, in a partial escape from the inward-looking policies that had held agriculture in their grip for forty years, the United States should not return to them.

The challenge to diplomatic and agricultural leadership is to minimize these and other threats to trade, all of which are more or less responsive to the public policy process. To the degree that these dangers are reduced, American farmers improve their economic position, the trade balance is improved, and the world's people have a better diet.

THE IMPORT SIDE

Up to this point the focus has been mainly on the food and feed grains and on soybeans, for the production of which the United States enjoys comparative advantage and is on a strong net export basis. But the United States also imports agricultural products. Appendix table 4 shows imports by country of origin for the year 1977. Imports are of two kinds. First, there are mostly tropical products that are not competitive with our own production: coffee, rubber, bananas, cocoa beans, tea, and spices. In 1977 imports of these noncompetitive products, called "complementary," totaled $6.8 billion. There are relatively few controversies involving importation of these products. Policy issues center on imports of those agricultural products, called "supplementary," of which the United States itself produces substantial amounts. In 1977 imports of such products, competitive with crops and animals produced by our own farmers, were valued at $6.6 billion. Table 15 shows imports by commodity groups. The position of United States farmers with regard to imports of competitive products is next examined.

Sugar

Rivals have risen to challenge the traditional sugars. During the past seventeen years, corn sweeteners have increased two and a half times, now supplying one-fourth of the United States' caloric sweetener supply. Saccharine, on a sugar-equivalent basis, provides almost one-third as much sweetening as comes from domestically produced sugar beets. Of actual sugar consumption in 1977, domestic beets provided 32 percent, domestic cane 24 percent, and imported sugar 44 percent (U.S. Department of Agriculture 1978*e*, p. 31). Imported sugar is the least costly to produce. Beets, corn, and domestic cane cannot match tropical cane, the greatest of all converters of sunlight into biomass (Calvin 1976, pp. 270–78).

One of the first acts of the United States Congress, in the early days of the country (July 4, 1789), was to pass a tariff on the importation of sugar (Johnson 1974). Sugar has been a protected crop ever since. Horton says that in the absence of protection United States sugar production would shrink to from 20 to 25 percent of the volume it enjoys with its protected status (1970, p. 187). The industry is protected by a complex system of tariffs, quotas, and payments, most of which we criticize when they are used by other countries.

Protection of the sugar industry in the United States is rationalized on the basis of the need for a domestic supply in case of war. Another rationale for the sugar program is the desire for more stable prices than come from the highly volatile behavior of an open competitive market. The sugar program has generally demonstrated its ability to help stabilize the retail price of sugar in the United States. But this internal stability has been achieved at the cost of destabilizing the world price. We took a relatively stable amount of sugar out of the world market, whether world production was high or low, and forced the full adjustment of price and quantity onto nations that were not able to protect themselves.

Table 15. Value of United States Agricultural Imports, 1977 (in millions of dollars)

	Complementary Commodities
Coffee	$4,288
(green)	3,974
Rubber, crude dry form	571
Bananas, fresh	310
Cocoa beans	475
Drugs	133
Spices	133
Tea	178
Wool, unmanufactured	26
Other	689
Total	6,803
	Supplementary Commodities
Animals and animal	
products	$2,310
(meats)	1,289
Sugar, cane and beet	916
Oilseeds and products	639
Vegetables and preparations	616
Wines	384
Tobacco, unmanufactured	339
Fruits and preparations	373
Nuts and preparations	214
Grains and preparations	172
Other	616
total	6,579
Total agricultural	$13,382

SOURCE: U.S. Department of Agriculture (1978c, p. 6).
NOTE: Fiscal year, October–September.

This is the same destabilizing policy as is employed by the Common Agricultural Policy of the European Economic Community, which we denounce.

The decisive consideration that drives the sugar program is the political power of Western beets, Southern cane, Midwestern corn, and Eastern refineries. Policy issues related to sugar imports have been contentious for at least two hundred years and will continue to be so. Many countries of the Third World are able to produce sugar efficiently and look hopefully at the American market.

Beef

Most American beef is readied for the market by a period of grain feeding. The American resource base is a combination of rangeland for growing the cattle and feed grain production for finishing them. The American taste, pocketbook, and agricultural endowment are well suited to this kind of beef.

But at the same time there is a growing market for lean beef, coming to market directly off grass, especially for hamburger. We do not produce as much of this as the market demands. Australia, a dry country with much rangeland and little capacity for producing feed grain, is well adapted to the production of lean beef. Other countries, particularly in Latin America, are poorly suited for crop production whether because of climate, terrain, sparse population, or limited market outlets, and are adapted to grazing. Around the world, grass-grown beef is produced on land ill suited for crops. An American cattleman would have to give up profitable alternatives if he were to produce lean beef. An Australian cattleman would not. So, as the economist says it, the "opportunity cost" of producing lean beef is lower in Australia than in the United States. Australia enjoys a comparative advantage. Usually the United States imports about 7 or 8 percent of the beef it consumes, mostly lean beef.

American cattlemen resent these imports, especially when beef prices are low. Consumers want the imports increased, particularly when beef prices are high. A compromise import law has been worked out, allowing modest increase in the volume of imports as the American market grows. This law and its administration are subjected to much pulling and hauling as the beef market changes. And the United States is subjected to criticism, especially in Third World international trade conferences, for limiting access to its attractive market.

The beef import issue is unlikely to be "resolved." There are votes, for both farm and city congressmen, in demonstrating advocacy for one's constituents. There may be more votes in agitating the issue than in resolving it, if indeed there is a solution.

Dairy Products

In the United States, prices of manufactured dairy products such as butter, cheese, and nonfat dry milk are held above competitive world levels by a system of price supports. Were it not for a companion system of import quotas, we would suck these products out of the world market, away from their accustomed users, and impound them in American cold storage houses. Foreigners often demand that we relax or remove our import quotas, but we can never relinquish these so long as we support prices above competitive levels.

Imports of dairy products are small compared with our total production. Since 1974 dairy imports, on a milk-equivalent basis, amounted to between 1 and 2 percent of United States production.

What would happen if we were to give up both price supports and import quotas for manufactured dairy products? According to a study by the Department of Agriculture (1975), New Zealand and Australia are the countries with the lowest cost of production. European dairy production is heavily subsidized, so that production costs are difficult to ascertain. The volume of additional dairy products available for export from these countries is limited in the short run. Nevertheless, if the American price were at world levels and our markets were open, more dairy products would come in from New Zealand, Australia, and Europe. Prices of manufactured dairy products in the United States would fall, the volume of milk production would be diminished, incomes of American dairy farmers would decline, and some dairymen would go out of business. This is what the dairymen fear.

When markets get tight and retail prices rise, as they did during 1973–74, the government liberalizes the quotas to let in more dairy products. Usually enough additional supplies come in to anger the farmers but not enough to appease the consumers. Administering import quotas is a thankless proposition.

Dairy-state congressmen, who formerly ran for office against margarine, now run against imports of manufactured dairy products. Here, too, from the politician's standpoint, the issue may be worth more than a solution. Back in the 1950s, while the Department of Agriculture was working on import controls for dairy products, a dairy-state congressman told me, only half in jest, "I don't know what I would do for an issue if you fellows ever solve this problem."

Fats and Oils

The United States is a large net exporter of fats and oils, chiefly in the form of that marvelous crop, soybeans, in the production of which we enjoy comparative advantage. A considerable share of our exports moves out in the form of soybean oil subsidized under PL 480. But we do import some food oils, chiefly coconut and palm, that have somewhat different end uses than does soybean oil. The soybean industry seems to have convinced itself that it has much to fear from imports, especially palm oil. This is in spite of the fact that we export ten times as much oil-bearing material and products as we import. And the industry has also talked itself into a high state of apprehension about increased soybean production in Brazil. The American soybean industry is lusty and growing. Analysts project further growth despite overseas expansion of palm oil and soybeans (Hacklander 1976). But the controversy over imports of vegetable oils has proved rewarding to some individuals. Very likely we shall hear more about vegetable oil imports during the decade of the eighties.

Specialty Crops

Specialty crops like strawberries, tomatoes, mushrooms, flowers, fruits, and nuts require much human labor. American farm wage rates are high by comparison with those abroad. Other countries have comparative advantage for certain of these specialty crops and ship us increasing amounts. We get tomatoes and strawberries from Mexico, cut flowers by air from Colombia, and mushrooms from Taiwan. American producers of these crops are at a disadvantage; their problems are not imaginary. This is an expanding difficulty; it is likely to increase in importance as a policy issue.

When the American negotiator sits down with the people of other countries to bargain for the reduction of trade barriers, he would like to open markets wider for our export crops. But he must give up something if he wishes to make a gain. What can he give in exchange? Access to the United States for more European or New Zealand dairy products? A bigger share of the American sugar market? More beef from Central America? More specialty crops from Mexico? Acceptance of commodity agreements, sought by some of our trading partners, that carry price and quantity specifications that are objectionable to American farmers? The concessions he can offer are limited by law and by the economic and political facts of life.

SPECIAL ATTRIBUTES OF AGRICULTURAL TRADE

One of the basic issues is whether international trade in agricultural products is unique or whether it is similar to other kinds of trade. This argument has run through several rounds of tariff negotiations.

The case for agriculture's uniqueness rests on a number of contentions. First, food is the prime necessity of life. To be highly vulnerable to a cutoff of supplies is unacceptable. Food is thus especially imbued with public interest. So a greater degree of self-sufficiency is necessary for food than for other products. This calls for protectionist policies. Second, world market prices of farm products are highly volatile, with resulting difficulties for both farmers and consumers. Thus some form of insulation from competitive and wildly gyrating world prices is considered desirable. Third (or perhaps first), farmers are thought to wield political influence disproportionate to their numbers. In countries such as France, Japan, and the United States, some public officials believe that farmers hold the balance of political power. So their felt needs for protection are given more than ordinary consideration.

These views are deeply held, especially by the Europeans, who wish, in trade negotiations, to keep agricultural products separate from industrial goods. The United States, reflecting the views of an exporting nation with little fear for its food supply, minimizes these special attributes of agriculture and tries to keep farm and nonfarm products in the same negotiating package. The hope of the farm interests (and it is a vain hope) is that foreign markets for United States farm products can be opened by providing access to the American market for additional foreign manufactured products.

It is unrealistic to expect the free working of supply and demand for agricultural products in the setting here described. Often, in the battles on agricultural trade, the liberal trader makes the better logical argument but the protectionist wins the decision. Most of the liberalization of trade achieved in multilateral negotiations since 1934 has been in the nonfarm sector.

TOOLS OF THE TRADE

If price is not allowed to perform its normal function, alternative means of allocating resources and rationing supplies must be found. Various tools are available. Generally accepted methods of pushing exports are trade promotion, extension of government credit, government insurance against various hazards, and food aid. Export subsidies and other forms of dumping are disapproved. Tax rebates for exported commodities are a difficult-to-detect form of export subsidy. Exchange-rate manipulation for particular commodities is another device for pushing out exports. It is viewed with disfavor in international negotiations. To curb the out-shipment of crops it customarily exports, a country may impose an export embargo, as the United States did briefly for grain and soybeans during the food scare of the mid-seventies.

The most common policy objective regarding imported products is to keep them out. The historical device for doing this was the tariff of so many cents per pound or per bushel. But now new means have been developed (Hillman 1978). A subtle one is a ''health restriction.'' Some of these are legitimate, such as restrictions against the importation of beef from countries that have that highly contagious and destructive affliction foot-and-mouth disease. But some are intended more to protect the economic health of the domestic farmer than the physical health of the consumer. Another device is the variable tariff, the favored tool of the European Economic Community. If the world price of the protected commodity should drop by ten cents a pound, the tariff would increase by a like amount, so that the effect of price competition is canceled out. As a protectionist device an import quota is more effective than a tariff. With a quota there is precise control over the quantity imported and assurance that competition from abroad will be confined to prescribed limits. A tariff provides no such assurance. Quotas are of two kinds. One is the forthright quota, specified by law or by administrative edict. The other is the so-called voluntary quota, whereby the exporting country "agrees" to limit shipments. These "voluntary" agreements are negotiated under an unspoken form of duress; the exporting country understands that unless it limits shipments on its own, the importing country may enact more stringent quotas. Another device is the countervailing duty. International trade negotiating rules recognize the right of the importing country, if subjected to dumping, to increase its tariff rates on other products imported from the offending nation. Sometimes, and this is rare, an importing country earnestly wants more of a certain product from the exporting country. The ordinary way of getting the additional product would be by bidding up the price. But if price has been frozen by law or agreement, other ways may be invoked. One tool is a promise or threat of future action. Thus, when the United States needed more imported sugar and the domestic price was lower than the world market, the needed supplies were obtained by implying that countries that provided such sugar would be rewarded by generous quotas when market conditions changed. More imported beef was obtained in similar fashion during the mid-seventies.

To administer this complex mechanism takes an enormously involved bureaucracy, at both national and international levels. Ever since Cordell Hull, international trade matters have been a responsibility of the president, administered through the various departments of the executive branch. The legislative branch has a role in law and in practice that combines, in varying degrees, surveillance, advice, consent, and veto.

At the international level the main theaters of action are two. One is the General Agreement on Tariffs and Trade (GATT) at Geneva, Switzerland, where the multilateral trade negotiations (MTN) take place. This forum has been dominated, since its emergence thirty years ago, by the big trading nations like the United States, the European Common Market, and Japan. The other forum is the United Nations Conference on Trade and Development (UNCTAD), a relative newcomer. It is dominated by the nations of the Third World. For a long time the developed market countries refused to take UNCTAD seriously. They now must, so long as the oil-producing countries continue to lend their weight to the bargaining position of the Third World countries. The United States does most of its speaking in the GATT and most of its listening in UNCTAD.

THE LINEUP

The word ''liberal'' as used in this chapter means a general preference for open competitive international markets over markets that are regulated or strongly influenced by government action. ''Protectionist'' generally means the reverse. It is not possible to categorize with clarity either the general farm organizations or the commodity groups by this criterion. Gradations are more relevant than categories. Among the major general farm organizations, the Farm Bureau is clearly the most liberal on trade issues. The National Farmers Union is the most protectionist. The Grange takes a middle position. The National Farmers Organization and the American Agriculture Movement are domestically rather than internationally oriented.

Among commodity groups, chief advocates of liberal trade are the export-oriented producers of corn and other feed grains. Soybean growers were in the liberal camp but are flirting with the protectionists. Cotton growers have had a change of heart; they were strongly protectionist but more recently have come to look with greater favor on the competitive market. Wheat growers seem to favor a higher wheat price, whether this can be obtained by such ideologically incompatible devices as the competitive market, restricted output, price supports, deficiency payments, trade agreements, food aid, market promotion, export subsidies, or restrictions on imports. The most protectionist people probably are the sugar producers. Close on their heels are the dairymen. Cattlemen accept the market discipline domestically but can become livid about imports. Producers of the specialty crops—fruits, nuts, and vegetables—are likewise generally willing to accept the good and bad fortune dealt out by the domestic market but consider low-cost foreign competition to be unfair.

This setting is amenable to political exploitation. A political diatribe against imports is virtually a riskless undertaking. It is almost certain to win the applause of the special interest group to which it is delivered. The people who might be offended—foreign producers—are unlikely to hear of it, and if they do they cannot vote their disapproval. Tirades against imports have kept politicians in office and farm organizations in existence beyond their time of useful service. Opposition to imports helps assure political longevity. It is perhaps the best form of occupational Geritol available to the officeholder.

Political Responsibilities and Opportunities

Clearly, the open competitive market will not be allowed to exercise full discipline over international trade in farm products. It therefore becomes the responsibility of public officials, elected and appointed, to determine the degree and nature of the intervention. This is a weighty responsibility, as is evident from all that has been said. Involved are the incomes of farm people, the price of food to American consumers, the strength of the dollar, the food intake of people abroad, cost to the government, the congeniality or animosity of our trading partners, and the economic development of the Third World—not necessarily in that order.

International trade in farm products will be a major farm policy issue during the 1980s. I venture the judgment that the advantages of trade will more than offset such negative forces as have been described. Both our exports and our imports of farm products will increase during the decade ahead. We and our trading partners will gain thereby.

References

Calvin, Melvin. 1976. Photosynthesis as a resource for energy and materials. *American Scientist,* pp. 270–78.

Culver, David W. 1973. American agriculture: Its capacity to produce. *Farm Index* 12:8–16. Washington, D.C.: USDA.

Hacklander, Duane D. 1976. *The decade ahead for U.S. soybeans.* Economic Research Service Report 652, pp. 30–33. Washington, D.C.: USDA.

Hillman, Jimmye S. 1978. *Non tariff agricultural trade barriers.* Lincoln: University of Nebraska Press.

Horton, Donald C. 1970. Policy directions for the United States sugar program. *American Journal of Agricultural Economics* 52:185–96.

International Food Policy Research Institute. 1976. *Food needs of developing countries: Projections of production and consumption to 1990.* Washington, D.C.

Johnson, D. Gale. 1974. *The sugar program: Large costs and small benefits.* Washington, D.C.: American Enterprise Institute.

Koffsky, Nathan M. 1978. Food needs of developing countries. *International food policy issues: A proceedings.* Foreign Agricultural Economics Report 143, pp. 21–25. Washington, D.C.: USDA, Economics, Statistics, and Cooperatives Service.

Libbin, Susan A. 1977. U.S. agricultural commodity aid and commercial exports, 1955–1976. In *Foreign agricultural trade of the United States.* Washington, D.C.: USDA, Economic Research Service.

Malmgren, Harald. 1972. *International economic peacekeeping in phase II.* New York: Quadrangle/New York Times.

Martin, Marshall A., and Dunn, Lucia F., eds. 1978. The competitive threat from abroad: Fact or fiction? In *Proceedings: Conference on International Trade.* Lafayette, Ind.: Purdue University.

Murray, John W., and Atkinson, L. J. 1978. *An analysis of the UNCTAD integrated program for commodities.* Foreign Agricultural Economic Report 148. Washington, D.C.: USDA, Economics, Statistics, and Cooperatives Service.

National Research Council. World Food and Nutrition Study Steering Committee. 1977. *World food and nutrition study: The potential contributions of research.* Washington, D.C.: National Academy of Sciences.

Sanderson, Fred H. 1978. The role of international trade in solving the food problem of the developing countries. In *International food policy issues: A proceedings.* Foreign Agricultural Economic Report 143, pp. 69–78. Washington, D.C.: USDA, Economic, Statistics, and Cooperatives Service.

Tontz, Robert L. 1978. U.S. agricultural imports and trade balances: Short-term trends. In *Foreign agricultural trade of the United States,* pp. 5–14. Washington, D.C.: USDA, Economics, Statistics, and Cooperatives Service.

U.S. Department of Agriculture. 1953. *Statistical bulletin 112.* Foreign Agricultural Service. Washington, D.C.: USDA.

―――. 1974. *The world food situation and prospects to 1985.* Foreign Agricultural Economic Report 98. Washington, D.C.: USDA, Economic Research Service.

―――. 1975. *The impact of dairy imports on the U.S. dairy industry.* Agricultural Economics Report 278. Washington, D.C.: USDA, Economic Research Service.

―――. 1978a. *Alternative futures for world food in 1985. Vol. 1. World GOL model analytic report.* Foreign Agricultural Economic Report 146. Washington, D.C.: USDA, Economics, Statistics, and Cooperatives Service.

―――. 1978b. *Changing world agricultural trade.* Issue Briefing Paper no. 7. Washington, D.C.: Office of Governmental and Public Affairs.

―――. 1978c. The foreign connection: Imports. *Farm Index.* Washington, D.C.: USDA.

―――. 1978d. *Outlook for U.S. agricultural exports.* Washington, D.C.: USDA.

―――. 1978e. *Sugar and sweetener report,* vol. 3, no. 9. Washington, D.C.: USDA.

Valdes, Alberto, and Huddleston, Barbara. 1977. *Potential of agricultural exports to finance increased food imports in selected developing countries.* Occasional Paper 2. Washington, D.C.: International Food Policy Research Institute.

22. International Food Aid

Estimates of the Food and Agriculture Organization indicate that about 450 million of the world's 4,000 million people do not receive sufficient food (1974). This is something over 10 percent of the world population. Other estimates bracket this number.

From studies of the World Health Organization we know fairly well who these unfortunate people are. They are pregnant and nursing mothers, weanling children, landless laborers in the rural areas, the urban unemployed, the aged, the ill, and the infirm. Disproportionately they are women. Most of them are in Asia. Many are in Africa and in Latin America. There are some in every country—fewer, proportionately, in the United States than in most other places. With the increase in the world population, absolute numbers of malnourished people have increased, though the proportion has diminished (National Research Council 1977, p. 27).

Statistics are useful but are an inadequate means to portray hunger. Statistics are impersonal; they blur the true tragic nature of the problem. People who focus heavily on totals and averages sometimes note that food production has risen overall or that per capita consumption has increased and thus infer that everyone in the population is better off, which may not at all be the case.

People customarily think of the world food problem in terms of starvation. No one can estimate with acceptable accuracy the number of people who die each year from lack of food. Nutritional deficiencies aggravate disease and debilitation, increasing the death rate. What is then the direct cause of death? Acute and chronic infections and anemia reduce human effort. Loss of vitality undermines a person's capacity to savor life, and the human condition is de-

274

graded. It is this endemic situation that constitutes the more intractable part of the world food problem.

The major reason people receive insufficient food is that they are too poor to buy as much as they need. If the poor people were to become more productive they could earn more money and could bid food away from those who now consume it in kinds and amounts beyond their physical needs.

There are contentions over whether the world food problem is one of production or of distribution. This is a futile argument, like the debate over which blade of the scissors does the cutting. Both production and distribution are important. If production were vastly expanded and if the income pattern were unaltered, there would still be many hungry people (Schertz 1977, pp. 32–34). On the other hand, an improved pattern of distribution has greatest promise of success if it comes from an increment to production. There is no politically satisfactory way to redistribute a stagnant or diminishing total.

THE FOOD AID PROGRAM OF THE UNITED STATES

Large-scale American efforts to alleviate hunger abroad were first undertaken with Herbert Hoover's successful program to feed the people of devastated Europe after World War I. Food was shipped to Europe through Lend-Lease during World War II. After that war there were large shipments of food under the Greek-Turkish aid effort, through the United Nations Relief initiative, and with the help of the Marshall Plan. There were specific authorizations of food aid to Pakistan and to India. Section 550 of the Mutual Security Act required that certain sums be used to finance sales of food for local currency.

All of these were forerunners of Public Law 480, the Agricultural Trade Development and Assistance Act of 1954, the chief vehicle of food aid. The program became known as Food for Peace. While PL 480 is the chief vehicle for food aid, there are some additional shipments financed by the Agency for International Development. Strictly speaking, we should say "agricultural commodity aid" rather than "food aid" because part—a small part—of the aid has been in the form of nonfood commodities such as cotton and tobacco. But we shall forego some accuracy to gain some familiarity; we shall use the conventional term.

From 1955 through September 1976 our food aid totaled $25.5 billion. Over the twenty-one-year period it constituted 14 percent of our agricultural exports. Appendix table 5 summarizes the history of the program. The United States is by far the largest supplier of food aid. From 1960 to 1968 we supplied more than 90 percent of the world total. Recently the American share has diminished (Libbin 1977, p. 16).

Our food aid programs have undergone a quarter-century of evolutionary change. At this time they are of various kinds, briefly described in the paragraphs that follow.

Disaster Relief

Disaster relief is the most dramatic form of our food aid. The most noteworthy example of famine relief was our assistance during the 1966–67 failure of the monsoon in India, particularly in Bihar Province. Here is Alan Berg's description of that effort (1973):

During the crisis, the Indian government unloaded and moved an average of seven trains a day—fifty cars per train—an average of 550 miles. By the end of 1967, 153,000 fair price shops were operating in the country (20,000 in Bihar, benefitting forty-seven million Biharis) and six million people were involved in relief works projects (700,000 in Bihar). Programs for youngsters and destitutes reached nearly twenty million (seven million in Bihar) during the two years. The cost of all this: somewhere in the vicinity of $700 million (perhaps $200 million spent in Bihar). Help came from many foreign quarters, but the major flow came from the United States, which provided one-fifth of its wheat crop. This unprecedented movement of food from one country to another required an armada of 600 ships. Ships docked at the rate of three a day, depositing an average of two billion pounds per month. Sixty million Indians are estimated to have been sustained for two years solely by these shipments.

Other initiatives have helped meet food needs arising from other natural disasters such as floods and earthquakes. Food used in this form of aid moves through various channels: the voluntary agencies, the World Food Program, and, bilaterally, from the government of the United States to the government of the stricken country. In the government-to-government programs the recipient government typically makes the distribution, usually on a mass basis. Programs are terminated when the disaster has passed. In 1976 programs for disaster relief and economic development totaled $65 million (U.S. Department of Agriculture 1978a, p. 71).

Donations through Voluntary Relief Agencies

In addition to government-to-government aid, there is help on a people-to-people basis. In 1976 these programs totaled $192 million. Through these programs food is distributed directly to target groups: mother and infant clinics with in-clinic feeding, and schoolchildren. Food is also used as part payment for work by unemployed or underemployed people on small-scale development projects. In fiscal 1976, commodities were[1]shipped to about forty million recipients in seventy-eight countries and territories (U.S. Department of Agriculture 1978*a*, p. 58). Administration of the programs is through what are known as the voluntary agencies. Prominent among these are CARE, Catholic Relief Service, American Joint Distribution Committee, Church World Service, Lutheran World Service, United Methodist Commission on Relief, Seventh Day Adventist World Service, and UNICEF. There are others, some of them small. These agencies get their resources from individual donations, church budgets, and fund-raising projects. Most of this money is used in distributing government-donated food. Some is used for purchasing supplies. There are three parties to the operation, whose functions are outlined here.

The United States government donates the food, processes and packages it if need be, and pays ocean freight to the port in the recipient country. The mix of donated foods depends on availability, nutritive value, acceptability to the recipients, and cost. Major foods donated are the cereal grains, often enriched (vitamins and minerals) and fortified (with soy). Also important are nonfat dry milk and vegetable oils.

Congress has mandated a minimum allocation of 1.3 million tons of food annually to be provided to the voluntary agencies and the World Food Program. This amount is to rise by 50,000 tons a year beginning in fiscal year 1981, to a total of 1.8 million tons (Kathleen Bitterman, pers. comm.).

The government of the country for which the food is destined is a participant in the food donation programs. It usually waives any tariff duty, provides internal transportation, agrees on the identification of target groups, and often provides the buildings used for distributing food. In some cases the recipient country takes care of the internal expenses of the voluntary agency.

The voluntary agencies supervise the distribution to individuals in the recipient country. This is supplemental feeding; a participant receives only part of his food needs from this source. Distribution is made on the basis of need, without regard to race, religion, or political affiliation. Religious proselytizing is not permitted. To the maximum extent possible, the food aid is associated with health services, vocational education, help with family planning, and the donation of needed commodities other than food. The emphasis is on maternal and child health, food for work, and school feeding. Ninety-three percent of the voluntary agencies' programs are in countries with per capita gross national product of $580 or less.

World Food Program.

The Food and Agriculture Organization of the United Nations has a World Food Program in which fifty-three donor nations participate. An international board determines where and how the food is to be used. The United States contributes its share, specified as 25 percent of the total. The program, like disaster relief and distribution through the voluntary agencies, is budgeted under Title II of Public Law 480. The World Food Program put food into the Sahel district of Africa during the prolonged drought of the early seventies.

An advantage of the multilateral program is that it can get food to needy people in countries that, for political reasons, would refuse to accept food from a particular donor. From the standpoint of the United States, the multilateral program has the disadvantage that the use of our food may be determined not by ourselves but by an international group. For 1977 and 1978 the United States pledged $188 million to this program (U.S. Department of Agriculture 1978a, p. 9).

Long-term Credit Sales

By far the largest share of our food aid goes out under the long-term credit program, Title I of PL 480. A country that is judged too poor to buy needed food in the competitive market is given low-cost credit, usually 2 to 3 percent interest, for a long period (up to forty years), with a grace period (up to ten years) before repayment begins. The concessional terms are so generous that the grant element amounts to as much as two-thirds of the face value of the loan (Saylor 1977, p. 202). The credit is used to buy specified amounts of foods that have been declared currently available. This food may move through private channels and may be indistinguishable to the consumer from food of other origin. Or the food may be distributed by the government of the recipient country to designated needy people at below-market prices.

At various times this part of the program has been financed by sales for the currency of the receiving country, by long-term sales for dollars on concessionary credit terms, and by long-term sales for foreign currencies that can be converted into dollars. The public prefers sales for dollars, even though the terms may be so generous that the sale resembles a gift. In 1976 programs of this kind totaled $650 million.

All together, the Title I and Title II programs moved a total of $907 million worth of food in fiscal year 1976. Preliminary indications are that for calendar year 1977 the value of exports under PL 480 totaled $1,074 million, slightly up from the previous year. When food exports financed by the Agency for International Development are added, the total comes to $1.5 billion (Libbin 1978, p. 31). The size of the program has fluctuated around a level of about a billion dollars a year for the past quarter-century. As the value of the dollar has diminished, the real size of the program has been reduced.

Appendix table 5 shows, in dollars, the magnitude of the PL 480 program, with its various parts, from 1955 to 1976. Appendix table 6 indicates which countries have been the major recipients during the life of the program. Appendix table 7 reports the combined magnitude of Title II donation programs (disaster relief, work of the voluntary agencies, and World Food Program) in dollars and by number of recipients from 1969 to 1976.

OBJECTIVES OF FOOD AID

Our food aid programs have several objectives. The purist, who wants the program to be judged by a single criterion, finds the multiple objectives troublesome. The pragmatists, of whom I am one, are happy to see several purposes accomplished rather than one alone. These are the various objectives:

Humanitarian need—food for the hungry—is the best understood and most frequently asserted reason for the program. This is the objective subscribed to by church groups and concerned citizens. Advocacy comes through what is known as the hunger lobby.

Surplus disposal was the original reason for Public Law 480. This purpose has the support of farm groups who wish to avoid the price-depressing effect of surplus. It also wins the approval of government; this is a way of cutting storage costs for government-owned grain. In about six or seven years the cost of storage equals the value of the product. There have been times (supplies heavy over a protracted period) when giving away the food was the most economical thing the government could do; stocks could not be marketed without depressing prices below legally established levels. And paying farmers not to produce is surprisingly expensive.

Trade development is an objective to be achieved by acquainting foreign populations with American foods. As the recipients escape poverty, they may buy from us in the commercial market. This idea has worked with wheat in Japan. Farm commodity groups strongly support this objective.

Economic development is one of the purposes. The idea here is that if a country's food needs are met by this program, resources are released for development within the receiving country. It is a form of foreign-exchange support. Foreign exchange not spent for imported food can be used for imported capital goods. This effect of the program is looked on with misgiving by USDA officials. Their objective is to see that the shipments are in addition to food that would be imported for dollars, not a substitute for the dollar trade in farm products.

Support for diplomatic initiatives is sometimes achieved by food aid. Occasionally, through the granting of food aid, a country can be persuaded to support some arrangment sponsored by the Americans. During the first six months of fiscal year 1975, 30 percent of the total PL 480 long-term credit sales were proposed for Cambodia and South Vietnam, 19 percent for the adversaries in the Middle East, and 15 percent for Chile and South Korea (Saylor 1977, p. 204). These programs obviously had a major diplomatic-military component. The military, the State Department, and the National Security Council are the major advocates of initiatives of this kind.

GRADUATES OF THE PROGRAM

A distinctive feature of the food aid program is that a nation that once receives help does not necessarily continue to do so. Countries graduate from the program as their economic position improves. Six developing countries (Republic of China, Brazil, Iran, Peru, Chile, and Colombia) and two developed ones (Japan and Spain) are examples of former PL 480 Title I sales recipients that became good United States commercial customers. Figure 3 portrays graphically the transition from aid to trade for a dozen of the more dramatic cases.

Commendation seems merited by a program that has saved lives, alleviated hunger, avoided the growth factor characteristic of so many governmental activities, pushed out of the program countries that had reached the point at which they could help themselves, stayed out of partisan politics, helped build markets, lubricated American diplomatic initiatives, and earned the support of Congress and the people for a quarter of a century.

MYTHS ABOUT FOOD AID

Most Americans have never missed a meal except by choice. So we are poorly equipped to understand hunger or its alleviation. Into this vacuum of knowledge have rushed various myths, unproved collective beliefs that have enough truth to make them credible and enough error to make them dangerous. Here is a short list.

Myths of the Advocates

The common attribute of advocacy myths is that they are brimming over with laudable purpose. Three such myths are listed, with acknowledgment of such truth as they have and with what I hope is corrective comment.

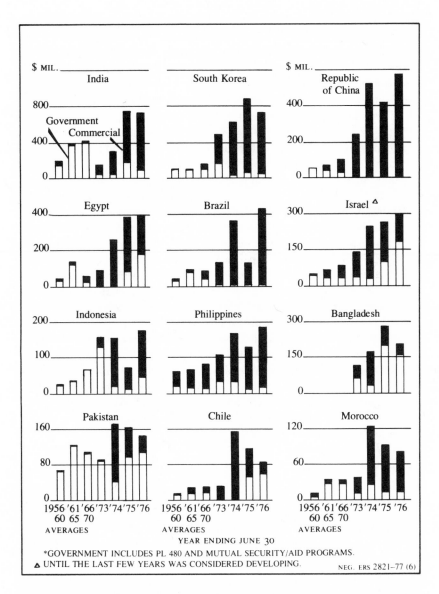

FIGURE 3. United States agricultural exports to developing countries, government and commercial, fiscal years 1956–76. From U.S. Department of Agriculture (1977*a*, p. 16).

Myth one: We could feed the world. A common view is that the United States could, if it resolved to do so, send overseas enough food aid to banish malnutrition. This view overstates our agricultural potential and reflects misunderstanding of the attitudes in the recipient countries. The FAO says there are 450 million people in the world who lack sufficient food. This is more than twice the population of the United States. We simply lack the resources that would be necessary to supplement the food supplies of that many people.

There are good reasons for not trying to feed the world, even if we could. A huge expansion of food aid would depress prices of farm products in the recipient countries, inhibit their agricultural development, and make them continually dependent on us for our gifts. They would become our permanent subsidized relief clients, losing their autonomy in international affairs, Out of their experience with hunger they can see this danger, though we may not. Contrary to popular belief, these countries want limited rather than openhanded food aid. They want help at a time of emergency, rather than help that will put them in a position of continuing deep dependency. If that is difficult to comprehend, maybe it can be understood if put in reverse. Would the United States, its farmers and its government officials, be pleased to see huge amounts of foreign food donated in this country, depressing prices of farm products and discouraging agricultural investment? The question answers itself.

The fact that we cannot feed the world, that we cannot by our aid banish world hunger, is not a valid indictment of the program. There is no program of any sort that can, by itself, solve the world food problem. It will take all that can be done through many undertakings—agricultural development, commercial trade, family planning, public education, food aid, and institutional change— to do the job. The main responsibility lies with the poor countries themselves.

Myth two: With food aid we could win friends. The concept held by some people is this: We should provide a bridge of ships, laden with donated wheat, bound for Calcutta. There on the dock will be the hungry Indian populace, waiting to receive this gift and, out of gratitude, voting with us in the United Nations.

There may be some thanks and some friendship resulting if the effort has the right blend of prudence and compassion. But if some quid-pro-quo is involved, the food is not a gift; it is part of a bargain, with no more reason for gratitude on one side than on the other. An undertaking that is contrived to put one country under obligation to another is unlikely to be the basis of enduring friendship. The motivation is wrong.

These people are poor. They are also proud. They regret being unable to supply their own needs. The fact of food aid makes obvious their dependent status. Few people, domestic or foreign, are grateful for being deprived of their self-reliance and having the fact flaunted before the public.

Myth three: American self-denial would solve the problem. Americans consume more total food than is required by their physical needs. They consume large quantities of livestock products, made from cereal grains that could be consumed by human beings. We are charged with having preempted more than our share of the world's food. We hear that if we would reduce our intake, much food would be available for poor people overseas.

There are good reasons for reducing and simplifying our diets: health, economy, and removal of a basis for invidious comparison. But it does not follow that if we cut back our intake the food foregone would be available to the poor people of the world. With demand reduced, prices would fall and farmers would curtail output. Self-denial is a means of meeting the food needs of the world's poor only if it is accompanied by a system of subsidies to get the food produced, coupled with a parallel system of subsidies to get it shipped, distributed, and wisely used overseas.

Myths of Those Who Oppose Food Aid

Here I shall list five widely held ideas that will win endorsement when voiced before a conservative audience. Myths, clichés, or half-truths, whatever one might call them, here they are.

Myth one: Food aid is injurious to the recipients. The argument is that food aid deprives people of their self-reliance and inhibits their agricultural development. That there is a degree of truth to this belief has already been acknowledged. Competent research has shown that it was true in Colombia, where we poured in very large amounts of wheat. From 1955 to 1963 the United States provided PL 480 wheat equal to more than one-third of Colombia's domestic production. During this period the real farm price of wheat in Colombia fell 25 percent and its wheat production declined 38 percent. For many decades Colombia had produced about half its wheat requirements, but during the heavy reliance on PL 480 wheat the gap between domestic production and utilization widened (Barlow and Libbin 1969, pp. 23–32; Adams 1964; Isenman and Singer 1975).

The Colombian case and a few others provide particular facts giving credibility to the belief that food aid is hurtful to the recipient country. The error comes when we generalize from a particular case. While an excessive amount of aid is harmful, a lesser amount can do much good. Most participating countries have received limited rather than excessive help. One should not condemn a medicine because an overdose has a bad effect.

The relationship between the volume of food aid and that unquantifiable something we might call "the general good" is in the form of a curve. With zero program, zero effect. At some intermediate program level, much good. At very high aid levels, the result is damaging. The difficulty is that people find it hard to conceive of such relationships. It is simpler to think that if some is good, more is better, and the largest amount imaginable is the best that could be. Or, conversely, if some is bad, more is worse, and the largest conceivable amount is the worst possible.

It is harder to give food away successfully than it is to sell it. Required are a level head and a warm heart, a rare combination. It is amazing that this immensely difficult job has been done as well as it has.

Myth two: Food aid is costly. There is truth, of course, to the assertion that food aid costs money. A billion dollars a year is a large sum. But some perspective is appropriate. International food aid costs about one-fifth as much as our domestic food program. It constitutes about 0.2 percent of the federal budget.

Myth three: Food aid misses the target groups. Every so often a congressman or a newspaper reporter traveling abroad sees some donated wheat or nonfat dry milk being sold in the black market rather than consumed by the needy person for whom it was intended. This does indeed happen. The newspapers feature such stories, and the public concludes that this is typical. I know of no careful studies of the degree to which food aid is diverted from the intended recipients. A fair guess is that overseas food aid reaches the target group about as well as does our domestic food program. For these programs, the USDA says 14 percent of the food goes to people who are either ineligible for it or receive more food than they are entitled to (U.S. Department of Agriculture 1977*b*). In the receiving countries, want is so widespread that even the food that misses the specified target group nevertheless often alleviates hunger.

Myth four: Corruption is widespread. There have been cases in which graft and corruption have crept into the PL 480 programs. The name of Tongsun Park immediately comes to mind. The belief has arisen that abuses of this kind are characteristic of the program. But scrutiny by the Government Accounting Office and other surveillance bodies keeps such cases from becoming general.

Myth five: We have the option of scrapping international food aid. Some people who oppose the food aid program conduct themselves as if eliminating it were a real alternative. The implicit belief such people hold is that we could say to the starving Biharis: "We know you are hungry and that we have the means to help. But if we help you, you might survive and have children. The problem some years from now would be even greater. It is better that you die." That might have been said a hundred years ago. In fact it was said and was decisive for public policy. But it cannot be a guide for public policy in the 1980s. Times have changed. This was proved during the food scare of 1973–76, when we continued supplying food aid though our own supplies were short and prices were high. There is little point in talking about options that are no longer available.

FOOD AID AND MALNUTRITION

An appraisal of our food aid programs from the standpoint of their effect on malnutrition was given by C. Peter Timmer, professor of the economics of food and agriculture at the Harvard School of Public Health (U.S. Department of Agriculture 1978*b*, pp. 29–35). Timmer gives high marks to famine relief programs, which he says have not only saved lives but also have "generated important lessons about the nature of the development process." He is less enthusiastic about the nutritional consequences of direct feeding programs such as those operated by the voluntary agencies. He says, "Only a handful have demonstrated a significant nutritional impact on the target population." The third type of aid, sales of food on favorable terms, he considers even more difficult to evaluate. Timmer says of this category, "Food aid becomes a form of foreign exchange support for the recipient country, and the uses to which the freed foreign exchange are put determine the long-run effectiveness of food aid."

Those people who have examined our international food aid programs most objectively very likely would agree with Timmer. Those who have analyzed the United States Food Stamp Program and the direct donation programs will note similarities between domestic and foreign food aid.

SOME TROUBLESOME MATTERS

Program appraisals such as those of Timmer raise a major question. If it is indeed true that, apart from famine relief, the effect of the program on nutrition of the recipients is marginal or modest, why continue it? As in the domestic food programs, improved nutrition is sometimes the rationale, while empathy and greater overall equity is the real motivation. Failure to demonstrate improved nutrition does not then indict the program. Many church people who are involved in food aid would reject nutritional improvement of the recipients as the sole criterion for success of the program. They would say, out of religious conviction, that the compassion motivating the giver has merit of its own, and that it is good to provide an outlet for this virtue. This is apart from and in addition to any measurable accomplishment of the program as far as the recipients are concerned.

The secular public has difficulty understanding this, particularly when presented with the bill. What is the compassion component of a program financed by the forced extraction of taxes? "Let those who feel compassion express it through private contributions to their own voluntary organizations." So say the opponents of public-supported food aid.

The food aid program troubles the conscience of one who is concerned with relieving world hunger. Existence of the program attests a measure of responsibility for the condition of less fortunate people around the world. But the limited size of the program and its modest accomplishment, objectively measured, witness how little accountability we accept. On the other hand, the program eases the consciences of those to whom symbolism is important. There the program stands, testimony to our concern, even though it alleviates a very small share of need.

Food aid has always been conceptually difficult for the economist. In his assumptions there is no place for the unrequited transfer of goods or services. He assumes, as part of the mind-set his discipline confers, that man is motivated by self-interest, that he is a maximizing animal, carefully attuned to the calculus of less and more. How can the economist understand motives that he has assumed out of existence? He can do so only by breaking out of the strictures imposed by his discipline.

Debates on the food aid budget bring out these sharp differences. On the one side are the budget officers with their questions about benefit/cost ratios. On the other side are the advocates of a larger food aid program, moved more by the spirit than by the dollar. But they need the dollars! The two have discourse without communication. The arguments slip by one another without making contact.

ISSUES

The central issue regarding food aid is this: Do we have responsibility for helping solve the food problems of people from other countries? Giving an affirmative answer to this question are many church people, considerable numbers of warmhearted citizens, the internationalists, many farmer-producers of the commodities concerned, and the government people who administer the programs. Opposition comes from those who mistrust the various forms of internationalism, who dislike the expanding role of government, and who are concerned with cost. The difference is essentially ideological. The arguments are so chosen as to serve whichever view one subjectively holds.

Confrontation has been going on for at least twenty-five years. The advocates have succeeded in keeping the program alive, even through a period of food shortage. The opponents have succeeded in keeping the program from growing. This confrontation, which has seesawed first one way and then another through times of abundance and shortage and through various changes in world view, seems likely to continue. It is only recently that government assumed responsibility for the food needs of our own citizens, and public acceptance of this principle is far from complete. The extension of this principle beyond our own borders is a major step, unlikely to win full or early support. The food aid advocates have won a beachhead, and the opponents have prevented a breakout. The debate is certain to be with us during the 1980s.

Granted that we have a program, what objectives should be pursued? The lineup here is predictable. Farmers say surplus disposal and trade development. The hunger lobby says humanitarian purposes. The State Department says support for United States diplomatic initiatives.

How much aid, and what commodities? A big program, say the advocates. A small one or none at all, say the opponents. As to the mix of commodities, the farm commodity groups push their wares into the program. By good fortune the commodities that are most often in surplus—cereal grain, manufactured dairy products, and vegetable oils—are also economical, nutritionally sound, and generally relished by the recipients.

A major policy question relates to whether food aid should be limited to countries judged to be friendly. Food aid advocates say no. Should we use food aid as a supplement to our military support? Again the advocates say no. Should we give food to people made hungry in an attempt to overthrow their government? Those who favor the existing government in the subject country are disinclined to provide food aid to rebel groups. Those who oppose such governments generally favor helping the dissidents. No other issue so vividly portrays the political aspects of food aid.

In addition to the foregoing questions, of a major policy nature, there are matters largely of an administrative kind:

What should be the breakdown between famine relief, aid through the voluntary agencies, and concessional food sales?

Should the cost appear in the budget of the State Department rather than in that of USDA, as at present?

Should the interagency machinery that develops and oversees the program be changed so as to give more power to some agencies and less to others?

What role should be assigned to grants and to sales for dollars on concessionary terms?

Should debts owed to us be canceled if it becomes clear that the country cannot pay?

In Washington, within the concerned agencies, these administrative issues are taken to be enormously important. Out in the country these issues, if raised, encounter bored silence. But the deeper questions regarding the degree of our responsibility for hungry people abroad are of great interest to most audiences.

The radius of human concern and responsibility has lengthened over time. The food aid programs project this concern beyond our own borders into the international area. For those who are interested in calibrating the extent of man's responsibility for his fellows, international food aid will be a good program to watch. I expect the volume to increase rather than diminish.

REFERENCES

Adams, Dale W. 1964. *Public Law 480, and Colombia's economic development. Medillin.* East Lansing: Michigan State University.

Barlow, Frank D., and Libbin, Susan A. 1969. *Food aid and agricultural development.* Foreign Agricultural Economic Report 51. Washington, D.C.: USDA, Economic Research Service.

Berg, Alan. 1973. *The nutrition factor: Its role in national development.* Washington, D.C.: Brookings Institution.

Brown, Peter G., and Shue, Henry. 1977. *Food policy: The responsibility of the United States in the life and death choices.* New York: Free Press.

Food and Agriculture Organization. 1974. *Assessment of the world food situation: Present and future.* Document C/Conf. 6 j/3. World Food Conference. Rome: United Nations.

Isenman, Paul, and Singer, H. 1975. *Food aid: Disincentive effects and their policy implications.* AID Discussion Paper 31. Washington, D.C.: Agency for International Development.

Johnson, D. Gale. 1975. *World food problems and prospects.* Foreign Affairs Study 20. Washington, D.C.: American Enterprise Institute for Public Policy Research.

Libbin, Susan A. 1977. U.S. agricultural commodity aid and commercial exports, 1955–1976. In *Foreign agricultural trade of the United States.* Washington, D.C.: USDA, Economic Research Service.

————. 1978. Calendar year 1977 government program exports estimated at $1.5 billion. In *Foreign agricultural trade of the United States.* Washington, D.C.: USDA, Economics, Statistics, and Cooperatives Service.

National Research Council. World Food and Nutrition Study Steering Committee. 1977. *World food and nutrition study: The potential contributions of research.* Washington, D.C.: National Academy of Sciences.

Pontecorvo, Guilio, ed. 1975. *The management of food policy.* C. W. Cook Lectures on World Food Policy, Columbia University School of Business. New York: Arno Press.

Saylor, Thomas Reese. 1977. A new legislative mandate for American food aid. In *Food policy,* ed. Peter G. Brown and Henry Shue, pp. 199–211. New York: Free Press.

Schertz, Lyle. 1977. World needs: Shall the hungry be with us always? In *Food policy,* ed. Peter G. Brown and Henry Shue, pp. 13–35. New York: Free Press.

Shuman, Charles B. 1977. Food aid and the free market. In *Food policy,* ed. Peter G. Brown and Henry Shue, pp. 145–63. New York: Free Press.

U.S. Department of Agriculture. 1977a. *Foreign agricultural trade of the United States.* Washington, D.C.: USDA, Economic Research Service.

———. 1977b. *Participation in the Food Stamp Program as shown by quality control reviews, July–December, 1976.* Washington, D.C.: USDA, Food and Nutrition Service, Food Stamp Division, Performance Reporting System.

———. 1977c. *P.L. 480 concessional sales.* Foreign Agricultural Economic Report 142. Washington, D.C.: USDA, Economic Research Service.

———. 1978a. *Food for Peace: 1976/TQ Annual Report on Public Law 480.* Washington, D.C.: Government Printing Office.

———. 1978b. *International food policy issues: A proceedings.* Foreign Agricultural Economics Report 143. Washington, D.C.: USDA, Economics, Statistics, and Cooperatives Service.

23. International Agricultural Development

In many of the poorer countries of the world considerable numbers of people exist at or slightly above the subsistence level; that is, food intake is close to the biological minimum below which healthy human life is impossible. These countries, chiefly in Asia, Africa, and Latin America, are overwhelmingly agricultural. In many cases agricultural practices are traditional, little changed for centuries. In the wealthier countries, including the United States, agriculture has become modernized. Levels of living, farm and nonfarm, are high and rising.

Thus the difference in living levels between the poor and the nonpoor have been increasing. And this has been occurring in a world in which distance has been reduced by air travel and knowledge has been increased by the media, a world in which the one half knows more and more about how the other half lives. This is a world in which invidious comparisons are increasingly invidious and are more likely to be made. A widening gap in a shrinking world is cause for concern not only on the part of the poor but also on the part of the wealthy.

At the turn of the century the poet Edwin Markham was moved by Millet's painting *The Man with the Hoe* to write these lines:

> How will the future reckon with this man?
> How answer his brute question in that hour
> When whirlwinds of rebellion shake all shores?

Markham's questions are already on the public policy agenda and will be so increasingly during the decade of the 1980s. The Third World countries, from their platform in the United Nations, will see to that.

290

Although the development process has political, diplomatic, and indeed military connotations, I shall focus primarily on its food and agricultural component. Agriculture is a key, not only because it must feed the world's growing population but also because in the developing countries the vast majority of the people are on the land. Genuine progress can occur only if it means progress for them.

THE WORLD FOOD SITUATION: A CONSENSUS

The world food situation is exceedingly complex. It is possible for a person of pessimistic mind-set to select (perhaps unknowingly) certain of its more dismal attributes, document these fully, and conclude that the world will be unable to feed its people. On the other hand, a person inclined toward optimism can, with equally honest intent, take some of the more hopeful aspects of the world food situation, summon irrefutable evidence in their support, and infer that the world will move out from the Malthusian shadow. There are thus great differences in appraisals that come from competent persons and research agencies.

There are also strong similarities in these assessments. In accordance with the well-known human tendency to focus on what is different rather than on what is common, the differences are the subject of more discussion. But, to the careful observer, the similarities in these appraisals outweigh the differences.

At the end of this chapter is a list of research studies of the world food situation, past and prospective. It is obviously impossible for me to review these many studies separately, and so I shall attempt to find a consensus among them. These studies embrace the full range from pessimism to optimism. At the pessimistic extreme are Garrett Hardin (1974), the Paddocks (1967, 1973), and the Club of Rome (Meadows et al. 1972). Believably pessimistic is the International Food Policy Research Institute (1977a). In the middle position, with numerous studies bunched around them, are the Food and Agriculture Organization of the United Nations (United Nations World Food Conference 1974a) and the United States Department of Agriculture (1974). Credibly optimistic are D. Gale Johnson of the University of Chicago (1975), Thomas Poleman of Cornell (1975), and Robert Evenson of Yale (1974). At the optimistic extreme is the futurist Herman Kahn (1976) with his glowing projections to the year 2176. Ranked by degree of optimism, this group of studies approaches a normal bell-shaped distribution.

To base public policy decisions on the analyses offered by one or the other of the two extremes would result either in fantastic success or in catastrophic failure. And the odds for a successful outcome would be adverse. Public policy is best based on the consensus of competent studies. This does not assure that the policy will be the right one, but it increases the probabilities.

What follows is a review of the studies that occupy the middle of this distribution. A statistician would say this embraces one standard deviation on each side of the mean—perhaps two-thirds of the studies.

The Situation in the Late Seventies

As of the late seventies—the jumping-off point for this book—the world food situation could be described as having half a dozen generally agreed attributes.

The disaster that had been feared during the poor crops of 1972–74 had been averted. The predicted onset of generally unfavorable weather had not occurred. Recovery had taken place, and stocks of food were being rebuilt.

Alarmed by the food crisis of the mid-seventies, the hungry countries had been stimulated to make a stronger commitment to agricultural development and to do more research. Almost everywhere the state of the art in agriculture was advancing, by different rates and from different levels.

Birthrates, though high, were dropping in a number of countries. Projections of world population made by the United Nations had been revised downward.

The average man in the developing countries was eating better than did his father or his grandfather. But the average was low, and many people were far below the average. Something like half a billion people were receiving less food than biologically desirable. An unknown number were starving. The gap in food availability between the rich and the poor was widening both within countries and between countries.

Public consciousness concerning the problem of hunger had been raised. Public commitment to overcoming world hunger, though still weak, had strengthened.

Despite the improvement, the situation was still precarious. The world lives mostly from hand to mouth for the major components of the diet and is always heavily dependent on next year's crop—an uncertain thing.

In other words, the world's larder was half full or half empty, depending on one's viewpoint. In any case, it was better stocked than it had been during the mid-seventies.

The Prospect for the 1980s

The eighties are the period to which this book is addressed. As an outlook for that decade, the consensus of reputable studies would probably support most of the following propositions:

Food production in the developing countries will increase. There will be modest increases, on the average, in real per capita incomes.

Birthrates, though remaining high in comparison with those of the developed nations, will probably fall significantly in many Asian and Latin American countries, and slightly in some African countries.

Average per capita food consumption in the developing countries therefore very likely will continue to increase. Food production in the aggregate is expected to keep a half-step ahead of population growth. Per capita food consumption is projected to increase at a rate of 0.5 percent per year, in line with the rate of improvement of the past twenty years. But increases will not be enough to meet nutritional needs or to satisfy aspirations or as much as has been promised by the politicians. Numbers of hungry people will be large, possibly increased, though probably reduced as a percentage of the total population.

The developing countries will need an increased quantity of foreign exchange with which to purchase larger amounts of food from abroad. How this foreign exchange will be earned is a major problem. Protectionist trade policies would be a major obstacle.

Even the more optimistic estimates foresee a widening of the gap between the rich and the poor.

Major hazards endanger the world's food supply during the eighties: uncertainty regarding the weather, economic instability that might result from inflation and the energy problem, the growing burden of debt service, political instability, and the danger of war.

Much depends on the motivation to raise living levels in the poorer countries. For real improvement to occur, political will must be marshaled in both the developed and the developing countries.

This consensus anticipates a prospect midway between the doom-sayers and those optimists who confuse desire with reality.

The Long Term

By the long term is meant beyond 1990—indeed, beyond the year 2000 and well into the twenty-first century. Population is half of the equation that balances food and people. Yet, until the publication of Ross's *Standing Room Only* in 1927, population problems received little attention. In the long run, unless the rate of population growth is reduced there can be no solution to the world food problem. Extrapolating from recent growth rates into the twenty-first century, the numbers of people not only become unmanageable; they become inconceivable. Indeed, without a reduction in the rate of population growth, many other problems would be encountered, including: overcrowding and consequent frictions, civil uprisings, depletion of natural resources, and degradation of the environment. These other hazards may, in fact, become the critical ones disciplining human numbers, while food supplies might still be adequate. In specifying food supply as the factor that ultimately limits population growth, Malthus may have erred.

The Green Revolution and similar agricultural advancements provide time—a decade, or two, or three—within which to cope with the population problem. This is their strong point. If this time is used wisely, the world may be helped to overcome its most ancient enemy, hunger. If it is not, the pessimistic predictions will prove to be right.

THE AMERICAN EFFORT AND THE CASE FOR IT

The first American experience with international agricultural development was in the early years of our country, when we were on the receiving end of the process. Private European capital and know-how came into the United States, helping develop our agriculture. Technical assistance and financial help worked well for us, which gives hope that they can work for others. After our agriculture had reached a fairly advanced stage, we, in company with other advanced countries, began offering and adapting our technology and our institutions to those who were less advanced. Commercial firms began developing fruit production in Central America. Agricultural missionaries brought American farm technology to people in various countries. The great foundations— Ford, Rockefeller, the Agricultural Development Council, and others— brought American agricultural science to all quarters of the globe. The land grant colleges provided agricultural education to foreign students almost from the beginning.

Public support for international agricultural development was first undertaken on a large scale thirty years ago. It was called "Point Four" because it was the fourth point in President Truman's 1949 inaugural address. The other three points in that internationally oriented statement were the United Nations, the Marshall Plan, and the North Atlantic Alliance. "Point Four" is of interest not only because of its intrinsic importance but also as an illustration of the role that happenstance often plays in the arcane mechanics of national policy formation. The story is that a State Department aide had the idea of providing assistance to the developing countries somewhat after the pattern of a technical assistance program that had been tried on a very small scale in Latin America. He could not interest his superiors and so sent a memo to Clark Clifford, White House special counsel. When President Truman wanted something appealing for his inaugural address, Clifford remembered the memo and showed it to him. Truman liked it and used it, though it had not been staffed out. It was picked up with more enthusiasm than either Clifford or Truman had expected (Phillips 1966, pp. 272–75).

Agriculture was a component of our technical assistance programs from the first. The case for agricultural assistance was persuasive. The United States has a great body of scientific knowledge, built up through a century of work by our agricultural experiment stations and the Department of Agriculture. This was an asset that we had, the developing countries needed, and our rivals lacked. Supplying it would be helpful to the developing countries and should reflect credit on us. So ran the argument.

The share of our effort devoted to agriculture within the aid program changed over time, depending on which idea or which person happened to be dominant. After the world food scare of the mid-seventies the agricultural share was increased.

Most of our technical assistance is provided bilaterally through the Agency for International Development—AID, an apt acronym. A recent and important part of the AID effort is in family planning, a program that grew in ten years from practically nothing to the $100 million level. This agency funds biological research and on request provides administrative help to the family planning programs of other countries.

Multilateral aid programs of technical assistance in agriculture are provided along with our bilateral efforts. This is done in part through the Food and Agriculture Organization of the United Nations, of which the United States is a founding member and the chief financial supporter. Multilateral forms of assistance are also supplied through the International Bank for Reconstruction and Development (World Bank) and other lenders such as the Asian Development Bank and the Interamerican Development Bank. The United States is a prominent—perhaps dominant—member of these lending institutions. These banks lend money on both hard and soft terms, often for agricultural projects. In addition, the United States participates in the work of other specialized agencies of the United Nations family, such as the World Meteorological Organization and the World Health Organization, that have agricultural significance. We contribute to the United Nations Development Program, which has a strong agricultural component.

The American effort to promote economic development in the Third World countries is small in comparison both with need and with our capability. In 1976 the total flow of resources from the United States to the developing countries and multilateral agencies stood at $12.3 billion, 0.7 percent of our gross national product. This covered all sectors including agriculture. The United

States ranked thirteenth among the seventeen developed countries in the percentage of its gross national product flowing to the developing countries (appendix table 8). After thirty years we experience what might be called compassion fatigue. Obviously our assistance is so small relative to the size of the job that it cannot be expected to quickly transform the world. The capacity of the developing countries to absorb outside help may also be limiting.

The nature of the development effort changed as theoretical concepts changed. We ran through the classical idea of "capital investment." We tried "big push" and "incremental change." We advocated "industrialization," then "balanced growth." We developed "two-sector models." "Institutional change" had its turn. We flirted with "small is beautiful" and moved in with (but did not marry) "intermediate technology." Obviously we were experimenting.

One strategy we did not try was "triage," recommended by the Paddocks (1967) and by Garrett Hardin (1974). The word triage comes from the medical strategy followed during the terrible carnage of World War I, when the battlefields were strewn with wounded, in numbers beyond the coping ability of the medical corpsmen. The wounded would be divided into three groups: those able to care for themselves in some fashion at least for a time, those beyond help, and those that would probably respond to medical treatment. The limited medical resources were confined to the third group. The reasoning in the triage strategy is that a similar situation prevails with respect to the food problem. Catastrophe has occurred or is impending. Some countries, like India, should be written off as beyond hope. Others, like Brazil, would be judged able to make it on their own. Our limited resources should be confined to the in-between countries, where our help could make the difference.

Sometimes voiced in the same context with triage is the "lifeboat" strategy. The idea is that the ship has gone down and there is only one lifeboat, without room for all. If too many get into the lifeboat it sinks and all are lost. The sensible thing to do (for those already in the boat) is to club off those who try to climb aboard.

The triage idea and the lifeboat strategy are deeply flawed in all respects: scientific, moral, and diplomatic. Good analysts tell us that no country is beyond hope. India, written off by the Paddocks in 1967, has increased its per capita food production since that time. The same is true of Bangladesh, which a few years ago was considered a "basket case." We could not accept the adverse diplomatic consequences of sitting in judgment over the nations of the world, making pronouncements about this or that country as a hopeless case. Nor is it clear that our technical assistance is potent enough to make the difference between success and failure for those countries we would choose to help. The "triage strategy" and the "lifeboat strategy" are good examples of how an overdramatic analogy can be a trap instead of a help.

OBJECTIVES

What are we trying to accomplish with technical assistance in agriculture? Our purposes are multiple; they are similar to those discussed with respect to food aid. We are motivated by: the humanitarian desire to help less fortunate people; the effort to fight communism by demonstrating that there is a better way; the wish to win friends and the belief that technical assistance can help us do so; the belief that by providing technical assistance we can help build the developing nations into good trading partners; and the hope that technical assistance will help meet the aspirations of the people and so contribute to political stability.

The detractors say these objectives have not been met. They note that the spread of communism has not been checked, that we perhaps have fewer friends overseas now than when the program began, and that political stability in the Third World has not been achieved.

Supporters of the program point out that agriculture has advanced in the countries we have helped. Some combination of forces—the efforts of the countries themselves, development initiatives undertaken by private multinational firms, the work of the great foundations, loans of the World Bank, the multilateral efforts of FAO and other such agencies, plus technical assistance through AID—these, together, have improved the state-of-the-arts in agriculture fast enough to keep ahead of the population explosion. This is a great achievement, a sustained rate of increase in agricultural production, worldwide, that has never previously occurred. The contributions of the various initiatives cannot be separately identified. Undoubtedly most of the credit belongs to the developing countries themselves.

WHAT HAVE WE LEARNED?

Here are listed a limited number of points on which most supporters and detractors would agree.

Expectations were too high. In Europe, with the Marshall Plan, there was a motivated populace and an institutional base. A known and valued economic system was being restored. What was lacking was capital; when capital was supplied everything moved forward. But in the developing countries motivation is often lacking. The people cannot easily visualize something they have never experienced. The institutional base is suited to the old rather than the new technology. For meaningful progress to occur almost everything has to change. We should not be surprised. The United States established the agricultural experiment stations in 1887 and the agricultural extension service in 1914. But it was not until the 1940s, many years later, that really rapid agricultural change occurred. How could we expect quick results from a small attack on a major problem in an alien culture? Expectations had been too high, and the let-down was painful.

Some things work. The greatest achievement in international agricultural development very likely has been the international research network and associated endeavors. This is the effort that produced the Green Revolution and saved the Third World from disaster during the bad weather of the mid-seventies. The international research network is a system that brings together a great team: the foundations, the universities, the FAO, the World Bank, AID, the national research institutions, and the extension services in the developing countries. Add to this the private agribusiness firms. Central to the system are the international research centers, such as the International Center for the Improvement of corn and wheat (CIMMYT) in Mexico, Norman Borlaug's base, where high-yielding wheat was developed, and the International Rice Research Institute (IRRI) in the Philippines, from which came the so-called miracle rice. There are now a dozen of these research centers in various stages of planning, development, and service.

The pattern of cooperation, which is informal more than rigidly specified, is, in concept and to some degree in actuality, as follows: the colleges and universities of the world supply scientists, schooled in the relevant agricultural disciplines such as agronomy, genetics, and pathology. At the international research centers these scientists, with financing from a consultative group including AID, work on improving the performance of a specified food crop or livestock species. The national research institutions of the developing countries take the germ plasm and the technology from the centers, testing and adapting these under local conditions, feeding back their improved materials into the global system. Governments of these countries retail the improved practices to farmers through their extension services. AID and FAO workers in the field are in position to tie in their projects with the technology that flows from this system. The World Bank helps finance the needed capital investments. Agribusiness firms supply the necessary inputs and marketing facilities.

The international research network is an institutional invention of the first order—voluntary, coordinated, interdisciplinary, international, and mission-oriented. Very likely the historian of the twenty-first century will look back on the international research network and compare it to an important predecessor invention—the American land grant college system. The international research network is well described by Wortman and Cummings (1978).

Another thing that works is the price incentive. "Farmers in the developing countries may not be able to read, but they can figure," says F. F. Hill, formerly of the Ford Foundation. If the price of wheat or rice is high, farmers respond by increasing production. If prices of food are held low in the supposed interests of consumers, production declines.

The Food Crisis Workshop of the Ramon Magsaysay Award Foundation puts the case at its emphatic best (Wortman and Cummings 1978, p. 371):

Whether in Taiwan, the Philippines, Thailand, Burma, or other developing countries, farmers respond most of all to the price their product brings. To assume farmers can be encouraged to expand production without it being profitable is one of the most serious miscalculations in government policy. Understandably, governments are anxious to protect the consumer by controlling the price of rice. And city dwellers are more articulate, organized, and closer to the center of decision-making than farmers. As prices of petroleum products, fertilizer, and insecticides have escalated during the past three and a half years, farmers' costs have risen radically. Unless governments recognize promptly the diminishing economic margin available to farmers, Asia's grain production will be crippled. The alternatives of subsidy for farm inputs or gradually rising prices for consumers are neither one attractive. Yet, the controlling principle must be maximizing production.

Obstacles to agricultural development are discussed by twenty distinguished authors in an excellent book titled *Distortions of Agricultural Incentives,* edited by Theodore W. Schultz (1978). Commodity price policy is considered in depth by Krishna (1967) and Mellor (1975).

Some things do not work. We have learned—or, more accurately, we have been exposed to the lesson—that American farm technology cannot be exported as such. It has to be adapted and transformed to meet conditions in the developing countries. American methods of wheat production, suited to a thousand-acre Kansas farm, cannot be adopted by a farmer in India with three acres of irrigated cropland. Corn-belt feed grain/livestock agriculture cannot be transplanted to a country too poor to afford meat. But the basic agricultural sciences—genetics, pathology, plant nutrition—are applicable.

Another lesson we have been exposed to but have not adequately perceived is this: that American methods of education, lending, and marketing cannot be directly transplanted overseas. These institutions are a part of our history, culture, and tradition; they do not take root readily in countries of sharply different background. Accepting this has been painful to people who hold our institutions in high regard.

The Case against Technical Assistance

The Case Made by the Opponents

Argument one: It's no business of ours. This argument comes from those who dislike international efforts as a matter of principle. Their strong belief is that we should take care of our own and that other countries should do likewise.

Argument two: It costs too much. This contention arises from the conviction that government is too large and should be pruned back. Appendix table 8 shows that the total net flow from the United States to the developing countries in 1976 was $12.3 billion. Much of this was in the form of loans that will be repaid. The AID program and the international lending agencies are preeminently eligible for budget cuts. The Department of Agriculture and the Labor Department have their domestic constituents, who rally in support of threatened programs. Not so AID or the World Bank; their constituents are overseas and do not vote.

Argument three: It doesn't work. William and Elizabeth Paddock state this case vigorously in their book *We Don't Know How*. Errors and ineptitude in our effort—these do occur—are flagged. Our claims of success are critically examined and reported as faulty. The charge is made that we simply do not know how to bring about agricultural development in other countries. While the Paddocks make some legitimate points, they greatly overstate their case. Something must have worked, or agricultural production in the Third World would not have increased, as in fact it has.

Argument four: We put our rivals in business. The Paddock charge is that international agricultural development does not work; the opposite charge, put forward with equal vehemence, is that it works too well. We are accused of putting the Malaysians in the oil palm business and of helping the Brazilians develop their agriculture to the injury of American soybean growers; of helping Turkey with its wheat production, thus reducing our wheat exports; of assisting the African countries to solve their cotton problems, thereby damaging our own cotton industry. Similarly with tobacco in Rhodesia and mushrooms in Taiwan. In its most blatant form the argument becomes "Keep 'em poor and feed 'em on PL 480." Undoubtedly there is truth to the allegation that some American farmers are injured. American producers of mushrooms have clearly been hurt by increased output of mushrooms in Taiwan, which occurred in part with our help. But, overall, economic development in Taiwan has helped make that island, in 1977, a $611 million customer for exported American farm products, up from practically nothing before technical assistance began.

Argument five: We upset an adapted culture. This argument comes from the anthropologists and the sociologists. Some of these people consider technical agricultural assistance to be a form of cultural aggression. Why should we intervene and push our own pattern of living onto these people? What evidence do the social scientists have that our system will generate more happiness and contentment than the people of the developing countries now enjoy? The defensible answer to these charges is that it cannot be cultural aggression to help people achieve the goals to which they themselves aspire.

Criticism from the Recipients

Dissident groups in the developing countries fault United States–assisted agricultural development projects on several counts:

Argument one: They are mostly production-oriented. The allegation is made by some that the major problem is inequitable distribution of food rather than lagging production, and that the American programs focus almost entirely on the lesser problem, production.

Argument two: They are an extension of the American economic system. The conviction of some left-leaning groups in the developing countries is that real progress can come only if capitalistic institutions are replaced by a socialistic system. American efforts are seen as an attempt to export capitalism as it exists in the United States and to prop up institutions the revolutionists wish to overthrow.

Argument three: We promote energy-intensive and capital-intensive agriculture. This, it is alleged, is ill suited to countries poor in both energy and capital. The Green Revolution is faulted on this and other counts by Lappé and Collins (1977, p. 142). Vernon Ruttan makes a much more careful and favorable evaluation of the Green Revolution (1977). Hayami and Herdt, in their award-winning article (1977), discount the allegation that the Green Revolution works a hardship on small farmers.

Despite criticisms from dissident groups, American overseas programs are undertaken only with the support of the host government. If the host government disapproves of some project it is closed out, as has occurred in a number of cases.

American agricultural scientists at work on development projects generally respond to these criticisms by contending that their work is politically and socially neutral. In the tradition of the land grant college system, where most of them got their training, they try to stay out of political battles. But there is no denying that if overseas technical assistance in agriculture is effective, it will bring changes in the social, political, and institutional fabric of the countries concerned, as it did in the United States.

THE ISSUES

The main issue regarding agricultural development (foreign aid, technical assistance, Point Four; pick your own label) is between the internationalists, who favor it, and the nationalists, who oppose. There are other criteria for delineating the two positions, but this is the major one. Arguments are mostly subservient to these ideological positions.

For thirty years the argument has been resolved in favor of having a publicly supported program of modest dimensions to assist the development of agriculture in other nations. The questions then become: How much help? What kind of assistance? Whom are we to help? How much bilateral and how much multilateral aid? Which agency should have operating responsibility? Should technical agricultural assistance be linked with the requirement that the receiving country follow some prescribed agricultural policy or initiate a family planning program?

The lineup on these issues is fairly predictable. The internationalists and the government people who run the program generally want a large operation, wide administrative latitude as to its content, and many eligible countries. They want a large multilateral component in the program and a strong hand for the State Department. They dislike tying aid programs to specific performance by the receiving nation. The nationalists generally take an opposed position on each of these issues.

Some American commodity groups are ready to help these poor countries with agricultural development, but not in commodities that compete with us. But persuading them to produce crops and livestock for which they are not well adapted may be more injurious than helpful.

An immense and very deep issue, which I have touched on occasionally but which is really beyond the scope of this book, is the question whether agricultural development in the Third World is to rely primarily on market forces or whether it should proceed along Marxist lines. The case for market orientation is implicit in Wortman and Cummings (1978). The socialist case is made explicitly by Lappé and Collins (1977) and by George (1977). Charles Hardin of the University of California offers a review of these respective cases in his unpublished paper "Conflicting Views on the World Food Problem—A Socialist or Capitalist Orientation: Which Is Preferable?" (1978). Hardin gives full exposition of the rival views and supports the capitalist approach.

PROGNOSIS

The battlelines on international agricultural development programs have been essentially stable for thirty years. Both sides are dug in. A principle is at stake—

the degree to which responsibility should transcend national borders—and neither side intends to give in.

Thirty years are too few to establish acceptance of so major a matter as extension into the international realm of principles that have only recently won acceptance within our own borders. In this respect, technical assistance is like food aid. So for the decade of the eighties the standoff very likely will continue.

But time probably is on the side of a broadened rather than a narrowed feeling of responsibility and a better perception of enlightened self-interest. International agricultural development is not a zero-sum game in which someone's gain involves a loss to someone else. It is a positive-sum game, from which can come long-run gains for all. The legitimate hope is that in time the players will come to realize that fact.

REFERENCES

Agricultural development. 1969. Proceedings of a Conference at the Villa Serbelloni, Bellagio, Italy, April 23–25. Published in the United States by the Rockefeller Foundation. New York.

Aziz, Sartaj. 1975. *Hunger, politics and markets: The real issues in the food crisis.* New York: New York University Press.

Bhagwati, Jagdish N., ed. 1977. *The new international economic order: The north-south debate.* Especially chapters 10, 11. Cambridge: MIT Press.

Blakeslee, Leroy L.; Heady, Earl O.; and Framingham, Charles E. 1973. *World food production, demand, and trade.* Ames: Iowa State University Press.

Brandow, G. E. 1974. American agriculture's capacity to meet future demands. *American Journal of Agricultural Economics* 56:1093–1102.

Brown, Lester R. 1970. *Seeds of change: The Green Revolution and development in the 1970s.* New York: Praeger.

———. 1975. The world food prospect. *Science* 190:1053–59.

Chandler, Robert F., Jr. 1976. The physical and biological potentials and constraints in meeting world food needs. In *Proceedings of World Food Conference of 1976,* ed. Frank Schaller. Ames: Iowa State College Press.

Chou, Marylin; Harmon, David P., Jr.; Kahn, Herman; and Wittwer, Sylvan H. 1977. *World food prospects and agricultural potential.* New York: Praeger, in cooperation with Hudson Institute.

Dalrymple, Dana G. 1975. *Measuring the Green Revolution: The impact of research on wheat and rice production.* Foreign Agricultural Economic Report 106. Washington, D.C.: USDA, Economic Research Service, in cooperation with USAID.

Dams, T.; Hunt, K. E.; and Tyler, G. J., eds. 1978. *Food and population: Priorities in decision making.* Report of a meeting of the International Conference of Agricultural Economists held in Nairobi, 1976. Farnborough, England: Saxon House. Papers by:

S. Krasovec, T. Singh, J. P. Bhattacharjee, K. Campbell, J. Klatzmann, A. Valdes, I. I. May-Parker, L. P. Mureithi, J. O. Otieno, S. M. Essang, O. A. Hakim, V. M. Dandekar, S. Baharsjah, S. M. Kim, W. G. Farmer, F. C. Sturrock, N. Amerasinghe, A. R. Teixeira Filho, and B. B. Quraishi. Foreword by Denis K. Britton.

Edwards, Clark. 1977. *Strategies for balanced growth in developing countries.* Agricultural Economic Report 375. Washington, D.C.: USDA, Economic Research Service.

Evenson, Robert. 1974. "The Green Revolution" in recent development experience. *American Journal of Agricultural Economics* 56:387–94.

George, Susan. 1977. *How the other half dies: The real reasons for world hunger.* Montclair, N.J.: Allanheld, Osmun.

Hanson, Roger D., and staff. 1976. *The U.S. and world development: Agenda for action 1976.* New York: Overseas Development Council, for Praeger.

Haq, Mahbub ul-. 1976. *The Third World and the International Economic Order.* Development Paper 22. New York: Overseas Development Council.

Hardin, Charles M. 1978. Conflicting views on the world food problem—A socialist or capitalist orientation: Which is preferable? Unpublished. University of California at Berkeley.

Hardin, Clifford M., ed. 1969. *Overcoming world hunger.* Englewood Cliffs, N.J.: Prentice-Hall, for American Assembly, Columbia University.

Hardin, Garrett. 1974. Living on a lifeboat. *Bio Science* 24:561–68.

Hayami, Yujiro, and Herdt, Robert W. 1977. Market price effects of technological change on income distribution in subsistence agriculture. *American Journal of Agricultural Economics* 59:245–56.

Hayami, Yujiro, and Ruttan, Vernon W. 1971. *Agricultural development: An international perspective.* Baltimore: Johns Hopkins University Press.

Heady, Earl O. 1976. The agriculture of the U.S. *Scientific American* 235:106–27.

Hueg, William F., Jr., and Gannon, Craig A., eds. 1978. *Transforming knowledge into food in a world-wide context.* Proceedings of a seminar jointly sponsored by the American Academy of Arts and Sciences and the University of Minnesota, September. Minneapolis: Miller Publishing Company.

International Agricultural Development Service. 1978. *Agricultural development indicators: A statistical handbook.* New York: International Agricultural Development Service.

International Food Policy Research Institute. 1976. *Meeting food needs in the developing world.* Research Report 1. Washington, D.C.

———. 1977a. *Food needs of developing countries: Projections of production and consumption to 1990.* Research Report 3. Washington, D.C.

———. 1977b. *Recent and prospective developments in food consumption: Some policy issues.* Research Report 2, rev. ed. Washington, D.C.

International Labor Office. 1976. *Employment growth and basic needs: A one-world problem.* Geneva: International Labor Office.

Johnson, D. Gale. 1975. *World food problems and prospects.* Washington, D.C.: American Enterprise Institute for Public Policy Research.

Joseling, Tim. 1977. The world food problem. National and international aspects. *Food policy,* vol. 1, no. 1.

Kahn, Herman, with Brown, William, and Martel, Leon. 1976. *The next 200 years: A scenario for America and the world.* New York: William Morrow.

Krishna, Raj. 1967. Agricultural price policy and economic development. In *Agricultural development and economic growth,* ed. Herman M. Southworth and Bruce F. Johnston. Ithaca: Cornell University Press.

Lappé, Frances Moore, and Collins, Joseph. 1977. *Food first: Beyond the myth of scarcity.* Boston: Houghton Mifflin.

Lipton, Michael. 1977. *Why poor people stay poor: A Study of urban bias in world development.* London: Temple Smith.

Mayer, Jean. 1975. Agricultural productivity and world nutrition. In *Crop Productivity: Research imperatives,* ed. A. W. A. Brown et al., pp. 97–108. East Lansing: Michigan Agricultural Experiment Station.

Meadows, Donella H., et al. 1972. *The limits to growth: A report for the Club of Rome's projection on the predicament of mankind.* New York: Universe Books.

Mellor, John W. 1975. *Agricultural price policy and income distribution in low income nations.* World Bank Staff Working Paper 214. Washington. D.C.: World Bank.

————. 1976. *The new economics of growth: A strategy for India and the developing world.* Ithaca: Cornell University Press.

Mesarovic, Mihajlo, and Pestel, Eduard. 1974. *Mankind at the turning point: The second report to the Club of Rome.* New York: E. P. Dutton.

National Academy of Sciences. 1977. *World food and nutrition study: The potential contributions of research.* Washington, D.C.: National Research Council.

Nicholson, Heather Johnston, and Nicholson, Ralph L. 1978. *Distant hunger: Agriculture, food and human values.* Lafayette, Ind.: Purdue University Press.

Paarlberg, Don. 1974. The world food situation in perspective. *American Journal of Agricultural Economics* 56:351–58.

Paddock, William, and Paddock, Elizabeth. 1973. *We don't know how: An independent audit of what they call success in foreign assistance.* Ames: Iowa State University Press.

Paddock, William, and Paddock, Paul. 1967. *Famine 1975! America's decision: Who will survive?* Boston: Little, Brown.

Perrin, Richard, and Winkelmann, Donald. 1976. *Impediments to technical progress on small versus large farms.* Mexico City: CIMMYT.

Phillips, Cabell. 1966. *The Truman presidency.* New York: Macmillan.

Poleman, Thomas T. 1975. World food: A perspective. *Science* 188:510–18.

Proceedings of the Seminar on Agricultural Policy: A limiting factor in the development process. 1975. Washington, D.C.: Inter-American Development Bank.

Ross, E. A. 1927. *Standing room only.* New York and London: Century Company.

Ruttan, Vernon W. 1977. *The Green Revolution: Seven generalizations.* New York: Agricultural Development Council.

Schultz, Theodore W. 1964. *Transforming traditional agriculture.* New Haven: Yale University Press.

————, ed. 1978. *Distortions of agricultural incentives*. Bloomington: Indiana University Press.

Science. 1975. Special issue, Food. 188:503–651.

Scientific American. 1976. Special issue 235, Food and agriculture. 235:31–205.

Sen, S. R. 1976. Growth and instability in Indian agriculture. Address delivered at the Twentieth Annual Conference of the Indian Society of Agricultural Statistics, January, Waltair, India.

Society for International Development. 1978. *Survey of international development,* vol. 15, no. 1. Washington, D.C.

United Nations World Food Conference. 1974*a*. *Assessment of the world food situation present and future*. E/CONF 65/3. Rome: United Nations.

————. 1974*b*. *The world food problem: Proposals for national and international actions*. E/CONF 65/4. Rome: United Nations.

U.S. Department of Agriculture. 1974. *The world food situation and prospects to 1985*. Foreign Agricultural Economic Report 98. Washington, D.C.: Economic Research Service.

————. 1978*a*. *Alternative futures for world food in 1985*. Vol. 1. *World GOL model: Analytical report*. Foreign Agricultural Economic Report 146. Washington, D.C.: Economics, Statistics, and Cooperatives Service.

————. 1978*b*. *International food policy issues: A proceedings*. Foreign Agricultural Economic Report 143. Washington, D.C.: Economics, Statistics, and Cooperatives Service.

U.S. National Advisory Commission on Food and Fiber. 1967. *Food and fiber for the future*. Report to the president and eight volumes of technical papers. Washington, D.C.: White House.

U.S. President's Science Advisory Committee. 1967. *The world food problem: A Report*. Washington, D.C.: White House.

University of California. 1974. *A hungry world: The challenge to agriculture*. Berkeley: University of California Press.

Walters, Harry E. 1975. Difficult issues underlying food problems. *Science* 188:524–30.

————. 1977. Towards a world food policy: Progress and problems. In *Decision-making and agriculture*. Papers and reports of the Sixteenth International Conference of Agricultural Economists, Nairobi, Kenya, July 26–August 4, 1976. Lincoln: University of Nebraska Press.

Wharton, Clifton R., Jr. 1976. The role of the professional in feeding mankind: The political dimension. In *Proceedings of World Food Conference of 1976,* ed. Frank Schaller. Ames: Iowa State College Press.

Winkelmann, Donald. 1976. *Promoting the adoption of new plant technology*. Mexico City: CIMMYT.

Wortman, Sterling. 1976. Food and agriculture. *Scientific American* 235:31–39.

Wortman, Sterling, and Cummings, Ralph W., Jr. 1978. *To feed this world: The challenge and the strategy*. Baltimore: Johns Hopkins University Press.

24. A Concluding Comment

A recurring theme throughout this book has been the considerable degree of shared interest between farm and nonfarm people. Many of the issues between them have been shown to be either spurious or exaggerated. Farmers and nonfarmers have more in common than they have in opposition. Both groups are interested in a good environment, a wholesome food supply, wise resource use and a big export market for farm products. Neither likes burdensome governmental regulation. Repeated public opinion studies show that farmers are generally held in high regard by nonfarm people.

Unfortunately, confrontation has often been the strategy employed by leaders of both groups. The result has been to create issues where there were none and to escalate to major dimensions issues that were of minor importance. Farmers, with their declining numbers and eroding political power, can only lose by such strategy.

De-escalation, common ground, and trade-offs are the ingredients of good public policy. Each has its potential contribution to the development of good farm and food policy during the 1980s.

Issues might be de-escalated, for example, by searching out the facts about safety and the environment and supporting leaders who respect the facts. Both farmers and nonfarmers could elevate their understanding and lower their voices.

Acres of common ground could be found if sought out. Farmers and nonfarmers are interested in each other's well-being. As nonfarm people prosper, farmers have a better market for their products. If farmers are well-rewarded, they will provide a bountiful supply of wholesome food.

307

Trade-offs might be worked out. A better deal for hired farm labor could assist farmers in passing legislation to help reduce the gyrations in farm income. Needed nonfarm help on issues important to farmers might be obtained by reducing the big-farm bonanzas of present commodity programs. Operating as they do from a weakening political base, farm interests are likely to lose on these points anyway; it is a question of whether farmers get something for them before they are lost.

Farm leaders have fallen into the unfortunate habit of dividing the remnant. The farm scene is replete with issues that elevate small differences to such proportions as to weaken the whole. Large farmers versus small farmers; farm people versus rural nonfarmers; full-time farmers against part-time farmers; the general farm organizations against the commodity organizations; the farm organizations against one another; research and education people versus commodity program people versus the new agenda people; Virginia-type peanuts versus runner-type peanuts versus Spanish-type peanuts; fluid milk producers versus producers of manufactured milk. And so on. There are quarrels within the old agricultural establishment that ought to be abated—the land grant colleges versus the Department of Agriculture, for example. Intramural quarrels of this kind are a luxury, once tolerable because the overall position was strong. But that is not now the case.

This is not to say that any one of these subgroups should capitulate and "give away the store." It means that there should be more effort to find common ground and less effort to exploit differences. It means that farm leaders should reexamine, in the light of prospective circumstances, the historic tactic of unifying their subgroup by attacking some sector of the larger body. When, overall, agriculture was strong, such tactics were successful. Now that agriculture has lost strength they may be lethal. Farm leaders should not divide the remnant; they should stitch together a patchwork quilt.

Nonfarm people have succeeded in putting their issues on the agenda. They have demonstrated strength and skill in doing this. Some of the tactics used were more sensational than substantial. Some were hurtful to farm people and of questionable usefulness to the nonfarmers. There is little need for nonfarmers to further demonstrate their ability to influence the farm and food policy agenda. They have made their point.

For a hundred years farmers had the policy initiative. They called the signals, moved the ball, and put points on the scoreboard. But sometime during the past fifteen years there was a turnover. Like it or not, farmers must now play defense. There is one thing worse than losing the ball; that is to lose the ball and think you still have it.

Appendix

APPENDIX TABLE 1

Government Payments, by Program, 1933–77 (in millions of dollars)

Year	Conservation[a]	Soil Bank	Sugar Act	Wool	Feed Grain	Wheat	Cotton	Rental and Benefits	Price Adjustment and Parity	Wartime Production Subsidy	Cropland Adjustment	Miscellaneous[b]	Total
1933	—	—	—	—	—	—	—	131	—	—	—	—	131
1934	—	—	—	—	—	—	51	395	—	—	—	—	446
1935	—	—	—	—	—	—	15	558	—	—	—	—	573
1936	24	—	—	—	—	—	41	213	—	—	—	—	278
1937	324	—	—	—	—	—	—	11	—	—	—	—	336
1938	309	—	22	—	—	—	114	—	—	—	—	—	446
1939	527	—	28	—	—	—	8	—	201	—	—	—	763
1940	496	—	27	—	—	—	—	—	200	—	—	—	723
1941	382	—	27	—	—	—	—	—	134	—	—	—	544
1942	450	—	25	—	—	—	—	—	175	—	—	—	650
1943	332	—	36	—	—	—	—	—	254	22	—	—	645
1944	378	—	27	—	—	—	—	—	1	370	—	—	776
1945	259	—	24	—	—	—	—	—	—	459	—	—	742
1946	285	—	31	—	—	—	—	—	—	456	—	—	772
1947	277	—	37	—	—	—	—	—	—	—	—	—	314

Year	Conservation[a]	Soil Bank	Sugar Act	Wool	Feed Grain	Wheat	Cotton	Rental and Benefits	Price Adjustment and Parity	Wartime Production Subsidy	Cropland Adjustment	Miscellaneous[b]	Total
1948	218	—	39	—	—	—	—	—	—	—	—	—	257
1949	156	—	30	—	—	—	—	—	—	—	—	—	185
1950	246	—	37	—	—	—	—	—	—	—	—	—	283
1951	246	—	40	—	—	—	—	—	—	—	—	—	286
1952	242	—	33	—	—	—	—	—	—	—	—	—	275
1953	181	—	32	—	—	—	—	—	—	—	—	—	213
1954	217	—	40	—	—	—	—	—	—	—	—	—	257
1955	188	—	41	—	—	—	—	—	—	—	—	—	229
1956	220	243	37	54	—	—	—	—	—	—	—	—	554
1957	230	700	32	53	—	—	—	—	—	—	—	—	1,016
1958	215	815	44	14	—	—	—	—	—	—	—	—	1,089
1959	233	323	44	82	—	—	—	—	—	—	—	—	682
1960	223	370	59	51	—	—	—	—	—	—	—	—	702
1961	236	334	53	56	772	42	—	—	—	—	—	—	1,493
1962	230	304	64	54	841	253	—	—	—	—	—	—	1,747
1963	231	304	67	37	843	215	—	—	—	—	—	—	1,696
1964	236	199	79	25	1,163	438	39	—	—	—	—	—	2,181
1965	224	160	75	18	1,391	525	70	—	—	—	—	—	2,463
1966	231	145	71	34	1,293	679	773	—	—	—	51	—	3,277
1967	237	129	70	29	865	731	932	—	—	—	85	—	3,079
1968	229	112	75	66	1,366	747	787	—	—	—	81	—	3,462
1969	204	43	78	61	1,643	858	828	—	—	—	78	—	3,794
1970	208	2	88	49	1,504	871	919	—	—	—	76	—	3,717
1971	173	—	80	69	1,054	878	822	—	—	—	67	2	3,145
1972	198	—	82	110	1,845	856	813	—	—	—	52	6	3,961
1973	72	—	82	65	1,142	474	718	—	—	—	47	7	2,607
1974	192	—	78	—c	101	70	42	—	—	—	41	6	531
1975	193	—	61	13	279	77	138	—	—	—	37	9	807
1976	209	—	1	39	196	135	108	—	—	—	20	26	734
1977	328	—	65	5	187	887	89	—	—	—	—c	257	1,819

SOURCE U.S. Department of Agriculture, *Farm Income,* Statistical Bulletin 609 (Washington, D.C.: Economics, Statistics, and Cooperatives Service, 1978), p. 52.

NOTE: Details may not add to totals owing to rounding.

[a]Includes Great Plains and other conservation programs.

[b]Includes all other programs.

cLess than 0.5 million dollars.

Appendix Table 2

United States Agricultural Exports: Value by Country of Destination, Calendar Year 1977 (in thousands of dollars)

Country of Destination	Value	Country of Destination	Value
Greenland	0	French West Indies	6,130
Canada	1,550,411	Guyana	11,387
Saint Pierre and Miquelon	92	Surinam	16,279
		French Guiana	253
Total Latin America	2,218,732		
		Europe	10,005,978
Latin American Republics	1,903,453	Iceland	4,916
Mexico	664,405	Sweden	93,914
Guatemala	43,113	Norway	125,303
El Salvador	48,415	Finland	29,986
Honduras	26,045	Denmark	199,545
Nicaragua	20,665	United Kingdom	879,514
Costa Rica	30,220	Ireland	32,420
Panama	44,554	Netherlands	2,124,406
Cuba	0	Belgium-Luxembourg	460,936
Haiti	49,676	France	465,529
Dominican Republic	102,345	Federal Republic of Germany	
Colombia	134,845	(West Germany)	1,656,216
Venezuela	304,125	German Democratic Republic	
Ecuador	75,926	(East Germany)	31,197
Peru	124,753	Austria	17,409
Bolivia	19,543	Czechoslovakia	54,487
Chile	80,296	Hungary	33,890
Brazil	111,031	Switzerland	240,180
Paraguay	931	Estonia	0
Uruguay	11,243	Latvia	0
Argentina	11,322	Lithuania	0
		Poland	293,005
Other Latin America	315,279	USSR	1,036,764
Belize	6,409	Azores	2,305
Canal Zone	0	Spain	634,062
Bermuda	22,897	Portugal	413,217
Bahamas	47,896	Gibraltar	123
Jamaica[a]	81,063	Malta and Gozo	12,865
Turks and Caicos Islands	486	Italy	807,449
Cayman Islands	4,688	Yugoslavia	70,286
Leeward and Windward		Albania	270
Islands	17,499	Greece	165,052
Barbados	12,746	Romania	118,302
Trinidad and Tobago	42,694	Bulgaria	2,430
Netherlands Antilles	44,852		

Country of Destination	Value	Country of Destination	Value
Asia	8,049,439	Hong Kong	303,907
Turkey	3,273	Republic of China	611,870
Cyprus	11,745	Japan	3,856,756
Syria	22,831	Nansei Islands, n.e.c.[e]	—
Lebanon	27,561		
Iraq	62,798	Australia and Oceania	153,007
Iran	423,220	Australia	98,841
Israel	298,836	Papua New Guinea	440
Jordan	21,483	New Zealand[b]	28,118
Gaza Strip	147	Western Samoa[b]	697
Kuwait	15,866	British Pacific Islands	43
Saudi Arabia	171,073	Other Pacific Islands, n.e.c.	1,870
Qatar[b]	1,569	French Pacific Islands	11,374
United Arab Emirates[b]	12,539	Trust Territory of Pacific	
Yemen (Sana)[b]	682	Islands	11,624
Oman[b]	2,177		
Yemen (Aden)	340	Africa	1,364,450
Bahrain	4,862	Morocco	69,112
Afghanistan	1,281	Algeria	139,736
India	290,550	Tunisia	36,302
Pakistan	85,142	Libya	16,565
Bangladesh	129,391	Egypt	540,297
Nepal	1,815	Sudan	13,517
Sri Lanka (Ceylon)	42,483	Canary Islands	30,664
Burma	2	Spanish Africa, n.e.c.	37
Thailand	108,442	Equatorial Guinea	0
Vietnam[c]	0	Mauritania	2,718
North Vietnam	0	Cameroon	8,511
South Vietnam	0	Senegal	18,579
Laos	9	Guinea	4,963
Cambodia	0	Sierra Leone	5,379
Malaysia	52,441	Ivory Coast	13,645
Singapore	72,528	Ghana	32,696
Indonesia	241,968	The Gambia	2,231
Philippines	186,136	Togo	8,065
Macao	17	Nigeria	211,986
Southern Asia, n.e.c.[d]	186	Central African Empire	126
Brunei[d]	230	Gabon	233
People's Republic of China	63,982	Mali	286
Mongolia	0	Niger	1,557
North Korea	0	Chad	4,174
Korea, Republic of	919,301	Upper Volta	5,869

Country of Destination	Value	Country of Destination	Value
Benin (Dahomey)	4,968	British Indian Ocean Territory[f]	0
Congo (Brazzaville)	1,147	Tanzania	19,531
Saint Helena		Mauritius[f]	2,599
(British West Africa)	0	Mozambique	3,725
Madeira Islands	2,409	Malagasy Republic	3,013
Angola	12,559	French Indian Ocean Areas	18
Western Africa, n.e.c.	4,305	Republic of South Africa	56,175
Liberia	21,247	Southwest Africa (Namibia)[g]	49
Zaire	15,132	Zambia	3,674
Burundi	2,350	Rhodesia	3
Rwanda	1,565	Malawi	180
Somalia	2,737	Botswana	1,607
Ethiopia	4,767	Swaziland	23
Afars-Issas	828	Lesotho	3,178
Uganda	1,927	Destination Unknown[h]	328,894
Kenya	7,364		
Seychelles[f]	122	Total all countries[i]	23,670,994

SOURCE: U.S. Department of Agriculture, *Foreign Economic Trade of the United States* (Washington, D.C.: Economics Statistics, and Cooperatives Service, 1978), pp. 13–15.

NOTE: Because of transshipments, United States agricultural exports to certain countries such as Canada (before January 1, 1973), the Netherlands, and Belgium are overstated; exports to many other countries are therefore understated, particularly the United Kingdom, France, Switzerland, Ireland, Italy, Denmark, and Sweden. The data in these tables are not adjusted for transshipments.

[a]New classification effective January 1, 1976. Turks and Caicos Islands reported with Jamaica before January 1, 1977.

[b]Separately classified January 1, 1972.

[c]North and South Vietnam reported separately before January 1, 1977.

[d]New classification effective January 1, 1976. Previously included under the former designation "Southern and Southeastern Asia, n.e.c.," now classified as Southern Asia, n.e.c.

[e]Separately classified before June 1, 1972.

[f]New classification effective January 1, 1976. British Indian Ocean Territory reported partly with Seychelles and partly with Mauritius before January 1, 1976.

[g]Separately classified January 1, 1975.

[h]Transshipments through Canada where final destination was not known at the time of export.

[i]Particulars may not add to totals owing to rounding.

APPENDIX TABLE 3

United States Agricultural Exports: Specified Government-Financed Programs, Commercial Sales for Dollars, and Total (value by commodity group, calendar year 1977, in millions of dollars)

| Commodity | Government Programs | | | | | Commercial Sales for Dollars^d | Total Agricultural Exports |
| | Public Law 480 | | | AID | Total | | |
	Title I Credit Sales^a	Title II Donations^b	Total^c				
Animal and animal products	—	80.2	80.2	54.5	134.7	2,532.1	2,666.8
Inedible tallow	—	—	—	44.0	44.0	460.4	504.4
Meat and meat products	—	—	—	4.1	4.1	606.4	610.5
Poultry and poultry products	—	—	—	6.1	6.1	305.6	311.7
Nonfat dry milk	—	80.2	80.2	—	80.2	3.8	84.0
Other	—	—	—	0.3	0.3	1,156.0	1,156.2
Grains and preparations	549.9	247.1	797.0	204.3	1,001.3	7,679.1	8,680.4
Wheat	284.6	58.1	342.7	42.2	384.9	2,314.6	2,699.5
Wheat flour	74.1	37.1	111.2	—	111.2	71.9	183.1
Wheat products^e	6.9	46.2	53.1	—	53.1	—	49.7
Rice	134.3	10.2	144.4	—	144.4	553.4	697.8
Corn	47.9	3.3	51.3	162.0	213.2	3,886.6	4,099.8
Grain sorghum	1.5	4.9	6.4	—	6.4	585.6	592.0
Feed grain products	0.1	15.2	15.3	0.1	15.4	29.3	44.7
Blended food products	0.5	60.0	60.5	—	60.5	—	57.5
Other^f	—	12.1	12.1	—	12.1	244.2	256.3

Oilseeds and products	81.4	39.1	120.5	134.5	253.0	6,375.3	6,630.3
Soybeans	—	—	—	86.6	86.6	4,306.6	4,393.2
Soybean oil	81.4	15.8	97.2	1.9	99.1	344.1	443.2
Other vegetable oils	—	20.4	20.4	46.0[g]	66.4	324.8	391.2
Other	—	2.9	2.9	1.0	3.9	1,398.8	1,402.7
Tobacco	56.4	—	—	19.3	75.7	1,033.3	1,109.0
Cotton	17.8	—	17.8	—	17.8	1,511.7	1,529.5
Other	2.0	1.3	3.3	6.7	10.0	4,045.0	4,055.0
Total	706.3	367.7	1,074.0	419.3	1,493.3	22,177.7	23,671.0

SOURCE: U.S. Department of Agriculture, *Foreign Economic Trade of the United States* (Washington, D.C.: Economics, Statistics, and Cooperatives Service, 1978), p. 35.

NOTE: Particulars may not add to totals owing to rounding.

[a]Includes long-term dollar and convertible foreign currency sales.

[b]Includes government-to-government, voluntary relief agencies, and World Food Program.

[c]Preliminary.

[d]Includes, in addition to unassisted commercial transactions, shipments of some commodities with governmental assistance in the form of extension of credits and credit guarantees for relatively short periods and for tobacco, sales at less than domestic prices.

[e]Mainly bulgar.

[f]Mainly sorghum grits.

[g]Cottonseed oil.

Appendix Table 4

United States Agricultural Imports: Value by Country of Origin, Calendar Year 1977 (in thousands of dollars)

Country of Origin	Value	Country of Origin	Value
Greenland	35	Netherlands Antilles	232
Canada	672,468	French West Indies	670
Saint Pierre and Miquelon	0	Guyana	5,788
		Surinam	98
Total Latin America	5,672,436	French Guiana	18
Latin American Republics	5,613,086	Europe	2,126,191
Mexico	1,013,127	Iceland	1,085
Guatemala	352,454	Sweden	30,685
El Salvador	319,492	Norway	40,533
Honduras	184,586	Finland	47,287
Nicaragua	119,853	Denmark	238,609
Costa Rica	254,739	United Kingdom	92,791
Panama	71,763	Ireland	20,730
Cuba	—	Netherlands	316,845
Haiti	39,502	Belgium and Luxembourg	29,784
Dominican Republic	471,869	France	285,682
Colombia	616,799	Federal Republic of Germany	
Venezuela	55,527	(West Germany)	196,726
Ecuador	292,679	German Democratic Republic	
Peru	183,482	(East Germany)	1,704
Bolivia	14,601	Austria	23,885
Chile	26,432	Czechoslovakia	5,422
Brazil	1,384,643	Hungary	23,483
Paraguay	17,711	Switzerland	48,406
Uruguay	3,700	Estonia	0
Argentina	190,127	Latvia	27
		Lithuania	0
Other Latin America	59,350	Poland	125,377
Belize	7,608	USSR	10,855
Canal Zone	0	Azores	381
Bermuda	4	Spain	173,641
Bahamas	2,465	Portugal	34,084
Jamaica	11,321	Gibraltar	176
Turks and Caicos Islands	0	Malta and Gozo	0
Cayman Islands	724	Italy	198,699
Leeward and Windward		Yugoslavia	85,689
Islands	4,227	Albania	844
Barbados	8,757	Greece	48,807
Trinidad and Tobago	17,438	Romania	20,540

Country of Origin	Value	Country of Origin	Value
Bulgaria	23,414	Australia and Oceania	903,791
		Australia	519,133
Asia	2,572,061	Papua New Guinea	69,211
Turkey	140,903	New Zealand	308,601
Cyprus	1,552	Western Samoa	1,084
Syria	6,521	British Pacific Islands, n.e.c.	0
Lebanon	9,282	Other Pacific Islands, n.e.c.	4,130
Iraq	4,332	French Pacific Islands	97
Iran	78,115	Trust Territory of Pacific	
Israel	19,085	Islands	1,535
Jordan	1,859		
Gaza Strip	0	Africa	1,510,835
Kuwait	5	Morocco	4,435
Saudi Arabia	13	Algeria	471
Qatar	0	Tunisia	1,537
United Arab Emirates	1	Libya	0
Yemen (Sana)	483	Egypt	6,195
Oman	0	Sudan	4,340
Yemen (Aden)	754	Canary Islands	16
Bahrain	3	Spanish Africa, n.e.c.	0
Afghanistan	13,155	Equatorial Guinea	0
India	181,321	Mauritania	0
Pakistan	1,770	Cameroon	32,177
Bangladesh	3,528	Senegal	0
Nepal	74	Guinea	1,338
Sri Lanka (Ceylon)	50,730	Sierra Leone	17,649
Burma	5	Ivory Coast	311,921
Thailand	96,231	Ghana	85,093
Vietnam	0	The Gambia	0
Laos	341	Togo	179
Cambodia	6	Nigeria	65,423
Malaysia	332,834	Central African Empire	0
Singapore	43,668	Gabon	0
Indonesia	628,151	Mali	25
Philippines	599,036	Niger	0
Macao	12	Chad	138
Brunei	0	Upper Volta	43
Southern Asia, n.e.c.	0	Benin (Dahomey)	0
People's Republic of China	67,115	Congo (Brazzaville)	0
Mongolia	2,070	Saint Helena	
North Korea	0	(British West Africa)	60
Korea, Republic of	50,002	Madeira Islands	166
Hong Kong	18,848	Angola	12,814
Republic of China	141,020	Western Africa, n.e.c.	587
Japan	79,236	Liberia	71,694

Country of Origin	Value	Country of Origin	Value
Zaire	93,370	French Indian Ocean	
Burundi	25,270	Areas	3,438
Rwanda	33,028	Republic of South Africa	66,901
Somalia	24	Southwest Africa	
Ethiopia	88,903	(Namibia)	82
Afars-Issas	425	Zambia	4
Uganda	246,880	Rhodesia	0
Kenya	86,644	Malawi	16,991
Seychelles	160	Botswana	10
British Indian Ocean		Swaziland	11,603
Territory	0	Lesotho	0
Tanzania	73,307		
Mauritius	11,685		
Mozambique	59,414		
Malagasy Republic	76,395	Total all countries[a]	13,457,818

Source: U.S. Department of Agriculture, *Foreign Economic Trade of the United States* (Washington, D.C.: Economics, Statistics, and Cooperatives Service, 1978), p. 38–41.

[a]Details may not add to totals owing to rounding.

Appendix Table 5.

Value of United States Farm Products Shipped under Public Law 480 Compared with Total Exports of United States Farm Products, Fiscal Years 1955–76 and July–September 1976 (in millions of dollars of export market value)

Fiscal Year Ending June 30	Public Law 480							Total Agricultural Exports			
	Sales for Local Currency	Long-term Credit Sales	Government Donations for Disaster Relief and Economic Development	Donations through Voluntary Relief Agencies	Barter[a]	Total Public Law 480	Mutual Security (AID)[b]	Total Government Programs	Commercial Sales[c]	Total Agricultural Exports	Public Law 480 as Percentage of Total
1955	73		52	135	125	385	450	835	2,309	3,144	12
1956	439		63	184	298	984	355	1,339	2,157	3,496	28
1957	908		51	165	401	1,525	394	1,919	2,809	4,728	33
1958	657		51	173	100	981	227	1,208	2,795	4,003	24
1959	724		30	131	132	1,017	210	1,227	2,492	3,719	27
1960	824		38	105	149	1,116	167	1,283	3,236	4,519	24
1961	951		75	146	144	1,316	186	1,502	3,444	4,946	26
1962	1,030	19	88	160	198	1,495	74	1,569	3,573	5,142	29
1963	1,088	57	89	174	48	1,456	14	1,470	3,608	5,078	29
1964	1,056	48	81	189	43	1,417	24	1,441	4,627	6,068	23
1965	1,142	158	55	183	32	1,570	26	1,596	4,501	6,097	26
1966	866	181	87	180	32	1,346	42	1,388	5,359	6,747	20
1967	803	178	110	157	23	1,271	37	1,308	5,513	6,821	19
1968	723	300	100	150	6	1,279	18	1,297	5,086	6,383	20

Fiscal Year Ending June 30	Public Law 480							Total Agricultural Exports			
	Sales for Local Currency	Long-term Credit Sales	Government Donations for Disaster Relief and Economic Development	Donations through Voluntary Relief Agencies	Barter[a]	Total Public Law 480	Mutual Security (AID)[b]	Total Government Programs	Commercial Sales[c]	Total Agricultural Exports	Public Law 480 as Percentage of Total
1969	346	427	111	154	1	1,039	11	1,050	4,776	5,826	18
1970	309	506	113	128		1,056	12	1,068	5,650	6,718	16
1971	204	539	138	142		1,023	56	1,079	6,674	7,753	13
1972	143	535	228	152		1,058	66	1,124	6,922	8,046	13
1973	6	661	159	128		954	84	1,038	11,864	12,902	7
1974		575	147	145		867	76	943	20,350	21,293	4
1975	—[d]	762	148	191	—	1,101	123	1,224	20,354	21,578	6
1976	—	650	65	192	—	907	216	1,123	21,024	22,147	5
July-September 1976	—	316	18	51	—	385	138	523	4,830	5,355	10
1955 through July-September 1976	12,292	5,912	2,097	3,515	1,732	25,548	3,006	28,554	153,955	182,509	16

SOURCE: 1976/TQ Annual Report of Public Law 480, Food for Peace, USDA (Washington, D.C.: Government Printing Office), p. 72.

[a] Annual exports have been adjusted for 1963 and subsequent years by deducting exports under barter contracts that improve the balance of payments and rely primarily on authority other than Public Law 480. These exports are included in the column headed "Commercial Sales."

[b] Sales for local currency, economic aid, and expenditures under development loans.

[c] Commercial sales for dollars include, in addition to unassisted commercial transactions, shipments of some commodities with governmental assistance in the form of short- and medium- term credit, export payments, sales of government-owned commodities at less than domestic market prices, and, for 1963 and subsequent years, exports under barter contracts that benefit the balance of payments and rely primarily on authority other than Public Law 480.

[d] Less than $500,000.

Appendix Table 6

PL 480 Exports to Principal Developing and Developed Countries, June 1954–September 1976 (in millions of dollars)

Country	Title I Credit Sales[a]	Title II Donations[b]	Title III Barter	Total PL 480
Developing countries				
India	4,454.0	865.5	74.6	5,394.1
Pakistan	1,700.5	135.1	0.1	1,835.9
Republic of Korea	1,418.4	309.6	6.2	1,734.2
South Vietnam	1,308.8	155.7	—[c]	1,464.5
Egypt	1,037.4	146.1	12.3	1,195.8
Indonesia	993.6	84.3	1.7	1,079.5
Brazil	606.6	225.3	63.4	895.3
Israel[d]	620.7	23.1	47.1	690.9
Turkey	550.1	105.5	17.6	673.2
Bangladesh	394.2	51.8	—	446.0
Morocco	164.8	231.4	4.0	400.2
Republic of China	293.3	85.5	16.1	394.9
Other	2,151.8	2,323.9	202.1	4,677.8
Total developing	15,694.2	4,742.8	445.2	20,876.1
Developed countries				
Yugoslavia	847.9	153.0	19.6	1,020.5
Spain	474.1	116.5	31.6	622.2
Poland	498.2	60.3	9.1	567.6
Italy	140.0	232.1	34.2	406.3
Japan	135.0	38.0	193.7	366.7
Greece	144.0	88.3	12.7	245.0
Other	270.6	181.0	986.0	1,437.6
Total developed	2,509.8	869.2	1,286.9	4,666.9
Total PL 480	18,204.0	5,612.0	1,732.1	25,548.0

Source: U.S. Department of Agriculture, *Foreign Agricultural Trade of the United States* (Washington, D.C.: Economic Research Service, 1977), p. 21.

Note: Particulars may not add to totals owing to rounding.

[a]Includes sales for foreign currencies (which predominated until 1969) and long-term dollar and convertible foreign currency credit sales.

[b]Through government-to-government, international (World Food Program), and United States private voluntary agencies.

[c]Less than $50,000.

[d]During most of the PL 480 period, Israel was considered developing; in recent years it has generally been classified as developed.

APPENDIX TABLE 7

Public Law 480, Title II: Value of Exports and Number of Recipients, by Program, Fiscal Years 1969–76

Program	1969	1970	1971	1972	1973	1974	1975	1976
	Million Dollars							
Food for development								
School lunch	137.3	106.9	123.3	102.5	79.1	69.8	66.3	55.0
Maternal and pre-school feeding	31.4	37.4	51.3	48.8	45.0	54.3	90.5	146.3
Food for work	52.3	71.4	68.0	64.8	62.2	68.9	102.1	67.1
Total	221.0	215.7	242.6	215.1	187.3	194.8	258.9	268.4
Emergency and relief	55.7	47.3	60.2	182.7	103.7	88.1	57.9	45.3
Total, all programs	287.2	263.0	302.8	403.7	290.0	282.9	316.8	313.7
	Thousand Persons							
Food for development								
School lunch	35,376	34,437	33,696	35,645	36,584	27,045	18,940	12,976
Maternal and pre-school feeding	10,374	10,932	13,168	10,843	15,621	13,159	11,126	14,849
Food for work	12,884	14,193	10,992	15,260	10,970	8,799	8,481	8,175
Total	58,636	59,562	57,856	61,748	63,175	49,003	38,547	36,000
Emergency and relief	14,012	18,083	17,467	28,143	23,715	6,406	12,759	4,025
Total, all Programs	72,648	77,645	75,323	89,891	86,890	55,409	51,306	40,025

SOURCE: U.S. Department of Agriculture, *Foreign Agricultural Trade of the United States* (Washington, D.C.: Economic Research Service, 1977), p. 23

NOTE: Details may not add to totals owing to rounding.

APPENDIX TABLE 8

Total Net Flow of Resources from DAC Countries to Developing Countries and Multilateral Agencies (in millions of dollars and as percentage of GNP)

Disbursing Countries	1965–67 Average[a]		1970		1973		1974		1975		1976	
	$	%	$	%	$	%	$	%	$	%	$	%
Australia	163	0.68	394	1.15	354	0.55	544	0.69	591	0.70	527	0.57
Austria	48	0.47	96	0.67	145	0.53	202	0.61	169	0.45	372	0.92
Belgium	188	1.03	309	1.19	507	1.11	598	1.12	867	1.36	1,222	1.83
Canada	236	0.42	630	0.77	1,105	0.90	1,677	1.13	2,041	1.28	2,471	1.28
Denmark	20	0.18	86	0.54	202	0.74	207	0.68	275	0.78	485	1.27
Finland	6	0.07	25	0.24	27	0.16	60	0.28	89	0.34	66	0.24
France	1,320	1.22	1,835	1.24	2,773	1.09	3,363	1.22	3,942	1.16	5,316	1.53
Germany	889	0.74	1,487	0.79	1,807	0.52	3,176	0.83	4,962	1.19	5,314	1.19
Italy	395	0.61	682	0.73	645	0.47	418	0.28	1,625	0.95	1,476	0.87
Japan	637	0.61	1,824	0.92	5,844	1.44	2,962	0.65	2,880	0.59	4,003	0.72
Netherlands	240	1.15	428	1.34	612	1.03	909	1.31	1,255	1.55	1,727	1.96
New Zealand	11	0.20	23	0.38	36	0.33	50	0.40	73	0.59	60	0.48
Norway	29	0.37	67	0.59	95	0.48	186	0.81	273	0.98	462	1.51
Sweden	100	0.45	229	0.74	359	0.73	640	1.15	752	1.09	1,134	1.53
Switzerland	146	0.98	137	0.67	299	0.72	367	0.75	701	1.25	1,350	2.28
United Kingdom	915	0.86	1,247	1.01	1,473	0.82	2,386	1.23	2,353	1.02	(2,176)	(0.99)
United States	5,341	0.71	6,211	0.63	8,346	0.64	10,270	0.73	17,530	1.15	12,344	0.72
Total DAC countries	10,684	0.73	15,710	0.77	24,628	0.79	28,016	0.81	40,378	1.05	40,505	0.97

SOURCE: Society for International Development, *Survey of International Development* 15, no. 1 (January/February 1978): 6.

NOTE: Details may not add to totals owing to rounding.

[a] Excluding grants by private voluntary agencies included in the other years shown.

Acknowledgments

Especially helpful in the preparation of this book were Walter Armbruster, Barbara Chattin, Bruce Gardner, and Charles Hardin. They read and commented on early drafts of the entire manuscript.

The following people helped in the early stages with particular sections and chapters: Dawson Ahalt, Stan Barber, Joe Barse, Calvin Beale, John Berry, Robert Beukenkamp, Kay Bitterman, W. T. Boehm, D. W. Bromley, Clark Burbee, Earl Butz, William P. Butz, Lee A. Christensen, Bob Coltrane, Harold Cosper, Mel Cotner, Stan Daberkow, Velmar Davis, Herman Delvo, Otto Doering, Clark Edwards, Peter Emerson, Will Erwin, Earle Gavett, Wade Gregory, Don Griffith, Lowell Hardin, Steve Hiemstra, Dave Hume, Edward V. Jesse, Susan Libbin, Dick Magelby, Bill Manley, Emil Mrack, Paul Nelson, Carmen Nohre, Clay Ogg, Hoey Paarlberg, Robert L. Paarlberg, J. B. Penn, A. J. Randall, B. H. Robertson, Kenneth Robinson, John Schaub, Ed Schuh, Norman Starler, Paul Stewart, Bob Tontz, F. T. Turpin, Wally Tyner, Tom VanArsdall, Jim Vertrees, T. K. Warley, and Dick Willsey.

Typing was done by Eva Paarlberg and Lorraine Ostroot.

Special thanks go to the Krannert Library at Purdue University and to my students, with whom many of the ideas in this book were hammered out.

Financial assistance was provided by the Ford Foundation.

Value judgments are my own, and responsibility for errors rests with me.

Index

DATE DUE			
MAY 14 1986			
NOV 16 1989			